GOLF COURSES OF

IOWA

BIRDIE 3 EDITION
Roger Aegerter

Golf Courses of Iowa

Web Site: www.golfcoursesofiowa.com

Published by:
Golf Courses of Iowa
PO. Box 65
300 W. Harrison
Jefferson, Iowa 50129

ISBN   0-9622074-2X

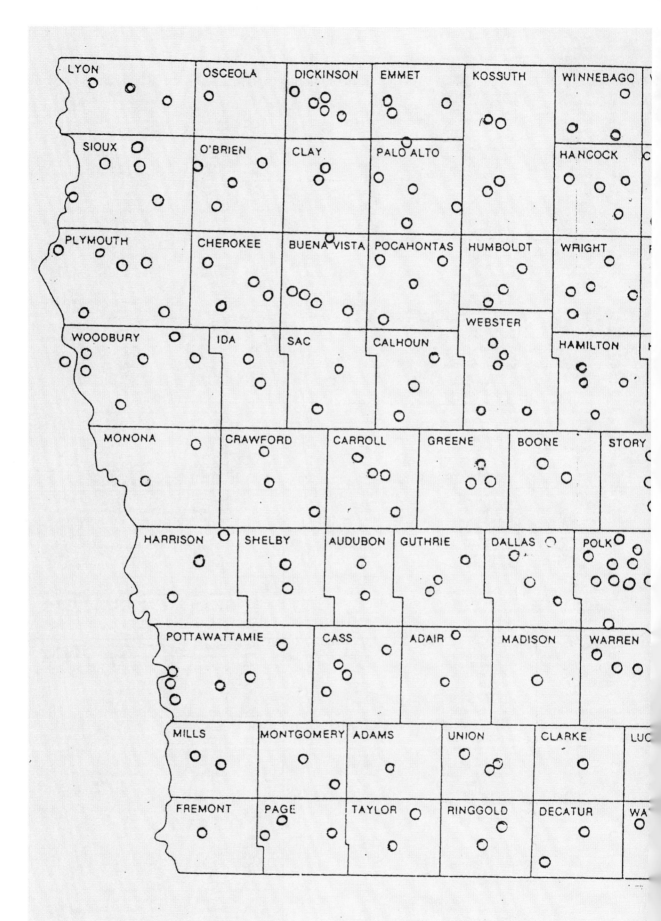

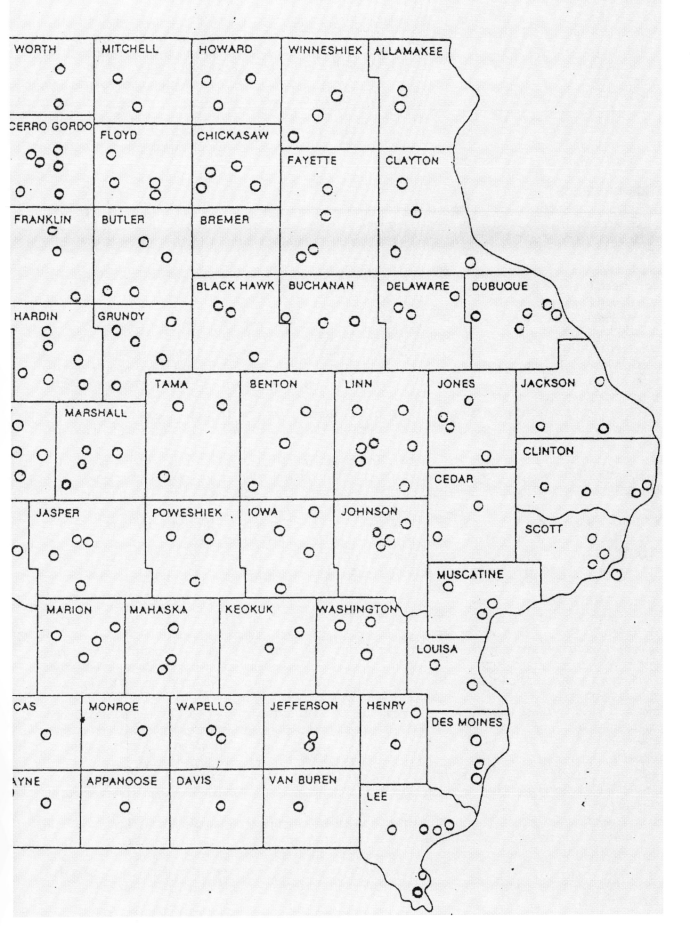

GLOSSARY

GOLF COURSES OF IOWA was initially written for the Iowa golfer who enjoys the unique golf offered around the state of Iowa. This golfer may be a weekend duffer who wants to play a different course near their home but has no knowledge of the difficulty or characteristics of that particular course. Or like thousands of other golfers around Iowa they want to keep current on all the new and expanded courses in the state. Since the first edition of GOLF COURSES OF IOWA in 1985 there have been over 63 new or expanded courses. In 1985 there were 4 sand green courses, that number slipped down to 2 but is now back up to 3 in 2004 with Pierson building a sand green course a couple of years ago.

Whatever the case, GOLF COURSES OF IOWA- Vol. 3 provides a comprehensive listing of all 407 golf courses in the state of Iowa, up from 365 in 1992. The purpose of the book is to provide information to Iowa Golfers about all the wonderful courses that they might not have the chance to play or even know about. The contents have evolved into a guide not only for golfers, but for people who believe that Iowa is a place of beauty and enjoyment.

EXPLANATION OF TERMS

Yearly golf dues and fees are included in many of the course descriptions. These prices may fluctuate from one year to the next. Green fees are described as being very reasonable, reasonable, average, or high. The rating takes into consideration the course size, location, difficulty, and the facilities offered by the course.

Very Reasonable Fees means that the fees are below average for a course this size.

Reasonable Fees means that a course is charging an appropriate amount for that size course.

Average Green Fees run from $10 to $15 for a 9-hole course.

Average Green Fees run from $20 to $30 for an 18-hole course.

High Green Fees indicates that the price is significantly above the average and with no extra perks.

Each of the 407 courses in the 2004 edition are compared and rated with all other courses in it's category. There are 263 – 9 hole courses; 124 – 18 hole courses; 5 – 27 hole courses; 1 – 36 hole course; 11 par 3 courses; and 3 sand green courses. When a nine hole course gets a three (***) star rating it doesn't mean that a rating would mean the same or be the same in the 18 hole category or the Par 3 category. It only means it is a *** course when compared to all the other nine hole courses in the state.

Throughout the book the terms poor, fair, good, very good, and excellent are used to describe everything from grass on the greens to lunch in the clubhouse. These terms are also used in the ratings of the individual courses. These terms include:

POOR – Not up to expectations, lacking in resource development, unsatisfactory, a detraction to the course.

FAIR – Passable, tolerable, resources not developed to their full potential, not desirable playing conditions.

GOOD – Adequate, satisfactory in quality, features that make the course fun but not exciting. Qualities and characteristics that can be found in a majority of courses in this size category.

VERY GOOD - Above average, resources incorporated into the course to enhance the golfing atmosphere. Qualities of this category make the time spent enjoyable and exciting, a new adventure.

EXCELLENT – Possessing superior qualities of courses in this category, superior to others in resource development, features, and golfing atmosphere. Excellent qualities, characteristics, and facilities.

EXPLANATION OF RATINGS

The ratings for each course contain eight different categories. The **Course** category just tells you how many holes this course has in its layout. **Par** and **Distance** gives the accurate course par and yardage distances.

Playability – Does the course test your skills and shot selection? Are you able to use a number of different clubs and types of shots? Are a variety of different shots available? How fair are the holes in the layout? Do the greens have good containment and is the grass condition conducive to accurate putting? In general Playability covers the individual characteristics of the course.

Aesthetics - Does the course use the natural surroundings to enhance the playability of the course? Is the landscaping used to enhance the atmosphere and playability? Does the layout contain an adequate number of trees, bushes, and natural land contours? Does the care-taking of the course promote a true golfing atmosphere? Does the clubhouse bring people back to the course or do people avoid it? Does the overall course have a sense of beauty?

Interest - Does the course keep you interested and motivated towards improving your golf game? Does the atmosphere of the entire operation make you want to come back and play again? Do the surroundings lend themselves to an enjoyable game of golf?

Worth the Trip - Does the course test your golfing skills and make the game of golf enjoyable? Is it worth your time and effort to come to this particular course? Is the course set up and run in the best interest and traditions of Iowa Golf?

Ratings - Each group of courses is rated as a group – 9 holes, 18 holes, Par 3 courses, and sand. A three star rating in one group does not mean the same rating will stand up in another group. The rating is based on playability, length, difficulty, condition of the course, aesthetics, golfing atmosphere, interest, price, location, clubhouse and facilities. There is a range from one (*) to five (*****) stars.

Forward

The first edition of Golf Courses of Iowa was dedicated to my father, Homer Aegerter. He could shoot his age at 84 and give me a lesson on the side. He has taught me a great deal about life in general, but he has given me two things that will last long after I par (birdie) that last hole, the love and respect for the game of golf and the love of a caring father.

Along with my father I dedicated the 2nd edition of the book to all the golf innovators in Iowa. From 1988 through 1992 there were 18 newly built or expanded courses in the state (from 1992 through 2004 there have been 45 newly built and 11 expanded courses). With this foresight, Iowa golf continues to grow and improve. My thanks to all of them for improving Iowa's golfing future.

For the 3rd Edition of Golf Courses of Iowa I would like to pay tribute to the past and future golfer. These are the lifelines of Iowa golf, those that have had the vision to build courses in the 1960's and in 2004, they are the ones that have made golfing accessible to all Iowa golfers and passed down their passion for golf to other generations. I would also like to encourage the younger generations around the state, some who probably can't even read this book yet, to take up the game, play it with a passion and give back as much as you take out. They are the future of golf in Iowa. The thousands of golfers in Iowa need to encourage these young players, they will carry on the passion and love for the game that all of us have. So to my generation of golfers, thanks, and to the new generations of hack...... I mean golfers "game on".

Ackley Country Club

Ackley

641-847-3475

The Ackley Country Club was built in the late 1950's as a short, but recreational course and it retains that spirit today. Total yardage for the course is only 2156 yards, with a par of 32. But don't expect to pitch and putt your way to glory on this course. It is a very picturesque course that has a medium number of trees, ranging from new plantings to large. These trees are placed where it will hurt you the most. Tree trouble is this course's middle name. They line the fairways, they guard the greens, they eat Top Flights for lunch. Beware. The appearance of the rest of the course is typical Iowa: flat fairways, a small creek that is there just for the beauty, some sand, and two inch rough. The greens are of medium size with rolling putting surfaces and the tee off boxes sport some nice grass. The clubhouse has a nice bar area with five round card tables. There are drinks and snacks to enjoy. Carts are available but the course is easy to walk. Green fees are very reasonable. The 140 members pay an annual fee of $299. This gives them the privilege to have a pleasant afternoon hitting into, around and through those darn trees. The course is located at 800 State St.

Course	9 Holes
Distance	2156 Yards
Par	32
Playability	Good
Aesthetics	Good
Interest	Good
Worth the Trip	Yes
Rating	★★

HOLE		1	2	3	4	5	6	7	8	9	Front
YARDAGE	Men	273	189	128	342	406	131	365	165	157	2156
	Women	264	180	124	337	395	123	360	157	141	2081
PAR		4	3	3	4	5	3	4	3	3	32
HANDICAP		9	1	6	3	7	2	4	5	8	
SIDE MATCHES	We										
	They										

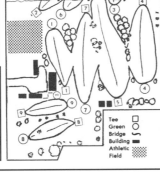

Tee		☐
Green		○
Bridge		⌣
Building		■
Athletic Field		▒

Hillcrest Country Club

Adel

515-993-3630

The Hillcrest Country Club is located one mile east and three miles north of Adel. Hillcrest is a private club that is open to the public on Wednesdays with green fees of $15.00. The clubhouse is suitable for a small, nine hole course and carries a full line of equipment. You can also get drinks and sandwiches at the bar. This course has two of the toughest finishing holes in the area. A severe dogleg on number eight and a pesky par 3 number nine. There are two ponds on the course and six bunkers. The rough has a distinctive look along the fairways and is cut to 2 inches and more in strategic areas. The trees can be found in all sizes and shapes. Poplars line some of the fairways while small elms are scattered along others. The greens are small, elevated and generally flat. With this description you can see why holding one of these greens is a major concern while touring the course. Added to this is the concern that the greens have a history of being very quick. Two greens were rebuilt in 2001. Fairways are narrow but have excellent landing area grass condition. The condition of the entire course is good thanks to the fairway watering system. Hillcrest is a very interesting, challenging, and hilly course. A little bit out of the way but well worth it.

Course	9 Holes
Distance	2887 Yards
Par	35
Playability	Fair
Aesthetics	Good
Interest	Good
Worth The Trip	Yes
Rating	★★★+

MEN'S YARDAGE	355	107	463	374	352	135	274	560	232	2852
HANDICAP	11	14	9	5	7	13	17	1	3	
PAR	4	3	5	4	4	3	4	5	3	35
HOLE	1	2	3	4	5	6	7	8	9	OUT
LADIES' YARDAGE	341	95	415	278	348	118	260	315	232	2402
HANDICAP	9	13	3	10	6	15	11	1	17	
PAR	4	3	5	4	4	3	4	4	4	35

Shady Oaks Golf Course

Ackworth

515-961-0262

Shady Oaks Golf Course is a public course located east of Indianola 5 miles and just east of Ackworth. The course was built in 1972 by John Martindale and is set among rolling and wooded hills. A second 9 holes was added during the 1993 season with fairway watering also being added to all 18. This is strictly a greens fee operation, with very low weekday fees. The clubhouse was remodeled in 1991 and offers snacks and supplies. They also have clubs and carts to rent. The course is quite numerous water hazards the on the course which affect eight holes. Trees range from 500 new plantings to old Oaks that are scattered along the valleys and along some of the fairways. The greens are in better shape than the past, but are still medium in size with flat putting surfaces. This is a hard course to walk and hard to play the first few times. It is a knowledge course, it helps to know where to put your tee shot for a decent shot to the green. Shady Oaks is an attractive country course and deserves consideration. The new back 9 was built out of the hills to the north of the original layout. The holes are carved into the hills and provide many uneven lies. When this 9 was built they incorporated many large trees. The new nine holes also have larger greens. These trees do not come into play much but provide a very scenic round. Weekday fees are $12.40 and weekends $14.20. It also boosts one of the longest hole-in-ones in the area, 383 yards by Bob Beeler.

Course	18 Holes	Aesthetics	Good
Distance	6252 Yards	Interest	Good
Par	71	Worth the Trip	Yes
Playability	Very Good	Rating	***

HOLE	1	2	3	4	5	6	7	8	9	Out	Total
White Tees	325	357	170	385	381	612	307	170	415	3122	
Handicap	15	9	11	3	7	1	13	17	5		
Men's Par	4	4	3	4	4	5	4	3	4	35	
Ladies' Par	4	4	3	4	4	6	4	3	5	37	
Red Tees	315	352	150	365	361	562	302	170	410	2987	

HOLE	10	11	12	13	14	15	16	17	18	In	Out	Tot	Hcp	Net
White Tees	330	175	410	365	499	315	351	510	175	3130	3122	6252		
Handicap	14	10	4	8	6	12	2	16	18					
Men's Par	4	3	4	4	5	4	4	5	3	36	35	71		
Ladies' Par	4	3	4	4	6	4	4	6	3	38	37	75		
Red Tees	325	100	380	345	394	295	331	500	170	2840	2987	5827		

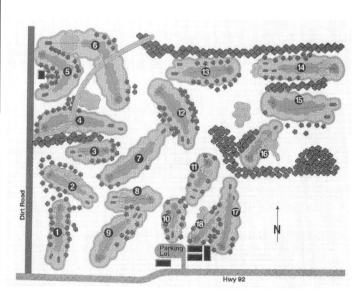

River Valley Golf Course
Adel

515-993-4029

River Valley can be found north of Adel at 2267 Valley View Trail. It can also be found at www.rivervalleygolf. com. This course was built in 1994 out of rolling farm land. There are many green fee and membership rates, but the normal daily rate is $34. Mulligan's Resturant is located upstairs of the spacious clubhouse and provides ample space for groups and corporate outings. This 6684 yard course has 22 sand traps and 14 grass bunkers scattered throughout the course. Water comes into play on 4 or 5 holes, depends on how you play. But the real challenge comes on the number 12 island green. This is a 160 yard hole that makes you think a little. A beautiful hole. Number 9 is also all water except fo the tee and green. This rolling course has a few new trees but relies on the cut rough to keep you honest. When the tree lined fairways mature it will be a different course. The shape of this course is good with distinctively cut fairways and a picturesque setting. No one said anything, but I would bet that the wind plays an important part of this course. River Valley is a nice addition to the central Iowa golf setting.

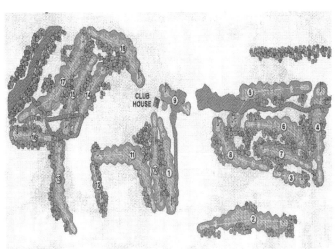

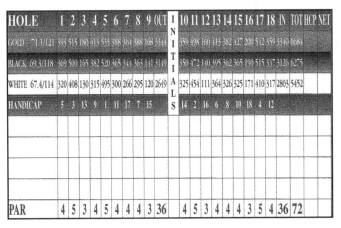

HOLE	1	2	3	4	5	6	7	8	9	OUT	INITIALS	10	11	12	13	14	15	16	17	18	IN	TOT	HCP	NET
GOLD 71.1/121	395	515	180	413	535	588	364	388	168	3544		359	498	160	413	382	327	200	512	359	3340	6684		
BLACK 69.3/118	369	500	165	382	520	565	344	365	141	3149		350	472	140	395	362	365	190	515	337	3126	6275		
WHITE 67.4/114	320	408	130	315	495	300	266	295	120	2649		325	454	111	364	326	325	171	410	317	2803	5452		
HANDICAP	5	3	13	9	1	11	17	7	15			14	2	16	6	8	10	18	4	12				
PAR	4	5	3	4	5	4	4	4	3	36		4	5	3	4	4	4	3	5	4	36	72		

Course	18 Holes	Aesthetics	Good
Distance	6684 Yards	Interest	Good
Par	72	Worth The Trip	Yes
Playability	Good	Rating	***

Lakeshore Golf and Country Club

Afton

641-347- 5221

The golfers in south central Iowa must have the best climbing legs in the state. Lakeshore Golf and Country Club on the northwest side of Afton, on Jefferson Street (old Hyway 34), is another example of up and down hills, uneven lies, and a lot of cart traffic: 90% of the 210 members of Lakeshore have carts. The characteristics of the course include three ponds affecting five holes, two bunkers, and a two inch rough that outlines the narrow fairways. As with many hilly courses there are a smaller number of trees and these are scattered in the fairways with a few in small groupings. The hilly fairways tend to be dry most of the summer. The greens are small to medium and have a flat putting surface. Tees are one of the highlights of the course; they are big, elevated and landscaped quite nicely. Lakeshore was built 1969-71 and opened in 1972 and is a nice small town course. The layout of the course is well thought out. The course is located in a scenic spot, not a lot of hazards to contend with, but is still a challenging course. The interest in the course has increased over the past 5 years due to the fine conditions. The green fees are average. Yearly memberships are $490 which includes access to a new brick clubhouse that has a lower level bar area and a dining area that is open only on special occasions. Lakeshore does have the laid back, down home feeling. It is neat and clean and represents the town of Afton well. A friendly course that puts the leisure part back into your golf game.

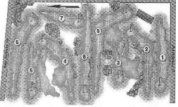

Course	9 Holes
Distance	2877 Yards
Par	35
Playability	Very Good
Aesthetics	Good
Interest	Good
Worth The Trip	Yes
Rating	★★★

HOLE	1	2	3	4	5	6	7	8	9	Out
WHITE YARDS	335	340	153	370	305	569	170	300	335	2877
Handicap	6	4	1	9	8	3	2	5	7	
Par	4	4	3	4	4	5	3	4	4	35
RED YARDS	335	340	111	320	305	520	170	300	270	2671
Handicap	6	3	9	5	2	1	4	7	8	

Akron Golf Club

Akron

712-568-3146

The Akron Golf Club has a very flat contour. This might be one of the easier courses to walk in western Iowa. Trees that were planted 7-10 years ago are now coming into play and will disturb play now and in the future. There are no water hazards on the course (unless you count the watering heads spread out in the fairways). There are six bunkers and a rough cut along the fairways and a deeper rough around the greens. Fairways have been narrowed down making accuracy a little more of a premium trait. Tees are adequate while the greens are a nice size, sloping and cut in distinctive patterns. The toughest green on the course is number nine. The surface is rolling and steep providing an opportunity to use the knowledge gained from previous experiences on the course. The Akron course, which was built in 1969, is located 1/2 mile south of town on Country Club Road, just off the highway and is comfortably busy most of the time. The grooming of the course has improved over the past three years and now has more of a professional look. The club has about 225 members. Green fees are a reasonable at $10 for 9 holes. Playing all day could result in a nasty sunburn on this course. This is an easy course to play and walk, plus it is an easy course to get on. They now have full time restaurant.

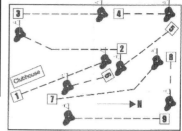

Course	9 Holes
Distance	2910 Yards
Par	36
Playability	Very Good
Aesthetics	Good
Interest	Poor
Worth The Trip	Yes
Rating	★★ -

PAR		4	5	4	4	4	3	5	3	4	36
YARDAGE	Men	384	456	422	271	278	118	448	156	377	2,910
	Women	357	446	356	261	268	108	438	146	307	2,687
HANDICAP		3	5	2	6	8	9	7	4	1	

Albia Golf and Country Club

Albia

515-932-5002

The Albia Golf and Country Club is a private club located on the east edge of Albia off Stanton Street. This nine hole course has a twenty mile radius for green fees, which are above average in price during the week and weekends. The 150 members pay a yearly fee of $800. The clubhouse has a limited full line of equipment along with carts to rent. The golfers have a selection of drinks and sandwiches in the clubhouse plus there is a full restaurant that is open to members and guests most of the week. The course has a pond, a lake, and a stream, affecting five holes in all. The trees come in all sizes and are mainly situated around or near the water. Eighty new trees were planted in 2003 along with a lot of pampas grass. The fairways are narrow where the trees come into play. The general layout of the course has a rolling contour. There is no distinct rough on the course and sand is present on six occasions. The greens are medium in size and have a prevailing flat surface with an occasional rolling aspect. Three fairways were reshaped along with number 5 green. They also now have FW watering. This 1920 course is a hard course to walk and a fairly tough course to score well on. This is an easy course to get on and rewarding to play if you can keep the ball in the fairway.

Course	9 Holes
Distance	3230 Yards
Par	36
Playability	Good
Aesthetics	Very Good
Interest	Good
Worth The Trip	Yes
Rating	***

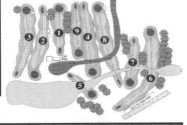

Par	4	4	4	5	3	4	3	5	4	36
Ladies Par	4	5	5	5	3	5	4	4	4	39
Distance Yards	325	430	424	425	125	434	227	484	356	3230
Handicap	8	2	4	9	7	1	3	5	6	
Hole	1	2	3	4	5	6	7	8	9	OUT

Algona Country Club

Algona

515-295-7308

The Algona Country Club is a tough course to play for the first time. It has a hilly contour and contains a variety of different lies that seem to create havoc with every shot. The course has few hazards except for the hills. There is one stream, no sand, no rough, and a medium number of trees. The trees that do exist are medium in size and scattered throughout the course. New trees are being planted each year. Fairways are wide and in good shape despite the hills that lay bare to the sun. Tees are elevated and medium in size. Greens are medium in size and flat. The greens also have a reputation of being hard to hold and fast. The Algona Country Club was built in 1920. This private course has a green fee radius of the Algona School District, anyone outside that area can pay the reasonable fees. The clubhouse sits on top of a hill overlooking the course. Inside you will find a meager assortment of supplies but they do have carts for rent, this is truly a cart course. The bar area is very nice and serves drinks and microwave sandwiches during the day. There is also an attractive restaurant in the clubhouse open to the public year round. The restaurant is informal with a very nice dining area over-looking the course and most importantly has good food. There is also a pool located in the complex. The Algona Country Club has a social, get together atmosphere. It is an interesting course to play and is located one mile west and then 1/2 mile south on Highway 18 on Country Club Rd.

Course	9 Holes
Distance	2888 Yards
Par	36
Playability	Good
Aesthetics	Good
Interest	Good
Worth The Trip	Yes
Rating	***+

WHITE TEES	YARDAGE	357	345	361	148	526	340	271	315	275	2938
	PAR	4	4	4	3	5	4	4	4	4	36
HANDICAP WHITE		3	9	7	17	1	5	15	11	13	
HOLE NO.		1	2	3	4	5	6	7	8	9	OUT
HANDICAP RED		2	5	4	9	1	3	6	8	7	
RED TEES	YARDAGE	320	271	274	138	452	241	251	108	211	2266
	PAR	4	4	4	3	5	4	4	3	4	

River Road Golf Club

Algona

515-295-7351

River Road Golf Club is a public course located two miles north of Algona on River Road. This 3080 yard course contains one pond, one stream and no sand. Trees throughout the course are medium in size with new trees planted every year. The contour of the course is hilly with fairways wide and generally tree lined. There is a two inch rough running the length of the fairways and with fairway watering it keeps fairly green all summer. Tees are elevated and medium in size, greens are medium to large and have rolling putting surfaces. River Road was built in 1973 and is owned and operated by Kent and Kevin Hoover. The 225 members pay a family membership of $310 with daily green fees very reasonably priced. The clubhouse has a golfing atmosphere and contains a full line of equipment, especially a large supply of clubs and shoes. For golfers the bar has drinks and sandwiches during the day. River Road is an easy course to walk and an easy course to score well on. This is a family operation that is family oriented. It maintains that easy going, fun golf feeling throughout the operation. The Hoovers built the course themselves and take a great deal of pride in its' conditioning and reputation.

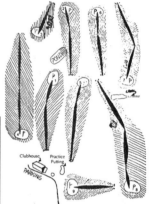

Course	9 Holes
Distance	3080 Yards
Par	36
Playability	Good
Aesthetics	Average
Interest	Good
Worth The Trip	Yes
Rating	★ ★ ★

Hole	1	2	3	4	5	6	7	8	9	OUT
Handicap	⑨	②	⑤	⑥	①	⑧	④	⑦	③	
White Tees	324	361	159	505	392	314	383	472	170	3080
Men's Par	4	4	3	5	4	4	4	5	3	36
Red Tees	306	342	150	490	380	294	372	428	157	2919
Ladies Par	4	4	3	5	4	4	4	5	3	36

Alta Golf & Country Club

Alta

712-200-2442

Northwest Iowa has its share of beautiful 9 hole courses. One of the best designed and manicured is the Alta Golf and Country Club on the east edge of Alta. Built in 1930, this 3106 yard course has 9 sand bunkers and 2 grass fairway bunkers to impede the golfer. The medium size trees line all the fairways and do pose a threat when you get off the beaten path. The greens are small in size with rolling surfaces. A rule of the course is to play below the pin on your approach shot to avoid the tilted surfaces that are good to catch incoming, but not so good to putt down from. The tees are slightly elevated and are landscaped very nicely. The grass condition on the greens is in excellent condition along with the fairway grass with the addition of FW watering. The general layout of the course is flat and is an enjoyable course to play. Alta is a family oriented course that is fairly busy on the weekends, but no tee times are needed even during heavy play. The 255 members enjoy this tight course and pay $365 a year for a family membership. The clubhouse is fairly typical of Iowa courses, a nice bar area, spacious seating in the dining area used mainly for special events, a limited amount of food and golfing supplies. But it is also typical in the sense that it has that true friendly golfing atmosphere. Alta Golf & Country Club is a very aesthetically and financially sound course, one that is well worth the trip. Green fees are $11 for 9 during the week.

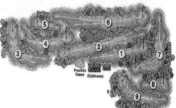

Course	9 Holes
Distance	3106 Yards
Par	36
Playability	Good
Aesthetics	Very Good
Interest	Good
Worth the Trip	Yes
Rating	★ ★ ★ +

MEN'S TEE	272	492	368	359	182	542	375	135	333	3058
MEN'S PAR	4	5	4	4	3	5	4	3	4	36
HANDICAP	6	8	3	2	4	1	5	9	7	
LADIES' TEE	264	435	318	306	149	440	325	125	293	2655
LADIES' PAR	4	5	4	4	3	5	4	3	4	36
HANDICAP	9	2	3	4	5	1	6	7	8	
HOLE	1	2	3	4	5	6	7	8	9	Out

Terrace Hills Golf Course

Altoona

515-967-2932

Terrace Hills Golf Course is a placement course. Someone who relies more on finesse rather than strength can score well on this layout. It is not an exceeding long course at 6416 yards, but makes up for it with other hazards. There are two ponds on the course and one stream; affecting play on eight holes. Eighteen bunkers also create problems for errant shots. Trees are medium in size and are scattered along the narrow fairways. The rough is cut just less than two inches along the fairways but becomes waist deep as you venture out into the wild. Terrace Hills is the first course in the area to have uncontrolled rough; sometimes becoming three to four feet high. The contour of the course is rolling on the front nine and hilly on the back nine. Tees are elevated and big. Greens average 6,500 square feet and generally have a very subtle slope to putt over. The grass condition on the greens is good; plus they have a reputation of being fast. The front nine was built in 1964 and the backside in 1970. The clubhouse is a small brown structure that has a bar area with microwave sandwiches and a nice selection of golfing supplies. This semi-private club has a green fee radius of outside the immediate area. Green fees are Very reasonable for an 18 hole course. The 100 members pay an annual fee of $770. Terrace Hills has a front nine holes that is easy to walk and play. The back nine is tougher to conquer. There is no one over-powering hole; but seven holes have out-of-bounds that tend to destroy scores. Terrace Hills has a mixture of all players. It has more of a public course feeling where non-members come to enjoy a different layout. The course is not very busy during the week but tee times are needed on the weekends. The course is located two miles straight east of Altoona at 8700 NE 46th Ave. .

Course	18 Holes	Aesthetics	Good
Distance	6416 Yards	Interest	Good
Par	36-36-72	Worth The Trip	Yes
Playability	Good	Rating	★★★

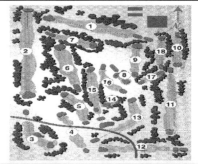

HOLE	1	2	3	4	5	6	7	8	9	OUT
BLUE YARDAGE	430	506	350	165	363	377	411	196	383	3181
WHITE YARDAGE	413	483	300	145	352	370	395	160	349	2967
HDCP MEN/WOMEN	2/16	17/14	8/6	14/10	10/18	11/2	4/4	13/12	12/8	
MEN'S PAR	4	5	4	3	4	4	4	3	4	35
WOMEN'S PAR	5	5	4	3	4	4	4	3	4	36
RED YARDAGE	400	395	270	130	258	333	327	140	284	2537

10	11	12	13	14	15	16	17	18	IN	OUT	TOT
405	349	393	463	208	507	405	160	345	3235	3181	6416
389	332	355	443	200	485	395	134	335	3068	2967	6035
1/1	6/9	7/5	15/11	3/13	18/15	5/3	16/17	9/7			
4	4	5	5	3	5	4	3	4	36	35	71
4	4	4	5	3	5	4	3	4	36	36	72
329	292	230	410	153	398	333	104	325	2574	2537	5111

Sioux Golf and Country Club

Alton

712-756-4513

One of the oldest courses in N.W. Iowa and the entire state is the Sioux Golf and Country Club located in Alton, also serving Orange City. This course was built in 1889 and has been a fixture in these communities ever since. It was voted Iowa's 9 hole course of the year in 1993. This is a nine hole private course with 200 members paying an annual fee of $500. Green fees for this 2,974 yard course are reasonable. The characteristics of the course include one stream running in the valley and affecting four holes, three bunkers, and no rough. An average number of trees line many of the wide and hilly fairways, there are also a lot of scattered trees on the hills. Tees are satisfactory, greens are small and tilted. Many of the members feel the greens are the best ingredient of the course, they are always in top shape and offer some fun and challenge. The grass condition on the fairways is good except for a few spots on the sides of some hills. This is a friendly course, a place where people play golf and have a fun social life too. Golfers during the day can get drinks and sandwiches in the clubhouse. The pro shop has a full line of equipment including clothes, and clubs. This is a hard course to walk but a fun place to play. There are a lot of side hill lies and not very much of a green to hit. This is a very nice course with a lot of history.

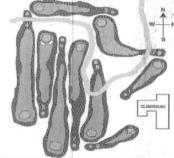

Course	9 Holes
Distance	2,974 Yards
Par	36
Playability	Fair
Aesthetics	Good
Interest	Good
Worth The Trip	Yes
Rating	★★★+

HOLE	1	2	3	4	5	6	7	8	9	OUT
MEN'S YARDS	173 157	330	354	506	315	469	397	290	140	2974
MEN'S PAR	3	4	4	5	4	5	4	4	3	36
MEN'S HANDICAP	15	9	7	1	13	5	3	11	17	
LADIES' YARDS	138	290	266	457	315	430	387	226	140	2649
LADIES' PAR	3	4	4	5	4	5	5	4	3	37
LADIES' HANDICAP	15	11	13	1	9	3	5	7	17	OUT

Homewood Golf Course

Ames

515-239-5363

One of the shorter finesse courses in the area is the Homewood Golf Course located at Duff and 20th in Ames. The course is built inside a park area and has a large number of trees, some can grab your ball at any time. The contour of the course is gently rolling with a few ravines thrown in. There are no water hazards on the course but there are 3 sand bunkers and some rough that does not affect play much. There are new tee boxes and 7 of the greens were redone. The tree size is medium to large and trees can be found in large numbers on six holes. The character of the course is shaped by the trees and the small greens. The greens are flat, with a little slope, and are very difficult to hit and stick. Homewood does have a fairway watering system so the condition of the course is good throughout the summer. There are 250 members on this course paying various season ticket prices from $125 to $560. Because of the student population this is more of a green fee course, with very reasonable prices, 21,000 rounds were played in 2003. This city owned course has a gray clubhouse that has beer and pop plus a few snacks. The clubhouse maintains a selection of golfing supplies. The course was built in 1928 and is tough for its size. The trees and small greens make it a thinking persons course, one that you need to be concerned about your next shot before you make it. The atmosphere is more like a family, all coming together for a short intimate time.

Course	9 Holes
Distance	2283 Yards
Par	34
Playability	Fair
Aesthetics	Good
Interest	Fair
Worth The Trip	Yes
Rating	★★+

HOLE	1	2	3	4	5	6	7	8	9	Out
BLUE TEES	244	361	317	165	255	242	317	252	130	2283
HANDICAP	7	4	1	2	5	8	3	6	9	
PAR	4	4	4	3	4	4	4	4	3	34
RED TEES	239	356	312	160	250	237	317	252	100	2223
HANDICAP	7	4	1	2	5	8	3	6	9	
PAR	4	4	4	3	4	4	4	4	3	34

Ames Golf & Country Club

Ames

515-232-8334

One of the outstanding courses in central Iowa is the Ames Golf & Country Club. A well designed course that has all the trappings of a future championship course. The course was build north and a little west of Ames, 3 miles on George Carver country road. It was brought to life on flat farm land but was converted into a semi-rolling course that has matured into a challenging course for anyone. This private course has some length at 6530 yards from the blue tees. But the length of the course may lengthen if you encounter any of the hazards. There are 3 ponds on the course that come into play on 4 holes. There is an average of 2 sand bunkers per hole, six new ones in the last 2 years and tiered rough that runs in front of tees and greens. One of the most outstanding characteristics of the layout are the greens. They are large in size, rolling and undulating to the last one. They are also noted for being exceptionally good greens to read and putt. Considering all the turns and dips you need a third year course in Engineering from Iowa State to read them. The condition of the grass is very good throughout the course. The FW watering system helps to keep the hot, dry winds form baking the fairways during the summer. The openness of the course also lends itself to the brisk wind conditions that can affect play. The tree size on the course is medium, most of the larger trees being evergreens that line the fairways. The course was built in 1975 and is a pleasant course to walk if you have the time. Local knowledge might suggest that you keep the ball in the short grass and out of the rough, leave the ball below the hole on your approach shot and keep in mind that the greens are fast and always have some kind of break. To play on Ames Golf & Country club you must be one of the 300 members or a guest. The clubhouse and facilities are very nice. The modern looking clubhouse has elegant dining for members. A beautiful lounge area upstairs and a full line pro shop downstairs. The pro shop also offers lessons on the practice range. This is a distinctive course, one that has elements of fun and challenging golf. It has an atmosphere of new time country club golf and a 30 year tradition of grandeur.

Course	18 Holes	Aesthetics	Excellent
Distance	6530 Yards	Interest	Excellent
Par	36-36-72	Worth the Trip	Yes
Playability	Excellent	Rating	★ ★ ★ ★

Hole	1	2	3	4	5	6	7	8	9	Out	10	11	12	13	14	15	16	17	18	In	Total
Blue 71.2/118	420	355	190	475	165	520	370	375	435	3305	395	400	160	490	395	355	225	390	430	3225	6530
God 69.9/115	405	335	175	455	150	495	355	355	395	3120	370	390	140	465	385	335	185	380	415	3065	6185
Gold 66.7/111	385	325	155	435	135	460	320	335	315	2870	360	315	130	460	345	320	165	285	400	2780	5650
Par	4	4	3	5	3	5	4	4	4	36	4	4	3	5	4	4	3	4	4	35	71
Red 71.2/116	385	305	155	420	120	400	320	335	315	2770	345	305	130	430	340	315	165	285	400	2715	5485
Par	5	4	3	5	3	5	4	4	4	37	4	4	3	5	4	4	3	4	5	36	73

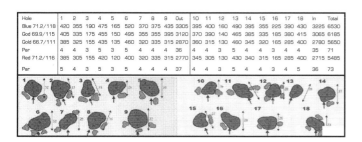

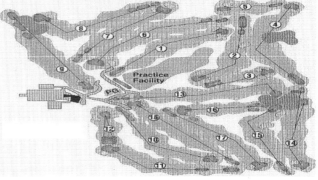

Coldwater Golf Links

Ames

515-233-4664
www.coldwatergolf.com

Coldwater Golf Links in Ames is one of the great additions to the metro area. This is an 18 hole 6787 yards course located on South 16th Street, 1 mile west of Duff and Sam's Club. The course opened in 2003 in a flood plane and wildlife preserve. The course used to be parking for Jack Trice Stadium. Now it is a natural golf course with Pampas grass, natural mounds and bent grass fairways and greens. As you might guess the rough is high and thick, all natural and beautiful. Since it used to be a grass parking lot there are very few trees on the course, but large trees to line the borders. None of the trees come into play unless you hit your ball out-of-bounds. The green sizes are above average with undulating surfaces. Most greens are tiered and oval in shape. The natural conditions provide grass bunkers on every hole and an average of 3 sand bunkers on every hole, generally in the FW. The unique feature of the course is the links layout with natural grasses incorporated into the design. This has been declared a wetlands area and so all the nature and beauty were incorporated into the design. The course is affiliated with the Audubon Society because of the wetlands and wildlife. The course has a wide variety of tee box situations. It has a fun and unique layout that used variety to keep you interest. The course also offers different sets of tees that vary the length of the course from 5,000 to 6,787 yards. This is more of a walker course. But the concrete paths make it good for carts also. The layout and location of the course make it a very interesting course. Coldwater is one that I would recommend for anyone.

Course	18 Holes	Aesthetics	Great
Distance	6787 Yards	Interest	Good
Par	336-36-72	Worth The Trip	Yes
Playability	Good	Rating	***+

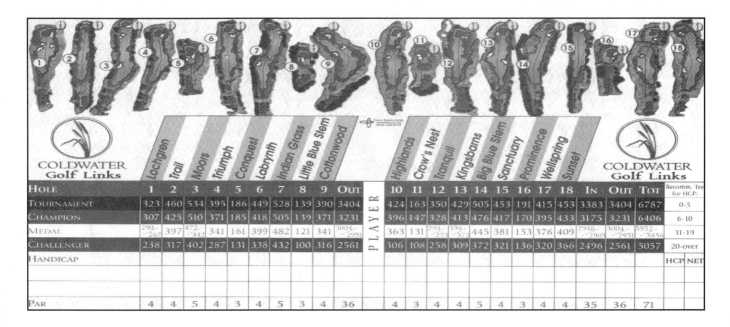

HOLE	1	2	3	4	5	6	7	8	9	OUT		10	11	12	13	14	15	16	17	18	IN	OUT	TOT	Recomm. Tee for HCP:
TOURNAMENT	323	460	534	395	186	449	528	139	390	3404		424	163	350	429	505	453	191	415	453	3383	3404	6787	0-5
CHAMPION	307	425	510	371	185	418	505	139	371	3231		396	147	328	413	476	417	170	395	433	3175	3231	6406	6-10
MEDAL	290-267	397	472-442	341	161	399	482	121	341	3004-2951		363	131	294-272	399-371	445	381	153	376	409	2948-2903	3004-2951	5952-5856	11-19
CHALLENGER	238	317	402	287	131	338	432	100	316	2561		306	108	258	309	372	321	136	320	366	2496	2561	5057	20-over
HANDICAP																								HCP NET
PAR	4	4	5	4	3	4	5	3	4	36		4	3	4	4	5	4	3	4	4	35	36	71	

Veenker Memorial Golf Course

Ames

515-294-6727
www.veenkergolf.com

One of the top ten courses in the state is located on the Iowa State University Campus in Ames. Veenker Memorial Golf Course is a public 18 hole course that offers a challenge to all levels of golfing ability. The course is divided by a river, the north section is flat with fewer and smaller trees, the south section is much hillier, bigger trees, and very challenging. The general contour of the course is very hilly on the front nine and the back nine not so bad. There are two ponds on the course, which are deep gullies in the summer, these affect 4 holes. Your play is interrupted by six river crossings, some of the crossings are critical while others are not if planned right. The rough is cut two to three inches and is saturated with trees. This course is packed with trees, the N.E. corner holes have new plantings. The remainder of the course has old mature trees lining all the fairways and scattered in the valleys to make things interesting. Greens are medium to large in size and have a variety of rolling and sloping surfaces. The condition of the greens and fairway grass is good, considering the amount of play this course gets in the early spring when the grass is greening up. Complete FW watering makes this an even better course. Many of the tees have been or will be rebuilt to accommodate the heavy play. The driving range has also been expanded with 2 tee areas, a large practice green, and practice bunker. Veenker is a challenging course with a gambit of situations. It is an easy course to walk, but not so easy to score well on. It is a very scenic course that is very busy while the students are in town, but much easier to get on during the middle of the summer. Weekday green fees are $16 for 9 and $21 for 18. You can buy a season pass for $785 or a 10 round card for $185. There is a whole range of fees for students, faculty, seniors, and public. The clubhouse is a small structure with a full line of equipment with carts for rent and pros to help. Food consists of snacks and beer. This is one of the outstanding courses in the area. This course has matured into a beautiful course. A layout that can hold major Iowa tournaments and yet let the average golfer enjoy a relaxed game of Iowa golf.

Course	18 Holes	Aesthetics	Excellent
Distance	6543 Yards	Interest	Excellent
Par	36-36-72	Worth the Trip	Yes
Playability	Excellent	Rating	★ ★ ★ ★

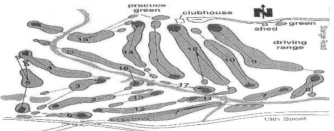

HOLE		1	2	3	4	5	6	7	8	9	OUT		10	11	12	13	14	15	16	17	18	IN	TOT	HCP	NET
BLUE	72.2/125	435	334	308	349	402	210	590	174	508	3310		481	155	330	160	416	420	544	190	534	3235	6545		
GOLD	70.1/122	419		289	340	350		570	157	495			473	134	306	144	397	386	485	152	521	2998			
RED	65.6/108	400		203	330	319	145	550	123	481			459	98	290	125	346	311	368	132	407	2569			
MEN'S PAR		4	4	4	4	4	3	5	3	5	36		5	3	4	3	4	4	5	3	5	36	72		
MEN'S HANDICAP		3	9	13	11	5	15	1	17	5			6	14	12	16	10	8	2	18	4				
GOLD	75.3/134	419		289	340	350		570	157	495	2998		473	134	306	144	397	386	485	152	521	2998			
RED	71.0/122	400		203	330	319	145	550	123	481			459	98	290	125	346	311	368	132	407	2569			
LADIES' PAR		5	4	4	4	4	3	5	3	5	37		5	3	4	3	4	4	5	3	5	36	73		
LADIES' HANDICAP		7	9	13	11	3	15	1	17	5			6	10	12	16	14	8	2	18	4				

Oaks Golf Club

Ames

515- 232-9862

The Oaks Golf Club offers an alternative to ISU Veenker and Homewood. It is a moderate course that is basically flat, except for one big hill and offers a friendly, slow paced atmosphere that is relaxing and rewarding. The entire course received a face lift recently and is on the way to improvement. This is a public course with a small clubhouse with a limited amount of supplies, plus a bar and grill for food items. There are no tee times required, it is very easy to get on during weekday afternoons. The 100 members pay $345 for the first member of a family and $150 for additional members. Green fees are $9.00 for 9 and $16.00 for 18 during the week. There is one pond and one creek on the course affecting play on two tee shots. There are two sand traps and no rough except for some natural rough areas on two holes. Trees range from new plantings to large mature trees. Many of the trees line the fairways. Greens are medium in size and all are flat. This is easy course to walk and plays with medium difficulty. It is a wide open course that was built in 1956. Oaks allows for a full swing without much penalty. The landscaping is very nice and the course is watered a great deal to maintain the plush look. The course is located two miles north of Ames on Highway 69. The picture shows a big tree, this tree is dead center in front of number 9 green !!!!

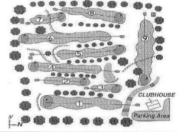

Course	9 Holes
Distance	2935 Yards
Par	36
Playability	Good
Aesthetics	Good
Interest	Fair
Worth the Trip	Yes
Rating	★★+

Men's Yardage	472	275	145	370	400	455	160	340	318	2935
Men's Par	5	4	3	4	4	5	3	4	4	36
Men's Handicap	7	17	15	1	3	9	5	13	11	
Ladies Yardage	452	255	125	345	320	430	145	320	308	2692
Ladies Par	5	4	3	5	4	5	4	4	4	38
Ladies Handicap	7	17	15	1	3	9	5	13	11	
HOLE NUMBER	1	2	3	4	5	6	7	8	9	OUT

Fawn Creek Country Club

Anamosa

319-462-4115

Fawn Creek Golf Course north of Anamosa is the number one evergreen course in the state. Ninty-nine per cent of the trees, and there are a lot of them, are 20 to 35 foot evergreens. The entire clubhouse was remodeled in 1988. Fawn Creek is a long course, 3211 yards, and yet easy to walk. Green fees are $15 for 9 holes. There are carts for rent at the clubhouse. Water is an important part of the course, one pond comes into play on two holes and a stream affects the play on four holes. The wide fairways are lined entirely with evergreens. Fairway watering was added in 2000. There are no hidden dangers on the course, no hidden shots and no doglegs. The greens are large in size and sloping, and are in excellent condition. The greens do possess minor breaks that are easy to see and true to putt. The course was built in 1963. Fawn Creek has a lot of repeat golfers beside the members. It is an informal course that is easy and stimulating to play, plus visually pleasing. The moderate green fees are worth the price just to play alongside all the evergreens.

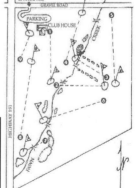

Course	9 Holes
Distance	3211 Yards
Par	37
Playability	Good
Aesthetics	Very Good
Interest	Good
Worth The Trip	Yes
Rating	★★★

HOLE	1	2	3	4	5	6	7	8	9	TOTAL
BLUE YARDAGE	366	335	347	391	549	469	159	405	170	3211
BLUE PAR	4	4	4	4	5	5	3	4	3	36

Wapsipinicon Country Club

Anamosa

319-462-3930

The only log cabin clubhouse found in the state can be enjoyed in Anamosa at the Wapsipinicon Country Club, located in the Wapsipinicon State Park. This course is set in beautiful surroundings. The trees are plentiful and very large. The rule is, if you can find your ball in the trees you can play it. The course was built in 1923 and is a family and socially oriented course for the 250 members. The log cabin clubhouse has a big fireplace room and is very majestic. There is a big bar area in the back and the restaurant is open all the time. Weekday green fees are reasonable,$10.00 weekdays, and the clubhouse has a full line of supplies. This is a short, tight course. Only two holes can be considered flat with the course generally described as rolling. If you can keep it in the middle and out of the trees, it is an easy course to score well on. The trees make the fairways narrow and the two inch rough also closes the gap. The greens are tiny in some cases and medium in others, most are flat and fast. Greens #2 and #9 were rebuilt recently. There are three blind approach shots to make so you might want to play this course more than once to get the right feel for it. Wapsipinicon is an old established course that is a treasure. If nothing else make the trip to see the log cabin clubhouse. The course is located on the south edge of town on E34.

Course	9 Holes
Distance	2362 Yards
Par	33
Playability	Fair
Aesthetics	Excellent
Interest	Very Good
Worth The Trip	Yes
Rating	★★★+

BLUE	110/120	362	398	125	277	292	174	394	251	2393
PAR	3	4	4	3	4	4	3	4	4	33
HDCP	5	1	4	8	7	6	3	2	9	
HOLE	1	2	3	4	5	6	7	8	9	OUT
WHITE	115	352	384	120	267	282	170	320	235	2245
PAR	3	4	5	3	4	4	4	4	4	35

Ankeny Golf and Country Club

Ankeny

515-964-3647

The Ankeny Golf and Country Club is a very picturesque golf course located on the S.W. corner of Ankeny. The layout includes one lake that comes into play on two holes, a creek that catches three holes and an average of one sand bunker per hole. There are 25 acres of rough and 25 acres of fairway on the Ankeny course. The Ash trees lining the fairways are medium in height and act as a boundary for the regulation PGA fairways. The greens are medium in size with a total of 50,000 square feet of surface. They are generally flat with a few breaks that tend to be difficult to read. The greens are also noted around the area as being fast and hard to hold, several of the greens have been rebuilt. The Ankeny Country Club is a control course — to play this course well you must keep the ball down the middle. The course was built in 1961 and has the ability to lull a player into submission. The contour of the course is flat except for one big hill. It also boasts many doglegs. This is a private club that has 260 members. You can play on this course with a member or if you belong to another private club. Green fees are $18 for 9. The clubhouse has a full line of clothes, plus carts, and it also has a bar and grill. New cart paths were added and several ladies tee boxes were redone. This is one course that you would not get tired of playing; there's always something different.

Course	9 Holes
Distance	2849 Yards
Par	35
Playability	Good
Aesthetics	Very Good
Interest	Very Good
Worth The Trip	Yes
Rating	★★★

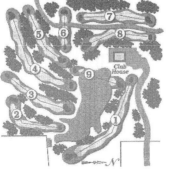

HOLE	1	2	3	4	5	6	7	8	9	Out
WHITE/BLUE	406	343	347	464	337	148	328	306	159	2838
HANDICAP	5	13	11	3	9	17	1	7	15	
PAR	M/L 4/5	4	4	5	4	3	4	4	3	35/36

Crestwood Hills Golf Course

Anita

712-762-3803

Course	18 Holes	Aesthetics	Good
Distance	5427 Yards	Interest	Good
Par	71	Worth The Trip	Yes
Playability	Good	Rating	* * *

The Crestwood Hills Golf Course in Anita is built along side Turkey Creek and many of the holes slope down to the water. A new clubhouse was built in 1989 and a new 9 holes was built in 1994. Seven of the front nine holes are built on the hillside, only the two by the creek are flat. The new 9 holes are hilly and are built to the west. There are mature trees that do come into play and new trees are being moved in every year. The layout does contain one pond, no sand, and a very deep rough that runs down the middle of the course. The greens are medium to large in size and generally flat giving you some relief from climbing up or downhill to get to them. The condition of the greens is good, they are soft, slow and cross cut to give a nice appearance. Holes 3 and 8 are sever doglegs to the right , which means you slicers have the advantage. Crestwood has developed into a beautiful course. The clubhouse has carts to rent, plus balls and gloves for sale. Green fees are average in price. The 320 members pay an annual fee of $340 for a family. Some things to remember about Crestwood Hills, which was built in 1965, there are lots of uphill and downhill lies, the rough is a bear to get out of, the greens are slow, and don't be concerned if an airplane makes its final approach over the course, the airport is right across Turkey Creek. The course has been identified as an easy course but a fun course to play. Green fees are $15 during the week. The course can be found on the south edge of Anita, 1/2 mile on Michigan Ave.

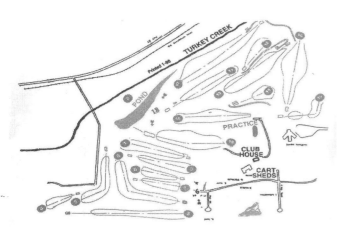

HOLE	1	2	3	4	5	6	7	8	9	OUT
YARDS	308	117	290	128	485	206	223	448	263	2468
HANDICAP	16	4	8	10	2	6	18	14	12	
PAR	4	3	4	3	5	3	4	5	4	35
YARDS	293	112	278	123	422	200	220	386	253	2287
Womens Par	4	3	4	3	5	4	4	5	4	36

10	11	12	13	14	15	16	17	18	IN	TOT
320	360	145	462	155	255	355	485	422	2959	5427
15	5	17	13	9	3	11	7	1		
4	4	3	5	3	4	4	5	4	36	71
315	300	140	410	148	215	352	383	362	2625	4912
4	4	3	5	3	4	4	5	4	36	72

14

Briarwood Public Golf Course
Ankeny
515-964-4653

Briarwood Public Golf Course is one of the metro area's new courses. The 18 hole 7019 yard course was opened in June of 1995 and is located on 3405 NE Trilcin Dr. which is in NE Ankeny off NE 26th street. The course was developed on farm land and could be called a links style course. All the trees on the course have been brought in and planted. One of the unique features of the complex is the grainery on the location, that was also brought in. This is a nicely laid out course with only one dogleg. The greens are bent grass, come in all kinds of shapes, and are in the 8,00 to 9,000 square foot range in area. Most of the greens are flat and big. There are several manmade fairway bunkers and 42 sand bunkers on the course. The course is fairly flat, remember it is farmland, but there is water everywhere. A creek comes into play on 10 and 18, a pond affects holes 8,9,3,17, and 14. There is rough, but only one level if you get off the beaten path. This is a well kept course and is in better shape since it has matured the last few years. The water is one of the most challenging aspects of the course and as the score card says on the front cover "don't be short". The clubhouse has a full line of equipment and food consists of drinks and a grill. There are approximately 100 members that pay $1,100 for a single membership. Green fees are $36.50 on a weekday that includes a cart. This is a heavily played course with 30,000 rounds played in 2003. This is certainly a nice addition to the north metro area.

Course	18 Holes	Aesthetics	Good
Distance	7091 Yards	Interest	Good
Par	36-36-72	Worth The Trip	Yes
Playability	Very Good	Rating	****

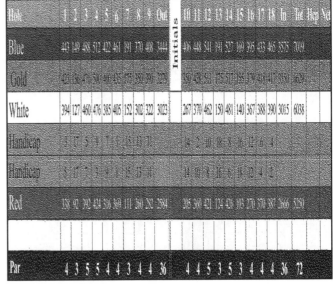

Hole	1	2	3	4	5	6	7	8	9	Out	10	11	12	13	14	15	16	17	18	In	Tot	Hcp	Net
Blue	443	140	488	512	422	461	191	370	408	3444	406	448	541	191	527	169	395	433	465	3575	7019		
Gold																					6629		
White	394	127	460	476	385	405	152	302	322	3023	267	370	462	150	481	140	367	388	390	3015	6038		
Handicap																							
Handicap																							
Red	338	92	392	424	316	369	111	360	252	2594	205	340	421	124	426	105	270	370	387	2666	5250		
Par	4	3	5	5	4	4	3	4	4	36	4	4	5	3	5	3	4	4	4	36	72		

Otter Creek Golf Course

Ankeny

515-965-6464

Otter Creek Golf Course, 2 miles northeast of Ankeny, was built in 1980 and has improved a tremendous amount over the past ten years. To start with this public course built an inviting and modern clubhouse a couple of years ago and now provides a complete line of supplies with a spacious snack area. Yearly dues are $550 for an adult single. Green fees are very reasonable for an 18 hole course, $14.00 during the week and $25.00 on the weekends with. There are mandatory tee times on Otter Creek but there is no problem getting on almost any time you want to. The layout has 3 ponds affecting five holes, a creek on two holes, and sharply mowed rough that definitely comes into play on this wide open course. Fairway grass is good thanks to the double row watering system. The cut rough defines the fairways and presents an aesthetic picture. The trees line all the fairways and are starting to present a problem. Now it is possible to cut corners on the doglegs, but in a few years the course will get a lot longer. The greens are small to medium in size and are flat. The greens have the reputation as being easy to read but lightning fast. Hidden breaks can lead to a three putt more than once as you traverse the course. This is a very nice landscaped course that has made a dramatic turn-a-round the last three years. The contour of the course is varied, flat on the west side and rolling on the 5 or 6 holes on the east side. Basically this lets the hitter spray the ball around and not get hurt too much. Otter Creek is a challenging course, the greens will test you, and I guarantee that you will be pleased with the condition of the course. The city of Ankeny has a jewel that it has polished to a brilliant shine.

Course	18 Holes	Aesthetics	Good
Distance	6473 Yards	Interest	Good
Par	35-36-71	Worth The Trip	Yes
Playability	Very Good	Rating	★★★★

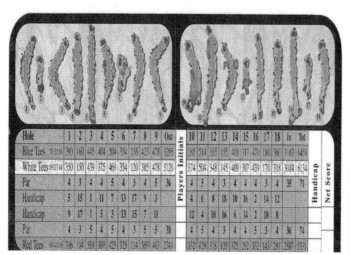

Hole	1	2	3	4	5	6	7	8	9	Out	Players Initials	10	11	12	13	14	15	16	17	18	In	Tot	Handicap	Net Score
Blue Tees	391	160	445	404	504	354	125	425	478	3295		305	514	355	155	418	317	479	180	360	3.63	6458		
White Tees	350	150	439	375	469	354	120	385	478	3120		374	504	348	145	409	307	439	170	318	3014	6134		
Par	4	3	4	4	5	4	3	5	4	35		4	5	4	3	4	4	4	3	4	35	71		
Handicap	5	15	1	11	7	13	17	9	3			6	8	18	10	16	2	14	12					
Handicap	9	17	1	5	3	13	15	7	11			12	4	10	16	6	14	2	18	8				
Par	4	3	5	4	4	5	3	5	5	38		4	5	4	4	4	5	3	4	36	74			
Red Tees	306	104	359	309	425	325	114	369	403	2714		332	429	318	135	325	262	352	143	291	2587	5301		

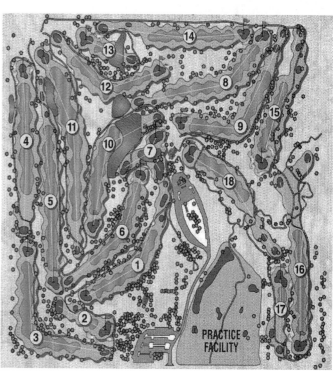

PRACTICE FACILITY

Anthon Golf Club

Anthon

712-373-5774

The Anthon golf Club is located south of Anthon and was built in 1997. This is an interested piece of land, part of the course was built on farmland and part of the course was built on the site of an old dump. There are rolling hills and some mature trees so the thought of playing on top of garbage does not come up. The greens are generally oval in shape and medium in size. There are no sand or grass bunkers on the course. There are mature trees but there are basically 10 foot trees lining the fairways. The only water on the course is the Fairway watering system, and a dried up creek bed that does become active in heavy rain. There are two doglegs on the course that turn a brisk 90 degrees. The local golfer says that Anthon is a fairly long course, has a very interesting par 3 that shots over a valley and the greens hold very good. The clubhouse has no equipment but they do have snacks. Yearly dues are $325 and daily green fees are $10 for 18 holes.

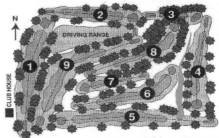

Course	9 Holes	Aesthetics	Good
Distance	2930 Yards	Interest	Good
Par	35	Worth The Trip	Yes
Playability	Good	Rating	★★★

HOLE	1	2	3	4	5	6	7	8	9	Out
Blue Tees	427	285	114	390	367	330	175	330	512	2930
White Tees	419	278	108	382	347	318	170	315	487	2824
Handicap	3	9	5	1	4	6	7	2	8	
Par	4	4	3	4	4	4	3	4	5	35
Red Tees	410	270	93	368	322	305	125	300	462	2655
Handicap	5	9	7	2	4	6	8	1	3	
Par	5	4	3	4	4	4	3	4	5	36

Aplington Recreation Complex

Aplington

319-347-6059

The Aplington Recreation Complex is a public course located on the west of Aplington on Highway 20. The yardage of 3307 yards makes this a long driver layout. A straight drive and a hot putter will make this course play much easier. There is one pond that comes into play in fairway four. There is an average of one sand bunker per hole and a two inch rough lining the wide fairways and fronting the tees and greens. The scarcity of trees is apparent with the majority of these being small or new plantings. The contour of the course is flat near the clubhouse but rolling out on the southern part of the course. Tees are elevated and big. Greens are large in size and have a variety of putting surfaces. The greens have many hidden breaks and are difficult to read. They are also fast and tricky to putt. The greens are the best feature of the course though. Aplington Recreation Complex was built in 1976. This is a wide open course that rewards the long ball. It is easy to walk and fairly easy to score well on. Green fees are very reasonable during the week and on the weekends. The clubhouse has golfing supplies and a bar that serves sandwiches and drinks. Aplington is a young course that has developed into more of a relaxed, pleasure seeking course. Drive for show and putt for dough would fit the description of Aplington Recreation Complex.

Course	9 Holes
Distance	3307 Yards
Par	36
Playability	Fair
Aesthetics	Fair
Interest	Good
Worth The Trip	Maybe
Rating	★★

Men's Course	YARDAGE	465	502	327	132	533	400	395	383	170	3,307
	PAR	4	5	4	3	5	4	4	4	3	36
HANDICAP		1	5	7	8	6	4	2	3	9	
Ladies Course	YARDAGE	372	417	305	117	454	375	332	365	180	2897
	PAR	4	5	4	3	5	4	4	4	3	36
HANDICAP		1	5	7	8	6	4	2	3	9	
HOLE		1	2	3	4	5	6	7	8	9	OUT

Country Greens Golf Course

Armstrong

712-868-3048

The Country Greens Golf Course in Armstrong is noted for its large, rolling greens that have humps and a lots of subtle breaks. This public course added an additional 9 holes in 2002 Country Greens has one stream running along the edge of the course and three bunkers. The trees are small with a few new plantings, they are generally along the fairways. The contour of the fairways is rolling with a two inch rough guarding the edges. Fairway watering keeps this N.W. Iowa course green throughout the summer. Tees are elevated and big just like the greens. Grass condition all over the course is good. Green fees on this public course are reasonable. The course has a great atmosphere and is easy to get on and play. The greens are quick but true to putt. A new clubhouse was built in 2003. There are also carts to rent. The clubhouse serves drinks and grilled sandwiches. In addition to the course food there is a full time restaurant on the complex, which used to be the clubhouse, and is open to the public serving very good food. This is a family oriented course. Yearly fees for a family are $700, weekday green fees are $14.80. A high percent of the golfers playing are bogey shooters. This is not a layout for hookers, there are out-of-bounds stacks on the left all the way around the layout. Country Greens is a very pleasurable course that has very active members and stays busy most of the summer.

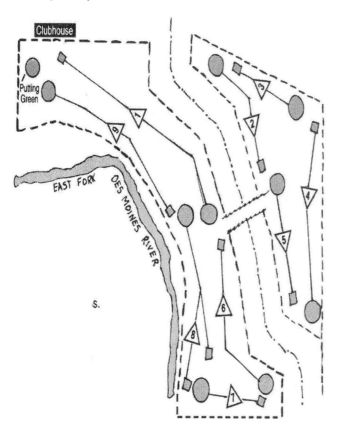

Course	18 Holes	Aesthetics	Good
Distance	5980 Yards	Interest	Good
Par	36-36-72	Worth The Trip	Yes
Playability	Good	Rating	***

Yardage	483	330	183	416	251	358	170	473	390	3054
Mens' Par	5	4	3	4	4	4	3	5	4	36
Mens' Handicap	9	15	3	1	17	7	13	11	5	
Ladies' Par	5	4	3	5	4	4	3	5	5	38
Ladies' Handicap	5	15	1	11	17	13	3	7	9	
We										
Side Matches	1	2	3	4	5	6	7	8	9	Out

18

Emerald Hills

Arnolds Park

712-332-7100

Emerald Hills is an 18 hole public course located in the lakes region of N.W. Iowa. This 1971 course can be found along Highway 71 in Arnolds Park. The course is located across the road from Okoboji Lake and has five ponds of its own. Golfing hazards include an average of three bunkers per hole and fairway rough. An above number of full size trees line most of the fairways with new planted trees scattered throughout the course. The fully automated fairway watering system keeps the grass green during dry summers. The contour of the course is very gently rolling hills. Tees are big and seeded with bent grass. The greens are large, rolling, and have some of the nicest surfaces in the area. Three greens were rebuilt in 91. The wide fairways encourage heavy hitting, and such hitting is possible without much penalty. Emerald Hills is easy to walk and fairly easy to score well on. Trees are not so much of a factor now but the 5,000 trees that are planted will become a force to reckon with in a few years. The atmosphere of the course is low pressure, high fun. Many vacationers to the area take advantage of such a nice 18 hole course and keep Emerald Hills busy most of the summer. The clubhouse has just been remodeled and is very nice and has a very nice view of the course and practice area. The dining area is open and bright with drinks and grilled sandwiches. Golf supplies include balls, gloves, and a few clothes. There are also 45 new carts to rent. The most unique thing about Emerald Hills are the large greens and with undulating putting surfaces. Emerald Hills is a busy course that has nice clubhouse facilities and good playing conditions.

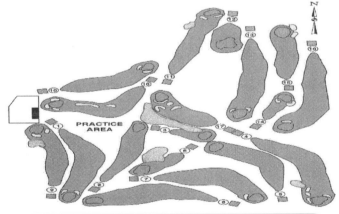

Course	18 Holes	Aesthetics	Good
Distance	6389 Yards	Interest	Good
Par	36-36-72	Worth The Trip	Yes
Playability	Good	Rating	★★★★

WELCOME TO EMERALD HILLS GOLF CLUB – ENJOY YOUR ROUND

Hole	1	2	3	4	5	6	7	8	9	OUT		10	11	12	13	14	15	16	17	18	IN	TOT	HCP	NET
Blue Tee	482	415	162	528	439	181	407	420	415	3449		360	430	158	513	163	354	531	306	397	3202	6651		
White Tee	470	400	147	514	408	150	392	410	399	3290		335	416	143	497	158	344	501	286	380	3060	6350		
Gold Tee	447	359	138	500	331	133	375	377	351	3011		320	365	130	427	153	335	463	270	328	2801	5812		
Red Tee	392	342	130	472	319	131	352	344	341	2823		310	349	123	417	148	326	419	250	328	2670	5493		
Handicap	17	5	15	9	1	13	11	3	7			14	2	16	10	18	8	6	12	4				
Par	5	4	3	5	4	3	4	4	4	36		4	4	3	5	3	4	5	4	4	36	72		

Atlantic Golf and Country Club

Atlantic

712-243-3656

The Atlantic Golf and Country Club is another fine course located in S.W. Iowa. This course has long been known as one of the best maintained and most challenging courses in the state. One of the major tournaments in Iowa, Tournament of Champions, has been held here each of the past 26 years. The course record was set during this tournament in 1985 by Jim Curel and Dick Saybert with an eight under par 61. The course is located on So. Chestnut in Atlantic and utilizes some of the beauty that the S.W. part of town has to offer. Green fees for weekdays are very reasonable when playing with a member. If you live outside a 50 mile radius of Atlantic the fees are still quite reasonable for an 18 hole course. This outstanding 18 hole course is 5950 yards long and carries a par of 69. The course is laden with big beautiful trees which line some fairways but are basically scattered throughout the course. The contour of the course ranges from flat to rolling to hilly in some areas. The greens are of medium size and also have a rolling putting surface. A stream cuts through a section of the course and affects play on 3 holes. A new pond was dug which now affects holes 14 & 15. They have also added fairway watering. Numerous sand bunkers guard the greens with a few fairway grass and sand bunkers placed to trap a few drives. The length of the course makes this more of a finesse layout. Iron control will bring your score down faster than your power draw. The front nine is hilly and mature. The clubhouse is spacious and can accommodate large numbers of people, especially during tournament time. There is also a bar and snack area that is available to golfers during the day. The pro shop carries a full line of equipment plus carts to rent. Atlantic Country Club is designed to challenge all levels of abilities. If you are not a club champion but plan on becoming one in the future you might want to try this course out and see how you measure up with the big sticks.

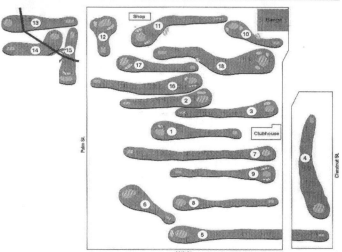

Course	18 Holes	Aesthetics	Good
Distance	5950 Yards	Interest	Excel.
Par	34-35-69	Worth The Trip	Yes
Playability	Excel.	Rating	★★★★

Starting Hole	BLUE	349	176	365	365	401	158	402	285	315	2816	377	406	147	367	330	185	426	342	558	3138	5980	Starting Hole
	WHITE	338	163	342	351	395	146	396	271	305	2707	367	382	137	361	320	177	423	338	540	3045	5730	
	PAR	4	3	4	4	4	3	4	4	4	34	4	4	3	4	4	3	4	4	5	35	69	
	HANDICAP	15	5	11	3	1	9	7	13	17		14	10	12	4	8	6	2	18	16			
Please	LADIES' PAR	4	3	4	4	4	3	4	4	4	34	4	4	3	4	4	3	5	4	5	36	70	
Replace	LADIES' HANDICAP	9	7	5	13	3	11	1	17	15		8	12	16	6	10	18	2	14	4			
Divots	RED	320	153	324	245	345	128	335	256	277	2383	259	356	126	356	305	122	410	318	408	2660	4948	
	HOLE	1	2	3	4	5	6	7	8	9	OUT	10	11	12	13	14	15	16	17	18	IN	TOT	HCP	NET

Men's Rating
Back - 68.6
Reg. - 67.5

Slope
Back - 118
Reg. - 113

Ladies' Rating
69.5

Slope
113

Nishna Hills Golf Club
Atlantic
712-243-9931

Nishna Hills Golf Course in Atlantic is located in the S.E. part of town on E. 14th. This is one of Atlantic's two fine golf courses. Nishna Hills was opened in 1963 and has grown to a membership size of 325. Over the 5456 yard course you can find a variety of unique characteristics that can only be found in Iowa. The fairways are lined with medium to large trees, a creek runs down the middle of the course and comes into play on five holes. The general contour of the course is rolling to hilly due to the location of the creek. But the well maintained fairway grass and rough makes the course fair and fun to play. The greens are generally small and flat but are elevated and tilted a few degrees to improve your control on the approach shot. The clubhouse view of the course is panoramic and the condition of the course is neat and green. A new sprinkler system has added to the beauty of the course. Weekday green fees are very reasonable. If you desire to become a member of Nishna Hills a yearly family membership will cost $600. The large and spacious clubhouse includes a pro shop with a full line of supplies. There is also a large dining and bar area that serves sandwiches and drinks during the day. There are some major tournaments that are held here each year; the S.W. Iowa Mens Tournament is held in July and the S.W. Iowa Ladies Open is also held at Nishna Hills. Nishna Hills is a challenging course but fairly easy to score well on. The small greens and tough approach shots make this a course to bring out the best in each golfer. Nishna Hills is a high traffic course. The members exhibit that "play till you drop" atmosphere, or at least play till you can't see the ball anymore.

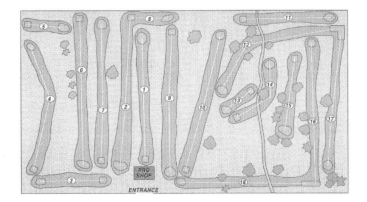

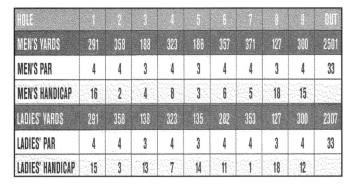

Course	18 Holes	Aesthetics	Good
Distance	5456 Yards	Interest	Good
Par	33-36-69	Worth the Trip	Yes
Playability	Excellent	Rating	★★+

HOLE	1	2	3	4	5	6	7	8	9	OUT
MEN'S YARDS	291	358	188	323	186	357	371	127	300	2501
MEN'S PAR	4	4	3	4	3	4	4	3	4	33
MEN'S HANDICAP	16	2	4	8	3	6	5	18	15	
LADIES' YARDS	291	358	138	323	135	282	353	127	300	2307
LADIES' PAR	4	4	3	4	3	4	4	3	4	33
LADIES' HANDICAP	15	3	13	7	14	11	1	18	12	

10	11	12	13	14	15	16	17	18	IN	TOTAL
359	329	510	163	323	206	296	267	502	2955	5456
4	4	5	3	4	3	4	4	5	36	69
9	12	13	10	11	1	14	17	7		
359	329	430	163	216	206	296	267	455	2721	5028
4	4	5	3	4	3	4	4	5	36	69
9	5	6	8	17	4	10	16	2		

Audubon Country Club

Audubon

712-563-2348

The Audubon Country Club is located on the west side of Audubon 1/2 mile on Division Street. . This is a rolling and hilly course that plays easy if you keep your ball on the beaten path. There are no water hazards and only two sand bunkers. The rough is cut wide and deep causing some problems only if you hook your tee shots. Trees are medium in size and are scattered in the rough with some along the fairways. One of the things that you will remember about this course are the greens. They are very small, postage stamp size. Many are flat but a few are rolling on the surface and all are cut short and putt quite fast. Whichever surface they have it is almost impossible to stop your approach shot on the green. This is a fairly open course with wide fairways suitable for someone who sprays the ball. The fairways have a mildly rolling surface but once in the rough the angle of attack becomes much steeper. This is a fairly easy course to score on but not the best to walk. It is set up for a straight hitter and any hooker will find things difficult. The course was built in the 1920's and has a clubhouse with balls and gloves, carts and a bar area. The 200 members pay $400 for a family membership with green fees very reasonable on weekdays and weekends. This is not a very busy course with few green fees taken in during the week. It is a members course, developed and kept to their needs, a nice home town course.

Course	9 Holes
Distance	2793 Yards
Par	35
Playability	Fair
Aesthetic s	Good
Interest	Fair
Worth The Trip	Maybe
Rating	★★

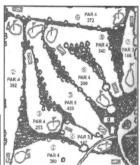

HOLE	1	2	3	4	5	6	7	8	9	OUT
YARDAGE	360	392	253	147	453	372	186	340	290	2793
MEN'S PAR	4	4	4	3	5	4	3	4	4	35
LADIES' PAR	4	4	4	3	5	4	3	4	4	35
HANDICAP	3	1	9	5	8	2	4	6	7	

Aurelia Golf Club

Aurelia

712-434-5498

The Aurelia Golf Club was started in 1960 and has developed into a likable small town course. The course is laid out on the N.E. side of Aurelia and is spread over 3038 yards of flat land. There is one pond on number 6 and an average of one sand bunker per hole. There are a large number of small and medium size trees lining the fairways which cause a great deal of difficulty throughout the round. The landscaping of the course is very nice especially around the clubhouse and tee boxes. An ongoing development program with traps, bunkers, and expanded greens makes this a growing course. The tees are big and slightly elevated while the greens are small and tilted to a small degree. Four new greens were opened late in the summer of '91' and a new pond was added in 2002. The greens also have a reputation as being hard to hold, mainly due to the crowned surfaces. The greens and fairways have a high quality of grass. This east-west course is more of a short iron approach course, an iron shot in the right spot on the green creates opportunities for a lower score. The 175 members pay $370 per year with an additional $100 entry stock. Green fees are average, $9.00 for a weekday. The clubhouse was remodeled in '91' with an expanded kitchen and patio areas. An out and back course that is well suited for pleasure golf.

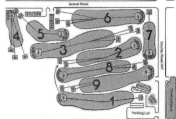

Course	9 Holes
Distance	3038 Yards
Par	35
Playability	Good
Aesthetics	Good
Interest	Fair
Worth The Trip	Yes
Rating	★★+

Hole Handicap	1 3	2 7	3 5	4 8	5 9	6 4	7 6	8 1	9 2	OUT	TOTALS
BLUE TEES	353	364	526	176	323	368	168	380	380		3038
WHITE TEES	348	344	512	163	319	362	158	373	364		2943
RED TEES	337	323	450	133	283	307	138	309	309		2589
PAR	4	4	5	3	4	4	3	4	4	35	35

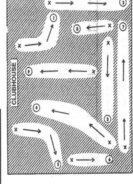

Avoca Golf & Country Club

Avoca

712-343-6979

The Avoca Golf and Country Club is located at the north edge of town at 1920 Willow. This is a city owned course that was built in 1975. The clubhouse sits on the west edge of the course and carries a few supplies and has normal bar and grill items available for golfers. Green fees are average in price, $16.00 all day weekdays and $14.00 all day on the weekends. The 206 members pay an annual fee of $406. The hazards on the course include seven sand bunkers, an above average number of small trees, 2 1/2 inch rough, and one pond on #5. The contour of the layout is hilly by the clubhouse and flat as you proceed farther to the east. Tees are medium in size and slightly elevated. Greens are medium to large and generally flat with a few dips to keep your interest. Avoca is an open course that rewards control off the tee. The par fives are fairly short making this a course that your overall score can turn out fairly low. Fairway watering was added in 2001. Also 500 trees have been added in the last 5 years. This is an interesting course to play. It is easy to walk, until you trek back up to the clubhouse. It is easy to score well on, if you have the right attitude about your shot selection. It is also an easy course to get on during the week. Overall it is a good small town course that offers members a chance to play something challenging and well maintained.

Course	9 Holes
Distance	3147 Yards
Par	36
Playability	Good
Aesthetics	Fair
Interest	Good
Worth The Trip	Yes
Rating	★★+

HOLE	1	2	3	4	5	6	7	8	9	OUT
PAR	4	4	4	5	4	3	5	3	4	36
HANDICAP	11	15	1	5	13	7	17	9	3	
Red Yardage	317	287	307	410	335	124	414	148	309	2651
White Yardage	331	346	368	465	347	165	484	148	365	3019
Blue Yardage	344	359	377	477	384	190	497	159	376	3163

North Kossuth Golf Club

Bancroft

515-885-2352

The North Kossuth Golf Club located on the east edge of Bancroft. This is a nine hole public course that has average weekday and weekend green fees. The clubhouse is typical small town, a big bar area serving drinks and sandwiches, but there are a good number of carts for rent but only a scant amount of golfing supplies. This course has the minimum number of hazards to worry about and fewer hills to encounter. There is no water on the layout but 10 sand bunkers and a three inch rough runs parallel to the wide fairways. Trees are medium in size with new plantings going in each year. The contour of the course is flat with barely a ripple to be seen anywhere. Tees are flat to the ground and not very big. Greens are medium to large and sloping. The greens also have the reputation of being fast and true to putt. North Kossuth was built in 1963 and is easy to walk and fairly easy to score well on. It is a well groomed course that is a pleasure to play and has a small town, friendly atmosphere. The thing most enjoyed by the members is the flatness of the course and ease of play.

Course	9 Holes
Distance	2785 Yards
Par	35
Playability	Poor
Aesthetics	Fair
Interest	Fair
Worth The Trip	Maybe
Rating	★★

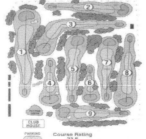

Course Rating 32.6

Hole	1	2	3	4	5	6	7	8	9	1st	2nd	TOT
Yards	476	277	366	200	352	141	327	358	288	2785	2785	5570
Par (Men)	5	4	4	3	4	3	4	4	4	35	35	70
Par (Women)	6	4	5	3	5	3	5	5	4	40	40	80

Bedford Golf Course

Bedford

712-523-3550

The Bedford Country Club is located one mile north of Bedford on Highway 148. The course's character is shaped by the ever-present water hazards. One pond comes into play on three holes and a stream affects play on five additional holes. Make sure you bring your ball retriever. There are no sand bunkers but the rough is cut to three inches and has many chances to swallow your ball. There are about ten big trees on the course with the remainder new plantings. The big trees are scattered and the small trees line the fairways. The greens are medium in size and flat. The general shape of the course is a little rough. Landscaping is shaggy around the tees and greens plus the paths are half overgrown. The Bedford course was built in 1923 and is a deceptive course. It is a placement course, with irons an important ingredient. There are out-of-bounds on the right on the first five holes, a real eye opener for the slicer. This is an easy course to walk, and an easy course to get on. Green fees are reasonable. The clubhouse has a very nice buffet that is open the year round. There are also sandwiches and drinks in the bar area for golfers. There is a full line of equipment but no carts. Bedford is one of those courses that you know you could do well on if only they would get rid of that darn water.

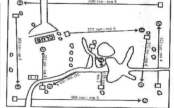

Course	9 Holes
Distance	2572 Yards
Par	35
Playability	Good
Aesthetics	Good
Interest	Good
Worth The Trip	Yes
Rating	★★+

HOLE	1	2	3	4	5	6	7	8	9	OUT
YARDS	272	409	268	408	323	272	123	241	251	2572
PAR	4	4	4	4	4	4	3	4	4	35
HANDICAP	9	1	7	2	4	6	5	3	8	
LADIES PAR	4	5	4	5	4	4	3	4	4	37

The Country Club

Belle Plaine

319-444-3113

Belle Plaine Country Club is a 3008 yard par 36 semi-private course located on the north edge of Belle Plaine on North 13th Ave.. The 175 members pay a yearly fee of $525 with green fees reasonable on weekdays and weekends. The pro shop has a small sampling of supplies. The clubhouse was renovated in 2000. There is a bar area serving drinks and microwaved sandwiches. The course has one stream, no sand, but rough has been added separating the fairways. Belle Plaine does have a fairway watering system, keeping the grass green throughout the summer. Evergreens have been planted around the course, along with additional trees and 150 yard bushes. The trees that do exist on the course are of medium size. Fairways are wide and in good shape. The general contour of the course is flat with a few gentle rolls. Tees are flat and are being improved with additional landscaping. Greens are small, flat and in some cases sloping. The grass condition on the greens is good and is noted for its quickness. The course was built in the 1930's. Belle Plaine is a wide open course that is easy to walk, challenging only in the sense of approaching the small greens, and not very busy. The course has purchased an additional 38 acres for future expansion.

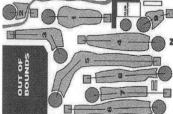

Course	9 Holes
Distance	2857 Yards
Par	36
Playability	Fair
Aesthetics	Fair
Interest	Poor
Worth The Trip	No
Rating	★★

HOLE	1	2	3	4	5	6	7	8	9	OUT	TOT	HD CP	NET
BLUE TEE	359	144	445	320	463	372	286	296	172	2857	2857		
HANDICAP	2	7	9	1	5	3	8	4	6				
MEN'S PAR	4	3	5	4	5	4	4	4	3	36	36		

Bellevue Golf Course

Bellevue

563-872-4262

The Bellevue Golf Course is a public course located two miles north of Bellevue on River Road. A treat for the 270 members is the view from the clubhouse overlooking rolling waters of the Mississippi River. Daily green fees are reasonable. The new clubhouse, built in 1976, sits on a hill overlooking the course to the west. There is a limited supply of balls and gloves and a few sets of clubs in the clubhouse. The bar and grill area serves drinks and sandwiches. Characteristics of Bellevue include two ponds and four bunkers. The trees are young like the rest of the course and do not come into play much. The fairways are wide open and rolling. The greens are medium to small in size and have a rolling putting surface on many of them. Jeff Frank is the greens superintendent and says that he is in charge of and upkeep of the great view of the Mississippi. This is not a real busy course and tee times are not needed. If you like to spray the ball a little and still score well, Bellevue should be a stop on your schedule.

MEN - HDCP	7	5	4	1	8	2	9	6	3	
WHITE/BLUE COURSE	340	510	165	410	490	380	140	350	360	3130
MEN - PAR	4	5	3	4	5	4	3	4	4	36
HOLE	1	2	3	4	5	6	7	8	9	OUT
LADIES - PAR	4	5	3	4		4	3	4	4	36
RED/GOLD COURSE	275	450	165	290	490	260	115	300	310	2655
LADIES - HDCP	7	3	9	5	2	4	8	1	6	

Course	9 Holes	Aesthetics	Good
Distance	3130 Yards	Interest	Fair
Par	36	Worth The Trip	Yes
Playability	Fair	Rating	★★+

Belmond Country Club

Belmond

641-444-4183

A new clubhouse has become a major asset to the Belmond Country Club. The course was built in 1970 and the present clubhouse was finished in 1983. The clubhouse has a large dining area that is open to the public the year round and serves exceptional food. This semi-private course is located on the east edge of Belmond along 3rd street. There are no carts to rent on this 3345 yard course, but it is very flat and easy to walk. There is one stream that runs down the middle of the course and comes into play on six of the holes. There are two new bunkers, and the trees are few in number and small in size except for a few medium-sized ones scattered throughout the course. The tee boxes are big and flat. The greens are medium size and flat with a little slope occuring on a few of them. There are 230 members that pay a $200 entry stock and $420 annual membership fees. Weekday green fees are very reasonable. This is a fairly busy course so it might be wise to plan a little extra time. Belmond is yet another example of a flat north central Iowa course that is fairly easy to walk, fairly easy to score well on, and has good Iowa hospitality.

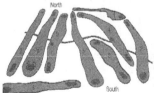

MENS TEES	320	366	172	414	490	195	533	465	390	3345
HDCP	7	5	4	1	8	3	6	9	2	
MENS PAR	4	4	3	4	5	3	5	5	4	37
HOLE	1	2	3	4	5	6	7	8	9	OUT
+ 0 -										
LADIES PAR	4	4	3	4	5	3	5	5	4	37
HDCP	8	5	6	7	4	3	1	2	9	
LADIES TEES	320	306	172	273	430	195	533	405	265	2899

Course	9 Holes	Aesthetics	Fair
Distance	3345 Yards	Interest	Average
Par	37	Worth The Trip	Yes
Playability	Good	Rating	★★

Hidden Hills Golf Course

Bettendorf

563-332-5616

One of the newer golfing and recreation complexes in the Quad Cities area is the Hidden Hills Golf Course located at the intersection of Middle Road and I-80 in Bettendorf. This public 18 hole course was built in 1981 and features a 6105 yard golf course. Although if you pay for 18 holes you can play 4 bonus holes just completed, 19,20,21,& 22. This budding course has 200 members who pay an annual fee of $500. The green fees are very reasonable for an 18 hole course. The course is built at the intersection of two streams, coming into play six times. There are also two ponds on the course and nine sand bunkers. The course is laden with new trees, none of which will cause you any problems during your tour of the course. The contour of the course is flat with some mild hills thrown in by the streams. This is a wide open course with fairway grass bunkers defining the lay of the fairways. Rough is cut along the fairways and will catch your ball. Greens are small and flat and can be counted on for straight putts. This family operation is run out of a log cabin clubhouse which is open all year and has just expanded its facilities. Hidden Hills seems to be growing in popularity and is fairly busy most of the time. They average 35,000 players per year. Given a few more years of growth and operating know-how this should develop into a very challenging and interesting course.

Course	18 Holes	Aesthetics	Good
Distance	6105	YardsInterest	Good
Par	35-35-70	Worth The Trip	Yes
Playability	Good	Rating	***

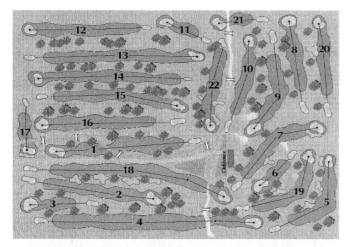

1	2	3	4	5	6	7	8	9	OUT	19	20	21	22
390	345	185	610	305	175	350	290	350	3000	310	300	130	290
345	320	140	460	270	110	285	250	320	2500	255	275	115	270
4	4	3	5	4	3	4	4	4	35	4	4	3	4
3	13	9	1	17	11	15	7						

10	11	12	13	14	15	16	17	18	IN	18 TOT	19-22 TOT	22 TOT
335	140	345	435	370	395	370	175	540	3105	6105	1030	7135
275	115	320	390	340	365	315	130	470	2720	5220	915	6135
4	3	4	4	4	4	4	3	5	35	70	15	85
10	18	16	4	6	8	14	12	2				

Palmer Hills Municipal Golf Course
Bettendorf
563-332-8296

Palmer Hills Municipal Golf Course is a public course located in Bettendorf. This 6583 yard course has no yearly membership fees, only green fees which are very reasonable. The clubhouse has a moderate amount of supplies, including balls and clothes. They also have carts to rent to tackle this fairly hilly course. The snack bar has general foods such as drinks, snacks, and grilled sandwiches. The characteristics of the course include one pond that must be traversed three times and one stream that runs the length of the entire course and must be crossed eight times. Palmer Hills also has an average of one sand bunker per hole, some being fairway traps. In 2003 bunkers were added on holes 4 & 11. The fairway watering system keeps the two inch rough thick and a little tough, plus the watering adds to the quality of the fairway grass. The trees are generally medium to large throughout the course except on the east side where they are much smaller. Trees line some of the wide fairways and are average in number. Tees are quite plush on the course, being large and elevated with exceptional grass conditions. The greens are medium to large in size and also possess very nice grass and have a reputation of being easy to hold but harder to putt over the rolling surfaces. This par 71 course was built in 1974. The condition of the course is nice, it is well maintained for a public course, it provides an assortment of challenges, and it seems to be fairly cheap. This looks to be a wide open course that allows tee shots to be sprayed without severe penalty. It is a hard course to walk until you get by the shag area; by then it is too late to turn your cart back in. Palmer Hills is moderately busy but moves people through quite rapidly. It is a course that has that wide open public flair, where people have fun and enjoy the game.

Course	18 Holes	Aesthetics	Very Good
Distance	6583 Yards	Interest	Very Good
Par	36-35-71	Worth The Trip	Yes
Playability	Good	Rating	★★★★

HOLE	1	2	3	4	5	6	7	8	9	OUT	10	11	12	13	14	15	16	17	18	IN	TOT	HCP
BLUE	402	503	418	186	349	528	369	163	383	3301	380	500	381	196	406	538	339	169	373	3282	6583	
WHITE	395	490	410	170	340	515	355	150	325	3150	373	475	370	180	390	430	330	160	360	3068	6218	
MEN'S PAR	4	5	4	3	4	5	4	3	4	36	4	5	4	3	4	5	4	3	4	35	72	
HANDICAP	4	18	5	11	14	3	12	17	6		7	2	10	9	8	1	13	15	16			

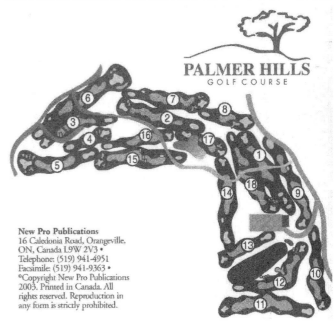

PALMER HILLS
GOLF COURSE

New Pro Publications
16 Caledonia Road, Orangeville, ON, Canada L9W 2V3 •
Telephone: (519) 941-4951
Facsimile: (519) 941-9363 •

27

Sunrise Golf Course

Bettendorf

3563-332-6386
www.gctimes.com/sunrise

One of the more interesting courses in Bettendorf is Sunrise Golf Course located at 3947 Moencks Road, deep in the heart of the city. One good thing about this course is that there are signs to direct you to the course. This is another family operation that rose out of farmland and became a public nine hole course. The barn from the farm serves as the clubhouse and is very nice inside with a moderate amount of supplies and a nice bar area that serves drinks and grilled sandwiches. Sunrise was built in 1983 and has 100 members who pay an annual fee of $750 for a family. Daily green fees are $12 for 9 holes. This former farm has three ponds affecting five holes, five bunkers, and no rough. The lay of the land by the clubhouse is flat but farther to the east it becomes hilly and uneven, due mainly to the ponds in the area. New trees are planted each year and medium size ones by the water do create some hazard. The greens are medium in size, with a few flat putting surfaces and a few rolling ones. Fairway watering has recently been added. This is an easy course to walk and is landscaped very nicely. Sunrise is a charming family operation. The course deserves some play and recognition; it has a relaxed atmosphere, and a down home feeling.

Course	9 Holes
Distance	2963 Yards
Par	35
Playability	Fair
Aesthetics	Good
Interest	Good
Worth the Trip	Yes
Rating	★★+

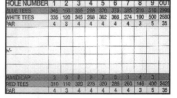

HOLE NUMBER	1	2	3	4	5	6	7	8	9	OUT
BLUE TEES	345	120	355	208	370	375	385	216	510	2968
WHITE TEES	335	120	345	268	362	366	374	190	500	2680
PAR	4	3	4	4	4	4	4	5	35	
+/-										
HANDICAP	2	5	6	6	7	1	4	3		
RED TEES	310	119	320	275	329	285	260	146	400	2420
PAR	4	3	4	4	4	4	4	3	5	35

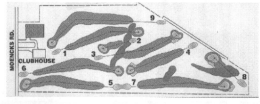

Bloomfield Country Club

Bloomfield

641-664-2089

One of the most picturesque courses in S.E. Iowa is the Country Club located east on old Highway 2 in Bloomfield. This course has a little bit of everything found in Iowa. There is one pond, a creek, sand bunkers, plus an abundance of large leafy trees lining the fairways and filling the valleys. The contour of the course is rolling and seems to have been cut out of a wooded area when built in 1928. The greens are small and fast. They are divided between tilted with flat surfaces and crowned with a little tilt. In either case they are hard to hold and tough to putt. Many tees point down a narrow fairway that is tree lined and rolling. It is a short course that is remembered for its tree trouble, hills, shortness, and natural beauty. This is a private club that does allow golfers from outside Davis County to play. Green fees are reasonable during the week; you must be a guest on the weekend to play. The 200 members support a clubhouse that has a small bar, an anytime grill, and a limited amount of supplies. Don't come to Bloomfield for the country club feeling; come here to play some inspired golf. Play conservative golf and you will have a memorable game on a beautiful course.

Course	9 Holes
Distance	2969 Yards
Par	35
Playability	Good
Aesthetics	Very Good
Interest	Very Good
Worth The Trip	Yes
Rating	★★★+

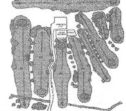

Blue Tees	360	345	355	445	375	196	130	405	358	2969
White Tees	348	333	343	421	367	188	120	396	328	2844
Par	4	4	4	5	4	3	3	4	4	35
Handicap	8	5	7	6	4	1	9	2	3	

Boone Golf and Country Club

Boone

515-432 -6002

The Boone Golf and Country Club is one of the oldest courses in the central Iowa area. The original course was built in 1899 and maintains the character of an old course. But a new nine has been built and opened in the fall Of 2003. This 9 holes is devoid of trees but does have 2 ponds. The layout of the land is flat but some additional length makes this more of a hitters nine. There are large old trees on the west side of the course but many new trees have been planted replacing some of the older ones. These trees line some of the fairways but many are also scattered. The hazards of the course include one pond, one creek, and six bunkers. There is also an abundance of ground bunkers around greens and in the fairways. Greens are medium in size with a variety of putting surfaces, generally flat to gently rolling. The contour of the course is flat, with medium width fairways and very little rough. Tees are big and nicely cut creating a high quality driving area for each hole. The clubhouse has a limited supply of balls and gloves. There is a full time restaurant that is open every day except Sundays and Mondays. The 280 members pay an annual fee of $549 for a family. Green fees are average for a 9 hole course. This is an open, flat course that is kept in top shape and not very busy. The course is located on the east side of town, and the entrance for the course is on the east side of the course. Boone has a private country club atmosphere and has many years of tradition to build the future on.

Course	18 Holes	Aesthetics	Very Good
Distance	6676 Yards	Interest	Very Good
Par	72	Worth The Trip	Yes
Playability	Good	Rating	★★★

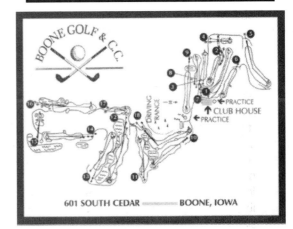

601 SOUTH CEDAR ——— BOONE, IOWA

HOLE NO.	1	2	3	4	5	6	7	8	9	OUT
BLUE	553	350	320	175	389	335	152	329	550	3153
WHITE	548	347	318	154	385	331	147	323	545	3098
GOLD	485	347	318	154	339	331	147	323	497	2941
RED	485	311	318	138	339	331	147	275	497	2941
PAR	5	4	4	3	4	4	3	4	5	36

10	11	12	13	14	15	16	17	18	IN	TOT	HCP
376	350	580	423	406	197	458	198	535	3523	6676	
352	330	536	403	373	175	451	178	504	3302	6400	
315	305	450	330	352	129	427	173	476	2957	5898	
309	300	443	320	318	119	358	163	426	2756	5597	
4	4	5	4	4	3	4	3	5	36	72	

Honey Creek Golf Club

Boone

515-432-6162

Honey Creek is a 2003 addition to Boone area golfing. The course is located just south of Boone on the Ledges Park Road. The original land was 87 acres of tillable land and about 170 acres of woods. That might be the signature of this course. They cleared 55 acres and put in a golf course. The cleared acres are rolling and the holes were bulldozed right through the woods. There are also 34 housing lots along fairways 1 and 2. Many of the holes seem to be isolated from the rest of the course. You roll down one fairway and loose track of where the other golfers are around you. The undulating greens are about 7,500 square feet in area with every green having a sloe of 2 to 3 feet from back to front. There is bent grass all through the course. There are 43 bunkers on the front 9 and 21 on the back nine. Every hole has mature trees except 1 & 2. This course has been carved out of the woods. The course architect created hills, rolling fairways, and no blind shots. There are 2 ponds with a creek on the back 9. Every hole has an adequate landing zone, at least they would be adequate for anyone that hits straight. This is a course that is similar to Amana. The back nine is hillier and hole 11 has a 130 foot drop to the green. Honey Creek is a little tougher than many of the other local courses. In the near future there will be a 5,000 square foot restaurant overlooking 9 & 18 with banquet room for 250. Honey Creek is a fair course there are no hazards that you can not see. But your vision is full most of the time. There are season pass rates of $450 for a single and of course carts and a driving range. This is a course that I think will become a premier course in central Iowa, something to look forward to when it gets on its feet.

Course	18 Holes	Aesthetics	Very Good
Distance	6800 Yards	Interest	Very Good
Par	36-36-72	Worth The Trip	Yes
Playability	Good	Rating	★★★★

HOLE	1	2	3	4	5	6	7	8	9	OUT
BLACK	530	432	180	381	544	190	395	366	382	3400
BLUE	500	404	155	350	515	165	365	324	355	3133
WHITE	480	382	141	330	493	141	345	306	334	2952
SILVER	456	358	115	312	473	116	328	286	314	2758
RED	405	333	101	291	423	110	285	259	298	2505
PAR	5	4	3	4	5	3	4	4	4	36

10	11	12	13	14	15	16	17	18	IN	TOT	HDC	NET
530	432	180	381	544	190	395	366	382	3400	6800		
500	404	155	350	515	165	365	324	355	3133	6266		
480	382	141	330	493	141	345	306	334	2952	5904		
456	358	115	312	473	116	328	286	314	2758	5516		
405	333	101	291	423	110	285	259	298	2505	5010		
5	4	3	4	5	3	4	4	4	36	72		

Breda Golf Club

Breda

712-673-4653

Breda Golf Club is a very recent example of small town tenacity and fund raising ability to provide recreation for the community. This 9 hole course is built on 72 acres of former farm land on the east edge of town in west central Iowa. The 230 members come from the surrounding 8 towns. They enjoy a course that is gently rolling, greens that are large, averaging 7,500 square feet in size, no sand traps but a number of grass bunkers and mogels in the rough and guarding greens. This is an irrigated course that has water hazards on 2 holes. This is an open course but is affected by gusty winds throughout the summer. The clubhouse crowd added that it is a good course for seniors to play and has good grass conditions for eay lyes. The clubhouse is big and serves noon meals and has a full kitchen for a year round restaurant. This is also one of the small courses that encourages student memberships. A very nice small town course that is worth playing.

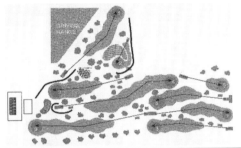

CHAMPIONSHIP	380	178	350	501	191	351	355	357	438	3046
MEN'S TEES	360	156	319	474	166	333	325	332	420	2840
PAR	4	3	4	5	3	4	4	4	4	35
HANDICAP	3	2	7	8	5	6	9	4	1	
HOLE	1	2	3	4	5	6	7	8	9	OUT

Course	9 Holes	Aesthetics	Good
Distance	2840 Yards	Interest	Good
Par	35	Worth The Trip	Yes
Playability	Good	Rating	**+

Britt Country Club

Britt

515-843-9295

One of the more pleasurable courses in northern Iowa is the Britt Country Club located on the north edge of Britt. This course was voted the best nine hole course in Iowa in 1982. It is known for its beauty, course condition, and pleasure attitude. The course is usually busy but tee times are not needed. It is an easy walking course and a course that an average or below average player can score well on and have a good time. The contour of the course is flat with poplar, birch, and pine trees lining all the fairways. There no water hazards on the course but the ten sand bunkers guard the big greens. The greens are elevated and have a slight slope or roll to them. The course was built in 1968. The clubhouse has a limited amount of supplies plus a nice bar area that serves sandwiches and drinks. Green fees are very reasonable. This is a beautiful, well rounded club. They have a junior program that meets on Monday mornings, a pool for the members and the public, and a clubhouse with a relaxing restaurant and good food.

Course	9 Holes
Distance	2894 Yards
Par	36
Playability	Excell.
Aesthetics	Good
Interest	Good
Worth The Trip	Yes
Rating	****

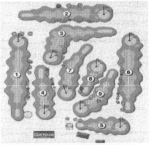

HOLE	1	2	3	4	5	6	7	8	9	Out
Men's Yards	497	251	310	301	163	490	389	173	320	2894
Handicap	3	17	11	15	13	5	1	9	7	

31

Brooklyn-Victor Country Club

Between Victor and Brooklyn

641-522-7608

The Brooklyn-Victor Country Club is located between Brooklyn and Victor on F29. This public course is dominated by very large trees. There were only a very few trees smaller than 20 feet on the course; the remainder were the gigantic, wide spread variety. This would seem to be more of a local's club for the 200 members. The building that resembled a clubhouse is a changing room for the pool that is located here. There were no supplies or snacks and you could pay your $15 green fee on the first tee. This gently rolling course has no water or sand hazards, it relies on the trees to make it difficult and interesting. These green monsters make the fairways very narrow in some parts. Your options are two — go over the trees or roll it on the ground under them. The tees are small and flat, the greens are small to medium and are also flat. This golf course is an average course to walk except for a few holes on the north end of the course where a ravine makes the hills a little steeper. Brooklyn-Victor is a beautiful course. If you want a day of relaxing, slow moving golf then try this one out. But make sure that you don't come with the misconception that trees are 90% air; on this course they are all leaves.

Course	9 Holes
Distance	2638 Yards
Par	35
Playability	Good
Aesthetics	Very Good
Interest	Good
Worth The Trip	Maybe
Rating	★★

BROOKLYN-VICTOR COUNTRY CLUB

HOLES	1	2	3	4	5	6	7	8	9	OUT
MEN'S YARDS	293	180	474	297	138	284	373	348	251	2638
MEN'S PAR	4	3	5	4	3	4	4	4	4	35

Prairie Rose Golf Club

Brunsville

712-533-6774

Prairie Rose was opened in 1994 and is located at 600 Oak Street on the east side of Brunsville under the blue water tower. This is a family owned course that has open membership and daily green fees. This is a very nice course and people in the clubhouse called it the "premier" 9 hole course in NW Iowa. It is a nice course with bent grass tees and greens. Greens run about 5,000 Square feet and run a fast 10.0. There are no water hazards on the course and new bunkers are being added in 2004. The full irrigation system gives this gently rolling course a good look. Players say the grass is lush, the fairways are thick and look carpeted, and the course is more difficult than it looks, maybe in part to its longer than average length.. There are approximately 12,000 rounds played each year, so the 450 members keep busy. Green fees ar $13 for 9 and $18 for 18. This is a very green course and I don't doubt that it is one of the best course in NW Iowa, you need to play it yourself to make that decision.

Course	9 Holes
Distance	3302 Yards
Par	36
Playability	Good.
Aesthetics	Very Good
Interest	Good
Worth The Trip	Yes
Rating	★★★

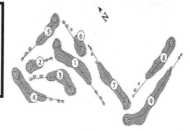

HOLE	HCP	1	2	3	4	5	6	7	8	9	OUT
BLUE		509	165	318	378	330	187	427	418	570	3302
WHITE		469	131	295	349	305	155	377	387	549	3017
PAR		5	3	4	4	4	3	4	4	5	36
HANDICAP		11	15	17	7	9	13	3	5	1	

Burlington Golf Club

Burlington

319-752-3720

Burlington Golf Club is a private golf course located at 2124 Sunnyside Avenue in Burlington. Annual fees are $300 per month for the 300 member families. You must play with a member or be a member of another club to pay the reasonable green fee. The clubhouse is large with a year round restaurant that is open to members and guests. The clubhouse was updated in 1992 and offers small meals. The pro shop is separate from the clubhouse and has a full line of equipment. The characteristics of this top ten course include seven ponds and an average of one sand bunker per hole. This is a very scenic and densely wooded course. The size of trees runs the gambit from new plantings to large and mature. The fairways are narrow, averaging 25 to 35 yards wide, and all the fairways are lined with trees. The grass on the course is excellent, fairway watering is present, and the rough is cut just below three inches along fairways and in front of many greens and boxes. The contour of the course is rolling to hilly. It is a very up and down course. Tees are elevated and have a surface of bent grass. Greens are medium in size, tilted and undulating. The greens also have a reputation of being very firm and fast but true and easy to read despite having very little grain in grass. Burlington Golf Club was built in 1970, a fairly young course for such a good reputation, and has been written up as one of the top ten courses in Iowa. This is a hard course to walk and a hard course to score well on. It can be defined more as a position course. Accuracy can benefit you tremendously off the tee. If you like challenges then Burlington is for you: dense woods, lots of water, lots of sand. What more could you ask for? It is a beautiful course to play, one of the finest clubs in eastern Iowa.

Course	18 Holes	Aesthetics	Excell.
Distance	6514 Yards	Interest	Very Good
Par	36-36-72	Worth The Trip	Yes
Playability	Excell.	Rating	★ ★ ★ ★ ★

COURSE / SLOPE RATINGS
Blue: 71.4/128
White: 69.6/124
Men's Gold: 67.4/119
Ladies' Gold: 73.2/136
Red: 72.6/127 • 72.3/126

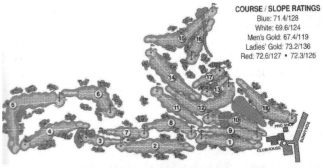

HOLE	1	2	3	4	5	6	7	8	9	OUT
BLUE TEES	370	490	158	443	550	394	192	346	380	3323
WHITE TEES	359	470	136	360	525	345	172	309	367	3043
GOLD TEES	347	428	136	345	452	322	118	283	317	2748
HANDICAP	9	7	17	1	5	13	15	11	3	
PAR	4	5	3	4	5	4	3	4	4	36

10	11	12	13	14	15	16	17	18	IN	TOT	HCP	NET
388	349	518	164	386	496	340	169	384	3206	6529		
382	342	500	142	372	483	327	155	380	3083	6126		
368	331	425	136	362	433	291	135	350	2833	5581		
4	12	10	18	6	8	14	16	2				
4	4	5	3	4	5	4	3	4	36	72		

Flint Hills Municipal Golf Course
Burlington

319-752-2018

Flint Hills Municipal Golf Course in Burlington is a public course located three miles north of town on Irish Ridge Road. This is an 18 hole course that was built in 1946 on a land fill. There are 200 members of Flint Hills that pay $356 for a single membership. Green fees are very reasonable. This is not a real busy course and tee times are not needed. The clubhouse is one big long building that has a puny amount of supplies, but they do rent carts, plus there is a bar and grill serving drinks and microwave sandwiches. The general contour of the course is flat making it easy to walk. There are three water hazards on the course in the form of ponds. Other hazards include fifteen sand bunkers and a two inch rough. Trees are generally located around the perimeter of the course and are large in size. The interior of the course has fewer trees and they are new in size. The fairways are laid out in a straight manner and are narrow with a few tree-lined. The grass condition is spotty in some places, especially along cart paths and tees. The greens are small in size but easy to hold most of the time. The putting surface can be flat, rolling, or sloping. You have many choices, sometimes on the same green. The course is at the end of a major rebuilding project. This is a course that is easy to walk, not very difficult to play, except for a few of the greens, and with a reputation of being short and fast to play. This seems to be one of the bargains in the east, cheap to play, 18 holes, easy to get on, easy to play yet with some interesting situations that arise during play. In 2000 4 holes were totally remade making it a more interesting and challenging course. Number 17 is totally new from tee to green. Because of the changes nearly 500 yards were added to the back 9.

Course	18 Holes	Aesthetics	Fair
Distance	6236 Yards	Interest	Good
Par	36-35-71	Worth The Trip	Maybe
Playability	Good	Rating	★★

319-752-2018
Club House

Ratings/Slope
Men 66.7 110
Woman 66.7 103

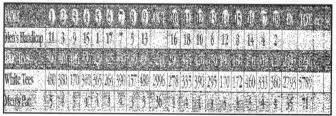

34

Spirit Hollow

Burlington

319-752-0004

Spirit Hollow in Burlington gets my vote as possibly the best new course in the state of Iowa. A lot of planning and thought went into this course. It is a long course at over 7,000 yards and incorporates all the natural settings and makes every hole a new and exciting experience. This is a privately owned course carved out of the gently rolling countryside. The entire course has bent grass. The greens average 5,000 square feet and are tiered, sometimes with several different levels. The blue grass rough is lush and cut to several heights. There are 60 sand and grass bunkers, and they come into play on every hole. There was 235,000 tons of dirt moved to create this bunkered feeling. Many of the holes are cut out of the Hickory and Oak trees and each holes stands along shielded from sight and sound of the other holes. Every hole is different and each does its own character. Each hole has a set of 6 tee boxes. North Spring Creek runs through the course and comes into play on several holes. This is a beautiful new course that looks hard and is hard, many looks from the tee are intimidating, but aren't we all up for a challenge once-in-awhile? The landing areas are generous and the beauty of the course includes fesque in several areas. Spirit Hollow has a full restaurant and is available for parties and gatherings. There is a full pro shop with a great practice green and driving range. All carts are equipped with GPS, and you might need it as you get farther from the clubhouse. This is a fantastic course and is great shape. Green fees are $45 during the week with seniors $25. I would highly recommend this course if you are looking for a great round of golf.

Course	18 Holes	Aesthetics	Excell.
Distance	7021 Yards	Interest	Very Good
Par	36-36-72	Worth The Trip	Yes
Playability	Excell.	Rating	★★★★★

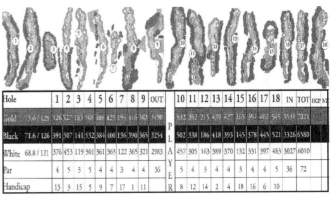

Hole	1	2	3	4	5	6	7	8	9	OUT		10	11	12	13	14	15	16	17	18	IN	TOT	HCP NR
Gold 73.6/129	126	327	183	566	408	425	151	116	383	3490	P	532	352	215	439	427	165	394	462	565	3551	7021	
Black 71.6/126	391	507	141	532	384	408	136	390	365	3254	L	502	338	186	418	393	145	378	445	521	3326	6580	
White 68.8/121	376	453	119	501	361	365	122	365	321	2983	A Y E	457	305	163	389	370	132	331	397	483	3027	6010	
Par	4	5	3	5	4	4	3	4	4	36	R	5	4	3	4	4	3	4	4	5	36	72	
Handicap	13	3	15	5	9	7	17	1	11			8	12	14	2	4	18	16	6	10			

Gruis Recreation Area

Buffalo Center

641-926-5393

The land for the Gruis Recreation Area was a complete farm donated in 1976 to be used by Winnebago and surrounding counties as a recreation facility. This public course is located on the Forest City to Bancroft road; A-42. Green fees are reasonable. Annual family membership fees of $225 are paid by the 297 members. The clubhouse is the original red barn from the farm and carries gloves and balls; plus there are carts to rent. The barn also has one of the best eating facilities in the area. The restaurant is open to the public year round and has a full menu with an excellent salad bar. The characteristics of the course include two ponds; coming into play on three holes. There are six sand bunkers that guard the fronts of four greens. Trees on the layout are small in size and medium in number; new plantings are made each year. The fairways are wide with new trees scattered in the two inch rough. Gruis has fairway watering so the grass condition is good throughout the summer. The contour of the course is flat to the south and gently rolling farther to the north. Tees are flat on the ground and medium in size. Greens are medium to large with tilted flat putting surfaces. This is an easy course to walk and a fairly easy course to score well on. It is a wide open course that allows you to spray the ball around in a controlled manner. Golfing on Gruis is good but the eating is better.

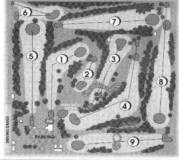

Course	9 Holes
Distance	3234 Yards
Par	36
Playability	Good
Aesthetics	Good
Interest	Good
Worth The Trip	Yes
Rating	★★+

Hole		1	2	3	4	5	6	7	8	9	Out
Par		4	3	4	5	4	3	4	5	4	36
Blue	70.2/114	375	180	357	542	399	130	399	484	364	3230
White	68.1/110	355	169	298	485	381	124	372	424	356	2964

Wapsi Oaks Country Club

Calamus

563-246-2216

Wapsi Oaks Country Club is located on Highway 30 1/2 mile west Calamus. This is a course that has a little bit of everything that Iowa golf has to offer. It has a clubhouse that looks a little like a Morton building, but looks are deceiving. Inside they have a year round restaurant that is open to the public, and the food is good. The view over the golf course is through a solid wall of windows. The 250 members enjoy a course that has a stream, eight sand bunkers, scattered medium and large trees and wide enough fairways that you can take a full swing and not get hurt too often. The green's putting surfaces are rolling and have a reputation of being some of the better greens in the area. The course was built in 1970 and the larger trees nearer the stream can cause major troubles on second shots. Wapsi Oaks is a fairly easy course that is semi-flat and easy to walk. It just strikes me as a typical small town Iowa course. Nothing fancy but ingredients that make an enjoyable golf game.

Course	9 Holes
Distance	3020 Yards
Par	35
Playability	Good
Aesthetics	Very Good
Interest	Good
Worth The Trip	Yes
Rating	★★★

Men	350	360	155	375	380	385	185	510	320	3020
Handicap	8	6	4	5	1	3	2	7	9	
Par	4	4	3	4	4	4	3	5	4	35

South Winn Golf and Country Club

Calmar

563-562-3191

South Winn Golf and Country Club is one of those courses that is cut out of the woods and hills and pretends to let you play golf and enjoy it. The contour of the course is flat near the clubhouse but adds some rolling holes to the east. There are no water hazards in the layout, only two sand bunkers, and a two inch rough that is cut along the base of the trees along the fairways. Trees are medium to large in size, line all fairways, and sometimes creep into the fairway itself. This is a course that you have to be accurate off the tees to avoid the funneling affect of the trees. There are a few holes that do widen out and offer a reprieve from branches, but not many. The course was built in 1960 and has 200 members. This is a private which allows green fees on M-T-F-S. Green fees are reasonable. The clubhouse is a nice brick structure that has a dining area plus a bar area that serves drinks and microwave sandwiches. There are carts to rent but very few supplies to buy. This is an easy course to walk and play. The only obstacles would be the trees and rough underneath the trees. South Winn is a very scenic course that is set in an area of beautiful shade trees and rolling hills. It is not very busy at all, so playing time is no problem. South Winn is located 2 miles west on 175th off Hwy. 52.

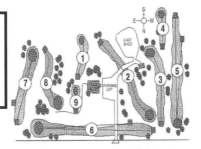

Course	9 Holes
Distance	2835 Yards
Par	36
Playability	Fair
Aesthetics	Very Good
Interest	Good
Worth The Trip	Yes
Rating	★★+

BLUE	233	445	329	130	414	495	361	309	119	2835
PAR	4	5	4	3	4	5	4	4	3	36
HANDICAP	8	9	4	6	1	2	3	5	7	

Fillmore Fairways

Cascade

563-852-3377

Fillmore Fairways, located five miles east of Cascade on Fairway Road, celebrated its 25th anniversary during the summer of 1991. This is one of the best-stocked pro shops in the tri-state area. The course has only 110 members who pay a family membership of $450, but the club has a large number of green fee players every day. The clubhouse also has a nice selection of sandwiches and bar items. This public course has one stream that comes into play on three holes. There is a medium number of trees, many new plantings. The fairways are wide and rolling and offer some wide open rounds of golf. Fairway watering was added in May 1991 and cart paths added in 2002. The greens are some of the largest in the eastern part of the state and hold approach shots nicely. This is basically a 3195 yard cart course. It is challenging and you can get into hazard trouble 6 out of the 9 holes. This is a busy public course, registering over 20,000 rounds of golf in 2001. Tee times are advisable. Stop by Fillmore and browse through the pro shop. If you find something that you like, try it out.

Course	9 Holes
Distance	3195 Yards
Par	36
Playability	Good
Aesthetics	Very Good
Interest	Good
Worth The Trip	Yes
Rating	★★★

MEN'S TEES	381	488	403	146	351	386	461	209	370
MEN'S HANDICAP	15	5	1	17	3	13	7	11	9
PAR (MEN/WOMEN/JR)	4	5	4	3	4	4	5	3	4
HOLE NUMBER	1	2	3	4	5	6	7	8	9

Carroll Country Club

Carroll

712-792-9206

One of the best clubs in west central Iowa is the Carroll Country Club located three miles east of Carroll on Highway 30. This is a private club that has a green fee paying radius of 15 miles, with fees being reasonable. The course was initially laid out in 1913 and remodeled and expanded to 18 holes in 1968. A new pool area was added in 1999. The unofficial logo of the course is the windmill on number three. This little symbol creates kind of a down home atmosphere for the entire course, relaxed and a challenging place to play. The general contour of the course is flat to gently rolling. There are five ponds on the course that come into play on six holes; there is also an average of two sand bunkers per hole which create some pressure around the greens. The 15 to 20 foot trees line many of the narrow fairways making accuracy a worthwhile goal on your drives. The condition of the grass throughout the course is excellent; fairway watering helps late in the summer, and it also helps the two-inch rough which becomes a little longer during tournament play. This well-landscaped course has large and elevated tees that lead to medium size greens that are flat and tilted. One of the positive factors on the course are the greens; they are in good condition and offer a putting surface that is true with very few hidden breaks, they are also known among the members for their speed. The Carroll Country Club is a course of the future, although it is an exceptional-looking course now. The trees will mature a little, the course will develop more of a competitive atmosphere and it may become one of the top courses in the state. It does have one of the top clubhouses in the state now, a sprawling structure that has excellent dining facilities for members and guests, a large snack and bar area for golfers, and a pro shop that has a full line of equipment and instruction. It is a course that is not too busy, unless they have one of their many special functions, and a course that is fun and relaxing to play. Green fees are $30 for 18 holes. A personal note about this course: during a tournament a few years back I saw two holes-in-one within ten minutes on consecutive holes. We did not lack for refreshments that day.

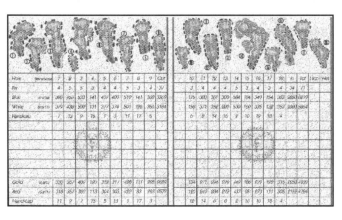

Course	18 Holes	Aesthetics	Very Good
Distance	6219 Yards	Interest	Very Good
Par	37-34-71	Worth The Trip	Yes
Playability	Good	Rating	★ ★ ★ ★

38

Carroll Municipal Golf Course

Carroll

712-792-9190

Carroll Municipal Golf Course is the public course in Carroll and is one of the busiest in the entire area, averaging around 30,000 rounds of golf a year. This 9 hole course was converted into an 18 hole course in the spring of 87; spreading out a little of the business. The original nine holes are quite short and void of any major hazards. The entire course has a flat contour with only a few dips near the east end. The yardage is much longer on the back side, 2500 yards compared to 3299 yards. The greens are medium to big on the old course and have rolling surfaces. The new greens are bigger, have the same undulating surfaces but are not quite in top shape yet. There is no sand on the entire course but there is fairway rough to outline the fairways. Trees consist of many new plantings on the back nine and small to medium size trees and evergreens on the front. Many of these trees line the wide fairways. This is a fairly easy and open course, which may account for the fact that there are 558 members. Over the past 10 years this course has grown and changed. The trees are now becoming an important part of the course. This is a city operated course with green fees being very reasonable. The small clubhouse has no supplies but did have an adequate snack and bar area and the people were very friendly. This course is well maintained by the city and provides a course for many people in town. Carts are now allowed on this course. If you are going to try this 18 hole course come early, lines form around 7:00 a.m. The course is located on the far north end of town on N. West Street.

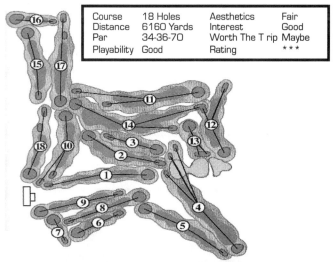

Course	18 Holes	Aesthetics	Fair
Distance	6160 Yards	Interest	Good
Par	34-36-70	Worth The Trip	Maybe
Playability	Good	Rating	* * *

Championship	480	350	200	540	412	167	107	304	299	2859
Men's Tees	467	340	180	513	399	145	99	295	289	2727
Par	5	4	3	5	4	3	3	4	4	35
Handicap	9	14	8	4	1	11	18	17	16	
Hole	1	2	3	4	5	6	7	8	9	Out
Ladies' Tees	444	270	160	423	385	136	86	281	273	2458
Par	5	4	3	5	5	3	3	4	4	36
Handicap	1	7	9	3	5	13	17	15	11	

360	498	387	196	536	383	159	402	380	3301	6160		
341	482	372	196	516	364	148	384	362	3165	5892		
4	5	4	3	5	4	3	4	4	36	71		
13	10	5	6	7	12	15	2	3				
10	11	12	13	14	15	16	17	18	IN	TOT	HCP	NET
287	375	265	144	421	309	137	315	283	2536	4994		
4	5	4	3	5	4	3	4	4	36	72		
14	10	2	16	4	8	18	6	12				

Shoreline Golf Course

Carter Lake

712-347-5173

A nice addition to the Council Bluffs area has sprung from the shores of the Missouri. Shoreline in Carter Lake is a 6657 yard 18 hole course that has been a big success in the Metro golfing community. The course is located at 210 Locust in Carter Lake, just find the river. This is a municipal course with approximately 90% of play coming out of the Omaha area. The course opened in June 1990 and in 2001 there were 40,000 rounds played, a busy place, reservations are required and are taken a week ahead green fees are reasonable . The clubhouse is small, future plans for a bigger one are now on the board, but the supplies are large. They also serve fresh sandwiches and beverages. Pros are available for lessons on the driving range. As you might imagine the contour of the course is generally flat, with a few ground bunkers rising up in a few locations and 8 sand bunkers to catch your shots near the greens. There is a combination of narrow and wide fairways but all of them have big old Cottonwood trees that come into play quite often. There is a 2-inch rough along the fairways but is fair to play in. There is one pond that affects two holes and the river comes into play on two other holes, two real LONG holes if the wind is in your face. Greens are elevated and medium in size. They already have the reputation of having subtle breaks and are tricky to read. Tee boxes are medium in size and at this time don't add a great deal to the course. The best feature of Shoreline is the layout, it uses the river, the trees and the general beauty of the shore area to its best advantage. In the summer of 2003 a tornado went through the course and knocked down a number of trees, but there has been a tree planting plan in effect for a number of years so these will be replaced. You will use almost every club in your bag on this course and still need more. This is one of the more challenging public courses in the area and is a nice addition to the area. An addition in 2000 was laser link distance computers on each cart.

Course	18	Aesthetics	Good
Distance	6609 Yards	Interest	Very Good
Par	36-36-72	Worth the Trip	Yes
Playability	Good	Rating	★★★+

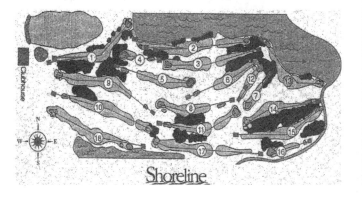

Shoreline

Hole	Rating/Slope	1	2	3	4	5	6	7	8	9	Out	10	11	12	13	14	15	16	17	18	In	Tot	Hcp	Net
Blue	72.0/127	433	567	448	176	368	364	185	357	500	3398	490	391	155	365	398	369	138	516	465	3211	6609		
White	69.1/117	398	503	415	141	333	321	158	310	465	3042	455	356	130	330	311	347	118	481	397	2925	5967		
Red	72.0/118	363	468	380	194	312	309	129	291	401	2770	420	309	104	306	293	306	106	446	359	2669	5439		
Handicap		5	3	1	15	9	7	17	13	11		18	14	16	8	12	6	10	4	2				
PAR		4	5	4	3	4	4	3	4	5	36	5	4	3	4	4	4	3	5	4	36	72		

Beaver Hills
Cedar Falls
319-266-1975
www.beaverhills.com

Beaver Hills in Cedar Falls is considered one of the top 10 courses in the state. It has a little bit of everything that a golfer could want during a day on the links. There are five ponds that come into play on five holes, one stream that affects eight holes, and an average of two sand bunkers per hole. This par 72, 6824 yard course is a gently rolling course with many contoured fairways. There are an above average number of medium size trees that line the fairways and are also scattered throughout the three inch rough, over 200 trees have been planted in the last two years. The tees are semi-elevated and big, the greens are tilted and rolling and large in size. The grass condition on the course is plush the year round because of the fairway watering system. The pro shop is located in the big modern clubhouse. It has a full line of equipment and has quite a few nice items. There is also a snack bar in the basement that serves bar items and sandwiches also a refreshment stand out on the course. The full restaurant is very nice but is only open to members and their guests. The 300 members pay an annual fee of $500 for a single junior to $2500 for a family. Although this is a private course, non-members can play if invited by the pro, $30.00 for non-members. This course has a little of everything, and you often use everything that you have in your bag. Beaver Hills is a course that is hard to score well on and is considered a challenging course. There is a lot of tree trouble that you can get into if you are not accurate off the tees, yet the big greens are easy to hold and have a true putting surface. Beaver Hills does have a family atmosphere but is a very busy private course, logging 21,000 rounds per year. The course is located 2 miles north of W. 1st St. on Union Rd.Beaver Hills is one of the courses in Iowa that must be seen and played to be appreciated.

Hole	Rating/Slope	1	2	3	4	5	6	7	8	9	Out
Blue	73.2/129	388	514	373	197	413	423	535	148	396	3387
White	71.8/127	380	502	362	176	389	411	521	134	359	3234
Gold	M 69.9/122 L 75.3/129	372	462	346	163	365	362	456	124	347	2997
Men's Handicap		5	15	9	13	1	3	7	17	11	
Par		4	5	4	3	4	4	5	3	4	36

10	11	12	13	14	15	16	17	18	In	Total	Hcp	Net
353	526	444	405	200	568	421	161	383	3461	6848		
344	509	428	389	182	550	405	141	368	3316	6550		
335	465	392	350	169	496	370	124	332	3033	6030		
14	12	10	8	16	2	6	18	4				
4	5	4	4	3	5	4	3	4	36	72		

Course	18 Holes	Aesthetics	Excell.
Distance	6848Yards	Interest	Very Good
Par	36-36-72	Worth The Trip	Yes
Playability	Excell.	Rating	★★★★★

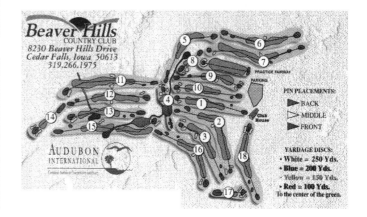

Pheasant Ridge Golf Course

Cedar Falls

319-266-8266

Pheasant Ridge Golf Course is a city owned course that was built in 1972. The course is located at 3205 W. 12th street in Cedar Falls and has a total yardage of 6730. There are over 300 members that have purchased a city pass for the two public courses and they pay $560 per year. The green fees are very reasonable for weekdays and weekends. The new clubhouse has a pro shop with a full line of equipment and clothing plus they sell snacks and drinks. This course is void of any hills or valleys; it is very flat and very open. Because it is such a young course the trees are very immature and pose no threat to your game. There are 45 sand bunkers to make up for the lack of trees, plus there is one pond that comes into play on two holes. The fairways are wide but the rough can be very severe if you venture too far off the beaten path. The greens are of medium size and provide the only rolling landscape in the area. Pheasant Ridge is easy to walk although the length of some holes can make it a bit tiring. There are carts for rent. It is a hard course to score on because of the greens speed and severe breaks. Your approach shot is very important if you want to play the hole in regulation. The wind also aids in the demise of your score. The changing direction of the wind and the gusts coming out of the north make each hole play a little differently each day. This course does tend to dry out late in the summer making drives go on forever. The future landscape development and growth of this course will make it an interesting addition to the golf courses in the area.

Course	18 Holes	Aesthetics	Poor
Distance	6730 Yards	Interest	Fair
Par	36-36-72	Worth The Trip	Yes
Playability	Good	Rating	★★

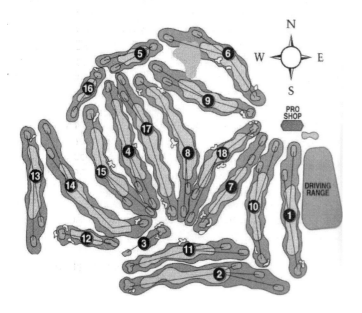

BLUE COURSE	410	570	150	420	180	400	370	510	380	3390
ORANGE COURSE	400	560	140	410	150	390	360	500	370	3280
HANDICAP	5	11	13	3	7	1	17	15	9	
PAR	4	5	3	4	3	4	4	5	4	36
+/-										
HOLE	1	2	3	4	5	6	7	8	9	OUT
RED COURSE	330	502	135	364	145	277	272	423	326	2774
WHITE COURSE	325	407	130	358	140	275	266	420	323	2644
HANDICAP	3	1	15	9	11	13	17	5	7	
PAR	4	5	3	4	3	4	4	5	4	36

400	425	185	370	535	415	150	480	380	3340	6730		
390	415	175	360	525	405	140	470	370	3250	6530		
8	2	6	18	10	4	14	16	12				
4	4	3	4	5	4	3	5	4	36	72		
10	11	12	13	14	15	16	17	18	IN	TOT	HCP	NET
330	351	170	311	415	357	135	427	329	2825	5599		
323	343	165	302	409	350	130	424	323	2769	5413		
8	18	4	16	2	12	10	6	14				
4	4	3	4	5	4	3	5	4	36	72		

Walters Ridge

Cedar Falls

319-266-8266

A new par 3 course opened in 1998 next to Pheasant Ridge Golf Course is Walters Ridge. This is a unique par 3 course. Each hole has a range of 2 to 4 tee boxes so you have a wide variety of choices on how to play this course. Shortest hole is 105 yards and the longest is 155 yards. There are 7 sand bunkers, many grass bunkers gently sloping to the rough and water comes into play on 2 holes. It is a very nice little course. The condition of the course is good, very similar to the bigger Pheasant Ridge. Players remarked that the course is wide open and plays long for a par 3. Fairways are lined with 20 foot trees and they do come into play in this compact layout. The facilities for Walters Ridge are the same as Pheasant Ridge. You register in the clubhouse, you can use the driving range and the parking lot separates the 2 layouts. Overall this is a very nice par 3 course. The numerous tees make it different every time you play it. This is a nice addition for the golfers in the Cedar Falls area.

Course	Par 3
Distance	2680 Yards
Par	32
Playability	Good
Aesthetics	Good.
Interest	Good
Worth The Trip	Maybe
Rating	★★

	1	2	3	4	5	6	7	8	9	OUT
BLUE COURSE	145	140	160	140	130	130	145	155	145	1290
ORANGE COURSE	120	120	140	105	135	105	120	145	155	1145
PAR	3	3	3	3	3	3	3	3	3	27
+/-										
HOLE	1	2	3	4	5	6	7	8	9	OUT
RED COURSE	100	100	115	90	115	100	90	120	135	965
WHITE COURSE	70	80	95	70	90	70	75	105	110	765
PAR	3	3	3	3	3	3	3	3	3	27

Washington Park Municipal

Cedar Falls

319-277-1764

Washington Park Municipal Golf Course in Cedar Falls is city owned along with Pheasant Ridge. They are operated by the city and are open to the public at all times. Washington Park is located at Main & E. 12th Street in Cedar Falls and is a short, 2025 yard, course that is a great way to spend an evening after work or an early morning. Annual dues for a city pass are $200, which is good on Pheasant Ridge also, and the green fees are $2.25 for 9 holes. The clubhouse is a smaller building that has a full line of supplies, beverages, and a snack bar. Washington Park is located by the Cedar River and takes some its character from it. There are all sizes and varieties of trees but the big oaks become more apparent as you get closer to the river. The contour of the course is very flat; even the tees and greens are flat. There are no bunkers on the course and two ponds offer the only other hazards. This is a very scenic course cut out of the woods by the Cedar River. It is very popular with seniors and women because of its shortness and beauty. If you want something that is easy to walk, short, and yet somewhat challenging, then Washington Park Municipal Course is what you should try.

Course	9 Holes
Distance	1981 Yards
Par	31
Playability	Poor
Aesthetics	Excell.
Interest	Fair
Worth The Trip	No
Rating	★★

1	2	3	4	5	6	7	8	9	IN	TOT	HCP	NET
270	303	375	162	140/126	343	171	123	94		1981	3962	
12	8	2	10	14	4	6	16	18				
4	4	4	3	3	4	3	3	3		31	62	

Airport National

Cedar Rapids

319-848-4500

Airport National is called the fastest growing public golf complex in Iowa. This is a 27 hole facility that emphasizes the short game. The three nine hole layouts are basically overgrown par 3 courses. The longest hole in the complex is 480 with most holes in the low to mid 200's. The course is located at 3001 Wright Brothers Blvd., east of the airport exit 4 miles. This is a wide open course with gently rolling contours. There are few trees on the west side of the complex , with three holes on the east side having several trees and a few sand bunkers. This is a good place for beginners and there is a driving range with lessons available. Players coming off the course said National is pretty open, easy to play, and there are some tough climbs if you are walking. Green fees are $10.45 for 9 and 15.24 for 18. Airport National was built in 1993 to give a high quality experience in a peaceful Christian country setting for the average public golfer. The average 9 hole round takes less than 2 hours. The complex consists of a 27 hole family course, huge driving range, adult and junior lessons, custom club fitting, miniature golf, family fun clubhouse, P.G.A. teaching pros, corporate, charity, and church outings. The clubhouse has a sports bar and grill and serves sandwiches during the day. This is a nice friendly , laid back course to relax and enjoy the game. Web site is www.airportnationalpublicgolf.com

Course	27 Holes	Aesthetics	Good
Distance	2096-1944-2001 Yards	Interest	Good
Par	32-31-33	Worth The Trip	Yes
Playability	Good	Rating	**

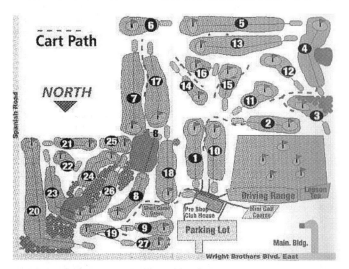

Hole	19	20	21	22	23	24	25	26	27	OUT	Ttl
White	119	480	243	100	324	248	95	283	109	2001	3945
M. Par	3	5	4	3	4	4	3	4	3	33	64
Handicap	11	1	7	13	3	9	17	5	15		
W. Par	3	5	4	3	4	4	3	4	3	33	64
Red	114	465	232	97	315	238	89	272	100	1922	3687

Hole	1	2	3	4	5	6	7	8	9	OUT		10	11	12	13	14	15	16	17	18	IN	Ttl
White	294	175	139	283	238	105	384	329	149	2096		298	120	197	281	201	162	83	338	264	1944	4040
Men's Par	4	3	3	4	4	3	4	4	3	32		4	3	3	4	3	3	3	4	4	31	63
Handicap	11	3	5	9	15	17	1	7	13			12	14	6	10	4	2	16	8	18		
Women's Par	4	3	3	4	4	3	4	4	3	32		4	3	4	4	3	4	3	4	4	31	63
												280	104	188	259	185	155	70	329	239	1763	3603
Match	+/-																					

Cedar Rapids Country Club
Cedar Rapids

319-362-4878

This is one of the few remaining old time country clubs left in the state. The clubhouse facilities are outstanding, one of the top two or three in the state. The red brick clubhouse restaurant is noted for its elegant dining. The pro shop has a full line of supplies including a rack of clothes extending around the room. This private course is only open for members and guests, which also applies to the restaurant. Green fees reasonable for this championship course. The 500 members can also play a few sets of tennis or hit a bucket of balls on the big practice range. Besides the full restaurant there is a snack bar with grilled sandwiches by the pro shop on the lower level. This is truly one of the most beautifully landscaped and designed courses in the state. The huge old trees line the narrow fairways making accurate tee shots a must. There are a few rolling hills throughout the course but it can best be described as generally flat. Not only will the trees catch an errant ball, but the tiered rough will make it nearly impossible to find relief. The rough also is painstakingly cut in front of the tees and around the greens. The greens are small and rolling with exceptional grass condition. The plush tees are elevated and landscaped with flowers and shrubs. The course was constructed in 1904 and is rated among one of the finest in the state today. The Cedar Rapids Country Club is a challenging course, beauty surrounds you on every hole. This is definitely not a hit and spray course; accuracy is at a premium. Tree trouble will make each and every hole something to remember, and if the trees won't take the wind out of your swing then the rough will. If you can find a means and a way to play this course, I emphatically recommend it. A fine experience on an exceptional course. It is truly an old time club experience.

Course	18 Holes	Aesthetics	Excell.
Distance	6819 Yards	Interest	Excell.
Par	35-36-71	Worth The Trip	Yes
Playability	Excell.	Rating	*****

PAR		4	4	4	4	3	5	4	3	5	36
BLACK TEES		342	364	395	400	149	438	405	200	547	3240
BLUE TEES		342	364	380	400	149	438	395	182	515	3165
WHITE		342	353	343	380	132	424	374	147	498	2993
GOLD		321	335	327	314	115	407	304	145	425	2693
HANDICAP	BLACK BLUE WHITE GOLD	11 9	5 3	3 11	9 7	17 17	15 13	1 1	13 15	7 5	
HOLE		1	2	3	4	5	6	7	8	9	OUT

4	4	3	4	4	5	4	4	4	36	72
374	437C	205	422	360	614	410	404	353	3587	6819
374	415	192	404	350	564	374	397	336	3406	6571
363	379	179	389	323	539	339	372	317	3200	6193
345	366	160	329	305	480	266	297	272	2820	5513
18 18	2 6	12 14	6 4	16 12	4 2	14 16	10 10	8 8		
10	11	12	13	14	15	16	17	18	IN	

Ellis Municipal Golf Course
Cedar Rapids
319-286-5589

Ellis Municipal Golf Course, located in Ellis Park in Cedar Rapids was completely redone in 2002. The city rebuilt the tees and greens plus reshaped the fairways in some areas. The layout remained the same so Ellis Muni still is essentially two completely different courses under one 18 hole setting. The front nine is an open free swinging course. It has small trees that are few in number and pose little threat. The front nine is also fairly flat and easy to walk making it more fun and leisurely to play. The back nine looks a little different now but is still hilly and difficult to maneuver around. It has an abundance of side hill lies and carries a reputation of having greens that are elevated, hard to reach, and difficult to read accurately. The back nine makes your iron game the one to use; many times a wood will not or should not leave your bag and accuracy is at a premium. The back nine at Ellis Park is all hills, lots of trees, tight, and more of a finesse course. So you must decide which course you want to play, a free-swinging, leisurly 9 holes or a tight, mind-grasping 9 holes that might leave you shaking in your spikes. An overall description of the course would be rolling with tree-lined fairways. Greens are of medium size and flat. Tees are big and elevated and the landscaping is very nice. Sand traps were also added to every hole in 2002. The city manages and operates the course. A city membership is $495 which allows you to play on the three city courses in Cedar Rapids. Green fees are very reasonable. The Ellis Municipal Course has a full line of equipment and clothes in the clubhouse and a full line of snacks and beverages. Ellis Municipal will test yours skills in all areas and if you make it back to the clubhouse you can always say that you survived the back nine at Ellis Municipal Golf Course.

Course	18 Holes	Asthetics	Very Good
Distance	6502 Yards	Interest	Excell.
Par	37-35-72	Worth The Trip	Yes
Playability	Excell.	Rating	★★★★

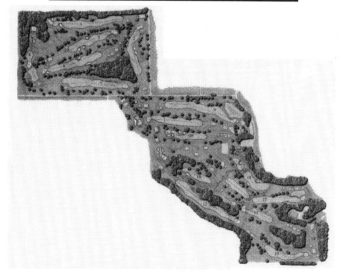

HOLE	1	2	3	4	5	6	7	8	9	Out	P L A Y E R	10	11	12	13	14	15	16	17	18	In	Tot	Hcp	Net
PAR	4	4	5	3	4	4	4	3	5	36		4	3	5	4	3	4	4	5	4	36	72		
MEN'S HANDICAP	12	14	6	16	10	8	2	18	4			9	17	3	7	15	13	11	1	5				
BLUE	395	365	481	202	385	420	463	150	534	3395		321	155	519	350	155	306	314	569	418	3107	6502		
WHITE	383	348	472	189	366	390	434	144	502	3228		303	143	497	338	132	283	303	536	386	2921	6149		

46

Elmcrest Country Club
Cedar Rapids
319-363-7980

Elmcrest is one of the younger country clubs in Cedar Rapids. The spacious new clubhouse has elegant dining facilities available for members and guests only. In 1991 a tennis and swimming facility was added to the complex. In 2001 a new addition was added to the clubhouse with a new pro-shop and sports bar. Elmcrest is located at 1000 36th street N.E. and is a private club that has approximately 650 members. You may play the course as a guest while paying above average green fees. The restaurant is open the year round and additional bar and snack items are available near the pro-shop. This is a compact course that is 6120 yards long. There are six ponds that affect play on seven holes plus there are approximately three sand bunkers per hole. The trees on the course are growing and range from new plantings to 30 feet. The narrow fairways that seem to be cut right out of the rough are lined with a moderate number of trees and do present a definite hazard. The rough is deep at four inches and is cut in front of greens and tee. The contour of the course is flat and provides a beautiful golf outing. The tees are elevated and flat and are beautifully manicured with bent grass. Green size is large with the general contour being flat. Many of the greens are tilted to hold the approach shot. Grass condition on the fairways and greens is plush, maybe none better in the area. The outstanding feature of this course would have to be its scenery. Elmcrest is designed with championship status in mind: lots of deep rough, fairways that are mowed and manicured to reflect the contour of the ground, tree lined fairways and spacious greens that make putting an integral part of your game. The remainder of the course is also beautifully landscaped making it a pleasure just to walk.

Course	18 Holes	Aesthetics	Excell.
Distance	6362 Yards	Interest	Very Good
Par	35-35-70	Worth The Trip	Yes
Playability	Excell.	Rating	****

HOLE	1	2	3	4	5	6	7	8	9	OUT	10	11	12	13	14	15	16	17	18	IN	TOT
BLUE 71.0/129	387	505	181	343	160	372	550	219	435	3152	190	506	386	416	185	550	437	144	396	3210	6362
WHITE 68.1/127	348	469	139	328	134	305	508	196	368	2795	178	489	373	344	168	502	424	134	364	2976	5771
Blue / White Hcp	9	1	15	13	17	5	3	11	7		16	6	10	8	14	2	4	18	12		
PAR	4	5	3	4	3	4	5	3	4	35	3	5	4	4	3	5	4	3	4	35	70

Hunters Ridge

Cedar Rapids

319-377-3500

The home of the Greater Cedar Rapids Open is the new 18 hole Hunters Ridge complex on the north side of Cedar Rapids. Hunters Ridge was built in 1997 and has developed into an outstanding addition to the Cedar Rapids community. What once was a pasture is now a rolling championship golf course surrounded by a housing development. This 7007 yard course is long and challenging. The green tees have holes of 520, 590, 523, and 613. From the blue tees the course draws back to 6527 yards. Four ponds come into play on the front nine and water can be found on 4 holes on the back nine. Number 13 has water on both side of the 361 yard fairway. Needless to say water, fesque grass and natural slough areas are a big part of this course. There are also 100 bunkers scattered throughout the course. Hunters Ridge does not have any trees to block the wind or even catch your ball, members claim it is a very windy course that can effect your shots. The 100 members pay $1,800 for a yearly membership. The greens are another unique feature of Hunters Ridge. Greens are generally oblong or kidney shaped. You need to read the big breaks and it might take you a few rounds to learn not to get on the wrong side of the hole. There are 6 tiered greens. The course has Bent grass from tee to green. The expansive clubhouse has a full line of supplies and clubs. There is a spacious snack area that offer sandwiches. Hunters Ridge is trying to offer the services and atmosphere of a private club yet still be open to the general public. Green fees are $26 for a weekday and $35 for a weekend. This is a very nice course, it is challenging but the layout and character of the course makes it fun to play. I would certainly say that this is a must course to try in the Cedar Rapids area.

Course	18 Holes	Aesthetics	Excell.
Distance	7007 Yards	Interest	Very Good
Par	36-36-72	Worth The Trip	Yes
Playability	Very Good	Rating	★★★★

HOLE	1	2	3	4	5	6	7	8	9	OUT	10	11	12	13	14	15	16	17	18	IN	TOT	HCP	NET
GREEN	398	520	422	166	392	590	423	170	231	3502	420	435	523	361	189	335	201	613	428	3505	7007		
BLUE	365	506	367	147	361	558	389	152	220	3272	395	398	504	346	178	302	189	544	409	3255	6527		
WHITE	348	480	372	109	336	538	361	119	382	3039	378	386	481	323	134	253	134	500	380	2969	6008		
SILVER	331	176	334	105	735	492	366	119	325	2861	361	339	416	275	132	250	138	418	340	2544	5395		
GOLD	292	426	319	88	275	447	306	102	317	2574	318	321	410	263	123	225	126	401	330	2516	5090		
PAR	4	5	4	3	4	5	4	3	4	36	4	4	5	4	3	4	3	5	4	36	72		

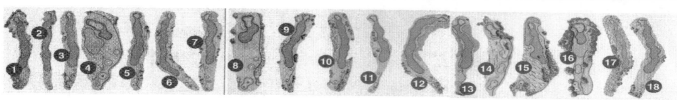

Jones Municipal Golf Course
Cedar Rapids
319-398-5181

One of the public courses found in Cedar Rapids is Jones Municipal Golf Course laid out in Jones Park off Fruitland Blvd. S.W. This was made into an 18 hole course in 2000 and now enjoys more golfers during the week. This is a shorter layout than most 18 hole course but was limited in space by the surrounding attractions in the park. There are picnic areas, a pool, courts and lots of flat grasslands. The course itself is basically flat. Hazards include one stream 9 additional water hazards and twenty-six bunkers. The trees line many of the narrow fairways and are of medium size. The Jones course runs in generally a diagonal direction catching many cross winds. Green size is in the medium range on the old nine but run bigger on the new 9 holes and are generally flat in contour. Jones Muni has been modified to become a more challenging course. All fairways are watered now so grass condition is better, the new greens are bigger and elevated. The trees are still an important factor on the course. Many of the fairways are lined and trees do come into play. This is an easy course to walk and a fun course to play. Green fees are very reasonable. A family city membership is $495. The clubhouse is basically there to collect green fees. They do have a small amount of refreshments and a few balls and gloves. The course is managed by the city. The park surroundings make this a delightful course to play, and if your game goes to the dogs, you can go for a long walk in the park.

Course	18 Holes	Aesthetics	Good
Distance	6009 Yards	Interest	Good
Par	35-35-70	Worth The Trip	Yes
Playability	Good	Rating	***

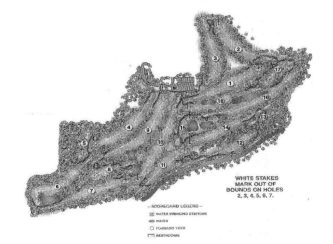

WHITE STAKES
MARK OUT OF
BOUNDS ON HOLES
2, 3, 4, 5, 6, 7.

— SCORECARD LEGEND —
WATER DRINKING STATIONS
WATER
FORWARD TEES
RESTROOMS

PAR	4	4	4	4	3	4	4	3	5	35	P L A Y E R	5	4	4	3	4	3	5	3	4	35	70
BLUE	376	339	355	389	136	347	416	198	509	3065		498	314	353	131	426	151	526	197	348	2944	6009
WHITE	362	322	337	373	122	334	386	173	499	2908		482	301	338	124	399	140	500	166	328	2778	5686
HANDICAP	2	10	14	4	18	8	6	16	12			11	7	5	15	1	17	3	13	9		
+/− PARTNERS																						
HOLE	1	2	3	4	5	6	7	8	9	OUT		10	11	12	13	14	15	16	17	18	IN	TOT
PACE OF PLAY	:14	:26	:39	:52	:60	1:13	1:27	1:36	1:56	Maximum Break 7 Min		2:12	2:24	2:38	2:46	3:04	3:13	3:30	3:39	3:52		

49

St. Andrews Golf Club

Cedar Rapids

319-393-9915

Some courses are cut out of the woods, or designed around a river or lake, but there are some that start as a corn field. St. Andrews Golf Club in Cedar Rapids is one of those. This public course, located at 1866 Blairs Ferry Rd., was a cornfield 25 years ago and is now a complex of office buildings, racketball courts, and a golf course. The course added an additional 9 holes in 1989. Only 5 of the original holes remain. The front nine is short and tight with a majority of the layouts big trees. The back nine is long and moderately open. The fairways are wide and the layout is flat, similar to a corn field. There is an abundance of two inch rough that catches a ball now and again. Fairway irrigation was installed in 88-89 making it much greener during the season. The greens are flat and of medium size. Some greens have an extreme slope to the surface while others are fairly flat. Greens regularly Stimp at 10 but go up to 11.5 for tournaments. This is a long course set up for a long hitting slicer. Family memberships are over $500 per year with reasonable green fees all week. The clubhouse was doubled in size with the addition of the extra 9 holes and has a full line of equipment and clothes on hand. There is also a selection of clubs to rent. Eats include snack foods, sandwiches and bar items. St. Andrews also has a public driving range. This is a long, hard, and challenging course that is flat and easy to walk. It is a free swinging course that lacks restricting hazards. The most outstanding feature would be the tough greens. They are fast and are full of hidden breaks. You literally use every club in your bag on the back nine at St. Andrews. If by chance you play this course, be a free swinger all the way to the green then putt for dough.

Course	18 Holes	Aesthetics	Fair
Distance	6100 Yards	Interest	Good
Par	35-35-70	Worth The Trip	Yes
Playability	Good	Rating	★★★

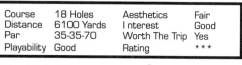

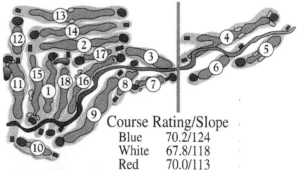

Course Rating/Slope
Blue	70.2/124
White	67.8/118
Red	70.0/113

Blue	343	422	347	475	286	380	139	224	412	3028
White	278	400	327	452	265	342	130	155	395	2744
Men's Par	4	4	4	5	4	4	3	3	4	35
Men's Handicap	13	5	15	7	11	3	17	9	1	
Hole	1	2	3	4	5	6	7	8	9	Out
Red	258	359	280	417	200	262	120	105	373	2374
Ladies' Par	4	4	4	5	4	4	3	3	4	35
Ladies' Handicap	11	5	7	1	13	9	17	15	3	
Date:	Scorer:									

165	421	155	487	425	362	502	210	345	3072	6100
160	382	150	470	395	340	482	190	330	2899	5643
3	4	3	5	4	4	5	3	4	35	70
16	2	18	8	4	12	6	14	10		
10	11	12	13	14	15	16	17	18	In	Total
146	342	145	406	333	320	410	165	285	2552	4926
4	4	3	5	4	4	5	3	4	35	70
16	6	18	4	10	12	2	14	8		
Attest:										

Twin Pines Municipal Golf Course

Cedar Rapids

319-286-5583

Twin Pines Municipal Golf Course on the northwest side of Cedar Rapids, has the distinction of having a regulation 9 holes lighted. They also have another 9 holes that are not. The back nine holes also have the misfortune of having numerous light poles scattered throughout the course, making some shots an enlightening experience. The front nine sports four ponds that come into play on four holes. There is only one bunker on the entire course, so leave your Lawrence of Arabia wedge at home. The medium size trees line some of the fairways but otherwise are planted in various locations. The contour of the course is flat and play is not hindered by any rough. Tees are big and lie flat on the fairways. The greens are also big and flat but are raised in some instances. The grass condition is good throughout the course and provides nice landing and hitting areas. The course was built in 1961 to a length of 5851 yards and has a par of 71. This public course has very reasonable green fees all the time and an annual family membership of $495. There were an estimated that 60,000 rounds of golf were played on the course in 2001, making it one of the busiest courses in the state, but the fact is that 9 holes have three to four more hours of playing time available in the evening. That's what's unique about this course; it is regulation size and is well enough illuminated that you can find your ball after a 200 yard drive. The clubhouse has a full line of equipment including carts, although this is an easy course to walk. It is also an easy course to score well on — not many hazards and a wide open driving area. Many golfers would like to play when it is a little cooler and maybe not so crowded. Twin Pines is the place where you can play a regulation game under the lights. But beware, night golf is a whole new type of game. By the way, I never did spot the twin pines that this course is named after. The course is located at 3800 42nd St. NE.

Course	18 Holes	Aesthetics	Poor
Distance	5851 Yards	Interest	Poor
Par	36-36-72	Worth The Trip	Yes
Playability	Good	Rating	**

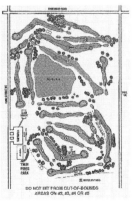

Rolling Acres Golf Course

Center Point

319-849-9917

Rolling Acres Golf Course is located two miles N.W. of Center Point. This is a public course that has 125 members paying $400 annual dues, green fees are reasonable. The clubhouse is located in a small structure that has a small bar with drinks and sandwiches. Supplies are few and seating is at a premium, but the atmosphere of the clubhouse is very friendly. There is one stream on the course coming into play mostly on number 7, a 510 yard hole that is the highlight of the layout. There are six bunkers, no rough, and very few trees. The trees that do exist are medium in size and scattered around the course, generally near the clubhouse. One of the first things that you notice about the course is how flat it is; barely a ripple is seen as you look to the north. Rolling Acres is a wide open course. You can spray the ball and be in just as good shape as down the middle. Greens are small in size and have smooth putting surfaces. The course was built in 1965 and is an enjoyable course to walk. It is short, has very few hazards, and is easy to score well on. Rolling Acres would be classified as a pleasure course, one where you don't have to think much about your game, just hit the ball and be sociable. Rolling Acres is a small town course that is not trying to win the hearts of all golfers, just provide a little pleasure for its local members. Rolling Acres is the home of the Iowa Boys 2A 1998 State Golf Champions.

Course	9 Holes
Distance	2730 Yards
Par	35
Playability	Poor
Aesthetics	Fair
Interest	Fair
Worth The Trip	Maybe
Rating	**

Rolling Acres Golf Course										
Hole	1	2	3	4	5	6	7	8	9	TOTAL
White	293	335	335	200	310	318	510	160	269	2730
Red	293	277	335	170	310	245	431	160	269	2490
Par	4	4	4	3	4	4	5	3	4	35
Handicap	8	2	4	3	6	5	1	7	9	

Appanoose Country Club

Centerville

641-856-2222

A grand clubhouse is the drawing point of Appanoose Country Club in Centerville. This expansive white structure has an elegant restaurant that is open to the public every afternoon but to just members and their guests in the evening. The food is the best in town and can be enjoyed April through January. This is one of the top ten clubhouses for looks in the state. The characteristics of this private course include one pond, five bunkers, and a rough that is void of any meaningful agony. The wide fairways are lined with medium size trees and have a gently rolling playing surface. Fairway watering has also been added recently. The medium size greens have a slight slope built in most of them. The 280 members enjoy a short course that plays fast and is easy to score well on. It plays easy if you place the ball where the approach shot can be accurately made. Appanoose is a busy course that was built in 1915. The clubhouse has a paltry amount of supplies and no carts for rent, although you can bring your own. Yearly family membership is $530 which includes $210 for food — well worth it. Green fees are reasonable for all day Monday, Tuesday , and Friday for the public; all other times you must be a guest. The course can be found on North Park Street, one mile northwest of Centerville.

Course	9 Holes
Distance	2929 Yards
Par	36
Playability	Fair
Aesthetics	Good
Interest	Good
Worth The Trip	Yes
Rating	**+

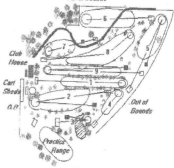

MEN (White)	426	375	144	187	312	328	244	444	469	2929
PAR	4	4	3	3	4	4	4	5	5	36
HANDICAP	1	7	11	9	13	3	17	15	5	
HOLE	1	2	3	4	5	6	7	8	9	OUT
WOMEN (Red)	426	295	87	172	204	320	192	435	409	2541
PAR	5	4	3	3	4	4	4	5	5	37
HANDICAP	3	7	11	9	13	1	17	15	5	

Meadowview Country Club

Central City

319-438-1063

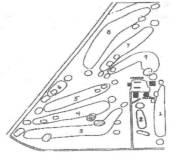

Course	9 Holes
Distance	3100 Yards
Par	34
Playability	Poor
Aesthetics	Fair
Interest	Poor
Worth The Trip	No
Rating	*+

Meadowview Country Club is a public nine hole course located one mile east of Central City. The Meadowview course was realigned and lengthened to 3100 yards — that is flat and wide open. It is easy to get on and a very good course for beginners. The 180 members of Meadowview pay $335 per year while daily green fees are reasonable for all day. The clubhouse is a refurbished barn that has a twenty foot bar offering drinks and grilled and microwave sandwiches. The characteristics of this small town course include one pond, two bunkers, and void of any measurable rough. The course has only a handful of medium size trees. The contour of the entire course is flat including the wide fairways. Some fairway watering has been added recently. The greens are medium in size and generally flat. The putting surfaces are also tilted a little and have some hidden breaks. Meadowview is an easy and short course to walk; it is also an easy course to score well on. Green fees are $9 for all day, a real deal. If you love to play a fast round this is where you belong: not very busy, a good drive may get you on, only one hole has yardage over 300 yards.

Hole	1	2	3	4	5	6	7	8	9	TOTAL
Yards	330	150	500	365	330	140	400	485	380	3100
Men's Par	4	3	5	4	4	3	4	5	4	36
Handicap	6	5	2	7	9	8	3	4	1	

Lakeview Golf and Country Club

Chariton

641-774-5964

An old course that is being rejuvenated is the Lakeview Golf and Country Club on Highway 34 West in Chariton. A new expansive clubhouse was recently built that has a fine restaurant that is open every day for lunch and three days a week for evening meals the year round. The proshop in the basement has a very nice sitting area overlooking the course and has sandwiches and drinks along with a small amount of golfing supplies. The clubhouse can be credited with having a very nice, relaxed atmosphere. There are carts for rent but the course is fairly easy to walk, if you don't mind gentle hills. The course is subject to a lake on three holes and a mere two sand bunkers. The course has established a new tree planting program and many fairways are now lined with twelve to twenty foot trees. There is a rough cut along the tree line but is only there for looks and inconvenience. Greens are small and generally flat. The greens are easy to read and putt but at times are very difficult to hold. Lakeview, which was built in 1920, has only one flat hole in the layout but is still easy to score well on. This is an open course that is easy to get on and has a rule that you can start anywhere on the course that there is an opening. The course has a new look to it, a feeling of fun golf.

Course	9 Holes
Distance	2891 Yards
Par	36
Playability	Good
Aesthetics	Good
Interest	Good
Worth The Trip	Yes
Rating	**+

Hole	1	2	3	4	5	6	7	8	9	Out
Men's Yardage	482	338	370	448	122	318	379	130	304	2891
Men's Par	5	4	4	5	3	4	4	3	4	36
Handicap	2	5	1	6	8	7	4	9	3	
Hole	1	2	3	4	5	6	7	8	9	In

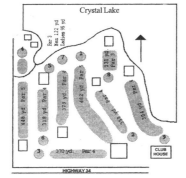

Charles City Golf Club

Charles City

641-228-6465

The Charles City Golf Club is located 3 miles east of Charles City on #57. The clubhouse also contains a big bar area, a small pro-shop and locker facilities downstairs. This 18 hole course stretches out for 3440 yards. This is now a public golf course. Green fees are $16.25 for a weekday and $18.75 for the weekend. Family membership is $800. The layout of course is very flat. Greens and tee boxes lay flat with the fairways, no elevation at all. The greens were of medium size and had no roll or pitch to them. The course was built in 1962 and the tree size indicated the lack of maturity on the course. The young trees were scattered throughout the course and were medium in number. The rough was cut to 2 inches along the wide fairways and there were no sand bunkers anywhere on the course. The course is very easy to walk and easy to score well on. This is a young course that you can spray the ball around and not be in too much trouble, but as with many courses in Iowa, in a few years the trees will present a real problem. The trees especially come into play on the front 9. If you are looking for a challenging game of golf you might want to try something else.

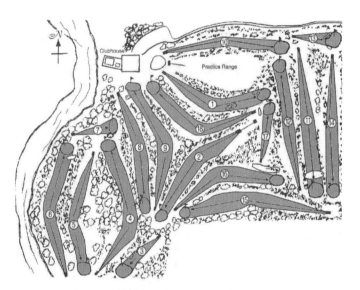

Course	18Holes	Aesthetics	Good
Distance	6765 Yards	Interest	Fair
Par	36	Worth The Trip	Maybe
Playability	Good	Rating	★★+

HOLE	1	2	3	4	5	6	7	8	9	OUT
BLUE	370	385	156	520	419	502	145	395	415	3307
WHITE	345	365	145	491	375	480	136	345	394	3076
MEN'S HCP (Blue/White)	15/13	11/9	17/17	7/5	9/7	3/15	13/11	5/11	5/...	
PAR	4	4	3	5	4	5	3	4	4	36
MATCH +/-										
LADIES' HCP	13	7	15	9	1	11	5	3	17	
GOLD	310	355	137	415	330	435	135	325	385	2827
RED	305	318	132	405	325	428	110	320	287	2630

10	11	12	13	14	15	16	17	18	IN	TOT	HCP	NET
405	500	415	153	436	570	386	203	390	3458	6765		
368	470	356	143	380	520	370	166	382	3161	6237		
6/14	18/8	2/12	16/18	4/6	8/10	12/2	10/16	14/4				
4	5	4	3	4	5	4	3	4	36	72		
6	12	8	18	4	2	10	16	14				
360	420	350	135	335	470	320	160	370	2920	5747		
320	416	307	135	330	445	314	140	300	2707	5337		

Wildwood Municipal Golf Course

Charles City

641-257-6322

Charles City has two golf courses, one being a municipal course on the west side of town called Wildwood. There is one distinctive feature of this course that catches your eye immediately - the sprawling white clubhouse. The outside has the look of country club but the inside has been worn down and now sports only a few of the bare necessities: balls, gloves, bar supplies, and sandwiches. But the clubhouse is on the National Historical Registry, and is worth the trip. The structure was a German Prisoner of War Camp. There are carts for rent but are not really needed on this course. Green fees are reasonable. The 256 members have little difficulty getting on this course during the week. The characteristics of the course include one sand bunker per hole and one stream that comes into play on three holes. There are an average number of trees, some new, some of medium size. The fairways are wide and you can spray your drive around a little without much trouble. The greens and tees are flat and both medium in size. This par 36, 2920 yard course is easy to walk and easy to score, basically a driver and wedge course. Wildwood is an inexpensive way to experience a little of the past elegance of golfing in Iowa.

Course	9 Holes
Distance	2920 Yards
Par	35
Playability	Poor
Aesthetics	Good
Interest	Fair
Worth The Trip	Yes
Rating	★★

Wildwood
Municipal Golf Course
3rd Rd. & North Iowa
Charles City
257-6322

HOLE	1	2	3	4	5	6	7	8	9	OUT
BLUE	287	285	486	360	146	305	329	345	377	2920
WHITE	274	240	464	294	107	271	315	339	366	2670
HANDICAP	6	5	3	7	9	8	1	4	2	
PAR	4	4	5	4	3	4	4	4	4	36

Cherokee Country Club

Cherokee

712-225-4687

The Cherokee Country Club has been developed in a very natural setting. The clubhouse sets on the crest of a hill and the course wraps around it in the valley below. But the layout of the course and the landscaping allow the natural weeds, wildflowers, and beautiful habitat to grow in co-existence right along with the green fairways. The course is in a beautiful wooded area with the original course being layed out in 1921 and revitalized and stretched out in 1963. A creek runs through the middle of three holes and sand guards two greens. The contour of the course is hilly on the holes down to the base and basically flat down at the bottom. There are lots of maple trees on the course, mainly medium in size and scattered throughout the rough. New trees were added in 1991 along with fairway watering. Greens average 5,000 square feet and are rolling. One of the most appealing parts of the course is the rough where the flowers and natural growth flourish. The clubhouse was built in 1981 and has a full line pro shop and a very nice restaurant, which is noted for its fine food. This is a busy course, averaging around 30,000 rounds per year. The 250 members pay $587 yearly for a family while green fees are reasonable for 9 holes. The outstanding characteristics of the course would be the beauty of the land that the course is built on and around. Cherokee is a true example of how nature can exist beside and among something man-made, very nice and fun to boot.

Course	9 Holes
Distance	3025 Yards
Par	36
Playability	Good
Aesthetics	Excell.
Interest	Good
Worth The Trip	Yes
Rating	★★★+

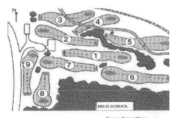

Course Rating/Slope
Men: 34.6/120   Ladies: 36.6/127

	1	2	3	4	5	6	7	8	9	OUT
BLUE TEES	415	492	333	175	409	441	338	126	296	3025
WHITE TEES	415	492	333	160	409	441	338	116	296	3000
PAR	4	5	4	3	4	5	4	3	4	36
HANDICAP	1	5	9	15	3	7	11	17	13	
HOLE	1	2	3	4	5	6	7	8	9	OUT

Clarinda Country Club

Clarinda

712-542-4010

The Clarinda Country Club was struck by a tornado in 1984 and lost many of its big beautiful trees; many others were partially destroyed. This did not diminish the beauty of this S.W. Iowa course. This 18 hole course was built in 1924 on the north edge of town amid some rolling countryside. The clubhouse is an old structure that has a lot of room inside for dining and meetings. The bar area serves sandwiches and the restaurant is open year round. Golf supplies are limited with only balls, gloves and carts available. The atmosphere inside the clubhouse is one of old time country club golf. There are no ponds on the course but a stream, sometimes wet, sometimes just a ditch, runs across six holes. Many of the fairways in the area of the stream slope down to the water and create some interesting lies on the course. The remainder of the course has a fairly flat contour. Fairway watering was added in 1999. A two inch rough follows the narrow fairways, but it is a rough that is easy to get out of and causes very few lost shots. The trees are big in most areas, many of them lining the fairways, but there are also 100 smaller trees that were planted after the tornado. Tees are big and elevated and greens are medium to large with slightly rolling putting surfaces. Overall this is an easy course to walk although some side hills may cause some heavy breathing. It is a challenging course with uneven lies, narrow landing areas, and meandering streams causing ever changing shot selection. The condition of the course is good and you will find the course busy most of the time. Daily green fees are $20 for 18. This is a pleasant course to play, one that has a feeling of golf inside and out.

Course	18 Holes	Aesthetics	Good
Distance	4986 Yards	Interest	Good
Par	33-35-68	Worth The Trip	Yes
Playability	Good	Rating	★★+

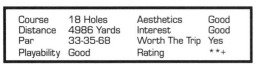

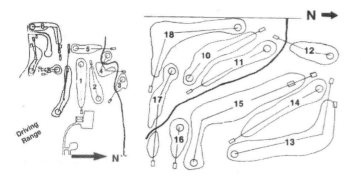

	1	2	3	4	5	6	7	8	9	out
PAR	4	4	3	4	3	4	4	3	4	33
Men's Handicap	6	14	13	7	3	5	10	17	11	
Women's Handicap	1	8	12	10	2	9	13	14	11	

10	11	12	13	14	15	16	17	18	in	Total
4	4	3	4/5	4	5	3	4	4	35	68
15	16	9	1	12	2	18	4	8		
18	17	5	15	4	7	16	3	6		

Clarmond Country Club

Clarion

515-532-2911

Lake Cornelia, seven miles Northeast of Clarion, is the home of Clarmond Country Club. This private course has a membership of 265 with family annual dues of $550 plus a $90 per year meal allowance. Green fees are average in price and cover the entire day. The brick clubhouse has a full restaurant and that is open to members. The restaurant has good food but is closed on Mondays and during the winter, January 2-April 1. This is a gently rolling course that is easy to walk. Carts are available for rent. The number of trees has increased, are of medium size and scattered along the fairways. The tees are plush, medium in size and elevated. Most of the greens are generally flat with a slight tilt to some and of medium size. Other greens are undulating and challenging. The only hazard on the course is the railroad track that runs through the middle of # 9. This is a quiet country course that offers peace and relaxation along with some fine golf. The course is located 6 miles from Clarion on R45. This course has made many improvements, bridges and trees, and is now one of the better courses in the area If the round doesn't turn out so good you can always stop at the clubhouse for a relaxing beverage and meal.

Course	9 Holes
Distance	3230 Yards
Par	36
Playability	Good
Aesthetics	Good
Interest	Good
Worth The Trip	Yes
Rating	★★★+

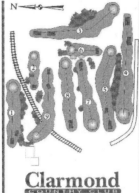

HOLE	1	2	3	4	5	6	7	8	9	OUT
BLUE	377	218	409	503	391	150	354	365	463	3230
WHITE	367	211	389	493	383	144	331	357	458	3133
HANDICAP	7	3	1	13	5	11	9	17	15	
PAR	4	3	4	5	4	3	4	4	5	36

Clarmond COUNTRY CLUB

Clarksville Area Recreation Development

Clarksville

319-278-4787

The course at Clarksville is an Area Recreation Development project. The par 36 course is 3065 yards long and provides an easy walking open course. Water hazards consist of two ponds that come into play on two holes and one stream that must be negotiated on the approach shot on number 9. The trees that are scattered throughout the course are small and few in number with new trees added each year. The tee off boxes are elevated a little, medium in size and have all been replanted. The greens are tilted and sloping and are of medium size. The greens are designed to create problems; you must leave your approach shot below the hole or suffer from Annie-Annie-Over syndrome coming down to the hole. You embark onto this level course from a modern brick clubhouse that has a very nice bar area with adequate seating. Golf supplies include only the necessities - balls, gloves, and golf carts for rent. This is a long hitter's course. There is very little tree trouble and the fairways are wide and open with very little rough. The 160 members pay an annual fee of $250 and green fees are reasonable. The grounds also has a pool open to the public. The Clarksville course has made a true effort over the past few years to make its course more competitive and beautiful. The course is located 2 miles south on Hwy. 188.

Course	9 Holes
Distance	3065 Yards
Par	36
Playability	Good
Aesthetics	Good
Interest	Fair
Worth The Trip	Maybe
Rating	★★

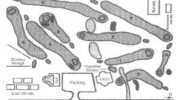

MEN'S & WOMEN'S PAR	4	5	3	4	4	4	5	3	4	36
MEN'S YARDS	375	470	150	360	365	375	460	120	390	3065
WOMEN'S YARDS	275	410	150	360	365	325	401	120	290	2737
HANDICAP HOLES	3	8	6	5	4	1	7	9	2	
HOLE	1	2	3	4	5	6	7	8	9	OUT

All Vets Golf Course

Clear Lake

641-357-4457

The All Vets Golf Course, formally the Clear Lake Country Club, was established in 1925 and still maintains the original small greens. This public course is located on North Shore Drive and is fairly busy during the summer months serving a membership size of over 200. Green fees for a weekday are average. The characteristics of this north/south course include 7 sand bunkers, no water hazards, and a fairway watering system that maintains a 2" rough. The rough comes into play in many popular landing locations of slicers and hookers. The contour of the course is gently rolling and supports a variety of medium size trees that line the narrow fairways. The old greens are small and flat but in good condition, they are also fast. The course is in good condition and presents a number of challenges to the average golfer. Take your clubs along while vacationing in the Clear Lake area and play one of the oldest clubs in Northern Iowa.

HOLE		1	2	3	4	5	6	7	8	9	Out
Blue		309	165	490	210	185	350	383	456	501	3049
White	66.4/112	300	159	468	190	165	340	375	449	490	2936
Handicap		13	17	5	3	15	11	7	9	1	
Par		4	3	5	3	3	4	4	5	5	36

Course	9 Holes
Distance	3049 Yards
Par	36
Playability	Good
Aesthetics	Good
Interest	Fair
Worth The Trip	Yes
Rating	***

Arrowhead

Clear Lake

641-357-7519

A new par 3 course was built in 1992 on the south shore of Clear Lake. Arrowhead is located on E. Finch one mile West of the State park. This par 33, 2071 yard course was built on a dried up slough. This is a typical par 3 course, the longest hole is 306 and the shortest 82. The course is basically an east/west course with the 2nd and 3rd holes running along the hillside to the east. The greens are good size. There are no sand bunkers and one pond comes into play on 3 holes. Arrowhead is a longer course than Oak Hill which is just down the road. The medium size Poplar trees line the fairways and provide some form of challenge. This is a course where you can use your woods to tee off with, unlike some other par 3's. The clubhouse is just a small structure where you can rent clubs and pay the green fees of $6 for 9 holes. This is a great course for people vacationing in the park that need a family activity.

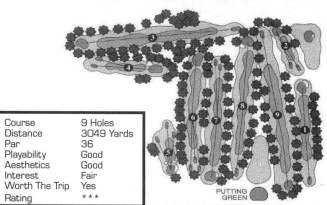

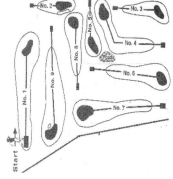

HOLE	1	2	3	4	5	6	7	8	9	TOTAL
MEN	4	3	4	4	3	4	4	3	4	33
LADIES	4	3	4	5	3	4	4	3	4	34
YARDS	260	82	251	302	115	296	306	155	304	2071

Course	9 Holes
Distance	2071 Yards
Par	33
Playability	Good
Aesthetics	Fair
Interest	Fair
Worth The Trip	Maybe
Rating	*+

Oak Hills Par 30 Public Golf Course

Clear Lake

515-357-2216

Oak Hills is one of the few public par 30 courses in Iowa. This is a short, 1637 yards, well manicured course that provides an easy and relaxing way to spend an afternoon. Green fees are $6 for weekdays and $10 for weekends. The clubhouse is an A-frame building that has the basic golf supplies, a bar and grill and a new lounge and kitchen. Characteristics of the course include 2 ponds that affect 4 holes, sand bunkers on five holes, and quite a few medium and new trees lining the fairways. The greens add a lot of character to the course, because they are kept fast with lots of interesting breaks. This par 30 course was built in 1972 and has a pretty steady flow of traffic. This course is designed for a player that wants a challenge and yet does not want to spend the whole day accomplishing the task. Oak Hills is an easy course to walk - they have no carts for rent- and is located one-fourth mile east of the Clear Lake State Park. It can usually be played in less than an hour and provides an opportunity to relax and enjoy the surroundings. This is a very nice course and is a fun course to play.

Course	Par 3
Distance	1637 Yards
Par	30
Playability	Good
Aesthetics	Very Good
Interest	Good
Worth The Trip	Yes
Rating	★★★

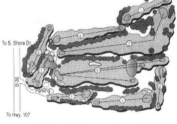

Hole	1	2	3	4	5	6	7	8	9	Out
Yellow Course	103	427	134	165	124	113	162	99	310	1637
Red Course	87	387	115	130	119	94	134	88	242	1396
Par	3	5	3	3	3	3	3	3	4	30

Canyon Creek Golf Club

Clinton

319-243-3534

As expected many of the courses near the Mississippi River tend to be hilly. This is the case for the Canyon Creek Golf Club that is located five miles north of Clinton on Highway 136. There are no level fairways in the layout, and if you ask many people, not a good lie in the place either. This public course has 90 members, paying $285 for a single, but relies on its green fees to survive. The golf shop has a limited amount of supplies and carts for rent to traverse some of the hills. The characteristics of the course include one big pond that glides along two of the holes and approximately one sand bunker per hole. What few trees that do exist are new plantings or medium size evergreens. This is a wide open course that is hilly and tends to dry out in the summer. The tees are cut and landscaped nicely, the greens are of medium size and possess a little rolling action with some tilt. The greens are also very true to read and putt nicely. The greens keepers have done a nice job of maintaining the course, considering the difficulty of working around the hilly terrain. Canyon Creek is not real busy and if nothing else walking the course will get you in shape after a couple of rounds.

Course	9 Holes
Distance	2665 Yards
Par	34
Playability	Fair
Aesthetics	Good
Interest	Fair
Worth The Trip	Maybe
Rating	★★

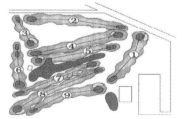

HOLE	1	2	3	4	5	6	7	8	9	OUT
YARDAGE	350	380	170	320	295	220	300	360	270	2665
MEN'S PAR	4	4	3	4	4	3	4	4	4	34
HANDICAP	3	1	9	4	6	8	5	2	7	

Clinton Country Club

Clinton

563-242-4961

The Clinton Country Club is a private club located on Harrison Drive in Clinton. This 18 hole course is one of the oldest in eastern Iowa. The initial course was started in 1911 with the present front nine built in 1922 and the back nine added five years later. There are 300 members of Clinton Country Club; each paying a yearly membership fee of $2,800, with an initial stock of $200. Green fees are only accepted from guests of members or card carrying country club members. The course has a very elegant clubhouse that maintains a full restaurant, serving members and guests. The clubhouse was remodeled in 1985. The pro-shop is located in the ground floor of the clubhouse and has a full line of golfing equipment. The course is divided by Harrison Dr. The front side, on the side of the clubhouse, is hilly. The back nine is flat and a little shorter. There is one water hazard on the layout but sand is in existence an average of two times per hole. Some of these traps are fairway bunkers. Trees are mature and line every fairway. The trees come into play a lot, they shape the courses character. The fairways are narrow with a two inch rough tiered along the edges. The grass condition of this club is plush; being maintained with a fairway watering system. Tees are elevated and big. Greens are medium in size and cover the range of surface contours. Clinton Country Club is an easy course to walk; but almost everyone uses carts. It can be a difficult course to score well on if you let the trees dictate your shot. This is more of a control course. It is not very long and rewards accuracy off the tees and on approach shots. The club also offers tennis and a pool for members. The Clinton Country Club looks like an old style country club but has taken on some of the new style features of championship golf. The facilities are tremendous, the course is in top condition, and it gives its members something to enjoy and use. This is a well rounded country club.

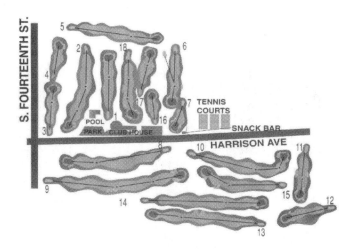

Course	18 Holes	Aesthetics	Very Good
Distance	6533 Yards	Interest	Very Good
Par	36-36-72	Worth The Trip	Yes
Playability	Excell.	Rating	★★★★

HOLE	1	2	3	4	5	6	7	8	9	OUT		10	11	12	13	14	15	16	17	18	IN	TOT	HCP	NET
BLUE 71.9/125	410	571	421	225	388	338	116	425	491	3385		474	369	163	397	466	328	175	307	469	3148	6533		
WHITE 71.2/123	404	566	397	193	373	335	111	418	481	3278		474	369	155	392	436	320	160	300	464	3070	6348		
GOLD 69.8/120 73.5/119	394	560	365	145	360	330	105	385	470	3114		460	369	150	375	374	320	110	300	464	2922	6036		
HANDICAP	7	1	9	15	13	11	17	5	3			2	10	16	8	6	14	18	12	4				

60

Valley Oaks Country Club
Clinton
563-242-7221
800-796-6187

One of the nicer public courses in eastern Iowa is the Valley Oaks Country Club on Heartsmill Road in Clinton. This is a spacious 18 hole course that was built in 1967 and is building its membership size on the aspect of quality golf. The 500 members pay $700 per year for a family and $400 for a single membership. Green fees are very reasonable for an 18 hole course. This is a fairly busy course even though it is a little out of the way, so you do need to call ahead for tee times. Green fees are $29 for weekdays, including cart. There is also a driving range. The pro-shop has a full line of supplies and equipment. Valley Oaks is a very well developed and scenic club. There are four ponds that come into play on four holes; there is one meandering stream that affects four additional holes. There are 46 sand bunkers throughout the course plus a number of ground bunkers located in the fairways. The fairway watering system keeps the fairways and the three inch rough in good shape all summer. One of the most impressive parts of the course are the tiered tees. They are elevated, big, and provide an inspirational starting point for each hole. The greens vary in size but are consistent in their surface contour, tilted and sloping. This is a very scenic course to play, which allows the tough conditions to slip up on you if you aren't prepared. There are a mixture of shots you must use and be prepared to use every club in your bag during the 18 holes. The most defined characteristic of the course is the length and the doglegs. More often than not when you get in trouble it will be because the length of a hole has caused you to be out of position for your next shot. I would not hesitate to go back and play this course. It offers challenges around every corner and yet you enjoy playing each hole challenging, tough, yet rewarding. Valley Oaks is a course of the future with good experiences available now.

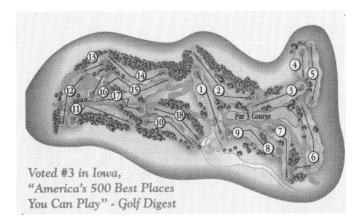

Voted #3 in Iowa,
"America's 500 Best Places
You Can Play" - Golf Digest

Course	18 Holes	Aesthetics	Excell.
Distance	7001 Yards	Interest	Very Good
Par	36-36-72	Worth The Trip	Yes
Playability	Excell.	Rating	***+

HOLE	1	2	3	4	5	6	7	8	9	OUT		10	11	12	13	14	15	16	17	18	IN	TOT	HCP	NET
BLUE	414	542	414	183	371	498	390	162	431	3405		413	538	361	207	493	607	151	370	456	3596	7001		
WHITE	350	502	362	155	339	473	334	145	398	3058		386	510	329	174	465	510	131	361	431	3297	6355		
GOLD	340	469	350	135	322	381	310	120	373	2800		280	363	293	162	334	495	120	343	365	2755	5555		
PAR	4	5	4	3	4	5	4	3	4	36		4	5	4	3	4	5	3	4	4	36	72		

Valley Oaks Little Links

Clinton

563-242-7221
800-796-6187

Adjacent to Valley Oaks Golf Club is a true par 3 course named Valley Oaks Little Links. Little Links uses the same address and phone numbers. All 9 holes are very consistent in length and provide a good short game fine tuning. The longest hole is 184 and the shortest 101. The course was built in 1995 to compliment the bigger course. Little Links is built down in the valley just south of the clubhouse and is generally flat. They have a great Junior league going and provide great instruction and experience for local kids. The condition of the course matches Valley Oaks and provides a good starter course on good conditions. Green fees can be paid in the clubhouse and they range from $6 for adults to $3 for kids.

Course	Par 3
Distance	1091 Yards
Par	27
Playability	Good
Aesthetics	Very Good
Interest	Good
Worth The Trip	Yes
Rating	**

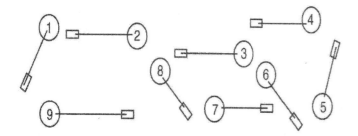

YARDAGE	101	139	161	115	102	94	119	76	184	1091
PAR	3	3	3	3	3	3	3	3	3	27

Lone Pine Country Club

Colesburg

319-856-3445

The Lone Pine Country Club is a public course owned by the city. It is located on the east edge of Colesburg on Deleware St. The 130 members pay annual family fees of $333 while daily green fees are reasonable for 9 holes. The clubhouse is on the north edge of the course and has a very open bar area inside. The twenty foot bar serves drinks and sandwiches during the week. The restaurant in the upper portion of the clubhouse is open to the public for meals Wednesdays and on the weekends all year round. Golfing supplies include bales, gloves, and some clubs. There are also carts for rent. The contour of the course is slightly rolling with wide and tree lined fairways. Almost all the trees on the course are twenty foot evergreens. These trees are spaced fifty feet apart on every fairway. A little boring but at least you know what you are up against. Tees are elevated and big. Greens are medium in size and tilted. The greens have a reputation of being fast but true to putt. Lone Pine is an easy course to walk and a very open course to play. It is ideal for the average golfer to play. lit is a family oriented course that has that small town atmosphere.

Course	9 Holes
Distance	2715 Yards
Par	35
Playability	Fair
Aesthetics	Fair
Interest	Poor
Worth The Trip	Maybe
Rating	**

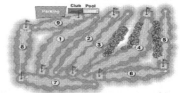

HOLE	1	2	3	4	5	6	7	8	9	OUT
MEN	375	385	405	455	255	275	165	245	155	2715
HANDICAP	2	3	1	4	6	5	8	9	7	
PAR	4	4	4	5	4	4	3	4	3	35

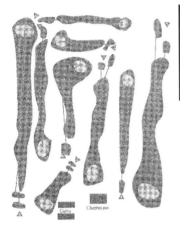

Colfax Country Club

Colfax

515-674-3776

The Colfax Country Club remodeled their clubhouse last year and greatly improved the first impression of the course. This public course is located on the S.W. edge of Colfax and is built on rolling ground. The fairway grass tends to have some bare spots on the hillsides, but the recent addition of fairway watering has helped.. The tee boxes are areas cut out of the fairway, not very conducive to good tee shots. The trees are medium in size with a few new plantings each year. The greens are small and flat, but the grass condition on the greens is good. The Colfax course is an open course, allowing you to spray the ball in any direction without much penalty. There have been additional trees planted since 2001. This is an easy course to walk and fairly easy to score well on. The green fees are very reasonable, $9.50 on weekdays and $12.50 on the weekends. Family membership is $488. This east-west course is trying to improve its conditions and aesthetics but still has some developing to do. The 200 members are getting what they want from this course, a place to hit a ball around.

Course	9 Holes
Distance	2980 Yards
Par	36
Playability	Poor
Aesthetics	Poor
Interest	Fair
Worth The Trip	No
Rating	*

HOLE	1	2	3	4	5	6	7	8	9	OUT	10	11	12	13	14	15	16	17	18	IN	TOT
CHAMPIONSHIP (RED)	335	380	128	512	355	330	170	270	500	2980	335	380	128	512	355	330	170	270	500	2980	5960
REGULAR (BLUE)	325	350	110	486	345	320	145	250	475	2806	325	350	110	486	345	320	145	250	475	2806	5612
WOMENS (WHITE)	315	285	92	380	335	310	130	240	400	2487	315	285	92	380	335	310	130	240	400	2487	4974
MENS - PAR	4	4	3	5	4	4	3	4	5	36	4	4	3	5	4	4	3	4	5	36	72
WOMENS - PAR	4	4	3	5	4	4	4	3	4	5	36	4	4	3	5	4	4	4	3	4	5	36	72

Cedarcrest Country Club

Columbus Junction

319-728-8461

Cedarcrest Country Club is a public course located southwest of Columbus Junction, turn at the intersection of X17 and 145th St. This is a compact course that radiates out from the clubhouse which sits on a hill. The holes to the east of the clubhouse are hilly, the holes to the west are flat. There are five sand bunkers on the course and one stream. Trees are generally small except around the stream and are not very plentiful. This is a wide open course that encourages free swinging but will penalize such maneuvers if taken advantage of. Because of the contour of the course this is a position shooting course; place the ball in a position to make your final approach shot. A new set of tees using 3 different locations has been added. Cedarcrest was built in 1962 and has a membership size of 200. Initial stock is $150 with annual fees of $400. This is a big green fees course, but is still not considered very busy during the week. Green fees for this 2810 yard course are reasonable. Cedarcrest is a fairly easy course to play but a hard course to walk if you are not used to long hills. The clubhouse was remodeled in 2000 and has a surprising amount of supplies. An impressive selection of clubs can be found along with balls and gloves. Cedarcrest has also added a driving range. Carts can also be rented. Food is not in such great supply, only drinks and a few snacks are available.

Course	9 Holes
Distance	2810 Yards
Par	35
Playability	Good
Aesthetics	Good
Interest	Good
Worth The Trip	Yes
Rating	** +

HOLE	1	2	3	4	5	6	7	8	9	OUT
YARDS	265	415	295	465	185	340	345	350	150	2810
PAR	4	4	4	5	3	4	4	4	3	35
HANDICAP	9	2	8	5	1	6	3	4	7	

Oakwood Golf Course

Conrad

641-366-2211

The Oakwood Golf Course is a semi-private course located 5 blocks south on main in Conrad. Oakwood has a small town country club atmosphere; concentrating most activity around the clubhouse. The clubhouse has a full line of equipment and supplies along with carts to rent. The dining room includes a nice bar area with tables to handle crowds on special occasions; which occur often. Green fees are reasonable. There is one pond on number seven and a stream that comes into play on two holes. Six sand bunkers guard the greens. Trees on the course are scattered along the wide fairways and are small to medium in size; with a few large willows near the water. The contour of the course is flat with grass height cut the same everywhere. Tees are big with a few elevated. Greens are medium in size and have flat putting surfaces. Fairway watering was added a few years ago. Oakwood was built in 1969 and has matured into a fine example of small town golf. It is a course that is easy to walk, easy to score well on, and has a reputation of being well groomed all through the summer.

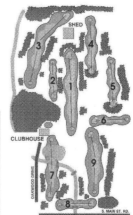

Course	9 Holes
Distance	2966 Yards
Par	35
Playability	Good
Aesthetics	Good
Interest	Fair
Worth The Trip	Yes
Rating	✱✱

Par	5	3	5	4	4	3	4	3	4	35
White	542	191	498	293	310	170	384	180	398	2966
Handicap	7	3	11	17	13	15	1	9	5	
Hole	1	2	3	4	5	6	7	8	9	Out

Coon Rapids Golf Course

Coon Rapids

712-684-2880

The Coon Rapids Golf Course is located on the south edge of town on Highway 141. The 2985 yards are spread over a fairly flat layout that is easy to walk and fairly easy to score well on. The course does have one pond, about 10 bunkers, and a cut of rough that is not very distinctive. The trees consist of small to medium pines and some very large cottonwoods planted in the middle of two fairways. The greens are medium in size, flat with a little tilt to some of them. The greens have a reputation of being slow but easy to read. The course was built in 1945, with the present brick clubhouse built in 1960. The clubhouse has a small sitting area looking over the putting green, the bar serves drinks and sandwiches plus a breakfast on the weekends is served out of the kitchen. The clubhouse has a full line of equipment, including clubs and carts for rent. The 200 members pay $285 for a family and $220 for a single. Green fees are average in price. This is an entertaining 9 hole course that stays fairly busy. It has a hard opening hole of 420 dogleg yards but eases up the rest of the round.

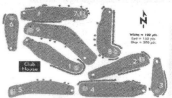

Course	9 Holes
Distance	2985 Yards
Par	35
Playability	Fair
Aesthetics	Good
Interest	Good
Worth The Trip	Yes
Rating	✱✱+

Hole	1	2	3	4	5	6	7	8	9	=/-	Total
White	420	300	200	380	375	160	380	305	465		2985
Par	4	4	3	4	4	3	4	4	5		35
HDCP	1	15	3	7	5	17	11	9	13		

Brown Deer Golf Club

Coralville

319-337-8508

Brown Deer in Coralville is a beautiful 9 hole course that has been expanding since its conception in 1992. A new clubhouse was built in 2003 and an additional 9 holes will be added in 2005. The course was designed around an existing lake and also is the home to an upscale housing development all over the course. This gently rolling course was a horse pasture on the north side of Coralville just off 1st Ave. N. Brown Deer has bent grass from tee to green. The greens average 5,500 square feet and come in all shapes. The rolling fairways have a large number of grass bunkers and every hole has sand bunkers also. The grass condition is excellent in the narrow fairways. This is a well designed course where you have to control your distance on your drive or you will be in the rough or in water. This is a very nice new course. There are only 95 members paying single yearly membership of $450. Green fees are $14 on a weekday. I would certainly recommend this course, its aesthetics are great, it holds your interest, and it present a lot of challenges.

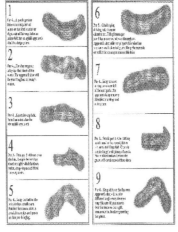

Course	9 Holes	Aesthetics	Excell.
Distance	3192 Yards	Interest	Very Good
Par	35	Worth The Trip	Yes
Playability	Good	Rating	★★★★

Happy Hollow Country Club

Corning

641-322-4333

One of the more interesting courses in S.W. Iowa is Happy Hollow Country Club located on the S.E. corner of Corning. This is a private club that has a green fees radius of the city limits, green fees are reasonable The 220 members pay an annual fee of $430 with a $100 initial stock. A new clubhouse was built in 1990 replacing the unique two story brick house. There are restaurant facilities in the new clubhouse. It is very well shaded clubhouse area with a large number of big Oak trees. These old Oaks line many of the fairways and cluster by the stream. There is one pond on the course and one stream that affect five holes. The contour of the course includes four fairways that are very hilly with the remaining five relatively flat. The fairway grass is in very good shape. Tees are flat and small while the greens are tiny and flat. The greens are almost unfair to the golfer because of their size. They are hard to hit and stick, plus hard to read and putt. Evidence of this is number 5, 210 yards straight up to an 11 degree sloped green, what a ride. This is truly a placement course with the trees and green size becoming a factor. The area around the greens is kept in excellent shape to encourage chip and run. Happy Hollow is a short, tight, and testy course. The trees are a real factor on four holes and the greens are a real factor on every hole. It is an interesting course that you should experience at least once, if it doesn't work out go inside and have a nice meal.

Course	9 Holes
Distance	2424 Yards
Par	33
Playability	Good
Aesthetics	Excell.
Interest	Very Good
Worth The Trip	Yes
Rating	★★★★

Handicap	9	5	15	11	13	1	3	7	17	2435
MEN TEES	318	318	169	271	200	406	352	261	140	33
MEN PAR	4	4	3	4	3	4	4	4	3	
HOLES	1	2	3	4	5	6	7	8	9	OUT

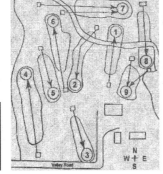

Correctionville Golf Club

Correctionville

712-372-4916

Correctionville Golf Club was built in the early 60's and serves a very important recreation purpose for the area. The clubhouse is a small white structure with one big room that maintains a feeling of small town golf. They have balls, gloves, snacks, drinks, and overflow with friendly conversation, if you can get them away from the card table. The layout of the course is very short, 2300 yards, and the contour of the land is flat. It is basically an east-west course that is wide open and designed as an iron course. The second shot is what lowers scores on many of the holes. There are five bunkers on the course and very little rough to stop your ball from leaving the fairway. The few trees present are medium in size and scattered along the fairways. The greens are elevated and small but have good surfaces to putt on. I must warn you that this is a tough course on slicers, there are out-of-bounds stakes on the right side on four holes. Correctionville is a small town course that is meant to be played for the fun of it, and it succeeds.

Course	9 Holes
Distance	2385 Yards
Par	34
Playability	Fair
Aesthetics	Fair
Interest	Poor
Worth The Trip	No
Rating	*+

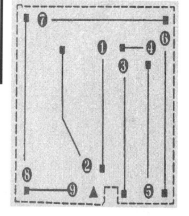

Hole	1	2	3	4	5	6	7	8	9	IN
Yards	250	300	267	108	271	352	354	358	125	2385
Par	4	4	4	3	4	4	4	4	3	34

Corydon Golf Club

Corydon

515-872-9969

One of the shorter courses in southern Iowa is the Corydon Golf Club in Corydon. This par 31, 2355 yard course is a wide open course that is flat, relatively free of hazards and yet is a tough one to score well on. There is one pond on the course, no sand, and very little rough. Trees range in size from new plantings to large and old. The medium number of trees are scattered throughout the course and cause few problems. There are five par threes on the course which would have to be considered an iron and second shot layout. The greens are small, flat, with a little tilt. They are hard to hold but putt true once you find the line. The course was built in 1920. The clubhouse is one big room that has no supplies and only pop and candy bars for refreshments. Green fees are very reasonable. The 130 members pay a little over $100 per year for a family. This is an intriguing small-town course. It is short, easy to get on, quick to play, and yet it offers some challenges that others don't. Maybe the challenge is that you must hit your irons well to score well. I hope you attack this course with more confidence in your five iron than I have.

Course	9 Holes
Distance	2355 Yards
Par	31
Playability	Fair
Aesthetics	Good
Interest	Fair
Worth The Trip	Maybe
Rating	**

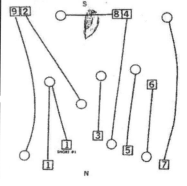

HOLE	HOLE NAME	YARDS	PAR	HANDICAP	LADIES
1	Dixons Open	226	3	6	3
2	Sunset	292	4	7	5
3	Trees	190	3	9	4
4	Piece A Cake	255	4	9	4
5	Shot Gun Alley	210	3	6	3
6	Hard Hat Area	224	4	5	4
7	One for the Road	365	4	1	5
8	Past Your Shot	220	3	4	3
9	Gotcha	374	4	2	5
	TOTAL	2355	31		36

66

Bent Tree Golf Club
Council Bluffs

712-566-9441   www.benttreegolf.com

Bent Tree Golf Club opened in July 2000. It is one of the latest editions to the prairie links type course that are being built around the state. This 18 hole, 7022 yard course, was built on top of an old course that has not been open for a while. Although when they started they plowed the entire course under, keeping only some of the natural grass terraces and starting over. Bent Tree has huge greens averaging nearly 9,000 square feet. They are varied in shape and undulating making them one of the unique features of the course. There is an average of 3 sand bunkers per hole, some holes have none others have 8. There are natural grass mounds on every hole, thus creating a prairie links style course. There are only 3 trees that come into play on this course and the signature 'bent tree' on hole 9 is dead. The course is located out in the country 2 miles east of I-80 on Hwy. 6. Because of its location the course succumbs to wind on a regular basis. There are some short par 4 holes which take advantage of the elevation changes. There is a lot of trouble everywhere you hit. The rough is fair but there is a great deal of it. The conditions are good and the players coming off the course say they enjoy the layout and the aesthetics very much. There is a full time pro and a very nice pro-shop. The clubhouse also includes a full time restaurant. The 130 members pay a yearly fee of $2,400. There were 25,000 rounds played in 2003 gathering in $40 green fees on a weekday and $48 on the weekend, including a cart. This is a great course that incorporates the existing topography of the land to make golf a true game of the land.

Course	18 Holes	Aesthetics	Excell.
Distance	7022 Yards	Interest	Very Good
Par	36-36-72	Worth The Trip	Yes
Playability	Good	Rating	****

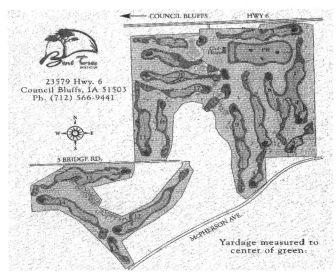

23579 Hwy. 6
Council Bluffs, IA 51503
Ph. (712) 566-9441

Yardage measured to center of green.

BENT TREE GOLF CLUB

HOLE	Rating/slope	1	2	3	4	5	6	7	8	9	Out	P	10	11	12	13	14	15	16	17	18	In	Tot	Hcp	Net
Black	74.1/126	390	375	426	524	180	433	463	224	542	3557	L	400	453	558	167	440	542	340	380	185	3465	7022		
Gold	72.4/123	373	348	403	500	155	418	435	205	522	3359	A	387	425	540	160	426	528	318	355	148	3287	6646		
Blue	70.6/119	310	325	380	482	150	400	395	171	500	3113	Y	373	400	524	142	420	515	302	347	125	3148	6261		
White	68.8/115	295	311	363	447	143	358	376	150	483	2926	E	305	383	517	137	400	468	280	327	113	2930	5856		
Green	63.6/100	255	283	330	412	135	318	328	124	427	2612	R	271	307	499	115	340	413	225	270	100	2540	5152		
PAR		4	4	4	5	3	4	4	3	5	36		4	4	5	3	4	5	4	4	3	36	72		

Cub Run Golf Course

Council Bluffs

712-366-4653

Cub Run golf Course is a par 3, 991 yard course build next to Fox Run Golf Course in Southern Council Bluffs. This is a course built on the old driving range of Fox Run, the old Scottish Links course. This course uses the Fox Run clubhouse, there are clubs to rent, with green fees at $5 on weekdays. The course was built in 1998 and one of it unique features are the big greens. Hole distances range from 94 yards to 154 yards. The greens and fairways are rolling and present some interesting lies. This is a golfer friendly course, it is set up nice and is in excellent condition. There are very few hazards and so becomes a casual place to play and enjoy your game. This is a very nice addition to the Council Bluffs area. I would recommend Cub Run to any beginner or someone that needs a relaxing hour of golf time.

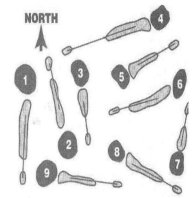

Course	Par 3	Aesthetics	Good
Distance	991 Yards	Interest	Good
Par	27	Worth The Trip	Yes
Playability	Good	Rating	**

HOLE	1	2	3	4	5	6	7	8	9	OUT	HCP	NET
BLUE	120	117	94	154	108	109	70	110	109	991		
WHITE	108	102	77	126	87	93	53	91	90	826		
HANDICAP	6	3	7	1	8	2	9	5	4			
PAR	3	3	3	3	3	3	3	3	3	27		

Westwood Park Golf Club

Council Bluffs

712-328-4675

Council Bluffs has six courses to play. Westwood is the par 3 course located at 37th St. and 9th Ave. This is a short course, 1136 yards, that has the added attraction of lights for night play. This is a public course that caters to beginners and older couples. The entire course is watered, but because of the heavy play some tees and patches of fairway are reduced to dirt by the end of the summer. Tee boxes and greens are flat and small in size. This course does have an abundant supply of trees that can make the fairways very narrow. The A-frame clubhouse has balls and gloves for sale, no carts, and a few snacks and drinks. The city operates this course, which is strictly a green fees course. The course was built in 1964 and is a nice compact par three layout. The grounds are a little worn in places but still offers a relaxing atmosphere to walk and enjoy the game of golf. The course opens at 8:00 a.m. and the last tee off times are usually around 9:45 in the evening. If you really want to challenge yourself the course record is a quick 23. A new option to Westwood is the floating casinos just to the west on the river. It's a gamble either way.

Course	Par 3
Distance	1136 Yards
Par	27
Playability	Good
Aesthetics	Fair
Interest	Good
Worth The Trip	Yes
Rating	**

HOLE	1	2	3	4	5	6	7	8	9	OUT
TEE	107	112	95	135	117	136	167	167	100	1136
PAR	3	3	3	3	3	3	3	3	3	27

Dodge Riverside Golf Club
Council Bluffs
712-328-4660

One of the nice things about courses built along rivers is that there are a lot of trees and scenic beauty. Dodge Park in Council Bluffs is no exception. There is an immense number of large trees lining the fairways on this course, providing some welcome shade on the hot dry days in S.W. Iowa. This 18 hole municipal course is found on 4041 W. Broadway in western Council Bluffs just off the interstate by the river. It is a fairly short course, stretching out only 6399 yards, but the trees and their looming reach sometimes make it play a few yards longer. The fairways are narrow and in good shape throughout the summer thanks to fairway watering. The rough is cut to two inches along the fairways and can seem much longer with a limb of a tree in your face. One water hazard was added on number 13. The course's character relies on the trees and course history. The course was built in 1910, and completely revamped in 1998. A new clubhouse was built with a full restaurant, the course was renumbered, all the tees and greens were rebuilt, a new irrigation system was added and approximately 250 new trees were added. This is strictly a greens fee course, no yearly members. This is a placement course; if you keep it straight and in position for the next shot, then you will score well, similar to all tough courses. But getting into the trees can make a long afternoon of it. Carts can be rented but this is an easy and flat course to walk. It is a challenging course that features accuracy as your top priority. The atmosphere seems to be let's play some serious golf and if that doesn't work let's get a saw and cut down some of the trees and if that doesn't work let's go back to the clubhouse. Dodge Park can also be credited with friendly people, people who want you to enjoy the game, not cut down the trees. The changes to the course have been fairly dramatic, if you have not played Riverside (Dodge Park) for a couple of years I suggest you re-acquaint yourself with the new course.

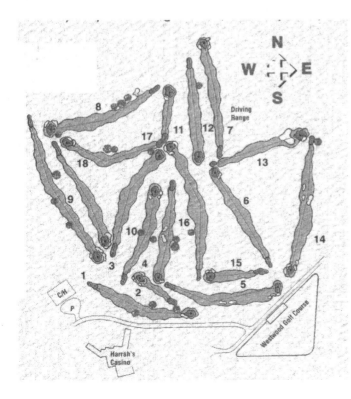

Course	18 Holes	Aesthetics	Excell.
Distance	6399 Yards	Interest	Very Good
Par	36-36-72	Worth The Trip	Yes
Playability	Good	Rating	★★★

DODGE RIVERSIDE GOLF CLUB

HOLE	1	2	3	4	5	6	7	8	9	Out	P	10	11	12	13	14	15	16	17	18	In	Tot	Hcp	Net
Black	379	151	352	351	391	362	383	398	545	3312	L	389	157	340	300	463	190	482	332	374	3027	6339		
White	353	129	319	327	368	337	356	369	516	3074	A	356	135	318	280	440	170	454	302	355	2810	5884		
Red	313	106	275	269	333	294	322	338	484	2734	Y	319	107	279	226	409	151	407	290	310	2498	5232		
HANDICAP	4	15	14	13	1	6	8	3	5		E	10	12	18	16	7	2	17	9	11				
PAR	4	3	4	4	4	4	4	4	5	36		4	3	4	4	5	3	5	4	4	36	72		

Fox Run

Council Bluffs

712-366-4653
www.golfllc.com

Fox Run Opened in June of 1987 as Scotish Links. This public course is located at the junction of Highway 25 and S. 31st in Council Bluffs. The huge white clubhouse houses a full line of equipment, a bar, and a snack area serving grilled and microwave sandwiches. Green fees are $30.50 for 18, including a cart. There is also a large fleet of carts for rent. The contour of the course is flat. The only relief from the pancake effect are the many ground bunkers that guard the greens or dot the wide fairways. The rough has been left a little longer to toughen up the course. There are four ponds on the course coming into play on five holes. There are no sand bunkers and the rough is now being kept low to give the grass a chance to spread out. There are groves of original trees scattered around the layout. Most of the 400 new leafy tree plantings line the fairways growing to 20-30 feet. The grass condition is good considering the age of the course. It will continue to improve thanks to the fairway watering system that has been installed. Tees are big with a few slightly elevated. Greens are medium in size, averaging 4,000 to 5,000 square feet in size. Putting surfaces are flat and hard to hold. Fox Run is an easy course to walk and a fairly easy course to score well on. This is a second shot course where length off the tee is not always that important. There is a driving range to the west of the clubhouse, the old driving range is now a par 3 course. Fox Run is a nice addition to the golfing community. You can play this 18 hole course in less than 4 hours. This course has matured nicely and has become a nice course. A nice addition has been the landscaping especially the wildflowers that appear on several holes.

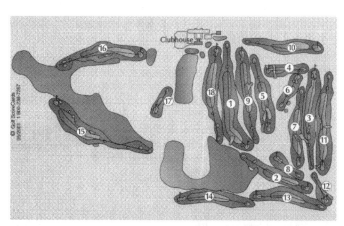

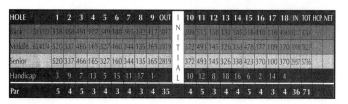

HOLE	1	2	3	4	5	6	7	8	9	OUT		10	11	12	13	14	15	16	17	18	IN	TOT	HCP	NET
Back	203	538	358	491	177	349	180	365	142	417	I	394	513	158	331	345	518	410	116	430	217	2937		
Middle	184	414	520	337	466	165	327	160	344	135	N	365	2819	372	493	145	326	338	478	377	109	370	3008	5827
Senior			520	337	466	165	327	160	344	135	I	365	2819	372	493	145	326	338	423	370	100	370	2937	5756
Handicap			3	9	7	13	5	15	11	17	T	1		10	12	8	18	16	6	2	14	4		
											A													
Par			5	4	5	3	4	3	4	3	L	35		4	5	3	4	4	5	4	3	4	36	71

Course	18 Holes	Aesthetics	Good
Distance	6234 Yards	Interest	Fair
Par	35-36-71	Worth The Trip	Yes
Playability	Fair	Rating	**

Lakeshore Country Club

Council Bluffs

712-366-1639

Lakeshore Country Club, located by Lake Manawa in Council Bluffs, is a private club that offers fine dining facilities, a marina, a fully equipped pro shop and an 18 hole golf course. The course has a membership of over 300 who pay a fee of $240 per month. Guests of members may pay the above average fee for green fees and enjoy one of the nicer courses in the area. The back nine was redone in 2000, reshaped with added bunkers. There are five ponds on the course that come into play on five holes. There are bunkers guarding the greens and rough is tiered 1.5 to 3 inches along most fairways. The trees are big and old, especially near the lake. These cottonwoods line many of the narrow fairways and offer shade to players during the hot summer months. The contour of the course was raised 5 feet to eliminate the threat of flood that has hindered the course in the past. The fairways are irrigated and now have a more rolling aspect with tees elevated slightly and greens level with the fairway. The greens are well-known in the area as being small, flat and fast. This is an easy course to walk with yardage being only 6234. If you can keep the ball out of tree trouble and stop your approach shots on the flat greens, then this is a fairly easy course to score well on. The outstanding feature of the course is the number and size of trees and what they can do to a good golf game. The location by Lake Manawa makes this course scenic. The most appealing quality is the extra facilities that make up the Lakeshore complex: the outstanding pro-shop, the lake with marina, and the luxurious supper club that is open to members and guests. Since the course underwent changes is has a lot more character and is more challenging. There is a true country club atmosphere surrounding Lakeshore.

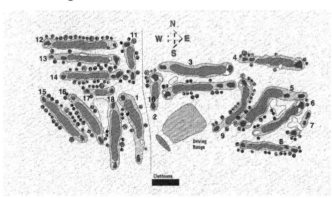

Course	18 Holes	Aesthetics	Very Good
Distance	6366 Yards	Interest	Good
Par	35-36-71	Worth The Trip	Yes
Playability	Good	Rating	★★★+

LAKESHORE COUNTRY CLUB

HOLE	1	2	3	4	5	6	7	8	9	Out		10	11	12	13	14	15	16	17	18	In	Tot
Black	359	137	430	397	506	359	171	380	379	3118	P	397	192	522	510	380	349	323	146	429/431	3248	6366
Men's Silver / Ladies' Silver	347	129	421	382	498	350	147	363	372	3009	L	381	174	510	492	368	334	296	122	334	3011	6020
MEN'S HANDICAP	13	17	1	3	5	7	15	9	11		A	8	14	4	2	12	6	16	18	10		
MEN'S PAR	4	3	4	4	5	4	3	4	4	35	Y	4	3	5	5	4	4	4	3	4	36	71
Green	262	120	612	320	381	341	95	311	301	2543		325	150	472	461/471	337	316	258	95	289	2623	5166
LADIES' HANDICAP	9	17	3	5	1	7	11	15	13			14	18	2	6	8	10	16	12			
LADIES' PAR	4	3	5	4	5	4	3	4	4	36		4	3	5	5	4	4	4	3	4	36	72

Cresco Country Club

Cresco

563-547-2374

The Cresco Country Club, located two miles South of Cresco on Vernon Rd., is a private course that has no restrictions. A unique thing about this course is that the Turkey River surrounds the course, coming into play on five holes. To add to this natural beauty is the man-made landscaping with flowers and shrubs that is featured around the tees and the clubhouse. The fairways have been narrowed and tree lined, mostly with 20-30 foot trees. Where there are no trees the rough becomes a hazard or one of the nine sand bunkers. This is an easy course to walk and fairly easy to score well on. You can spray your tee shot a little but beware of wood and water. The greens are medium in size and are generally tilted, providing good holding action on your approach shot. The 250 members have a very spacious clubhouse, remodeled in 2000, to hold their activities in. From the comfortable stone interior of the clubhouse you can sit back in a big chair and view the Turkey River and the entire nine holes. The clubhouse has a full line of golf supplies, microwave sandwiches and bar items for sale inside. Green fees are reasonable. Northeast Iowa is a great place to visit; made even a better by the beauty of its golf courses.

Course	9 Holes
Distance	2867 Yards
Par	36
Playability	Good
Aesthetics	Excell.
Interest	Excell.
Worth The Trip	Yes
Rating	***+

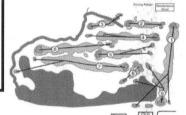

Yardage - White	517	279	179	475	316	321	408	124	257	2876
Par	5	4	3	5	4	4	4	3	4	36
Handicap	3	17	11	12	14	6	1	10	16	
Hole	1	2	3	4	5	6	7	8	9	Out
+/-										
Yardage - Red	497	275	164	454	268	312	402	114	245	2731
Par	5	4	3	5	4	4	4	3	4	37
Handicap	1	17	3	13	7	5	11	15		

Crestmoor Golf Club

Creston

641-782-2771

One of the older courses in southwest Iowa can be found in Creston. The Crestmoor Golf Club was built in 1900 and has a membership size of 200 today. This private course still has that old country club feeling with nice clubhouse facilities, mature layout, and a relaxed, serious golfing atmosphere. Crestmoor has a lake that extends itself over three holes. There are seven bunkers on three holes. Trees are medium to large in size and line most of the fairways, 150 tress were added in 2000. They can create many problems for a golfer who sprays his tee shot. Greens are medium in size and have a variety of surfaces — sloping, flat, tilted — a nice contrast. The greens are also fast and have a history of being hard to read and putt. Crestmoor does claim an Iowa Hall of Fame hole in number 8, a dogleg over water. The remainder of the course has a great many side hill lies and uneven stances. If you live outside of Union County you can pay the $12 green fee and enjoy this beautiful course. The members pay an annual fee of $1,058 including cart and enjoy privileges in the spacious clubhouse that has a big dining area for special occasions and a small intimate bar area. There are carts for rent and a few supplies, but the attraction of this course is the actual play — a beautiful course that has a lot of tradition and excitement to offer. If nothing else, come play their 582 yard number three, not just a driver and wedge.

Course	9 Holes
Distance	3176 Yards
Par	36
Playability	Excell.
Aesthetics	Very Good
Interest	Very Good
Worth The Trip	Yes
Rating	****

430	223	582	272	311	130	409	471	348	3176	6352
4	4	5	4	4	3	4	5	4	36	72
2	4	1	9	3	5	8	7			
5	4	6	4	4	3	4	4	4	38	76

Pine Valley Golf Club

Creston

641-782-4917

Pine Valley Golf Club is a public course located one mile west of Creston on Highway 34. This is a very short course stretching out only 1969 yards and is easy to walk making it a course to play when you are short on time. Green fees are very reasonable. Members pay $250 per year for a family. The clubhouse also houses a bowling alley. Golfing supplies include balls, gloves, plus carts for rent. The bar area serves both establishments, and there is a full time restaurant open to the public that has the best steaks in town! The characteristics of the course include one pond, no sand, and a two inch rough that is not too difficult. The contour of the course is rolling, leveling out near the clubhouse to the south. Trees on the layout are medium in size with 150 new plantings. These trees line some of the fairways but are mainly scattered in the gullies and around the pond. Tees are flat and a little shaggy, greens are small and flat, but the grass is in good condition. This is a complex that can't decide whether to be a golf course or a bowling alley. If the golf doesn't work out then try the food, it will.

Course	9 Holes	Aesthetics	Fair
Distance	1969 Yards	Interest	Good
Par	32	Worth The Trip	Yes
Playability	Fair	Rating	★★

HOLE	1	2	3	4	5	6	7	8	9	OUT
PAR	4	4	3	4	3	4M 3W	3	4	3	32 M 31 W
MENS YARDS	335	260	155	310	100	235	155	284	135	1969
LADIES YARDS	320	230	150	310	90	155	150	266	125	1819
HANDICAP	2	5	3	1	9	7	6	4	8	

Ladies Slope - 90
Ladies Course Rating - 29.9
Men's Slope - 88
Men's Course Rating - 29.6

Replace Divots • Repair Ball Marks

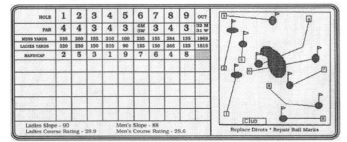

Credit Island Park Golf Course

Davenport

563-326-7820

One of the more unusual locations for a nine hole golf course is on an island. Davenport has two island courses located in the middle of the mighty Mississippi. Rock Island Arsenal Course is a beautiful 9 hole private course and Credit Island Park Golf Course is a nine hole public course located on Credit Island. Credit Island is strictly a greens fee course. A fee of $10 is collected every day of the week, second 9 is $3. There is a small amount of golfing supplies in the clubhouse. The snack area serves the entire park and has a wide variety of foods and drinks. Trees on the course are medium to large in size and line all of the wide fairways. The contour of the course is flat with some unattended rough growing along the fairways. Tee boxes are medium in size and flat to the ground. The greens are medium in size with flat putting surfaces; except for two greens away from the river. This is a very easy course to walk. It is very level with very few hazards and is easy to score well on. Senior players and women like to play Credit Island because of those reasons. The sight of the course was once an Indian trading post on the Mississippi. It was also once an eighteen hole course until a 1965 flood wiped out the entire course; just nine holes were rebuilt. Flooding is a major problem for this course, with the last major flood happening in 2001. Opening day for Credit Island is usually late in the spring after the water has resided. But sometimes you have to pay the price for a great view.

Course	9 Holes
Distance	2632 Yards
Par	34
Playability	Good
Aesthetics	Good
Interest	Fair
Worth The Trip	Yes
Rating	★★

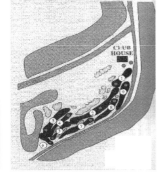

BLUE TEES	184	519	194	254	260	145	436	342	298	2632
PAR	3	5	3	4	4	3	4	4	4	34
HANDICAP	5	11	3	17	15	7	1	9	13	

HOLES	1	2	3	4	5	6	7	8	9	OUT
LADIES PAR	4	5	4	4	4	5	4	4	4	37
HANDICAP	5	11	3	17	15	7	1	9	13	

Crow Valley

Davenport

319-359-1676

One of the more exclusive courses and one of the nicest courses in eastern Iowa is Crow Valley in Bettendorf. This is a private club with 300 members paying $1,950 per year after a $7,500 stock entry fee. Guests of members are allowed to pay the expensive green fees but the chance to play is worth the money. The clubhouse at Crow Valley should be included in the top ten clubhouses in the state. It has elegant dining facilities for members and guests. Its expansive dining rooms and bar areas bring out the old country club tradition. A large pro shop is located in the lower level and has a complete line of clothes, clubs and bags. The pro shop has all the facilities to help you in every aspect of your game. Crow Valley is a moderately rolling course. It has nine ponds located throughout the layout and an average of three sand bunkers per hole, many being fairway bunkers. The fairways are narrow and lined with all sizes of trees. A beautifully tiered rough is present along the fairways and in front of tees and greens. The course has a fairway watering system that keeps the entire course green during the hot months of the summer. Tees are distinctively cut, elevated slightly and big. The greens are of medium size but are very undulating and difficult to putt. A key to success on Crow Valley is to leave your approach shot below the hole; sloping greens and pin placement make downhill putts impossible. This is an easy course to walk but a very unforgiving course where off-line shots are concerned. Accuracy off the tee is a must; the rough is deep, thick and tough to get out of. Once you get to the greens, they have a personality all of their own. Crow Valley is truly one of the finest all around courses in the state. It has a country club atmosphere and plays like a championship course, a real challenge to almost any golfer.

Course	18 Holes	Aesthetics	Very Good
Distance	6774 Yards	Interest	Very Good
Par	35-36-71	Worth The Trip	Yes
Playability	Excell.	Rating	★★★★

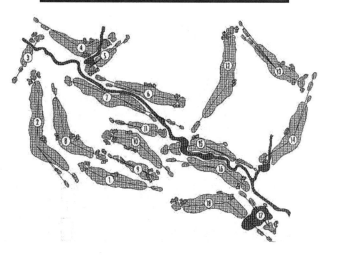

HOLE		1	2	3	4	5	6	7	8	9	OUT		10	11	12	13	14	15	16	17	18	IN	Total
Gold	73.1/139	380	589	191	389	187	422	569	425	203	3355		361	207	517	381	435	425	400	181	512	3419	6774
Blue	71.9/137	373	551	184	374	180	400	519	418	185	3184		344	196	490	363	414	391	379	160	484	3221	6405
Bl/Wh Combo	70.6/135	B	W	W	B	B	W	B	W	W	3076		B	W	B	W	W	W	B	W		3128	6204
White	69.9/133	359	531	146	360	166	384	500	404	165	3015		332	174	475	351	396	362	368	141	460	3059	6074
Silver	67.8/120	359	531	146	349	166	329	451	390	165	2866		332	174	475	300	348	271	368	84	380	2712	5578
Par		4	5	3	4	3	4	5	4	3	35		4	3	5	4	4	4	4	3	5	36	71
Handicap		17	9	15	5	11	1	7	3	13			16	10	18	8	4	2	6	12	14		
Ladies Handicap		11	7	17	1	15	9	3	5	13			8	16	4	12	6	2	14	18	10		
Par		4	5	3	4	3	4	5	4	3	35		4	3	5	4	4	4	4	3	5	36	71
Red	71.3/121	345	431	127	323	132	329	451	350	155	2643		319	158	429	300	348	271	292	84	380	2581	5224

Davenport Country Club

Pleasant Valley

563-332-5022

One of the best courses in eastern Iowa is the Davenport Country Club. It is located at 490 Valley Dr. in Pleasant Valley. This is a private course with 325 golfing members and 581 total members. Green fees, while playing with a member are a little expensive. The attractive and spacious clubhouse is built on top of a hill between the Mississippi and the course. Beside the clubhouse is a pool area; down in the valley below the clubhouse are tennis courts and the practice area. Inside the modern structure is an elegant restaurant that is open the year round to members and their guests. There is a snack and bar area on the lower level for golfers during the day that has a wide variety of food and drink. The pro shop is located on the lower level and has a full line of equipment and clothes. This is a very attractive and elegant clubhouse. The old time country club still has its roots embedded in this course but a transition is slowly taking place with the turn over of members. Davenport Country Club was site of the Western Open in 1936 and 1951. It was one of the Des Moines Registers five toughest courses in 1983. Number sixteen was awarded all American status. This is a course with tradition and facilities to carry it on. The layout has two ponds and one stream affecting eight holes. Trees on the hilly course are large and old and are scattered alongside the regulation fairways. Greens are small in size, flat, and sloping. The greens have been converted to bent grass. Davenport Country Club was designed by Charles Allison and built in 1924. The course has many walkers but is a difficult course to walk. It is a challenging course that was built within the terrain. The hills and trees were incorporated into the design and have become a trademark of the course. This is a beautiful course that is well landscaped and conditioned. Davenport Country Club is truly one of the championship courses of Iowa. DCC was rated the 2nd best course in Iowa in 1997, and their 16th hole has been awarded All American Status. It is a course that maintains that old country club feeling inside the clubhouse and out on the course.

Course	18 Holes	Aesthetics	Excell.
Distance	6458 Yards	Interest	Very Good
Par	36-35-71	Worth The Trip	Yes
Playability	Excell.	Rating	*****

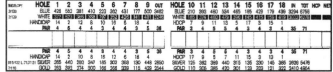

HOLE	1	2	3	4	5	6	7	8	9	OUT	HOLE	10	11	12	13	14	15	16	17	18	IN	TOT	HCP	NET
BLUE	426	582	381	410	223	362	431	177	500	3462	BLUE	210	393	480	534	465	185	429	179	439	3294	6756		
WHITE	392	523	366	388	197	352	426	141	481	3248	WHITE	165	374	450	475	396	159	419	159	419	3032	6278		
HANDICAP	14	2	12	8	10	16	6	18	4		HDCP	7	9	11	13	5	17	3	15	1				
PAR	4	5	4	4	3	4	4	3	5	36	PAR	3	4	5	5	4	3	4	3	4	35	71		
PAR	4	5	4	4	3	4	4	3	5	36	PAR	3	4	5	5	4	3	4	3	4	35	71		
HANDICAP	14	2	10	8	16	12	6	18	4		HDCP	9	5	11	13	3	15	13						
SILVER	365	440	280	347	185	302	359	130	448	2850	SILVER	125	382	399	440	315	135	330	145	385	2626	5476		
GOLD	263	392	270	300	166	266	339	115	429	2544	GOLD	110	306	385	420	301	129	323	121	322	2410	4954		

Duck Creek Park Golf Course

Davenport

563 -326-7824

Course	18 Holes	Aesthetics	Very Good
Distance	5787 Yards	Interest	Good
Par	35-35-70	Worth The Trip	Yes
Playability	Good	Rating	★★★

One of the busier public courses in Davenport is the Duck Creek Park Golf Course located off Locust Street in the center of Davenport. The course was built in 1935. It recorded 50,000 rounds of golf in 2001 and has been documented as one of the busiest public courses in the United States. This is an 18-hole course with total yardage of 5759 yards. The contour of the course is very hilly making it a hard course to walk. Duck Creek is basically a cart course, not many walkers, and the clubhouse has a fleet of carts that you can rent. There are no ponds on the course but a stream comes into play on four holes. There are no bunkers on the course and the rough only exists where it is too hard to get the mower to. There are a massive number of trees on the course; many of them line the wide fairways. But there are also a great many trees, mostly medium to large in size, that are scattered throughout the rough and around the tees and greens. Tees are in good shape and are elevated nicely on many of the holes. The greens are medium in size and generally flat. The greens also claim the reputation of being easy to stop an approach shot on and very slow to putt on. The grass condition on the greens and fairways is good; worn, but good. The clubhouse is typical big city and public. It has a complete selection of supplies, including clothes and clubs and a large snack area that has sandwiches and drinks and an ample sitting area. Green fees for this par 70 course are very reasonable, $15 for 18. Duck Creek is an easy course to play and score well on, but not easy to get on. The only major hazards are the trees and if you are careful you can avoid them all together. The course is situated in the middle of a park and takes on a park look and feeling. This course looks good and plays easy, but only play it if you like crowds.

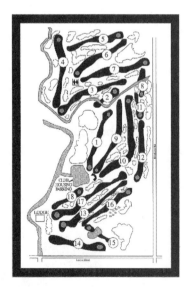

BLUE TEES	338	154	416	411	313	336	392	143	444	2949		532	122	328	441	300	143	321	478	174	2839	5788
WHITE TEES	323	140	402	394	298	320	370	129	429	2805		513	100	307	428	279	125	309	450	147	2658	5463
PAR	4	3	4	4	4	4	4	3	5	35		5	3	4	5	4	3	5	4		35	70
HANDICAP	13	15	1	3	9	11	5	17	7			6	18	10	2	8	16	12	4	14		
HOLES	1	2	3	4	5	6	7	8	9	OUT		10	11	12	13	14	15	16	17	18	In	Tot	HCP	Net
RED TEES	323	140	402	300	238	299	360	98	429	2589		441	100	307	428	279	104	309	388	112	2468	5057
PAR	5	4	4	4	4	4	5	3	5	37		5	3	4	5	4	3	5	4		36	73
HANDICAP	13	15	1	3	9	11	5	17	7			6	18	10	2	8	16	12	4	14		

Emeis Park Golf Course

Davenport
563-326-7825

One of the busier courses along the Mississippi is the Emeis Park Golf Course in Davenport. This is a public course that recorded 45,000 rounds last year. There are no yearly memberships, only green fees. Daily fees are very reasonable. Junior players and Senior Citizens can play for $12. The course is located at Locust and Emeis Dr. The clubhouse has a full line of equipment including carts and is very nice for a public course. The dining area includes drinks and snacks, not a real elaborate selection, but this is a golfer's course, not an eater's course. This 6463 yard course has two ponds and one stream that comes into play on four holes. In 2002 a lake was added on number 12. They also have 50 sand bunkers that affect play a great deal. An important element of the course is the number of trees. Sizes range from new plantings to very old and mature. They are mainly scattered throughout the three inch rough. The contour of the course is generally flat with some gentle slopes thrown in. Fairways vary in width but have good hitting surfaces throughout. Tees are cut nicely and are in good condition despite the heavy use. Greens are medium to large in size with flatness prevailing with a few tilted and sloping putting surfaces. The greens also have a reputation of being fast but holding well. Emeis Park sustains a lot of abuse from a great number of players but maintains a fairly good level of conditioning. This is a course that has a little bit of everything, but still lets you relax and play your game. This is an easy course to walk despite its long yardage and an easy course to score well on if you tend to business. This is a fun place to play, 45,000 people can't be wrong.

Course	18 Holes	Aesthetics	Fair
Distance	6463 Yards	Interest	Good
Par	36-36-72	Worth The Trip	Yes
Playability	Good	Rating	**+

BLUE TEES	548	550	436	357	149	441	413	322	515	3333
WHITE TEES	514	136	427	335	128	422	405	310	501	3174
PAR	5	3	4	4	3	4	4	4	5	36
HANDICAP	9	15	3	13	17	1	5	11	7	
HOLES	1	2	3	4	5	6	7	8	9	OUT
RED TEES	442	126	396	289	110	365	361	340	453	2930
PAR	5	3	5	4	3	4	4	4	5	36
HANDICAP	5	17	9	15	11	3	7	13	1	

549	357	524	162	334	385	454	185	522	3212	6463			
325	320	499	146	317	373	419	180	506	3086	6260			
4	4	5	3	4	4	4	3	5	36	72			
4	18	12	16	14	8	2	10	6					
10	11	12	13	14	15	16	17	18	In	Tot	HCP	Net
342	308	448	128	280	322	366	173	422	2731	5551			
4	4	5	3	4	4	4	3	5	36	74			
6	12	4	18	16	8	2	10	14					

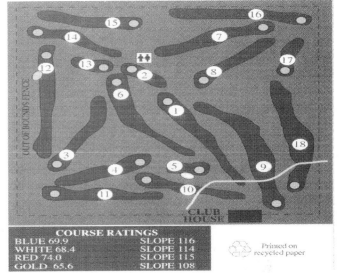

COURSE RATINGS	
BLUE 69.9	SLOPE 116
WHITE 68.4	SLOPE 114
RED 74.0	SLOPE 115
GOLD 65.6	SLOPE 108

Printed on recycled paper

Red Hawk Golf Course

Davenport

563-391-9711

One of the most versatile recreation areas in the Davenport area is Red Hawk Golf Course, formally Valley Golf and Recreation Center. In this complex you will find a 50-tee driving range, an 18 hole miniature golf course, and a 9 hole regular golf course. Red Hawk is also very involved with the First Tee Program. Daily green fees are very reasonable. The clubhouse has carts for rent, clubs for rent and other golfing supplies. Food includes drinks and pizza. The course is 2260 yards long with a par of 33. Valley was rebuilt during the past couple of years with a new green on 5 and holes 5 through 8 being rerouted. There are no water hazards but every hole has one looming sand trap. Trees are small in number and small in size. Greens are medium in size and rolling. Additional trees are being added every year. This is a good beginner's course. It is flat, easy to walk, and wide open. The course was built in 1972 and is located on the N.W. side of Davenport at 6364 N.W. Blvd. This is a family course; there is something here the whole family will enjoy. The busiest part of the complex is the driving range, but after you correct your problems there you can jump right on to the 9 hole course and see if you accomplished anything. This is a course that can be played after work or late in the evening.

Course	9 Holes
Distance	2260 Yards
Par	33
Playability	Fair
Aesthetics	Poor
Interest	Fair
Worth The Trip	Maybe
Rating	*

YARDAGE	175	261	241	253	321	350	176	350	133	2260
PAR	3	4	4	4	4	4	3	4	3	33
HOLE	1	2	3	4	5	6	7	8	9	OUT
FIRST TEE PAR	4	4	4	4	4	5	3	5	3	36
FIRST TEE YARDAGE	100	171	161	170	220	240	100	291	93	1546

Dayton Golf and Country Club

Dayton

515-547-2712

The Dayton Golf and Country Club was built in 1925 and had sand greens until 1975, one of the last courses in the state to convert to grass greens. The course is located just south of the rodeo grounds on Highway 175. The course, which is generally flat, does have a few exceptions. There is a small ravine that comes into play on two holes and there is one massive hill that comes into play on number nine. This particular hole is one of the finest and toughest finishing holes in the area. Number nine contains a blind tee shot, an approach shot over water up to an elevated green, a real challenge the first time around. The greens are small and flat but hold fairly well, the trees are few and far between and are scattered throughout the rough. The Dayton clubhouse is small but has everything that you might want in golf supplies and refreshments. The course was revamped in 2002 with 2 new holes built to the west. This is a course that runs east-west and is easy to play and walk, except for the last two holes. Try this course, it will get you in the end.

Dayton Golf & Country Club

Course	9 Holes
Distance	2973 Yards
Par	36
Playability	Fair
Aesthetics	Good
Interest	Fair
Worth The Trip	Yes
Rating	**+

MEN'S YARDAGE	501	506	284	365	135	155	375	191	461	2973
LADIES' YARDAGE	433	433	216	335	130	98	350	164	415	2574
HANDICAP	6	1	2	5	9	8	4	7	3	
HOLE	1	2	3	4	5	6	7	8	9	OUT
PAR	5	5	4	4	3	3	4	3	5	36

Oneota Golf and Country Club
Decorah
563-382-9347

Decorah has two fine courses and one of them is a beautiful 18 hole layout located east of Decorah on Old State A52 off Hwy. 9 called Oneota Golf and Country Club. This is a private course that has 285 members paying an initial $1,000 stock and $1,900 for a family membership. Guests of members can pay the above average green fees. The beauty of Northeast Iowa is also prevalent in Oneota. The Upper Iowa River runs along two sides of the course; it is a beautiful backdrop. The surrounding hills offer the beauty of the seasons throughout the year. There is two ponds on the course and an average of four sand bunkers per hole. A large number of small to medium size trees line the fairways and the fringes of the course. The narrow and slightly rolling fairways are also outlined with three inch rough that is thick and tough to get out of. A fairway watering system keeps the course in excellent shape late into the summer. Tees are elevated and big and landscaped very nicely. The greens are medium in size with rolling and sloping putting surfaces. The greens have been known for the last few years as being fast. Oneota was originally built in 1920 but was redesigned and rebuilt in 1984. The clubhouse has a full line of equipment. Oneota has a big new clubhouse that has a spacious sitting area that is very open and has a beautiful view of the course and hills to the north. Food includes drinks, snacks, and grilled sandwiches, no restaurant. This is an easy course to walk, but is a challenging course in which you need to be accurate off the tees and keep your head in the game at all times. The trees and rough can make your game last much longer on Oneota. This is one of the few 18 holes courses in the area. It is a very scenic course and a welcome addition to the Decorah area.

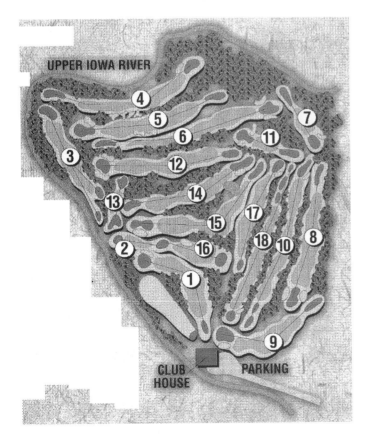

Course	18 Holes	Aesthetics	Excell.
Distance	6472 Yards	Interest	Very Good
Par	36-36-72	Worth The Trip	Yes
Playability	Good	Rating	***

HOLE		1	2	3	4	5	6	7	8	9	OUT
BLUE	70.6/122	337	150	375	497	430	536	192	393	357	3267
WHITE	69.5/118	335	135	357	468	412	515	180	376	345	3123
HANDICAP		17	15	3	9	5	7	11	1	13	
PAR		4	3	4	5	4	5	3	4	4	36

10	11	12	13	14	15	16	17	18	IN	TOT	HCP	NET
507	181	411	134	379	490	224	376	503	3205	6472		
488	162	400	124	368	466	201	362	473	3044	6167		
8	16	4	18	10	6	14	12	2				
5	3	4	3	4	5	3	4	5	36	72		

Silvercrest Golf and Country Club

Decorah

563-382-5296

Silvercrest Golf and Country Club is a semi-private golf course that is located on old Highway 52 north of Decorah 2 miles. The public can pay green fees and play on Monday, Tuesday, and Fridays. Weekday green fees are reasonable. The 150 members pay an initial stock of $540 with a yearly fee of $950 in 1991. The clubhouse has recently been remodeled and is nice with a big dining area with 30 tables. The proshop has a full line of equipment including carts. The clubhouse also has a short order restaurant that is open to members and guests. Silvercrest was built in 1935. The layout of this course can be described as an out and back course. The layout of the course is also set up to discourage hooking the ball out-of-bounds to the left. The contour of the course is rolling. Trees are large around the outside fringes with new plantings along the fairways and a few medium evergreens. Many new evergreens and leafy trees were added in '90 & '91. Fairways are wide and allow the spraying of tee shots, but they are also lined with these smaller trees. There are 8 sand bunkers and little evidence of rough. Greens are small to medium in size and flat with a little tilt in most of them. This is a hard course to walk, carts are in great demand, and it is also a very challenging course to play. A large number of couples' tournaments are played at Silvercrest. The most outstanding feature of the course is the beauty of the course and surrounding area. Many holes have a panoramic view of Luther College which increases in beauty as fall envelopes the hillsides surrounding the campus and course.

Course	9 Holes
Distance	2880 Yards
Par	36
Playability	Good
Aesthetics	Excell.
Interest	Good
Worth The Trip	Yes
Rating	* * *

HOLE	1	2	3	4	5	6	7	8	9	OUT
WHITE/BLUE TEES	344	310	486	134	360	290	310	144	502	2880
HANDICAP	6	4	12	14	2	18	16	8	10	
PAR	4	4	5	3	4	4	4	3	5	36

Willow Run Country Club

Denver

319-984-5762

Willow Run Country Club is located on the east edge of Denver on Fayette St. and is billed as a long hitters course. This private course, with a 20 mile green fee radius, has 2850 yards frequently interrupted by a stream. This stream comes into play on 7 of the 9 holes and guards the greens in four instances. Seventy-five trees per year have been planted over the past five years, financed by their 3-man best shot. The fairways are narrow and flat with a 2 inch rough cut making it a tougher course than in the past. Tees are flat but large and the greens are medium in size with a rolling contour. This is an easy course to walk and score on if you hit the ball fairly long. Because of the water and placement of trees you can count on some penalty strokes and some lost balls. The clubhouse has a few supplies including carts, and the bar area has snacks and sandwiches. Green fees are reasonable. The 240 members pay an annual fee of $480 for a family. This is a fairly busy course that can be frustrating. The openness tends to make you feel secure but the stream tends to make you reach into your bag for another ball. Willow Run was built in 1970 and is now mature enough to cause trouble.

Course	9 Holes
Distance	2850 Yards
Par	35
Playability	Fair
Aesthetics	Good
Interest	Good
Worth The Trip	Yes
Rating	* * *

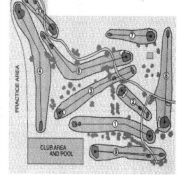

MEN'S		440	146	461	415	155	452	174	295	362	2850
PAR		5	3	5	4	3	5	4	4	4	35
HANDICAP		9	8	1	2	5	6	4	7	3	
HOLE		1	2	3	4	5	6	7	8	9	Out
LADIES		438	143	323	401	106	407	160	261	355	2590
PAR		5	3	4	5	3	5	4	4	4	35
HANDICAP		2	8	9	3	5	1	4	6	7	

Denison Country Club

Denison
712-263-5194

The contour of the land starts to succumb to rolling and wooded areas as you approach the S.W. corner of the state. The Denison Country Club has some of these characteristics surfacing on their course. The large clubhouse is located on the east edge of the course, on more of a level setting. The clubhouse contains a large bar area with a small amount of supplies available. An additional 9 holes was added in 1999. The general layout of the course is rolling with lots of medium and big trees lining the narrow fairways. There are water hazards and sand to add to the character of the course. Greens are medium in size and have a rolling element to them. One of the most pleasant things about the course is the landscaping; flowers adorn the tees and bushes accent the fairways and rough areas. The new 9 holes add some of the same rolling terrain. It is a beautiful course that presents a challenge to any golfer. The course is in terrific shape thanks to tot5al irrigation, even though hills sometimes dry out. The Denison course is an easy course to walk and challenging in the fact that the par 3 holes are difficult and long. The 200 members play a well-groomed course that has a golfing atmosphere supplemented by the friendliness of the members. Annual fees are $790 for a family. Daily green fees are a little above average. The course was originally built in 1931 and is located on the S.E. edge of town on M36. The Denison course is a nice example of what a little extra effort, care, and work can do in turning an ordinary course into a fine example of golfing in Iowa.

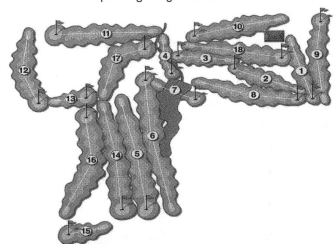

Course	18 Holes	Aesthetics	Very Good
Distance	6538 Yards	Interest	Very Good
Par	36-36-72	Worth The Trip	Yes
Playability	Good	Rating	★★★

HOLE		1	2	3	4	5	6	7	8	9	OUT		10	11	12	13	14	15	16	17	18	In	Tot	Hcp	Net
HANDICAP	BLUE/WHITE	14/14	17/17	5/6	18/16	9/9	1/2	11/11	8/4	5/7		P	2/3	3/4	13/12	15/18	13/13	1/6	19/10	7/15	4/5				
BLACK	71.5/118	308	290	211	161	519	585	185	505	392	3156	L	540	462	350	144	482	188	525	311	380	3382	6538		
BLUE	71.2/116	308	290	211	161	482	580	185	505	392	3114	A	540	393	345	140	480	184	520	308	380	3290	6404		
WHITE	68.5/112	305	285	208	140	454	544	170	411	382	2899	Y	535	370	328	110	472	157	480	290	376	3118	6017		
SILVER	66.3/108	280	275	208	130	426	506	140	299	380	2644	E	435	337	290	88	453	123	380	270	370	2746	5390		
PAR		4	4	3	3	5	5	3	4/5	4	35/36	R	5	4	4	3	5	3	5	4	4	37	72/73		
RED		280	275	208	100	424	460	110	299	380	2536		435	335	288	85	450	120	378	268	370	2729	5265		
PAR		4	4	3	3	5	5	3	4	4	35		5	4	4	3	5	3	5	4	5	38	73		
HANDICAP		14	16	3	17	2	4	15	10	1			8	9	13	18	5	6	11	7	12				

A.H Blank Municipal Golf Course

Des Moines

515-285-0864

Course	18 Holes	Aesthetics	Good
Distance	6745 Yards	Interest	Good
Par	36-36-72	Worth The Trip	Yes
Playability	Good	Rating	★★★

The A.H. Blank Municipal Golf Course was expanded to 18 holes in 1983. The original 9 holes course was built in 1971 at the location of S.W. 9th and County Line road in S.W. Des Moines. This is a public course that offers yearly memberships that are honored at all city courses; Blank, Waveland, and Grandview. To buy this $550 membership you must be a resident of Des Moines. Daily green fees for this public 18 hole course are very reasonable. The clubhouse is located on the south tip of the course and offers all golfing supplies except clothes. The area inside the clubhouse has been recently remodeled and expanded to include food service facilities. This is a maturing course that has come of age since the turn of the century, it has become a more interesting course to play. The basic layout of the course is good and with the addition of 600 tress the character of the course will take a new direction. Trees were added to number 7 so you can't cut the corner any more. In 2001 the layout of the course was changed and a new pond was added. There are 4 ponds on the course that come into play on 8 holes. There are a total of 24 sand bunkers o n the course with a few additional grass bunkers in the fairways. The rough is cut three inches outlining the fairways and in front of the greens. Fairways are wide with many of them tree lined. The contour of the entire course is gently rolling with a few hilly fairways to the north. Full fairway watering has kept Blank green most of the summer. The greens are large in size with sloping and rolling putting surfaces. A.H. Blank is an easy course to get tee times to play, it is easy to walk, with the addition of additional trees you have to use all your clubs in your bag to score well. This is a growing city course. One that affords many players the opportunity to play a long course close to home for a fair price.

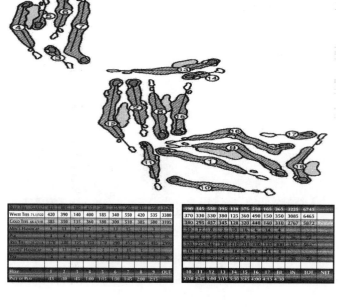

White Tees 71.1/122	420	390	140	400	185	340	550	420	535	3380
Gold Tees 68.1/118	385	350	135	360	180	300	510	385	500	3105
Men's Handicap										
Red Tees										
Ladies Handicap										
Hole	1	2	3	4	5	6	7	8	9	OUT
Pace of Play	:15	:30	:45	1:00	1:15	1:30	1:45	2:00	2:15	

390	345	550	395	410	375	510	165	365	3225	6745
370	330	530	380	125	360	490	150	350	3085	6465
340	295	457	345	120	320	440	140	310	2767	5872
10	11	12	13	14	15	16	17	18	IN	TOT	NET
2:30	2:45	3:00	3:15	3:30	3:45	4:00	4:15	4:30		

Echo Valley Country Club
Des Moines
515-285-0101

Another new course that is located on the south side of Des Moines is Echo Valley Country Club. This private 18 hole club was built in 1969 among the rolling hills and woods of south Des Moines. Green fees are only accepted when you are playing with one of the 500 members. The clubhouse is a modern structure that has a south wall of glass looking out over the entire course. Inside there is an elegant restaurant, open to members, and a bar area that is relaxing and quite high class. The pro shop is on the lower level and its full line of equipment is squeezed into a tiny area. The grill and bar on the lower level does have a dress code plus a nice selection of food and drinks. The atmosphere of Echo Valley is definitely country club. There are dress code bars, semi formal restaurants, and caddy's quarters for storage and maintenance. This course is in the maturing stages, but because it is well maintained and offers some challenging golf it is a course to consider in the Des Moines area. The characteristics of the layout include 10 ponds in which six hazards come into play, a creek that affects play on six holes. This is another example of a course laden with water hazards. To increase the difficulty of Echo Valley there are fairway, green, and earth bunkers, with an average of three per hole. The rough is cut three inches everywhere on the course, making it look and feel like a course that was designed and not just cut out of a hillside. The trees are small to medium with some new plantings. There is also a nice assortment of small bushes planted in the rough. The large greens have a variety of surfaces, flat, sloping, rolling; all have average speed and hold fairly well. The contour of this country club is gently rolling to flat in some areas. The course is noted for being a tough young course with lots of out-of-bounds possibilities plus there is a large quantity of hazard trouble. This section of Des Moines is a developing area and Echo Valley should develop into one of the better courses in the city.

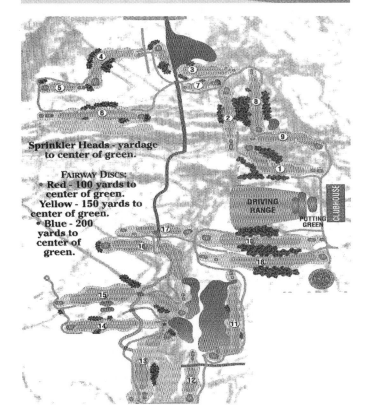

Sprinkler Heads - yardage to center of green.

FAIRWAY DISCS:
• Red - 100 yards to center of green.
Yellow - 150 yards to center of green.
• Blue - 200 yards to center of green.

Course	18 Holes	Aesthetics	Very Good
Distance	6819 Yards	Interest	Very Good
Par	36-36-72	Worth The Trip	Yes
Playability	V. Good	Rating	****

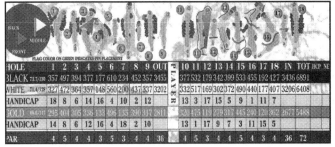

HOLE	1	2	3	4	5	6	7	8	9	OUT	10	11	12	13	14	15	16	17	18	IN	TOT	BCP	NC
BLACK 71.7/130	357	497	394	377	177	610	234	452	357	3455	377	532	179	342	399	533	455	192	427	3436	6891		
WHITE 71.4/128	327	472	364	357	148	560	200	437	337	3202	332	517	169	302	372	490	440	177	407	3206	6408		
HANDICAP	18	8	6	14	16	4	10	2	12		13	3	17	15	5	9	1	11	7				
GOLD 68.8/117	295	404	305	334	106	390	172	281			324	452	157	317	445	240	120	162	267	5488			
HANDICAP	14	8	6	12	16	4	18	2	10		13	1	17	9	7	3	11	15	5				
PAR	4	5	4	4	3	5	3	4	4	36	4	5	3	4	4	5	4	3	4	36	72		

Grandview Golf Course

Des Moines

515-262-8414

Course	18 Holes	Aesthetics	Good
Distance	5591 Yards	Interest	Good
Par	34-36-70	Worth The Trip	Yes
Playability	Good	Rating	★★+

The Grandview Municipal Golf Course is one of the older courses in the city, having been built around 1897. Today it is one of Des Moines city courses, and is located at E. 29th and Arthur. City passes are good on this course along with A.H. Blank and Waveland. Green fees at Grandview are very reasonable for an 18 hole course. The clubhouse is a large old white structure that is a privately run restaurant that has very good food. The clubhouse also has golfing items such as balls, clothing, clubs, gloves and there are carts for rent. In a separate building near the first tee is the starter for the course, a man you need to get close to. This is a fairly easy course to walk, thus making it a favorite place for seniors to play. The characteristics of the course include one pond, four bunkers, and rough that is mowed quite short, actually it never comes into play. The trees are medium to large in size and can be found in large numbers along many of the average width fairways. Fairway watering was added in 1991. The greens are small to medium in size and are flat with a little tilt to them. This public 18 hole course is an easy playing course, a course that is easy to read and requires very little control. Spraying the ball only gets you lost, not in very much trouble. The course has above average play and is kept in good shape for a municipal course. This is a scenic course to play: gently rolling hills on part of the course, beautiful trees to offer a little challenge and tradition to keep your mind off that bad shot you just made. The atmosphere is relaxed and one that stimulates pleasure golf.

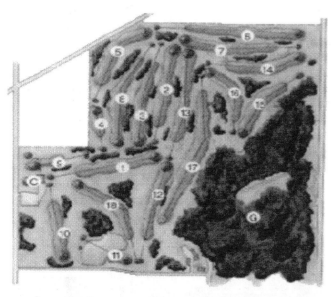

BLUE TEES 65.7/108	315	330	339	130	307	420	349	362	160	2712													
WHITE TEES 65.7/108	309	333	340	130	295	418	340	360	154	2679
MEN'S HANDICAP	13	11	5	17	7	1	3	9	15	
PAR	4	4	4	3	4	5	4	4	3	34
RED TEES 69.7/110	296	323	321	119	282	383	321	347	143	2535
LADIES' HANDICAP	15	11	5	17	13	1	7	9	9	
PAR	4	4	4	3	4	4	4	4	3	36
HOLE	1	2	3	4	5	6	7	8	9	OUT
PACE OF PLAY	:12	:25	:38	:47	:59	1:14	1:27	1:40	1:49	

268	154	450	370	278	280	244	517	443	2882	5591		
255	149	335	369	270	278	247	507	333	2743	5422	
16	10	2	6	18	14	12	2	4		
4	3	4	4	4	4	4	5	4	36	70
245	144	320	359	262	258	236	470	318	2612	5147
16	10	8	6	18	14	12	2	4		
4	3	4	4	4	4	4	5	4	34	70
10	11	12	13	14	15	16	17	18	IN	TOT	NET
2:00	2:09	2:22	2:36	2:47	2:58	3:09	3:25	3:38			

Wakonda Club
Des Moines
515-285-4962

One of the most exclusive and one of the best courses in the state of Iowa is the Wakonda Club in Des Moines. This private country club was built in 1922 and retains the old style country club atmosphere. The Wakonda Club complex has a spacious clubhouse that is one of the most exclusive and best in the city and was totally redecorated in 1991 to bring back the old traditional club look. It is open to members of the club and their guests. The pro shop for the course is in a separate building west of the clubhouse. It has a full line of equipment including carts for rent. Wakonda has approximately 440 members who enjoy many different aspects of country club living — fine dining, tennis, and an outstanding golf course. The course is located on Fleur Drive and is built on semi-rolling, wooded land. The fairways are all bent grass and are sloping in many cases and lined in every case with old oak trees that have been a highlight of this course for many years. A new landscaping plan is now in effect to interplant more oaks and maintain the oak character of Wakonda for future generations. In 2002 some greens were redesigned and 2 new bunkers added. These trees are why this may be the number one course in the state. There are six ponds on the course and one creek that comes into play a great deal as it meanders through the valleys. There are an average of three bunkers per hole and when combined with the three inch rough creates a very tough layout. A new number 9 hole has been designed to avoid errant shots ending up in the swimming pool! The greens are small to medium in size and take on an undulating characteristic. The greens are also known for their speed and trueness. Even though this may have all the aspects and design of a championship course the one thing that makes it become a true golfing pleasure is the landscaping. The rolling fairways are cut with the movement of the land making every little undulation look like a stroke of a sculpture. The trees are perfect in shape and look as though you are walking through a park rather than golf course. The greens and tees are cut to perfection, leaving little to the imagination of what a green or tee box should look like; they know on Wakonda. One of the best complexes in the state. Wakonda was also the site of the 1963 U.S. Amateur and 1963 Walker Cup.

Course	18 Holes	Aesthetics	Excell.
Distance	6881 Yards	Interest	Excell.
Par	36-36-72	Worth The Trip	Yes
Playability	Excell.	Rating	★★★★★

HOLE RATING/SLOPE	1	2	3	4	5	6	7	8	9	OUT
BLUE 74.1/135	437 [125] [163R]	441	416	542	422	365	549 [121] [153R]			3535
WHITE 72.3/132	410 [114L] [169R]	382	403	502	410	348	509 [129L] [153R]			3286
MENS HDCP	1	15	7	5	11	3	13	9	17	
RED 73.9/128	394 [114L] [116R]	370	400	446	353	315	436 [121L] [146R]			2976
GOLD 69.8/117	394 [114L] [116R]	312	328	424	353	246	363 [117L] [141L] [141R]			2677
LADIES HDCP	3	15	9	5	11	13	1	17		
PAR	4/5	3	4	4/5	5	4	4	5	3	36/38

10	11	12	13	14	15	16	17	18	IN	TOT	NET
441	408	361	530	201	500	425	169	311	3346	6881	
431	396	348	520	168	481	417	145	301	3207	6493	
2	10	12	6	16	8	4	18	14			
330	385	339	421	150	415	407	119	253	2819	5795	
310	324	266	421	114	415	300	100	253	2503	5180	
12	8	10	4	16	2	6	18	14			
4	4	4	5	3	5	4/5	3	4	36/37	72/75	

Waveland Golf Course

Des Moines

515-271-8725

There are a lot of nice municipal courses in the state but none are nicer or more respected than Waveland Municipal in Des Moines. The course is located at 4908 University and is built among rolling hills and wooded hillsides. The course is one of the oldest in the area, built in 1895, and has trees to prove it. Large mature trees line the narrow fairways and can be found wherever you try to go. This 18 hole course has one pond, one creek, very little sand and rough that fills in the valleys between the fairways. The greens are large and have a contour mirroring the hillsides they are built on. The greens have a reputation of being fast and difficult to read. The grass condition throughout the course is fair, mainly due to the many hillsides. This is definitely a cart course, the many hills make walking a real chore. Waveland has a reputation for being a short demanding course, one that is designed for good players that have excellent control of their irons and can place the ball in the correct position. This is also a course designed for a straight hitter; spraying the ball will only leave you fighting the trees and rough. Waveland has been developed into a course that is considered one of the top 75 municipal courses in the country. The pro has a full line of supplies and a full line of services for all golfers. The clubhouse is an old style red brick structure that looks like it belongs in a setting such as Waveland. There is an excellent eating facility inside that serves sandwiches and breakfast during the season. Waveland is part of the city network of courses and honors about 425 city season badges. These cost $600 for a resident. Daily green fees are very reasonable, $17 for 9 and $20 for 18. New cart paths were put in during the 2003 season. This is a course that you must play a few times to come out ahead. Playing it just once can leave you with a defeated feeling and a nice course like this has more to offer than rejection.

Course	18 Holes	Aesthetics	Excell.
Distance	6544 Yards	Interest	Excell.
Par	36-36-72	Worth The Trip	Yes
Playability	Excell.	Rating	****

	1	2	3	4	5	6	7	8	9	OUT
BLUE TEES 71.7/124	355	165	585	371	325	355	495	182	393	3226
WHITE TEES 70.6/121	308	147	558	361	318	345	486	175	384	3082
GOLD TEES 68.2/116	306	142	407	301	285	314	477	138	376	2746
MEN'S HANDICAP	9	17	1	7	13	15	11	5	3	
PAR	4	3	5	4	4	4	4	3	4	36
RED TEES 69.4/109	301	137	402	296	280	309	378	133	371	2607
LADIES' HANDICAP	9	17	1	7	13	15	11	5	3	
PAR	4	3	5	4	4	4	4	3	4	35
HOLE	1	2	3	4	5	6	7	8	9	OUT
PACE OF PLAY	:13	:22	:40	:54	1:06	1:19	1:35	1:44	1:58	

	10	11	12	13	14	15	16	17	18	IN	TOT	NET
	243	370	565	152	328	475	460	365	360	3318	6544	
	225	361	560	121	303	466	453	357	354	3200	6282	
	205	301	507	111	300	406	448	276	351	2905	5651	
	6	10	4	18	14	12	2	8	16			
	3	4	5	3	4	5	4/5	4	4	36/37	72/73	
	200	296	502	106	152	401	443	271	345	2716	5323	
	6	10	4	18	14	12	2	8	16			
	4	4	5	3	3	5	4	4	4	37	72	
	10	11	12	13	14	15	16	17	18	IN	TOT	NET
	2:08	2:21	2:39	2:48	3:00	3:16	3:31	3:44	3:57			

Woodland Hills Golf Course
Des Moines
515-289-1326

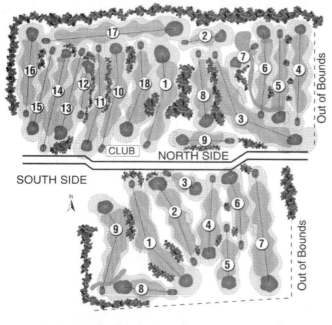

If you are looking for a change in scenery and terrain from the courses in Des Moines try the Woodside Golf Course located on Highway 69 north of Des Moines. The contour of this 27 hole complex is generally flat. Woodside sports an 18 hole course on the north side of the complex and a 9 hole course on the south side. There four ponds on the north side affecting eight holes, and one pond on the south course coming into play on six holes. New sand bunkers were added to 5 holes in 2001 and rough is cut at a two inch length along the fairways and around the greens. Tree size varies throughout the courses. There are many new plantings and there are also many large trees scattered mostly to the west. Green size is generally small with putting surfaces being flat. The back side of the north course has some tilted greens. The greens are also very easy to read and have a true putting surface. The grass condition of the greens and the fairways is fair, with some brown and bare patches visible. The fairway width is different on each hole. Despite the number and size of the trees the two courses are pretty open to erratic play. The only hills can be found on the back side of the north course, but otherwise the remainder of the course is flat. This is an easy course to walk but is heavily laden with carts. Woodside was built in 1928 and is generally busy throughout the summer. This is a good course for senior players to try, easy to walk, wide open, easy to read and score on. It is also a pleasure course that is run like a family operation. The clubhouse has a full line of equipment and offers bar items and snack food. They also have a dining area for special events and gatherings. The members pay an annual fee of $930 for a family, seniors pay $160. Weekday green fees are very reasonable. This is a great late afternoon course, one that you can play quickly and quietly. Not much trouble, not much tension. A enjoyable place to play and experience.

Course	27 Holes	Aesthetics	Good
Distance	5568 Yards	Interest	Fair
Par	34-36-70	Worth The Trip	Yes
Playability	Good	Rating	★★+

Springbrook Country Club

DeWitt

563-659-3187

Another old and beautiful course that can be found in eastern Iowa is the Springbrook Country Club located two miles northwest of DeWitt on 224th St.. This private course was built in 1916 and could be considered one of the top 10 nine hole courses in the state in both beauty and clubhouse facilities. The pro shop has a nice selection of clubs and golfing supplies. The restaurant is noted for its big salad bar and other menu items. The restaurant is open to members and their guests the same as the golf course. The 275 members pay an annual fee of $400 with reasonable green fees, only if you are a guest or a member of another country club. The water hazards on the course consist of one pond and one stream plus there is an average of one bunker per hole. There is an over abundance of large old trees that are scattered around the course. The fairways are cut narrow with a 2 inch rough guarding the sides. The fairway watering system keeps the course green throughout the summer. The tees and greens are small in size but have excellent grass. The layout has to contend with a high volume of cart traffic on the course wearing out the grass. This is a hilly course that is hard to walk and hard to score well on. The outstanding feature of the course is the elegant beauty of the course and clubhouse, truly a picturesque golfing scene.

Course	9 Holes
Distance	2893 Yards
Par	34
Playability	Excell.
Aesthetics	Excell.
Interest	Very Good
Worth The Trip	Yes
Rating	★★★★

HOLE		1	2	3	4	5	6	7	8	9	OUT
BLUE	67.1/126	212	130	425	531	365	140	469	351	270	2893
WHITE	65.3/121	202	120	405	506	355	125	360	339	270	2682
MEN'S PAR		3	3	4	5	4	3	5/4	4	4	35/34
HANDICAP		4	7	1	3	5	9	2	8	6	
LADIES' PAR		4	3	4	5	4	3	4	4	4	35
HANDICAP		6	7	1	3	4	9	2	8	5	
RED		212	130	350	435	340	105	285	325	260	2442

Green Acres Country Club

Donnellson

319-835-5011

Green Acres Country Club is a private course with a fifteen mile green fee radius that is located on the extreme N.W. corner of Donnellson. The facility also has a pool that is open to the public and a new clubhouse. The course was built in 1973 and has a big brown clubhouse that has a meager amount of supplies and a small bar area that serves drinks and sandwiches. They do have carts for rent but this is an amazingly flat course for being this close to the river. There is one pond on the layout but the course is void of additional hazards. The trees are small on the course and large around the perimeter. The fairways are wide and flat with a two inch rough lining the edges. The medium size greens are basically flat with a few having a slight slope. Green Acres was built in 1972 and has 200 members. Yearly membership is $320 for a family with green fees are very reasonable for all day during the week and weekends. This is an easy course to walk and an easy course to score well on. The holes have a nice contrast in length and offer varying shots during the round. This is a nice small town Iowa course that offers a relaxed atmosphere, not rushed; a nice place to start for beginners.

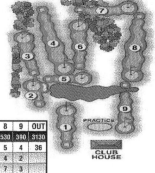

Course	9 Holes
Distance	3130 Yards
Par	36
Playability	V. Good
Aesthetics	Good
Interest	Fair
Worth The Trip	Yes
Rating	★★+

HOLE	1	2	3	4	5	6	7	8	9	OUT
MEN'S YARDAGE	340	140	340	500	160	420	310	530	390	3130
MEN'S PAR	4	3	4	5	3	4	4	5	4	36
HANDICAP 9 HOLE	7	9	5	8	3	1	6	4	2	
HANDICAP 18 HOLE	13	17	9	15	5	1	11	7	3	
WOMEN'S PAR	4	3	4	5	3	5	4	5	4	37
WOMEN'S YARDAGE	320	120	320	450	140	400	290	465	340	2845

Foxridge Golf Course
Dike
319-989-2213

A modern day small town golf course adventure is the Fox Ridge golf Course in Dike. The course is located on the east edge of Dike along highway 30. Many people watched as the front 9 was built and opened in 1998 and then the back nine came alive and was opened in early 2002. A farm field developed into a spacious course that is 6,809 yards long with a small town atmosphere yet big time golf. A season pass is $700 for the 220 members. Green fees are $15 during the week. They also have early bird specials. The bent grass greens are 5,000 square feet with undulating surfaces. There are 40 sand bunkers scattered throughout the course and innumerable grass bunkers and mounds making stances difficult if you land on one. The fairways are gently rolling, but one of the most unique features of the course are the grass mounds that frame many of the greens. Fortress greens would be more accurate. People in the clubhouse say the course is fun. The look of the course tells me it is great shape. Fox Ridge is also trying to develop a housing complex around the course. The clubhouse has several nice areas. You can get meals and all the equipment that you want. This is a very nice new course. It is one of the many courses around the state that have patterned their course after a links style course, using all the natural features available. I would highly recommend playing this course. Take charge of the course especially if the wind is blowing out of the north. A great new addition to small town golf.

Course	18 Holes	Aesthetics	Good
Distance	6809 Yards	Interest	Good
Par	36-36-72	Worth The Trip	Yes
Playability	Good	Rating	★★+

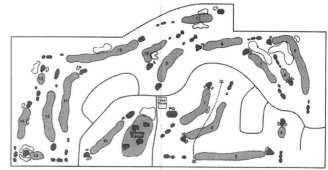

Hole	1	2	3	4	5	6	7	8	9	OUT	INT	10	11	12	13	14	15	16	17	18	IN	TOT	NET
Back	397	444	595	211	585	184	326	342	377	3461		342	548	440	226	315	185	622	348	322	3348	6809	
Middle	363	421	562	189	538	155	284	311	344	3167		324	520	409	195	288	155	588	317	294	3090	6257	
Men's Handicap	9	7	1	3	5	17	13	15	11			10	4	6	8	18	12	2	14	16			
Front	313	373	488	164	460	116	260	275	293	2742		285	456	359	156	249	123	480	269	248	2625	5367	
Ladies' Handicap	9	7	1	3	5	17	13	15	11			10	4	6	8	18	12	2	14	16			
Par	4	4	5	3	5	3	4	4	4	36		4	5	4	3	4	3	5	4	4	36	72	

Dows Golf Course

Dows

515-852-4751

The Dows Golf Course is located one half mile east of Dows on the site of an old farm, as are many of the courses in Iowa. The clubhouse is the farmhouse that was originally here and has been modeled in recent years and now has more seating and dining area. This short course has very reasonable green fees. The 200 members pay from $200 to $450 per year with a $100 initial stock. The greens are medium to small in size and most have a crested round shape. The fairways are wide and offer the hitter a chance to spray the ball around without getting into much trouble. This level course is easy to walk, although they do have carts for rent, easy to score, although the greens do present some problems, and easy to play on. One of the nice features of the Dows course is the small town atmosphere that you enjoy while playing the course. This course was built for that down-home relaxed feeling. It was built with volunteer town labor and the town and its members are proud of the course. If you are looking for a low pressure, relaxing, cheap time, then try this public course.

Course	9 Holes
Distance	2804 Yards
Par	35
Playability	Fair
Aesthetics	Good
Interest	Fair
Worth The Trip	Maybe
Rating	**

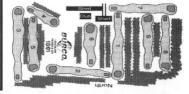

HOLE	1	2	3	4	5	6	7	8	9	OUT
WHITE TEES	470	160	454	133	384	308	183	348	364	2804
MEN'S HANDICAP	13	9	15	17	1	11	3	7	5	
MEN'S/LADIES' PAR	5	3	5	3	4	4	3	4	4	35
BLUE TEES	400	153	414	133	354	308	176	298	354	2590
LADIES' HANDICAP	15	13	11	7	1	9	17	5	3	

Dunlap Golf Club

Dunlap

712-643-5945

Dunlap is a local players course that has a little bit of everything. The creek that runs across the course has 5 bridges that make traversing the gulley an experience. They have just added on and remodeled their clubhouse, not many supplies but a nice sitting area. The gently-rolling layout is truly east-west with only one variation — number 7. The condition of the grass is average, and the number of trees are a little above average. Trees do line most of the fairways and have reached a height that impedes many shots. New trees are being planted every year. There are some new small evergreens planted. The fairways are sometimes narrow, but there is very little trouble to get into if you keep it in the middle of the course. Fairway watering was added in 1999. The greens are generally flat and an average size. Some interest is added with tilted and trapped greens. Tee boxes are big, landscaped and in good shape. Weekday green fees are very reasonable. Membership costs are $425 for a year. The Course is located on the south edge of town just off Highway 30.

Course	9 Holes
Distance	2814 Yards
Par	36
Playability	Good
Aesthetics	Good
Interest	Fair
Worth The Trip	Yes
Rating	**+

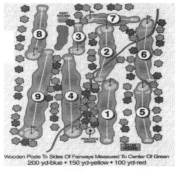

Wooden Posts To Sides Of Fairways Measured To Center Of Green
200 yd-blue • 150 yd-yellow • 100 yd-red

HOLE	1	2	3	4	5	6	7	8	9	Out
YARDAGE	304	342	174	481	230	392	107	294	490	2814
MEN'S HANDICAP	13	3	7	5	17	1	15	11	9	
PAR	4	4	3	5	4	4	3	4	5	36
LADIES' PAR	4	4	3	5	4	5	3	4	5	37
LADIES' HANDICAP	5	3	11	1	13	15	17	9	7	

Bunker Hill Golf Course
Dubuque
563-589-4261

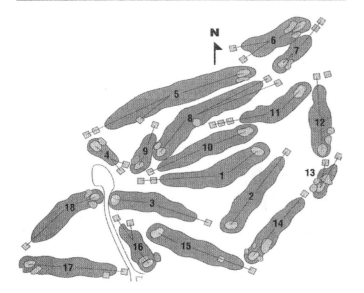

One of the busiest courses in the eastern part of the state is the Bunker Hill Golf Course in Dubuque, located on Bunker Hill Road. This is a public 18 hole course that is very busy much of the time. The 170 members pay $660 for a couple per year. Green fees are very reasonable. The clubhouse has a small snack bar and also serves drinks. The pro shop is quite small but does have a full line of equipment. Their main duty in the pro shop is to control tee off times and keep the crowd passing through. The course was built in 1911 but has been redone in recent years and all phases of the course are now just beginning to come into play. The trees line many of the fairways. Many of them small but some that are large and obstruct borderline shots. There is only one water hazard on the 5288 yard course, a pond on number 9. The fairways are narrow and guarded by some tough rough. The greens are of medium size and generally rolling. The general contour of the course is rolling and hilly. The staff in the clubhouse warned that this is a position course. But even if you think you are in the right spot for your approach, the pin placement can change each hole from day to day. This is a hard course to walk but the clubhouse and its enthusiastic staff have a fine line of carts for rent. This is a very busy course, which may be attributed to the low price to play. Or it may be that this is a challenging course that anyone and everyone can play and enjoy. The city should be commended for operating such a fine facility, probably one of the better municipal courses in the state. Before you do play this course call ahead and see where the pins have been placed that day. It could make a world of difference. This is a very nice course that is well maintained and a fun one to play.

Course	18 Holes	Aesthetics	Very Good
Distance	5316 Yards	Interest	Very Good
Par	35-34-69	Worth The Trip	Yes
Playability	Excell.	Rating	****

CHAMPIONSHIP	400	350	328	140	505	253	212	477	147	2851
REGULAR	385	311	316	135	535	226	162	459	147	2676
HANDICAP	5	3	7	17	1	11	9	13	15	
PAR	4	4	4	3	5	4	3	5	3	35
HOLE	1	2	3	4	5	6	7	8	9	Out
PAR	4	4	4	3	5	4	3	5	3	35
HANDICAP	5	3	7	17	1	11	9	13	15	
WOMENS	365	271	305	127	375	204	142	428	137	2345

	322	329	265	92/95	288	317	188	340	299	2665	2851	5516		
	323	288	216	92/95	272	320	180	308	289	2288	2676	4964		
	12	4	14	18	10	2	8	6	10					
	4	4	4	3	4	4	3	4	4	34	35	69		
10	11	12	13	14	15	16	17	18	In	Out	Tot	Hcp	Net
	4	4	4	3	4	4	3	4	4	34	35	69		
	12	4	14	18	16	2	8	6	10					
	312	355	181	82	251	244	149	224	275	1953	2345	4318		

Dubuque Golf and Country Club

Dubuque

563-583-9150

Dubuque Golf and Country Club pro is Fred Reider who had one of the top 100 pro shops in the United States in 1986. There of course is a full line of equipment and an exceptional line of clothes. The year-round restaurant, located above the pro shop, is open to members and their guests only, and it has some elegant eating. The 450 members also benefit from a pool and tennis courts, plus a fabulous golf course. The overall clubhouse has to rank as one of the top ten in the state and is truly an old time country club. The course layout has three ponds that affect play on four holes. There is also an average of two sand bunkers per hole. This course is very well stocked with trees, some of them new plantings, but most large and lining the fairways. The contour of the course is hilly, steep in some areas, and the fairways are guarded by tiered rough that extends out in front of the greens. Greens are medium in size and sloping, and have the added feature of very thick grass. The grass condition on the course is good, due mainly to the fairway watering system and the greens superintendent. The course appears to be very well maintained and enjoyed by the members. The course is very old, built around 1898, and was described as one of the ten old-time country clubs left in the state. Green fees are only accepted from guests of members or members of other private clubs. Dubuque is easy to walk, but hard to score well on. A challenging course due mainly to the hills, trees, and layout of the course. It is an accuracy course: be down the middle or suffer the consequences in a following shot. Dubuque Golf and Country Club is truly on of the best courses in the eastern half of the state. It is well maintained, offers a challenge, and carries on some of the old country club tradition that was so elegant many years ago. This is a majestic course that deserves all the praise and awards it can get.

Course	18 Holes	Aesthetics	Excell.
Distance	5852 Yards	Interest	Excell.
Par	35-35-70	Worth The Trip	Yes
Playability	Excell.	Rating	*****

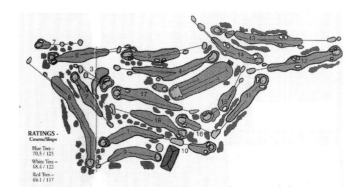

RATINGS -
Course/Slope

Blue Tees -
70.3 / 125

White Tees -
68.4 / 122

Red Tees -
68.1 / 117

HOLE NUMBER	1	2	3	4	5	6	7	8	9	OUT	10	11	12	13	14	15	16	17	18	IN	TOT	HCP	NET
BLUE TEES	344	269	156/168	442	356	368	190	543	293	2973	150	337	397	533	330	282	158	368	324	2879	5852		
WHITE TEES	331	262	140	377	349	328	182	535	281	2785	140	324	380	514	299	275	153	356	319	2760	5545		
HANDICAP	5	15	13	7	11	9	3	1	17		16	14	4	2	6	8	18	10	12				
PAR	4	4	3	4	4	4	3	5	4	35	3	4	4	5	4	4	3	4	4	35	70		
HANDICAP	3	15	13	5	11	1	17	9	7		18	6	2	8	4	10	16	12	14				
RED TEES	326	254	102	285	254	324	97	435	274	2351	130	313	310	441	289	243	147	332	315	2520	4871		

The Meadows
Dubuque
563-583-7385
www.meadowsgolf.com

Just seven miles west of the Mississippi is The Meadows located at 15766 Clover Lane, which is off NW Arterial. This is a new 1997 championship course that highlights the topography of the area . When the course was developed they used the existing trees and lay of the land. The rolling fairways offers a broad appeal for all devoted fans of the game of golf. The bentgrass fairways and superb greens makes this a must golfing destination. There are a number of sand bunkers on the course with number 5 having 7 bunkers stretched up and down the narrow fairway. The unique feature of the course are the numerable grass bunkers spread throughout the course. They offer a picturesque golf setting but also create some devastating lies. The evening shadows casting over these mounds make a beautiful sight. The layout of the course does resemble a links course with holes 1 through 9 going out and back. The entire course is landscaped to within an inch of its life. This is a public course that has approximately 200 members, with an $1,100 annual fee. Green fees are $23 on a weekday. The expansive two story clubhouse has a full line of equipment and a very nice bar area with sandwiches. The course is in great shape mainly to the fact that the owners are also in the irrigation business. The bottom line is that The Meadows is a great course. A course that offers a challenge and beauty. A course that uses the existing countryside to create a great course. I would highly recommend this course to anyone.

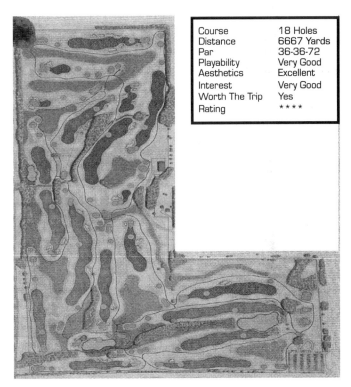

Course	18 Holes
Distance	6667 Yards
Par	36-36-72
Playability	Very Good
Aesthetics	Excellent
Interest	Very Good
Worth The Trip	Yes
Rating	★★★★

HOLE	1	2	3	4	5	6	7	8	9	OUT	10	11	12	13	14	15	16	17	18	IN	TOT	HCP	NET
BACK	392	349	559	224	327	446	181	392	503	3373	377	173	514	388	205	525	388	309	415	3294	6667		
MIDDLE	376	332	530	204/166	304	418	156	374	486	3180/3142	363	139/139	498	335	150/160	509	351	294	398	3037/3066	6217/5208		
FORWARD	276	268	468	132	262	352	132	336	429	2654	321	106	420	247	100	465	273	262	301	2545	5199		
HANDICAP	7	15	3	11	13	1	17	9	5		12	18	6	8	16	4	10	14	2				
PAR	4	4	5	3	4	4	3	4	5	36	4	3	5	4	3	5	4	4	4	36	72		

Dyersville Golf and Country Club

Dyersville

563-875-8497

The Dyersville Golf and Country Club is a private club with a 10 mile green fee playing radius that is located two miles north of Dyersville. You have to play with a member on the weekends. The clubhouse is quite interesting inside with a big dining room and nice bar that opens up to number one tee. A few carts can be rented and supplies include balls, gloves, and clothes can be bought. Out on the course there are no water hazards, two sand bunkers, and a two inch rough that is easy to recover from and is generally cut along the tree line. The trees on the course are large in many instances while new plantings are starting to fill in some of the gaps along the fairways. Fairways are wide and tree lined, there is also a watering system on the fairways that keeps them green late in the summer. The contour of the course is semi-hilly. Greens are medium in size and generally flat with two putting surfaces sloping. The greens are in good shape and are considered fast by the members. The course was built in 1928. This is an easy course to walk and score well on. Families are becoming more and more involved with the course. Dyersville Country Club can be considered a pleasure course with a country club atmosphere.

Course	9 Holes
Distance	2687 Yards
Par	35
Playability	Good
Aesthetics	Very Good
Interest	Good
Worth The Trip	Yes
Rating	**+

HOLE	1	2	3	4	5	6	7	8	9	OUT
MENS YARDS	146	318	155	361	493	271	339	311	293	2687
LADIES YARDS	135	318	96	354	493	255	327	300	278	2556
PAR	3	4	3	4	5	4	4	4	4	35

Rolling Knolls

Dyersville

563-875-7466

Rolling Knolls is a public golf course operated by Dick and Matt Mescher. It is located on Highway 420, or old Highway 30, 1 mile East on 2nd Ave. There is one pond on the course coming into play twice, four bunkers and a controlled rough. The trees are medium in size and are scattered throughout the course; except on number eight which is lined. There are new plantings of trees made each year to supplement the low number of trees now in existence. The contour of the wide fairways is flat with a few gentle rolls near the water. Tees are elevated and large in some cases. The greens are small with sloping putting surfaces. The greens also have a history of being slow and hard to hold; size must have an effect. Rolling Knolls was built in 1969 and is considered a family and couples pleasure course. It is an easy course to walk but relinquishes few good scores during the year. This is a wide-open 2522 yard course that the 200 members enjoy. Green fees are very reasonable. A yearly membership runs $390 for a family. The clubhouse has a full line of supplies but in small quantities. The bar area serves snacks and microwave sandwiches. This is a pleasant course that is relaxed and a little laid back. Rolling Knoll's course is a family backed course that has emphasized the play of family and friends.

Course	9 Holes
Distance	2555 Yards
Par	34
Playability	Good
Aesthetics	Good
Interest	Fair
Worth The Trip	Yes
Rating	**+

HOLE	1	2	3	4	5	6	7	8	9	TOT	HCP	NET
MEN'S YARDAGE	280	208	265	354	160	333	530	242	183	2555		
WOMEN'S YARDAGE	280	175	265	354	160	333	362	242	183	2354		
PAR	4	3	4	4	3	4	5	4	3	34		
HANDICAP	7	6	9	2	5	3	1	8	4			

Dysart Golf Club

Dysart

319-476-3274

One of the hilliest courses found anywhere in Iowa is the Dysart Recreation Golf Club three miles north of Dysart. Besides the severe hills on the course some of the other characteristics include a pond that comes into play on two holes, a few sand bunkers scattered about, and oak-lined fairways on six holes. These trees are mature and many in number plus they obscure the view of the green from the tee on three holes. The contour of the course is very hilly; add the rough and the trees and you have some fairways that are extremely challenging. One positive note: at the end of a hole are large greens. The surfaces are flat with some rolling features. This is a very busy course that has 170 families playing. The course also has very reasonable green fees. The clubhouse has a nice supply of supplies plus pizza and sandwiches in the bar area. The clubhouse was remodeled in 2000. This is a tough course to walk but a beautiful course to play. This course, which was carved out of the woods in 1968, has developed into a unique, entertaining, and scenic golf course. It might be wise to practice a little on your up and downhill lies before you encounter Dysart, formally the Milne Memorial.

Course	9 Holes
Distance	2803 Yards
Par	35
Playability	V. Good
Aesthetics	Excell.
Interest	Excell.
Worth The Trip	Yes
Rating	★★★★

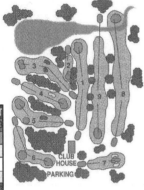

HOLE	1	2	3	4	5	6	7	8	9	OUT
MEN'S TEES	370	123	341	267	300	337	172	438	455	2803
HANDICAP	4	6	5	7	3	1	8	2	9	
MEN'S PAR	4	3	4	4	4	4	3	4	5	35
LADIES' PAR	4	3	4	4	4	4	3	5	5	36
LADIES' TEES	357	111	327	257	283	328	131	366	443	2603

Eagle Grove Country Club

Eagle Grove

515-448-4166

Hundreds of big trees dominate the Eagle Grove Country Club. Located two miles west of town, this course has a gentle rolling contour with a river running along the west edge. Most of the big trees are along the highway and the river. The rest of the course has small, scattered trees that present no problem, but when driving by on the highway it looks like a very rough and tree laden course. The raised greens are small, flat, and all are rolling with a slight tilt. Tee boxes are of medium size and slightly elevated. The three bunkers are the only hazards on the course, there are no ponds or streams and very little rough. The present course was rebuilt in 1982. Green fees are reasonable for the weekends and with only 225 members there is quite a bit of open playing time. The clubhouse is very nice on the inside and a limited amount of golfing supplies can be bought along with the rental of carts. Eagle Grove Country Club is no longer a private club. Any golfer can pay green fees and play. Ladies day is Wednesday till 3:00 and men's day is Thursday. The totally irrigated course is very wooded, hilly and plays like a nice small town course. The course seems to have the atmosphere of business golf: no time for frills, just basic golf.

Course	9 Holes
Distance	2959 Yards
Par	35
Playability	Good
Aesthetics	Very Good
Interest	Good
Worth The Trip	Yes
Rating	★★★

	1	2	3	4	5	6	7	8	9	OUT
BLUE			208	342	381	364			378	2959
WHITE	487	315	344	195	333	368	353	140	361	2896
RED										
MEN'S/WOMEN'S PAR	5	4	4	3	4	4	4	3	4	35
MEN'S/WOMEN'S HANDICAP	5	9	7			1	3	8		
HOLE	1	2	3	4	5	6	7	8	9	OUT

Woods Edge

Edgewood

319-928-6668

Woods Edge is a new course built on the west edge of Edgewood on Highway 3. But despite its young age it was named the Iowa 9 Hole Course of the Year in 2000. The course was designed by William Spear and brings some championship features to a small town course. The general layout of the course is fairly flat. Tee boxes are small but have good grass and are tiered to three levels. Greens are medium to large with sloping and undulating surfaces. Woods Edge has 23 sand traps, guarding many greens and landing areas, and are huge. There are 3 ponds that affect 5 holes and a stream that connects them adding additional stress to your driving game. When the town wanted a drawing card to bring new residents in town they found a gem in the rough, so to speak. They have a well designed and intriguing course that is long, 3286 yards, but fun to play and walk. A course that is challenging thanks to the greens and sand but gives players a break with open fairways and good grass condition, thanks partially to the fairway watering. There is also a housing development that is being established around the course. Many of the trees that were here initially were left with many others planted on the course and near the housing area. Membership is up to 140 with $500 annual dues. The clubhouse has all the necessities with daily fees of $15.00 for 18 holes. This is really a nice addition to N.E. Iowa.

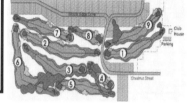

Course	9 Holes
Distance	3286 Yards
Par	36
Playability	Good
Aesthetics	Good
Interest	Good
Worth The Trip	Yes
Rating	★★★

HOLE	RATING/SLOPE	1	2	3	4	5	6	7	8	9	OUT
BLUE	71.6/121	400	504	416	160	364	498	364	193	387	3286
WHITE	70.5/120	385	489	400	151	350	483	364	175	376	3173
RED	71.9/114	372	421	382	121	336	468	345	158	354	2957
PAR		4	5	4	3	4	5	4	3	4	36
HANDICAP		7	17	3	15	5	11	13	9	1	

Pine Lake Country Club

Eldora

641-858-3031

For one of the most scenic 9 or 18 holes course in Iowa you should travel to Pine Lake Country Club in Eldora. The course was built in 1927 and designed by Leo F. Wolcott. The course is surrounded by Pine Lake State Park. The course is cut out of thick woods, which makes for narrow fairways and lots of challenges from trees and hills. There is a mixture of green size and running contour. Many would be considered small but easy to hold most of the summer. Fairway watering makes the entire course park like the entire summer. The general contour of the course is gently rolling making it an easy course to walk and enjoy. Pine Lake is blessed with the natural beauty of the area. The spacious clubhouse carries a full line of equipment, plus a dining room and bar area that serves sandwiches. The course also has another natural resource: Ivan Miller. Ivan has won over 130 tournaments, including the Iowa Masters, and was voted Player of the Year in 1980 and 1982. Pine Lake has also been recognized by the National Golfing Foundation as being one of the six best golf courses in Iowa. Annually it is mentioned by a variety of polls as being one of the most beautiful in Iowa. Number 9 is listed as one of the Hall of Fame holes. Not only does the course offer beauty but the surrounding park has many activities. Is this heaven? No, it's Pine Lake Country Club.

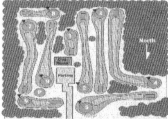

Course	9 Holes
Distance	2696 Yards
Par	35
Playability	V. Good
Aesthetics	Excell.
Interest	Excell.
Worth The Trip	Yes
Rating	★★★★★

10	11	12	13	14	15	16	17	18	In	Tot	Hcp	Net
151	340	360	438	306	162	427	115	397	2696	5392		
4	16	8	10	12	18	6	14	2				
3	4	4	5	4	3	5	3	4	35	70		

Rustic Ridge Golf Course

Eldridge

563-285-8119

Rustic Ridge Golf Course is a public nine hole course located on East Iowa Street, along the Interstate, in Eldridge. The course was built in 1973 and is a wide open course with a gently rolling to flat contour. There are two ponds on the course surrounding number seven, a stream that comes into play on two holes, and an average of one bunker per hole. All trees are new plantings except for the medium size ones in the gullies by the ponds and streams. There is a two inch rough cut along the wide fairways and sometimes becomes thick, deep and a lot of trouble. One of the unseen hazards of the course is the expectations of players. People come on to this course thinking that they can spray the ball all over the layout without getting into much trouble. Rustic Ridge does have its hazards and challenges and people tone down their swing the next time out. Most of the tees are elevated, big, and well taken care of. The greens are medium in size and have an undulating putting surface. The greens receive the most compliments and complaints. They are challenging to putt; very quick, true putting, slippery, and ruin many good scores. But the greens are still some of the best around. Rustic Ridge has 195 members who pay an annual fee of $827. Daily green fees for the public are reasonable. The course runs right along the interstate and can be the recipient of some interesting horn tooting.

Course	9 Holes
Distance	3230 Yards
Par	36
Playability	Fair
Aesthetics	Fair
Interest	Fair
Worth The Trip	Maybe
Rating	** +

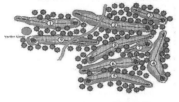

HOLE 34.7/113	1	2	3	4	5	6	7	8	9	OUT
BLUE	360	525	180	310	480	385	170	385	435	3230
WHITE	350	510	165	300	465	370	160	370	430	3120
MEN'S HDCP	5	2	7	9	8	3	6	4	1	
MEN'S PAR	4	5	3	4	5	4	3	4	4	36
RED	330	500	150	285	450	360	145	360	350	2930
LADIES' HDCP	3	1	5	6	2	7	4	8	9	
LADIES' PAR	4	5	3	4	5	5	3	5	5	39

Elkader Golf and Country Club

Elkader

563-245-2230

The Elkader Golf and Country Club is a semi-private course located one mile north of Elkader. Greens fees are average in price. The 230 members utilize a big red remodeled barn for a clubhouse. Inside there is a limited assortment of golfing supplies and a bar area that has drinks and sandwiches. The layout of the course has one pond affecting two holes. There are new sand bunkers and a one inch rough barely visible along the narrow fairways. The contour of the course is flat with a medium number of trees scattered throughout the course. Tees are flat and medium in size. Greens are large and sloping. The greens have a reputation of being tough to read and fast to putt. The course was built in 1966. Elkader is an easy course to walk but not so easy to score well on the first time around. The number and position of trees makes this course a little tighter than other courses near its size and layout. The condition and contour of the greens make the serious golfer concentrate on position and speed on all nine holes.

Course	9 Holes
Distance	2746 Yards
Par	35
Playability	V. Good
Aesthetics	V. Good
Interest	Good
Worth The Trip	Yes
Rating	***

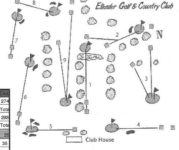

Elkader Golf & Country Club

Club House

HOLES	1	2	3	4	5	6	7	8	9	Out
Men's Front	297	338	160	445	155	362	307	170	485	2742
Handicap	11	7	15	3	17	5	9	13	1	Total
Men's Back	297	338	223	515	155	362	307	170	530	2897
Handicap	13	9	1	5	17	7	11	15	3	Total
Men's Par	4	4	3	5	3	4	4	3	5	35
Ladies' Par	4	4	3	5	3	4	4	3	5	35
Yardage	277	228	138	445	155	322	282	170	401	2323
Handicap	5	17	13	1	9	3	7	11	15	

Sun Valley Golf and Country Club

Ellston

641-772-4380

One of the newer courses in south central Iowa is the Sun Valley Golf and Country Club two miles east of Ellston. The course was built in 1982 and has nine holes playable with nine more being readied. The clubhouse is built on the north edge of the course on a lake and has a nice interior but nothing to offer: few snacks, a pop machine, and a few carts. This public course has 85 members who pay $250 per year. Green fees are reasonable. Sun Valley does have a unique watering system for its greens. Perwick self-watering supplies water to the greens from underneath and above, making a more complete saturation of the green. There is one outstanding characteristic of this course and that is the scarcity of trees. There are a few by the lake but the majority of the course just has small bushes. This tends to leave this course wide open, a course that is flat, wide and encourages gorilla swings. There are three ponds on the course, no sand and very little rough. Greens are medium and flat, and are in good shape. A drawback of this course is its location, away from people. It also has the disadvantages of being young and in need of a little maturity. I'd like to come back to this course in five years and see the changes. If you like straight away golf, Sun Valley might be for you now.

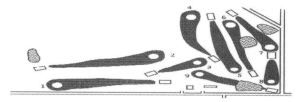

Course	9 Holes
Distance	2947 Yards
Par	35
Playability	Poor
Aesthetics	Fair
Interest	Poor
Worth The Trip	No
Rating	*+

SCORES

Men's Front Nine			Self Part.	Side Matches We They	Opp. Opp.	Women's Front Red Tees	
Yards	Men's Par	Hdcp. Stroke		HOLE		Women's Par	Yards
391	4			①		4	326
364	4			②		4	279
204	3			③		3	148
305	4			④		4	227
396	4			⑤		5	380
478	5			⑥		5	412
297	4			⑦		4	230
170	3			⑧		3	111
342	4			⑨		4	226
2947	35			OUT		36	2339

Maple Heights Golf and Country Club

Elma

641-393-2120

One of the new courses in the state of Iowa is the Maple Heights Golf & Country Club in Elma. This course was opened in July 1990, after being a cornfield since the beginning of time, and has matured into a very respectable course in just a short time. The 123 members pay a yearly fee of $250 and are looking forward to a new clubhouse to replace the farmhouse that serves them now. Maple Heights has three bodies of water that players go around, over, and through on three holes. There is an average of one sand bunker per hole and ground bunkers scattered throughout this gently rolling, almost like farmland, course. Trees on the course are medium around the water, big around the clubhouse, and newly planted ones line the fairways, although not many yet. The fairway grass has improved a great deal since opening day and has produced some very nice manicured fairways. Tee boxes are medium in size and elevated. Greens offer a little bit of everything. But most of all the greens are in good shape and challenging. This is a fun course that is a fine example of what is happening in Iowa. Maple Heights is located on the east side of town, at 1st & Wood, and runs right up to cornfields on two sides, so there is room for expansion. But for now this is a fun course that provides a great place to play.

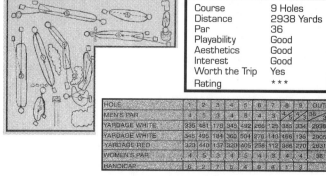

Course	9 Holes
Distance	2938 Yards
Par	36
Playability	Good
Aesthetics	Good
Interest	Good
Worth the Trip	Yes
Rating	***

HOLE	1	2	3	4	5	6	7	8	9	OUT
MEN'S PAR	4	5	3	4	5	4	3	4/5	4	36
YARDAGE WHITE	335	481	175	345	492	266	125	385	334	2938
YARDAGE WHITE	345	495	184	360	504	276	140	466	135	2905
YARDAGE RED	320	440	137	320	405	258	112	366	270	2631
WOMEN'S PAR	4	5	3	4	5	4	3	4	4	36
HANDICAP	6	2	7	5	4	8	9	1	3	

Emmetsburg Country Club

Emmetsburg

712-852-3422

The Emmetsburg Country Club is a course steeped with tradition and nestled in a very scenic corner of Emmetsburg. The 2695 yard course is located on the north edge of town on the west bank of the lake; on county road 40. The clubhouse is a massive structure overlooking the lake and containing a bar and dining area that is very traditional. The full restaurant is open to the public and serves some of the finest food in town. The course has 200 members paying a yearly fee of $435. Green fees are average in price. The lake that runs along the east side of the course can come into play on holes 6, 7, & 8; it is very nice addition to the aesthetics of the course. There are four sand bunkers on the course and rough cut along the tree line. The trees on the course are of medium size and more plentiful on the holes nearer the lake. Fairways are narrow in most cases and tree lined. The contour of the course is flat with very few swales. Tees and fairway grass are in good shape. A new irrigation system was installed in 2001. Tees are elevated and medium in size, greens are small to medium with sloping putting surfaces. The Emmetsburg course is an easy course to walk but the most pleasant features of the course are its' clubhouse and the beautiful area that it is situated in. Courses located near or along lakes always have a certain beauty and appeal. Emmetsburg has that feeling of light-hearted golf and relaxed surroundings.

Course	9 Holes
Distance	2695 Yards
Par	35
Playability	Good
Aesthetics	Excell.
Interest	Good
Worth The Trip	Yes
Rating	★★★

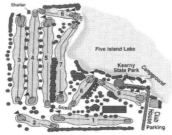

HOLES	1	2	3	4	5	6	7	8	9	OUT
Yardage - Men	340	148	363	415	405	140	428	154	302	2695
Yardage - Women	303	148	360	415	395	140	385	148	270	2555
Handicap	5	17	3	11	1	15	7	13	9	
Men's Par	4	3	4	5	4	3	5	3	4	35
Women's Par	4	3	4	5	5	3	5	3	4	36

Essex Golf & Recreation

Essex

712-379-3805

Essex Golf & Recreation is a public course located West on 150th St. in Essex, turn at the elevators. Now if that isn't a typical Iowa direction, turn at the elevators, then I don't know what is. This course was re-established in 1979. It had previously been an 18 hole course in another life but is now a 9 hole course with lots of rolling hills. According to the owners and the players it is also a great bird watching sanctuary. The greens are medium to large and are bentgrass. There is no fairway watering so some of the hills looked a little burned and thin. In 2000 they planted 1,000 new trees, many of them lining the fairways. The only other hazards are natural. They course has lots of natural grasses and scrub areas. This is a very hilly course, my cart had a hard time getting back up to the clubhouse. As you might guess there are very few flat lies. The clubhouse has snacks and friendly people. The membership of 75 pays $418 a year. Weekday green fees are $12 or $18 for all day.

Course	9 Holes
Distance	2892 Yards
Par	35
Playability	Good
Aesthetics	Fair
Interest	Fair
Worth The Trip	Yes
Rating	★★

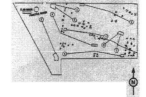

HOLES	1	2	3	4	5	6	7	8	9	
RED TEES	291	405	135	358	403	258	366	170	506	2892
BLUE TEES	276	395	128	343	388	243	356	162	491	2782
WHITE TEES	276	285	128	227	288	243	260	162	381	2250

Heartland Hills

Estherville

712-362-4755

Heartland Hills is a public course located on the north side of Ft. Defiance State Park west of town. . Weekends you must be a guest of a member and you can play all day for $10.00. The 250 members pay an annual fee of $735. A new restaurant called Deer Run has become a big hit in the area. The dining area has two different atmospheres, classic fine dining and a Bistro. Plus there is a pub style restaurant called the Watering Hole. A few balls and gloves can also be found in the clubhouse. The contour of the course is very hilly and hard to walk so you might want one of the carts that can be rented. There is one pond and one stream on the course affecting two holes. Sand can be found on each hole and the two inch rough is located along the fairways and is hard to get out of in certain places. Trees in this beautiful park are medium to large and line many of the wide fairways. The great number of trees do affect play, the sound of wood can be heard quite often from around the course. Greens are tiny and flat making them one of the most challenging aspects in the layout. The greens are also fast with a little tilt in places. The course was built in 1938. This is definitely a cart course. It is best known for its beauty, its tough greens, and it's trees. A beautiful 3255 yard course that is challenging and your answer to a good exercise program.

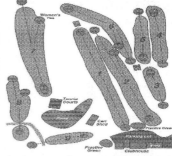

Course	9 Holes
Distance	3255 Yards
Par	36
Playability	Good
Aesthetics	Excell.
Interest	Excell.
Worth The Trip	Yes
Rating	★★★

HOLE	1	2	3	4	5	6	7	8	9	OUT
BLUE	475	450	160	373	334	428	568	327	140	3,255
WHITE	465	425	150	347	304	405	548	321	120	3,085
WHITE/BLUE PAR	5	4	3	4	4	4	5	4	3	36
HANDICAP	7	1	6	5	8	2	3	4	9	

River View Golf Course

Estherville

712-362-3911

River View Golf Course is a public course located 3 miles south and one mile east of Estherville. The characteristics of the course include one pond and one stream that affect a total of five holes. There are four bunkers on the course and a two inch rough cut under the fairway trees. There are an average number of trees that are small to medium in size. Many of the trees are lined up along the wide fairways. The contour of the course is flat with very little variance. The grass condition throughout the course is good, including the greens and tees. Tees are nothing special and the greens are small to medium in size, generally flat with a little slope apparent in some. The course was built in 1966 and has a total of 110 members. Green fees on this par 36 course are average in price. The members pay a yearly membership fee of $300. The clubhouse is a little run down with balls and gloves to buy and carts to rent. Inside the one room structure is a big bar and sitting area This is an easy course to walk and play, it is not very busy. The water hazards do come into play but the course would generally be considered wide open and an easy layout to play. The area in which the course is situated is very scenic and tranquil and this feeling carries over onto the course. This course has a nice, friendly atmosphere.

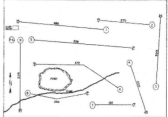

Course	9 Holes
Distance	2961 Yards
Par	36
Playability	Fair
Aesthetics	Fair
Interest	Poor
Worth The Trip	Maybe
Rating	★★

Par	5	4	4	3	5	5	3	4	3	36	5	4	4	3	5	5	3	4	3	36	72	Handicap	Net Score
Distance Yards	466	270	309	220	536	472	193	290	205	2961	466	270	309	220	536	472	193	290	205	2961	5922		
Holes	1	2	3	4	5	6	7	8	9	Out	10	11	12	13	14	15	16	17	18	In	Total		

Greenbrier Golf Course

Exira

712-268-2209

Greenbrier Golf Course which is located on Highway 71 three miles north of Exira. There are very few hazards on the course, it is wide open and forgiving. The trees are medium size poplars, some line the fairways but many are just scattered. The fairways are wide and have a few bare spots on them. The contour of the course is flat on most holes with a few hills to the N.W. The greens are medium in size with a few bare spots around the edges. The contour of the greens is flat with a gentle slope to a few. This is an open course that is fairly easy to walk and easy to score well on. The shape of the course was quite poor. But they are starting to make some progress with the conditions of the course. The course was built in 1962 and has limited use, mainly locals who want a relaxing game in the morning or late afternoon. Players are drawn from every direction play this course. The green fees are reasonable for all day play. The 150 members pay a family fee of $376. The clubhouse has microwave sandwiches and a bar; they do have carts for rent. There is a fully stocked pro-shop with a driving range to practice at. Greenbrier is under new ownership, a young, enthusiastic couple, that has already done some nice things.

Course	9 Holes
Distance	3090 Yards
Par	36
Playability	Good
Aesthetics	Good
Interest	Good
Worth The Trip	Maybe
Rating	★★+

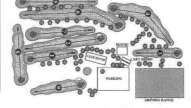

HOLE	1	2	3	4	5	6	7	8	9	OUT
MEN'S	320	475	160	350	405	510	350	190	330	3090
LADIES'	300	455	160	300	355	460	310	140	300	2780
PAR	4	5	3	4	4	5	4	3	4	36

Fairfield Golf and Country Club

Fairfield

641-472-4212

The Fairfield Golf and Country Club is located South on Highland Street in Fairfield. This par 35 course has 350 members that enjoy a very nice restaurant that is open the year round to members and guests. The pro shop is in a separate building and handles balls, gloves, clothes, and carts. The landscaping is the outstanding feature on this course. The tees are elevated and lined with fences and shrubs. The trees line six fairways and are old and very full. There is one stream on the course that comes into play on four holes. The fourteen bunkers also make play a little difficult. The contour of the course is quite hilly with many people hoping to find one of the few level lies on the course. Greens are medium to small in size with most tilted. The greens are also noted for being easy to hold but very difficult to putt, due in part to the many breaks on the putting surface. This course is one of the oldest in the area, being built in 1892, thus claiming to be one of the oldest west of the Mississippi. The maintenance people have done a fine job displaying the beauty of this course. It does rank as one of the most scenic in eastern Iowa. The course is easy to walk but not so easy to play. You must keep your tee shots straight or suffer the wrath of the trees. Fairfield is a challenging course that offers rewards both in execution and viewing.

Course	9 Holes
Distance	2791 Yards
Par	35
Playability	V. Good
Aesthetics	Excell.
Interest	V. Good
Worth The Trip	Yes
Rating	★★★★

Yardage	267	500	366	130	358	200	225	325	420	2791
PAR	4	5	4	3	4	3	4	4	4	35
Men's Hdcp	15	5	7	17	3	11	1	13	9	OUT
Ladies'/Hdcp	11	1	7	17	3	15	13	9	5	OUT
Ladies'/PAR	4	5	4	3	4	4	4	4	5	37
Holes	1	2	3	4	5	6	7	8	9	OUT

Walton Golf Club

Fairfield

641-472-4909

One of the more unusual courses in S.E. Iowa is the Walton Golf Course in Fairfield, North on D Street. The layout of the course is built entirely around a lake and has utilized the water as an integral part of the course. Green fees for guests are very reasonable. The clubhouse has a nice bar area and a full restaurant that is open to members during the summer and winter. The characteristics of the course include one sand bunker and four water crossings plus lots of lateral water hazards. The trees on the course are medium in size and scattered throughout the course along with some new plantings. This is a close course because of the water. Most fairways border the water and do not allow for any spraying of the ball. The greens are small and tilted, making approach shots very difficult. The general contour of the course is gently rolling, with many of the holes slanting down to the lake. The course was built in 1929. This is a fairly busy course that is easy to walk, easy to score well on, and an interesting sight to see. Many courses have a pond or lake as an optional feature, but Walton has a golf course that is an optional feature of the lake.

Course	9 Holes
Distance	2610 Yards
Par	34
Playability	Good
Aesthetics	Excell.
Interest	Excell.
Worth The Trip	Yes
Rating	★★★+

HOLES	1	2	3	4	5	6	7	8	9	Ttls	10	11	12	13	14	15	16	17	18	Ttls	Ttls
YARDS	455	180	458	190	449	185	340	170	183	2610	455	180	458	190	449	185	340	170	262	2689	5299
PAR	5	3	5	3	5	3	4	3	3	34	5	3	5	3	5	3	4	3	4	35	69
HANDICAP	8	6	7	2	9	3	4	5	1		4	6	7	2	9	3					
LADIES' PAR	5	3	5	3	5	3	4	3	4		5	3	5	3	4	3	4	3	4	35	70
YARDS	390	123	458	190	381	112	340	122	175	2291	390	123	458	190	381	112	340	122	175	2291	4582
LADIES' HANDICAP	4	7	1	3	5	9	2	8	6		4	7	1	3	5	9	2	8	6		

Fonda Country Club

Fonda

712-288-6419

There are many golf courses throughout Iowa that have an atmosphere that emphasizes family pleasure and play. The Fonda Country Club is this type of course. This is a public course located on the west edge of Fonda that has a very relaxed feeling and is not real busy. The course is not in business to pressure people to play a certain brand of golf. The 200 members pay an annual fee of $161; and to encourage participation, charge an additional $119 if you fail to work at some of the Sunday brunches — a good way to get people out and involved. Green fees are very reasonable. The clubhouse has snacks, beverages and supplies on the lower level with tables above for special occasions. The only hazards on this course are the two creeks that come into play on 5 of the 9 holes and the two inch rough that lines many of the fairways. The trees are mainly new plantings with a few medium size ones by the water. There are larger trees that enclose the course and catch many balls going out of bounds. For this part of Iowa the course is a little rolling; many of the courses in this area are flatter than flat. The course was built in 1965 and is generally well kept although there were a few dry spots located out in the fairways. The Fonda course is one that lets you enjoy the game at a leisurely pace, face few obstacles, and not be crowded or hurried at any time. A true small town Iowa course, a true Iowa treasure.

Course	9 Holes
Distance	2826 Yards
Par	35
Playability	Good
Aesthetics	Good
Interest	Fair
Worth The Trip	Yes
Rating	★★+

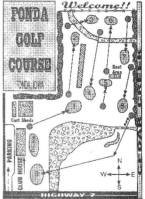

	HOLE	1	2	3	4	5	6	7	8	9		GROUP		
ROUND 1	Mens Yds	233	479	126	496	167	370	220	334	401	2826		HANDICAP	NET SCORE
	Ladies Yds	233	432	126	408	167	321	166	334	330	2517			
	Par	4	5	3	5	3	4	3	4	4	35			
	Hdcp	9	7	6	5	4	3	1	8	2	Score			

102

Big Rock Golf and Country Club

Fayette

563-425-3687

Big Rock Golf and Country Club is a semi-private course that will accept green fees. Big Rock was built in 1965 out of the natural surroundings and still maintains that back-to-nature feeling today. The course was made into an 18 hole course in 2002. The course is surrounded by a river and has many natural wooded areas in the layout. From the top of the back 9 you can see Fayette. There is no water on the course, but there are 18 sand bunkers. Rough is now being cut along the fairways. Trees are large in size and provide a nice outline for many of the holes. Four of the holes on the front 9 are tree lined while the remaining five are open and flat. The back nine was cut out of some rolling hills and have only planted trees. The back nine has been left as natural as possible, tall grassy areas and bushes dominate the rough. The tees are level to the ground and small. Greens are generally flat and in fair shape. Additional landscaping has been added over the past few years around the tee boxes. The clubhouse is a large brown structure located one mile west of Fayette on Big Rock Road. Inside there are balls and gloves for sale, carts for rent, and a bar area that serves drinks and microwave sandwiches. The 160 members pay an initial $100 stock and a yearly family fee of $750. Big Rock is a low pressure, relaxing course. The new 9 holes has added a new dimension and spread out the pressure of heavy play. It is an interesting layout with holes running upp the sides of hills and doubling back to the natural valleys below. The area is relaxing to be in but the conditions tend to be back to nature. It is an easy course to walk and a fairly challenging place to play; due mainly to the trees and their placement. It is a course that provides a place to gather and recreate. Big Rock would also have to be considered a very nature oriented course, which is something very positive.

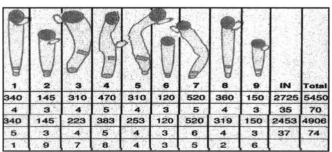

1	2	3	4	5	6	7	8	9	IN	Total
340	145	310	470	310	120	520	360	150	2725	5450
4	3	4	5	4	3	5	4	3	35	70
340	145	223	383	253	120	520	319	150	2453	4906
5	3	4	5	4	3	6	4	3	37	74
1	9	7	8	4	3	5	2	6		

Big Rock Country Club Fayette 425-3687									Yellow Bush 100 yd / Red Bush 150 yd / Key Ladies Tee / Sand Traps
HOLE	1	2	3	4	5	6	7	8	9	OUT
MEN	340	145	310	470	310	120	520	360	150	2725
MENS PAR	4	3	4	5	4	3	5	4	3	35
LADIES	340	145	223	383	253	120	520	319	150	2453
LADIES PAR	5	3	4	5	4	3	6	4	3	37
HANDICAP	1	9	7	8	4	3	5	2	6	

Course	18 Holes	Aesthetics	Good
Distance	5450 Yards	Interest	Good
Par	35-35-70	Worth The Trip	Yes
Playability	Good	Rating	** +

103

Bear Creek Golf Course

Forest City

641-582-3250

The Bear Creek Golf Course located in Forest City, is the type of course that looks easy as you tee off number one on the front 9 but becomes exceedingly difficult as you line up the fourth putt on the first green. The course expanded in 2003 and now measures 6575 yards. The font 9 is 2851 and the new back nine is 3724, long you say. Well the new back nine winds along and over a river that comes into play 6 times. The back nine stretches to the east all the way to the airport, among a new housing development. The front and back differ in other ways also. The front has small, crowned greens; the back are more expansive and sloping. The front has tree lined fairways and only one pond; the back has water almost on every hole and is more rolling and open. The back nine has 3 par 5's, 600 yards, 520 yards, and 589 yards, Those three holes come close to the total yardage on some smaller 9 hole courses. The course is still a drive for show, putt for dough type of atmosphere. The rolling backside offers different challenges and has had great reviews from playing members and guests. The number of sand traps has greatly increased with now approximately 2 per hole. The back nine is more of a links style course with grass bunkers in landing areas, unforgiving rough if you get off the fairway too far, and landing areas that play an important part of your scoring. The entire layout is watered, creating super conditions late into the summer. But the river has been know to flood and create other hazards, in fact the flooded river delayed the opening of the course. The original course was built in 1948. The clubhouse has a full line of equipment and a restaurant that is open most of the time. The bar area has a comfortable sitting area that looks out over number one tee and the pond on number seven. I personally have seen 2 holes-in-one on this course, SEEN not made. This course has an intertwined golfing and social atmosphere, it is located on the east edge of town on Country Club Road.

Course	18Holes	Aesthetics	Good
Distance	6575 Yards	Interest	Very good
Par	34/38-72	Worth The Trip	Yes
Playability	Very Good	Rating	***+

HOLE LOCATION
Front Middle Back

Stakes & Plates:
Red - 100 yds.
White - 150 yds.
Blue - 200 yds.
Yellow 250 yds.

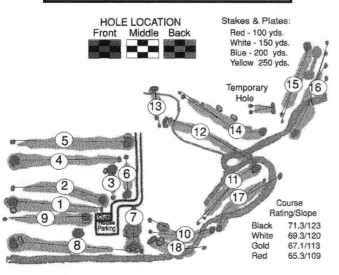

Course Rating/Slope

Black	71.3/123
White	69.3/120
Gold	67.1/113
Red	65.3/109

Hole	1	2	3	4	5	6	7	8	9	OUT
Black	378	403	151	383	395	194	141	476	330	2851
White	372	395	141	373	377	182	132	448	305	2725
Gold	364	385	134	363	363	176	108	419	297	2609
Handicap	10	8	17	11	6	14	18	15	12	
Par	4	4	3	4	4	3	3	5	4	34

10	11	12	13	14	15	16	17	18	IN	TOT		HCP	NET
355	393	600	179	520	379	589	453	256	3724	6575	185		
347	367	540	150	500	364	558	403	256	3485	6210	173		
322	360	428	101	442	349	519	307	256	3084	5693	101		
9	5	2	16	3	7	1	4	13					
4	4	5	3	5	4	5	4	4	38	72	3		

104

American Legion Post 130 Golf Club

Fort Dodge

515-576-4313

The American Legion Golf Course located two miles N.W. of Fort Dodge is a semi-private course, which means that members get priority on tee times. The course was built in 1927 and offers a challenging finishing hole with water and an uphill shot. There is a dry creek bed that runs through the course and is more of a rough hazard than a water hazard. The rough is cut short at one and one-half inches, plus there are three bunkers to guard some of the greens. There are many new plantings along the fairways and a smaller number of large trees around some of the greens and scattered throughout the course. These trees affect play very little. The greens are medium in size, have a slight tilt, and sloping. They also look very nice after being freshly cross cut. The putting surface is very true. The clubhouse sits on top of a hill on the south side of the course and has a nice view of the course and the surrounding countryside. The clubhouse has a bar with grilled sandwiches and a nice sitting area. The pro shop is in a separate building and has carts to rent and a few supplies. This is a cart course, mostly because it is hard to get down to the flat areas and back up. It is a fairly easy course to score well on and has very few hazards. The American Legion course has a relaxed golfing feeling, one that makes you feel like you belong and can play golf without anyone noticing how good or bad your score is.

Course	9 Holes
Distance	3161 Yards
Par	36
Playability	Good
Aesthetics	Good
Interest	Good
Worth The Trip	Yes
Rating	★★+

YARDAGE	365	336	280	196	447	518	499	366	154	3161
PAR	4	4	4	3	5	5	5	4	3	37
HANDICAP	6	2	9	3	8	5	4	1	7	
HOLES	1	2	3	4	5	6	7	8	9	OUT
LADIES' YARDAGE	365	300	280	196	355	409	396	366	154	2821
LADIES' PAR	4	4	4	3	5	5	5	4	3	37

Sunkissed Meadows Golf Course

Fort Dodge

515-576-4313

Another short and scenic par 3 course can be found by the river in Fort Dodge. This is a city owned public course that is strictly green fee oriented. Weekday green fees cost $5. There are monetary cuts for juniors and seniors. The clubhouse is only there to collect fees and offer pop and snacks, no sitting area. The course is located on Meriwether Dr. under the hospital bridge. This is not a very busy course, you can play at your convenience. Sunkissed Meadows has a pleasant setting among many shade trees and close to the river. There is one pond in the layout which entails all of the hazards on the course. The rough is cut the same as the fairways and is not a threat. Trees are of medium size and scattered throughout the course; they are well shaped and provide a great deal of shade. The greens are small, typical of a par 3 course, and are flat with slight elevation on some. The condition of the grass is good on fairways and greens. The fairways are wide and the contour of the course is flat. Sunkissed is the only beginner's course in Fort Dodge. It is a good course to learn on, short, flat, void of any real hazards, and has a very pleasant and relaxed atmosphere. The course was built in 1976. Try this one if you are a beginner or want to work on iron shots. You will be rewarded with a pleasant experience.

Course	Par 3
Distance	1243 Yards
Par	27
Playability	Fair
Aesthetics	Good
Interest	Good
Worth The Trip	Yes
Rating	★★★

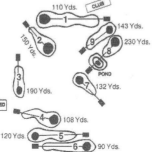

HOLE	1	2	3	4	5	6	7	8	9	TOT
YARDAGE	110	150	190	108	120	90	132	230	143	1243
PAR	3	3	3	3	3	3	3	3	3	27
HANDICAP	6	3	2	8	7	9	5	1	4	

Fort Dodge Country Club
Fort Dodge
515-955-8551

The Fort Dodge Country Club has to be considered one of the finest courses in N.W. Iowa and among the best in the state. This private course is located along Highway 169 on the west edge of Fort Dodge. The original course was built in 1926 and rebuilt in 1974. The clubhouse remains the same, a massive picturesque structure that offers country club dining and socializing. The food has a reputation of being some of the best in town. You must be one of the 350 members or a guest to enjoy it. There is also a snack bar in the clubhouse basement and a snack bar out on the course with sandwiches and bar items. The pro shop is housed in a separate structure nearer the course. It has a full line of equipment and clothes. They also have carts for rent. Green fees for guests are a little above average. The complex also offers a pool and driving range. Fort Dodge Country Club is a true championship course. It has all the tour quality features. There are three ponds on the course that come into play. The rough is cut over two inches and is beautifully manicured around tees and greens, and along the fairways. The rough has a reputation of being very thick and difficult, especially at tournament time. An expanded watering system now allows the rough to be watered. Sand is located on every hole and guards many greens from the pitch and run shot. Trees come in all sizes; variety is the spice of life. Only three fairways are lined with big trees, but many of the scattered trees throughout the course do come into play. Greens are small to medium in size and have a variety of putting surfaces. Grass condition throughout the entire course is good. The new watering allowed FDCC to convert their fairways from Blue Grass to Rye. This is a very scenic course built right on the edge of Fort Dodge near the river. The front nine holes has no water or out-of-bounds, the back nine both. This is a flat course that is easy to walk, but is considered a cart course. It is a championship course that hosts many major tournaments each year. This is a course that is worth it, big time golf.

Course	18 Holes	Aesthetics	Excell.
Distance	6573 Yards	Interest	Excell.
Par	35-36-71	Worth The Trip	Yes
Playability	Excell.	Rating	★ ★ ★ ★ ★

BLACK TEES	383	202	431	423	346	326	552	180	391	323	520	155	408	190	414	509	399	370	374	3339	6573	
BLUE TEES	371	175	403	376	337	298	540	153	386	303	510	147	376	184	389	502	355	345	366	3174	6213	
MENS HANDICAP	8	14	4	10	16	12	2	18	6		3	17	11	15	1	7	9	13	5			
WHITE TEES	321	160	395	369	315	209	526	146	335	277	478	130	357	150	314	480	327	315	350	2901	5677	
RED TEES	257	140	297	313	292	189	458	120	311	237	426	125	311	134	308	402	253	285	284	2528	4905	
LADIES HANDICAP	6	18	10	12	8	14	2	16	4		13	17	3	15	1	9	11	5	7			
PAR	4	3	4	4	4	4	5	3	4	35	5	3	4	3	4	5	4	4	4	36	71	
HOLES	1	2	3	4	5	6	7	8	9	OU	10	11	12	13	14	15	16	17	18	IN	TOTAL	

Lakeside Golf Course

Fort Dodge

515-576-6741

The only public 18 hole course located in Fort Dodge is Lakeside Golf Course located in Kennedy Park north of town four miles on Highway 413. This is a developing course that was built in 1978 and offers a wide variety of shots and situations in one location. The front nine holes are flat, easy to walk, and can be played using a free swing without any repercussions. The back nine holes are hilly, hard to walk, the fairways play much tighter, and you encounter a few blind doglegs. The complete layout has two ponds, one creek, and six bunkers. The trees on the course, especially on the front nine, are still immature and small. The front nine layout is on a flat area; the back nine stretches down towards a lake and contains hills and larger trees. The greens are large, tilted and rolling. They also have a reputation of being fast and easy to read. Players have to contend with a course that dries out in the summer and loses some of its grass. Lakeside is an easy course to walk and fairly easy to score well on. Trees do come into play on several holes, but like many other young courses, they will begin to reshape the character of the front nine in a few years when they get bigger. Tee times are needed at least a day in advance. This is a very busy course especially on the weekends. The pro shop has a complete line of equipment and also has lessons available on the driving range. The clubhouse is nice and has a public course feeling. It has fast food available along with bar items. It is a nice relaxing place to spend a few minutes between nines or after the round. Green fees are very reasonable.   The course has a reputation of drying out quickly and having spotty fairways. Lakeside is two courses wrapped into one setting. The front nine is basically flat and straight forward. The back nine has blind shots, severe doglegs, hills, creeks, and an original approach to a nine hole layout. The back nine is a real surprise; but a pleasant one once you decide to make the best of it.

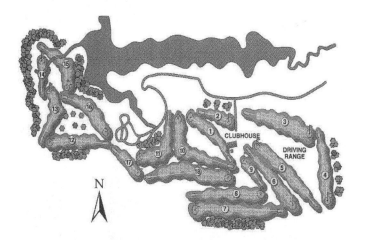

Course	18 Holes	Aesthetics	Very Good
Distance	6436 Yards	Interest	Excell.
Par	36-36-72	Worth The Trip	Yes
Playability	Excell.	Rating	***+

HOLE NUMBER	1	2	3	4	5	6	7	8	9	Out
BLUE TEES	350	203	422	370	495	395	544	422	157	3358
WHITE TEES	334	197	410	359	487	384	538	414	152	3275
HDCP	12	4	3	7	18	6	8	1	14	
PAR	4	3	4	4	5	4	5	4	3	36
RED TEES	320	183	327	344	472	369	467	366	143	2991
HDCP	8	12	4	6	9	1	10	3	17	

10	11	12	13	14	15	16	17	18	In	Tot
489	350	362	324	184	284	376	202	507	3078	6436
469	340	351	318	173	241	364	185	496	2937	6212
17	10	11	9	2	15	13	5	16		
5	4	4	4	3	4	4	3	5	36	72
414	330	338	269	154	208	268	116	452	2549	5540
7	2	5	14	13	15	16	18	11		

Sheaffer Memorial Golf Course

Ft. Madison

319-528-6214

The Sheaffer Memorial Golf Course is a public 18 hole course that is located on X-32 4 1/2 miles north of Ft. Madison. The course was built in 1960 on the site of a farm and is gently rolling with some man-made grass bunkers in the fairways. A new clubhouse was built in 1999 with a full grill and full pro shop which has a full line of equipment, including carts. This is mainly a greens fee course with 27,000 rounds being played each year. There are three ponds coming into play on four holes, a total of 43 sand bunkers strategically placed in the fairways and around greens. Sheaffer was built in 1960 and is now a mature course. The trees are medium to large in size with a continuing program of new plantings. Several new trees were planted on the back 9. The fairways are wide allowing for a certain degree of spraying of the ball. The rough along the flat fairways is cut just below two inches. The greens are large in size, some tilted, and all having some roll to them, many a severe case of roll. With the addition of fairway watering the grass condition throughout the course is very good. This is an easy course to walk and a fairly easy course to score, due mainly to it's topography. The front nine is a little tighter with more trees, several sloping fairways, and shorter distances. The back nine is wide open with rough that is easier to get out of and not as thick. This is a popular course in the Ft. Madison area, one of the nicer public courses in the area. Green fees are $13 for 9 holes. A family membership is $525. A driving range was also added in recent years. The outstanding feature would have to be the rolling greens and grass condition.

Course	18 Holes	Aesthetics	Good
Distance	6639 Yards	Interest	Good
Par	36-36-72	Worth The Trip	Yes
Playability	Good	Rating	* * *

HOLE		1	2	3	4	5	6	7	8	9	OUT
BLACK	71.5/125	492	438	528	371	195	354	347	131	347	3203
WHITE	70.5/123	477	428	513	361	170	293	339	126	337	3044
YELLOW	69.6/121	467	413	503	351	150	268	319	105	316	2892
HANDICAP		5	1	3	9	15	13	11	17	7	
PAR		5	4	5	4	3	4	4	3	4	36
RED	69.3/112	446	405	429	293	143	268	319	99	316	2718
HANDICAP		3	5	1	9	15	13	7	17	11	
PAR		5	5	5	4	3	4	4	3	4	37

10	11	12	13	14	15	16	17	18	IN	OUT	TOT	HCP	NET
398	187	376	463	391	378	225	441	577	3436	3203	6639		
388	175	364	458	371	368	200	378	557	3259	3044	6303		
378	165	354	435	361	358	185	368	542	3146	2892	6038		
8	18	12	6	14	4	16	10	2					
4	3	4	5	4	4	3	4	5	36	36	72		
298	152	290	435	279	304	177	304	484	2723	2718	5441		
12	18	8	4	14	6	16	10	2					
4	3	4	5	4	4	3	4	5	36	37	73		

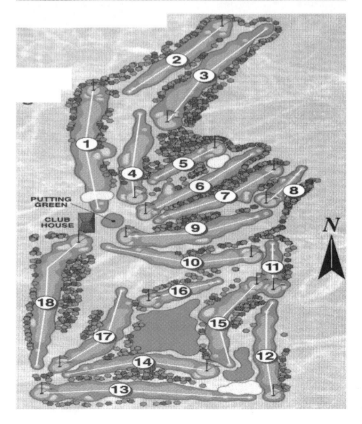

Spring Lake Golf Course

Ft. Madison

319-372-9937

Spring Lake Golf Course in Ft. Madison is located three miles north of town on X-32. This is a public course with 100 members who pay $450 for couples with reasonable green fees for non-members. This course has improved a great deal over the past two years. Rough has been introduced, sand traps dug and the condition of the course has generally improved. The clubhouse is a low structure that has balls, gloves, and a few clubs, plus an old thirty foot bar that spans one side of the building. Golfers can enjoy drinks and microwave sandwiches while watching number one tee. Four holes are affected on the course by two ponds, bunkers are being built and there is a two inch rough dividing the fairways. There are very few trees on the inside of the course but large old ones encompass the perimeter. This is a fairly wide open course with only three tight fairways. The fairway grass will dry out quickly in the summer leaving bare spots to contend with. The greens are small, crowned with humps and rolling, not a pleasant experience. The course was built in 1938 and has a flat contour with imposing humps in the middle of some fairways. This course is a slicer's delight — to the right is generally safe. Spring Lake is a family course that is easy to walk and easy to score well on. Traffic is not very heavy, so play when you get the notion. Make sure to bring your slice with you.

Course	9 Holes
Distance	2950 Yards
Par	36
Playability	Fair
Aesthetics	Fair
Interest	Good
Worth The Trip	Yes
Rating	★★+

HOLE	1	2	3	4	5	6	7	8	9	OUT
MEN'S YARDS	330	354	357	157	345	455	181	550	221	2950
LADIES' YARDS	318	342	300	137	333	425	155	470	180	2660
PAR	4	4	4	3	4	5	3	5	4	36
HANDICAP	5	3	2	8	6	7	4	1	9	

Plum Creek Golf Course

Fredericksburg

319-237-6401

Plum Creek Golf Course is located on the west edge of Fredericksburg. This is a private course with a 6 mile green fee playing radius. Green fees are $10 on weekdays. Membership size is 200 with annual fees of $400. Daily green fees are reasonable and even less when you play with a member. The general layout of the course is gently rolling with very few hazards, no water, very few trees, and one bunker. The wide fairways have only a few new trees scattered about and one cutting of the fairway is made over the entire course. Plum Creek is a course where you can let your fears of slice and hook go, swing away, nothing is stopping you, a wide open course. The tees are small and flat, the greens are also small and flat. The course was built in 1964. The clubhouse has carts for rent and a small amount of golf supplies on hand. There is a small kitchen area that reminds you of your childhood kitchen. They serve drinks at the bar and full meals are served from the kitchen. Fairway play is hampered by the lack of grass, hillsides are burned away by the normal summer heat. Local golfers keep the course fairly busy, but conditions need to improve to attract a bigger out of town crowd.

Course	9 Holes
Distance	3013 Yards
Par	36
Playability	Fair
Aesthetics	Poor
Interest	Poor
Worth The Trip	No
Rating	★+

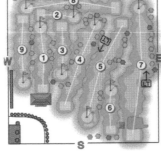

HOLE	1	2	3	4	5	6	7	8	9	Out
MEN'S TEE	320	170	257	381	547	145	492	335	366	3013
MEN'S HANDICAP	6	2	9	1	3	7	8	5	4	
PAR	4	3	4	4	5	3	5	4	4	36
LADIES' TEE	320	170	257	346	405	125	376	273	281	2523
LADIES' HANDICAP	6	2	9	1	3	7	8	5	4	

Garner Golf Club

Garner

515-923-2819

The Garner Golf and Country Club is a public course that is located on the northeast edge of town on Highway 18. The big brown clubhouse has a full restaurant that is open to the public the year round and has a nice variety of food. One of the nicest places to eat in the area. The pro shop, located in the basement, has the basic supplies plus a few clubs and will also rent you a cart for this 3232 yard course. Green fees during weekdays are reasonable but on the weekends are elevated a little. The 192 members pay $420 for an annual membership. The layout of the course is pretty wide open, with wide and slightly rolling fairways. There are 19 sand bunkers throughout the course and four ponds. There are approximately 300 trees on the course and they are now coming into play. Greens are large and flat with a little tilt to some of them. There is a 2" rough cut along the fairways and around some greens. The fairway watering system keeps the grass green throughout the course all summer. The course was built in 1975 and keeps fairly busy on the weekends and the evenings. Garner is a course that sells itself with appearance and facilities. Garner is also set up as a members course, pleasing the people that play it the most.

Course	9 Holes
Distance	3232 Yards
Par	36
Playability	Good
Aesthetics	Good
Interest	Good
Worth The Trip	Yes
Rating	★ ★ ★

Hole	1	2	3	4	5	6	7	8	9	Out
Blue	359	505	168	398	510	371	147	393	381	3232
White	343	480	150	336	492	357	132	376	349	3015
Par	4	5	3	4	5	4	3	4	4	36
Handicap	15	5	11	13	9	7	17	1	3	
Red	312	430	137	304	446	312	102	334	336	2713
Par	4	5	3	4	5	4	3	4	4	36
Handicap	11	1	15	13	3	9	17	5	7	

Otter Valley Country Club

George and Boyden

712-475-3861

Otter Valley Country Club is a young course, built in 1972, that serves the golfers of several small communities around the Boyden and George area. It was voted the Iowa 9 hole Golf Course of the Year in 2001. It is located 6 miles south of George on L14. The 210 members pay a membership fee of $345 for a family. Daily green fees are average in price, $10 on weekdays. The clubhouse is a compact new structure that overlooks the course and was remodeled in 2001. Inside there is a full line of equipment, a bar area with snacks, and kitchen facilities for special events. There are also carts for rent but the Otter Valley course is generally flat and easy to walk. The water hazards on the course consist of one pond that barely comes into play on two holes and a dried up creek bed that plays as a gully on four fairways. This is a wide open course that has little rough and is suited for a long ball hitter. There are many new trees scattered throughout the course and a few tall poplars located by a few greens and tees. Greens are medium in size but have dips on the surface that make them very difficult to read and putt. Otter Valley has that country feeling. Otter Valley is a great place to get away from the noise and business of a town and enjoy the sights of Iowa.

Course	9 Holes
Distance	3186 Yards
Par	36
Playability	Fair
Aesthetics	Good
Interest	Fair
Worth The Trip	Yes
Rating	★ ★

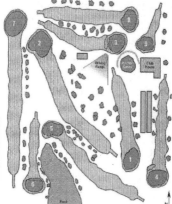

HOLE	1	2	3	4	5	6	7	8	9	OUT
YARDS	375	516	343	365	374	205	535	365	110	3186
MEN'S PAR	4	5	4	4	4	3	5	4	3	36
HANDICAP	7	5	15	11	9	3	1	13	17	
SCORE	/	/	/	/	/	/	/	/	/	
YARDS	360	482	313	327	342	173	432	333	95	2856
LADIES' PAR	4	5	4	4	4	3	5	4	3	36

Glenwood Golf Club

Glenwood

712-527-9798
glenwoodgc@aol.com

The Glenwood Golf Club was built by all volunteer labor. The course was built in 1963 on some rolling land on the N.E. edge of town, about one half mile east of the high school. There are no ponds on the course, but a creek that runs through the layout comes into play on three holes. The fairways are fairly narrow with large trees lining most of them. The greens are small and elevated making this a placement and approach course. The clubhouse has carts to rent for the person who dislikes climbing a little, plus the bar area has deli sandwiches and a limited supply of balls and gloves. The course has a membership of 200 with annual fees of $540 for a family. This is a public course that will accept daily green fees of reasonable amount. There are a couple of unique things about this course. One is that it is built on a parcel of land that is a true triangle, also Glenwood has an Early Bird Tournament late in April and their Last Chance Open in the first week of September, spreading the golf season out for local players. This is an interesting course that has all the right things to offer for a small town course.

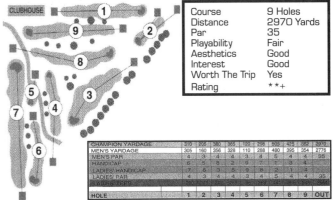

Course	9 Holes
Distance	2970 Yards
Par	35
Playability	Fair
Aesthetics	Good
Interest	Good
Worth The Trip	Yes
Rating	★★+

	1	2	3	4	5	6	7	8	9	OUT
CHAMPION YARDAGE	310	205	380	365	120	298	505	425	362	2970
MEN'S YARDAGE	305	160	356	328	110	288	480	395	354	2776
MEN'S PAR	4	3	4	4	3	4	5	4	4	35
HANDICAP	6	5	8	2	9	7	1	3	4	
LADIES' HANDICAP	7	6	3	5	9	8	1	2	4	
LADIES' PAR	4	3	4	4	3	4	5	4	4	35
LADIES' TEES										
HOLE	1	2	3	4	5	6	7	8	9	OUT

Oakridge Recreation Association

Goldfield

515-825-3611

Small town golf courses have loyal members and the Oakridge course at Goldfield is no exception. The 220 members are involved with the whole operation of the course. Green fees are reasonable for a community this size. The fairways are very wide on a very flat course. The trees are medium in size and come into play very little. Some of the medium size tee boxes are elevated and most of the medium size greens are flat. There is one pond that comes into play on one hole and one lone bunker on the course. The course was built in 1971. Inside the one-level clubhouse you can rent a cart and buy a few supplies. They serve snacks and microwave sandwiches. After a hot day on the course you can do a little swimming in their pool. Oakridge is located one mile northwest of town. Members take pride in the maintenance of the course and devote much of their time improving the entire facility. The course is an easy course to walk and score well on. The greens are true, the rough is fair and the people are nice, a good combination for a nice day. Course is located west of town on County 32.

Course	9 Holes
Distance	3018 Yards
Par	36
Playability	Good
Aesthetics	Good
Interest	Fair
Worth The Trip	Yes
Rating	★★★

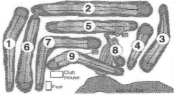

		1	2	3	4	5	6	7	8	9	OUT
MEN'S YARDAGE		385	511	290	165	375	365	448	125	354	3018
MEN'S PAR		4	5	4	3	4	4	5	3	4	36
LADIES YARDAGE		380	357	285	160	330	360	440	100	267	2719
LADIES PAR		4	4	4	3	4	4	5	3	4	35
HOLE		1	2	3	4	5	6	7	8	9	OUT
HANDICAP		2	4	9	5	1	7	8	6	3	

Gowrie Golf and Country Club

Gowrie

515-352-3320

Gowrie Golf and Country Club is located on the S.E. edge of town. The layout of the course is fairly flat to rolling. 100 new trees were planted in 1989 adding to the medium size trees already lining the fairways. New tee boes were built in 2001 and more trees added. Sand bunkers guard three holes and ponds are hazards on two other holes. The course does drain well which means that in the spring they are usually one of the first courses to open. The greens are some of the best ones in the area, being elevated and tilted to receive lofted shots. New sprinklers now water the tee boxes and have really made them nice to hit off of. The newly remodeled clubhouse has a restaurant that is open Wednesday, Saturday, and Sunday mornings. They do have a very nice snack and bar area to sit and view the course. The course which is located on the S.E. edge of Gowrie has 180 members that pay an annual fee of $400. Daily green fees are reasonable for a community this size. This is an easy course to walk, although there are carts for rent, and it is an easy course to score well on. This is just a nice example of a small town public course, one that members enjoy and you will too.

Course	9 Holes
Distance	3064 Yards
Par	35
Playability	Good
Aesthetics	Good
Interest	Fair
Worth The Trip	Yes
Rating	★ ★ ★

HOLE	1	2	3	4	5	6	7	8	9	Gross
Men's Yardage	375	347	154	375	381	486	387	184	328	3064
Handicap	6	7	9	3	2	4	1	5	8	
Par	4	4	3	4	4	5	4	3	4	35
Women's Yardage	336	307	131	372	330	448	337	167	281	2706
Handicap	5	4	6	8	3	2	1	7	9	
Par	4	4	3	5	4	5	4	3	4	36

Hillcrest Golf & supper Club

Graettinger

712-859-3766

For a town of less than 1,000 people Graettinger has one of the most distinctive nine hole courses in N.W. Iowa. The Hillcrest Golf Course is located on the S.W. edge of town on Cedar St. and has a membership of 200. This is a public course of 2800 yards that has reasonable daily green fees. Members pay an annual fee of $335. The clubhouse provides a full time restaurant to the general public the year round and is known as one of the finer eating establishments in the area. The supplies in the clubhouse are slim but made up for by the eating facilities. The characteristics of the course include a few sand bunkers, a little rough, fairway watering, and two ponds on #5 and # 1 and #2. Trees on the course are medium in size with yearly new plantings. Tees are in good shape, elevated a little and landscaped a little. Greens are medium to large in size. The grass condition on the greens is very good. The course was built in 1976. This public course is flat and easy to walk. It is a interesting course for the beginning to average player to enjoy. Accuracy is important; although the course would be considered wide open. The shape of the course is very good considering the population that the course draws from. A lot of love and care goes into the operation of Hillcrest.

Course	9 Holes
Distance	2800 Yards
Par	36
Playability	Good
Aesthetics	Good
Interest	Fair
Worth The Trip	Yes
Rating	★ ★ ★

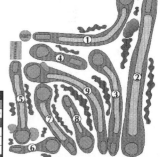

	1	2	3	4	5	6	7	8	9	OUT
MEN'S PAR	5	5	4	3	4	3	4	3	5	36
WOMEN'S PAR	5	5	4	3	4	3	4	3	5	36
MEN'S YARDAGE	433	535	317	170	274	139	280	215	437	2800
WOMEN'S YARDAGE	412	439	303	153	259	118	263	202	423	2572
WE										
SIDE MATCHES	1	2	3	4	5	6	7	8	9	OUT

112

Lakeside Golf Course

Grand Junction

515-738-2403

Lakeside Golf Course is another Iowa course that was developed out of necessity. Local players wanted a course they could call their own, the building of Lakeside brought life out of the depths of a corn field. The course is located by Spring Lake Park, two miles west and one mile north of Grand Junction. The 3090 yard course is basically flat laid out in a north-south direction. There is one stream that comes into play on two holes (four if you aren't careful). There are five bunkers on the course and the small trees that line the fairways usually don't come into play. This is generally a wide open course that allows you to play a free swinging game. A new watering system built in '84 has helped the grass condition throughout the course. Greens are medium in size with one very large green that is tiered to keep your interest late in the round. The clubhouse is new, replacing a smaller one destroyed by wind in '85. Inside they have a small amount of supplies and a good supply of snacks and drinks. The 200 members pay an annual fee of $400 for a family while green fees are reasonable. This is an easy course to walk but not that easy to score well on. It is generally played by local people, who like the pleasure of playing golf on a course they know. Lakeside is a good example of how people pulling together can create something that is useful and fun for all.

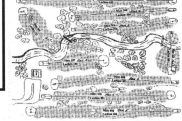

Course	9 Holes
Distance	3083 Yards
Par	36
Playability	Good
Aesthetics	Very Good
Interest	Good
Worth The Trip	Yes
Rating	★ ★ ★

HOLES		1	2	3	4	5	6	7	8	9	Total
YARDS	Men	418	478	197	294	489	340	314	152	401	3083
	Ladies	361	434	158	219	435	294	278	144	354	2693
PAR		4	5	3	4	5	4	4	3	4	36
Handicap		2	6	3	9	4	8	7	5	1	

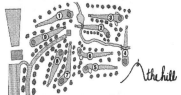

Course	9 Holes
Distance	2334 Yards
Par	34
Playability	Good
Aesthetics	Good
Interest	Fair
Worth The Trip	Yes
Rating	★ ★ +

MENS	247	425	250	101	310	270	335	206	190	2334
PAR	4	5	4	3	4	4	4	3	3	34
HANDICAP	17	15	13	7	5	11	9	3	1	
HANDICAP	17	15	13	7	5	11	9	3	1	
PAR	4	5	4	3	4	4	4	3	3	34
LADIES	247	330	250	80	310	270	325	150	170	2209

The Hill

Grand Junction

515-738-2571

When Cecil Rueter built a golf course in his own back yard, he hoped his friends and employees would use and enjoy it. He had no idea how much enjoyment he was dealing out! Today the employees and friends play the course with abandon; but there are also 100 members who enjoy the atmosphere of a small friendly course. The Hill Golf Course is located two miles west of Grand Junction on Highway 30. The course has developed into a public course with reasonable green fees. The yearly membership for a family is $200. The character of the course is shaped by the stream that runs the length of the course. It directly affects four holes and indirectly affects the terrain on another three. There are 4 sand bunkers on the course and no rough. Trees on the course are scattered along the fairways and are small in size with many new plantings, over 1000. Fairways are average in width with the contour of the course gently rolling; gently rolling right down to the stream. Tees are elevated and medium in size. Greens are small with a few sloping and a few tilted, 3 greens have been enlarged in the last two years. Large flower beds greatly enhance tee boxes. The Hill was built in 1985 and is used mainly by local golfers who like a short course to walk and play. A new clubhouse was built in 1998 and fairway watering was added the same year. The Hill was intended to be a private course; but the generosity of Mr. Rueter has enabled the entire community to enjoy his masterpiece of a backyard.

113

Jester Park Golf Course

Granger

515-999-2903

One of the busiest courses in the Des Moines area is Jester Park Golf Course located two miles east and one mile north of Granger, inside Jester Park. This 18 hole public course is set in a very scenic and tranquil area. Jester is also a very busy course recording over 60,000 rounds last year. This 6856 yard course has some long and challenging holes and some gigantic greens to finish off on. There are five ponds on the course that come into play on six holes, many affecting your tee shot. The twenty bunkers are also intended to catch your drives, many are placed at the landing area in the fairways. Rough is cut a very distinctive three inches and gives the feeling and look of championship holes. Trees are generally in the range of 20 to 30 foot evergreens and are scattered throughout the course, plentiful in number. Massive could describe the greens, maybe too big. They cover a large area, generally having flat putting surfaces. A heavy putter is a must on some of these greens. The grass condition on the greens is good, there are some worn spots on the fairways that have resulted from the wear and tear on the course, but overall the grass condition is very good. The tees also show some wear. The fairways are flat and narrow with trees dotting the rough. The rough along with the trees make the fairways average about 28 yards in width. The modern clubhouse was built in 1969 and offers a full line of equipment, including a nice selection of clubs and clothes. The staff also offers lessons on the practice range and has a fleet of carts to rent, which might be a good idea on this expansion layout. The clubhouse has a bar and sandwiches to eat, but the attraction on this course is the golfing. There are memberships that cost $400. They also have a junior membership for $1,150, a great way to get the younger generation started. Daily green fees are very reasonable for such a nice course. There are also special rates for senior citizens and juniors. This is a challenging course to play. Many USGA and PGA tournaments are held here and the Big 4 college tournament is held here each spring.

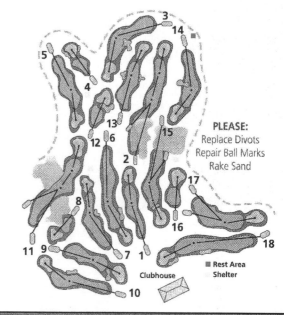

PLEASE:
Replace Divots
Repair Ball Marks
Rake Sand

Clubhouse

■ Rest Area
Shelter

Course	18 Holes	Aesthetics	Excell.
Distance	6856 Yards	Interest	Very Good
Par	36-36-72	Worth The Trip	Yes
Playability	V. Good	Rating	****

Hole Number	1	2	3	4	5	6	7	8	9	Out
Blue Tees	391	625	411	157	377	531	416	174	375	3457
White Tees	379	611	393	138	362	510	396	160	358	3307
Gold Tees	347	553	311	120	325	453	381	128	307	2925
Red Tees	302	428	284	98	286	400	343	111	285	2537
Par	4	5	4	3	4	5	4	3	4	36
Handicap	12	1	5	18	7	14	10	11	6	

10	11	12	13	14	15	16	17	18	In	Tot	Hcp	Net
418	501	170	395	370	507	220	423	395	3399	6856		
403	482	154	379	348	497	200	412	378	3253	6560		
359	307	139	346	327	477	163	327	357	2802	5727		
349	232	113	320	286	402	127	304	323	2456	4993		
4	5/4	3	4	4	5	3	4	4	36/35	72/71		
4	3	17	15	16	13	9	2	8				

Executive Par 3

Jester Park - Granger

515-999-2903

A very short par 3 course lies on the fringes of Jester Park Golf Course north of Granger. The Executive Par 3 course measures only 1077 yards but still has the beauty and terrain of its bigger neighbor. This is also a public course that has very reasonable charges for nine holes. All fees can be paid in the main clubhouse. You will also find any supplies you need for this par 3 course in the clubhouse. The starting hole for Executive is found at the east end of the main parking lot. There is one pond on the course affecting two holes. Two bunkers guard greens and one more is found in the fairway of number five. There are many trees on this course, generally scattered along the fairways. Some large willows make this a very scenic course to walk and play on. Tees are flat on the ground and medium in size. Greens are medium to large in size and generally flat. The fairways and greens are cut to perfection just like the championship course. What makes this such a nice course is the location in the park, the condition of the grounds, the number of big trees that come into play, and the greens. The greens are above average, compared to any other par three course in the state. Executive is quite short in length but long on beauty and fun. Next time instead of playing four hours on Jester play one hour on Executive. The relaxed atmosphere may do wonders for your iron game.

Course	Par 3
Distance	1140 Yards
Par	27
Playability	Good
Aesthetics	Excell.
Interest	Very Good
Worth The Trip	Yes
Rating	★★★

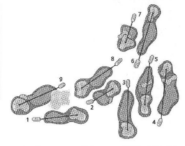

HOLE NO.	1	2	3	4	5	6	7	8	9	TOT
WHITE TEES	135	86	168	139	123	132	80	143	134	1140
RED TEES	126	73	136	124	105	115	70	126	121	996
PAR	3	3	3	3	3	3	3	3	3	27

Round Grove Golf and Country Club

Greene

641-823-5621

Green fees are accepted from out-of-town golfers at the Round Grove Golf and Country Club in Greene. Weekday fees are very reasonable. The 190 members pay $290 a year for the privilege to play this picturesque course that is located north on Highway 14 in Greene. This is a gently rolling course that has poplars lining the fairways, although they don't present much of a problem. There are four bunkers and one pond that come into play on three holes. The wide fairways are contained by one inch rough that is fair and easy to get out of. The greens at Greene are small to medium in size and are of the flat sloping variety. The clubhouse has a small variety of typical supplies, balls, gloves, plus the bar area serves microwave sandwiches and drinks. This course in fairly good shape although there is some burnout on some of the hillsides which is typical of side hills. The course is considered easy to walk (there are no carts for rent) and easy to score well on. Green fees are $10 during the week. Round Grove has a true small town Iowa atmosphere, something that goes well with this pleasing course.

Course	9 Holes
Par	36
Distance	3113 Yards
Playability	Good
Aesthetics	Good
Interest	Fair
Worth The Trip	Yes
Rating	★★

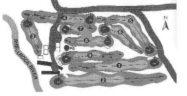

	1	2	3	4	5	6	7	8	9	Out
BLUE	510	548	175	400	395	290	155	285	355	3113
WHITE	500	508	155	360	375	275	140	260	335	2908
RED	455	478	145	347	350	259	120	260	315	2729
HOLE	1	2	3	4	5	6	7	8	9	Out

Beaver Creek Course
Grimes
515-986-3221

Everyone from N.W. Iowa traveling to Des Moines has watched the development of Beaver Creek. They have now added an additional 9 holes giving them a total of 27. The new 9 was added in 2001. The layout was cut out of a Christmas Tree farm and has a lot of elevation changes. The new nine is seeing 50% of play. This is a public 27 hole course that relies 100% on green fees, $26 on. Yearly memberships are $1,200 for a single and $1,000 for seniors. Evergreens dominate the course. 1525 six to eight foot trees were planted along with 570 leafy trees on the initial 18. . All of the bent grass fairways are watered and lined with trees. Although they may not present much of a problem now the one foot growth per year will bring them into play soon. There are 4 ponds on the course affecting 6 holes, there is an average of 1 sand bunker per hole. Tee boxes are tiered to three levels and are generally big and plush. Greens average 6,500 square feet in surface area, are generally flat, and got faster as they matured during their first summer. Beaver Run is a good mixture of holes. The new 9 has an island green. The average to high handicap player will enjoy the overall challenge of the course. For a few years you will be able to spray the ball around without much penalty, but there is a premium on being in the good grass rather than the 2" rough. This a very scenic course, one that will get better as the course matures. There were 25,000 rounds played the first year so tee times are needed. The clubhouse has a spacious interior with a full line of equipment and grilled sandwiches. Beaver Run has a full time pro to help you with your game, on the practice green or on the driving range. This 6779/3254 yard course(s) is a must for golf enthusiasts in the central Iowa area, beauty, challenge, and courteous service all in one place.

Course	18 Holes	Aesthetics	Very Good
Distance	6779 Yards	Interest	Very Good
Par	36-36-72	Worth the Trip	Yes
Playability	Very Good	Rating	***+

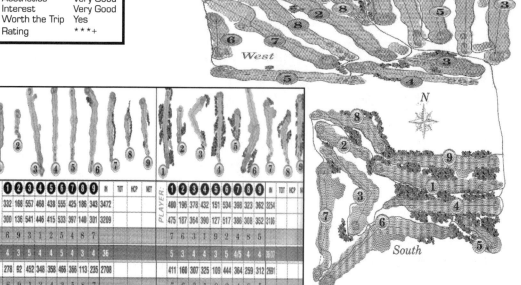

HOLE	1	2	3	4	5	6	7	8	9	OUT		1	2	3	4	5	6	7	8	9	IN	TOT	HCP	NET		1	2	3	4	5	6	7	8	9	IN	TOT	HCP
BLUE	330	577	180	336	351	176	432	501	424	3307		332	168	557	468	438	555	425	186	343	3472					400	196	378	432	151	534	398	323	362	3254		
WHITE	310	532	153	317	329	159	419	482	349	3050		300	136	541	446	415	533	397	140	301	3209					475	187	364	390	127	517	386	308	352	3116		
MEN'S HDCP	8	2	3	9	4	6	1	5	7			6	9	3	1	2	5	4	8	7					7	6	3	1	9	2	4	8	5			
PAR	4	5	3	4	4	3	4	5	4	36		4	3	5	4	4	5	4	3	4	36					5	3	4	4	3	5	4	4	4	36		
RED	275	464	127	258	303	147	276	416	271	2537		278	92	452	348	358	466	366	113	235	2708					411	160	307	325	109	444	364	259	312	2691		
LADIES' HDCP	6	1	3	9	5	4	8	2	7			6	9	1	3	4	2	5	8	7					7	6	3	1	9	2	4	8	5			

Greenfield Golf Club

Greenfield

641-743-2113

The Greenfield Country Club is located one mile west of Greenfield on Highway 92. The drive to the clubhouse is a steep one, but the view over the course to the west and south is worth it. Inside the clubhouse there are the general supplies; balls, gloves, a few clothes, and an assortment of carts to rent. The course was altered in 1995, with added length, new bunkers, and a different layout. This private course has a green fees radius of outside Adair county. Green fees for these people and guests are average for a 9 hole course. The 100 members pay a stock of $150 then a yearly fee of $530 for a family or $400 for a single. This is a short and hilly course. The only water hazard is the stream that is wet in early spring but becomes a dry creek bed affecting five holes the rest of the year. The rough is cut at two inches along the tree line and one sand bunker to catch approach shots. The contour of the course is hilly going away from the clubhouse and again as it rises in the west. The trees on the layout are above average in number and above average in size. Tees have been expanded and are slightly elevated. Greens are medium in size and generally flat. Five greens are being enlarged or rebuilt. The course was built in 1936. Greenfield is a second shot course. The short yardage makes your drive off the tee less important, it is how you get on the green that can make or break your game. It is a hard course to walk and a challenging course to play. The beauty of the hills and woods to the west make this family course an interesting place to play.

Course	9 Holes
Distance	2786 Yards
Par	35
Playability	Fair
Aesthetics	Good
Interest	Good
Worth The Trip	Yes
Rating	★★

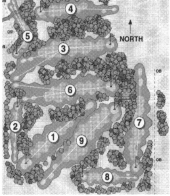

HOLE	1	2	3	4	5	6	7	8	9	Out
Blue 65.5/112	326	142	357	275	320	314	375	193	484	2786
White 64.9/111	326	122	319	275	275	276	375	180	472	2620
PAR	4	3	4	4	4	4	4	3	5	35
HANDICAP	7	15	3	17	5	11	1	9	13	

Grinnell Golf & Country Club

Grinnell

641-236-3590

The Grinnell Country Club is full of tradition. The club was first established in 1899, making it one of the oldest golf courses west of the Mississippi. The old country club style is changing with younger members having more influence over the decisions. In 1996 the layout of the course was changed. This private club is located on the north edge of Grinnell at 13th and Park. If you live outside a ten mile radius you can pay the above average green fees. The 250 members pay an initial $110 in stock and a family membership of $1,425. The clubhouse has just been remodeled and supplies full food service. The pro shop does carry a full line of equipment including carts for rent. Water is the dominant characteristic on the course coming into play on 6 holes. These hazards include three ponds, one stream, and seven new sand bunkers. Old mature trees are scattered throughout the gently rolling course with a one-cut rough outlining the wide fairways. tree plantings have number 300 in the last few years. The tee boxes are small but in good shape. The rolling greens are of medium size and have a true putting surface. With the new watered fairways and the addition of new sand bunkers Grinnell Country Club has been made more challenging. This north-south course plays differently every time you tee it up. It is an easy course to walk and fairly easy to score well on. Grinnell Country Club is a course laden with tradition and building on a bright future.

Course	9 Holes
Distance	3059 Yards
Par	35
Playability	Good
Aesthetics	Good
Interest	Good
Worth The Trip	Yes
Rating	★★★

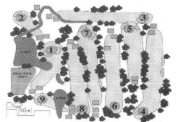

Par	4	3	4	5	4	4	4	4	3	35
Blue	265	162	321	487	322	394			171	3050
White	265	158	372	447	310	363	438	359	138	2850
Gold	229	129	315	405	285	279	351	310	115	2418
Hcp	15	13	3	9	11	5	1	7	17	
HOLE	1	2	3	4	5	6	7	8	9	OUT
Par	4	3	4	5	4	4	4	4	3	35
Red	229	129	315	405	285	279	351	310	115	2418
Hcp	15	17	1	3	11	9	5	7	13	

117

Oakland Acres

Grinnell

641-236-7111

One of the better conditioned courses in eastern Iowa is Oakland Acres located 6 miles west of Grinnell on Highway 6. The medium size greens are in great shape and provide a great putting surface for any golfer. There are two ponds on this 18 hole course that come into play on three holes. There is a noticeable absence of sand that might add to the layout of this course. Because of the soil condition the fairways tend to dry up on the south sides of the hills. There is some short and heavy rough guarding the tree lined fairways. The trees are small in stature and do not pose a problem to the average golfer. What does present a threat is the hilly contour and the absence of level shots. The hills on the course can create some blind approach shots to many of the holes. The greens are soft and thick with a lot of subtle breaks, with most having a sloping contour that adds just a little extra drama to your game. Even though this course is hilly it is still considered an easy course to walk. Oakland Acres is a busy course and rightfully so. A very nice challenging course that also maintains a beautiful clubhouse and restaurant. The Oakroom has some of the best food in the area and is open to the public year round. The golf course is also open to the public with green fees reasonable in price. The pro shop has a full line of equipment plus a very nice area to sit and relax. Sandwiches can be ordered throughout the day from the pro shop. Oakland Acres is a course that is a challenge on the fairways, on the greens, and in the clubhouse (you have a hard time deciding what to order to eat).

Course	18 Holes	Aesthetics	Good
Distance	5878 Yards	Interest	Good
Par	35-34-69	Worth The Trip	Yes
Playability	Good	Rating	★ ★ ★

HOLE	1	2	3	4	5	6	7	8	9	Out
WHITE YARDS	419	138	368	339	344	475	421	430	209	3143
HANDICAP	7	17	9	15	11	13	3	1	5	
PAR	4	3	4	4	4	5	4	4	3	35
RED YARDS	399	138	360	330	330	463	349	334	209	2912
HANDICAP	9	17	5	13	11	3	1	7	15	
PAR	5	3	4	4	4	5	4	4	4	37

10	11	12	13	14	15	16	17	18	In	Tot	Hcp	Net
373	439	160	325	331	315	302	96	394	2735	5878		
6	2	8	10	14	12	16	18	4				
4	4	3	4	4	4	4	3	4	34	69		
361	300	139	319	316	304	284	95	380	2498	5410		
4	14	16	8	6	10	12	18	2				
4	4	3	4	4	4	4	3	4	34	71		

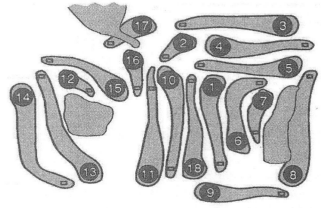

Nishna Valley Recreation Area

Griswold

712-778-4104

The Nishna Valley Recreation Area, which includes a golf course, is located one mile east of Griswold. This is another young course built around 1970. The clubhouse has carts for rent and a small supply of balls and gloves. The clubhouse was remodeled in '91 with snacks and drinks and the restaurant portion is open for special occasions only. The Nishna Valley Club has a membership of 190, each paying a family fee of $470. Green fees are average, $12 weekdays. The contour of the course is gently rolling, receding all the way down the hill away from the clubhouse. The club does offer a remodeled pool and a practice range for its members. The trees are now coming into play and will become a factor in the years to come, the perimeter of the course is covered by larger trees. The fairways are wide and open to long hitting. The large greens hold approach shots well and have a true putting surface. Fairway watering was added in the late 90's and grass bunkers were placed to provide some resistance. The facilities on this young course are attractive and nice. In a few years this might be one of the finer courses in the area.

Course	9 Holes
Distance	3125 Yards
Par	36
Playability	Good
Aesthetics	Good
Interest	Fair
Worth The Trip	Yes
Rating	★★+

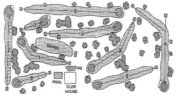

PAR	4	3	4	5	4	3	4	5	4	36
YELLOW	300	150	385	470	325	200	375	525	395	3125
HANDICAP	17	13	1	15	7	3	11	9	5	
HOLE	1	2	3	4	5	6	7	8	9	OUT
HANDICAP	17	13	1	15	7	3	11	9	5	
RED	300	150	310	359	325	200	375	392	395	2806
PAR	4	3	4	5	4	3	4	5	4	36

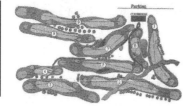

Town and Country Golf Club

Grundy Center

319-824-3712

The green fees at Town and Country Golf Course reasonable for a community this size. The 220 members pay an annual fee of $400 for a family. The new clubhouse offers a limited amount of supplies but has a very complete bar and dining area. The contour of the course is flat with little rough guarding the wide fairways. Fairway watering was added in the late 90's. Water hazards come into play on four holes with a good size pond waiting for approach shots on number 9. There are a small number of small to medium size trees scattered in the rough, presenting few problems to the average golfer. The greens are of medium size and most have a flat putting surface. This course was built in 1965 and is still a developing course. Two unusual facts about this course are that there were four holes-in-one during one week in 1985 and also that Patty Berg gave an exhibition at Town and Country in 1975. You will find the Grundy Center course easy to walk, easy to score well on, not very challenging and easy to get on, with a friendly clubhouse atmosphere. The course is located on So.12th Street, just south of the high school.

Course	9 Holes
Distance	3337 Yards
Par	36
Playability	Good
Aesthetics	Fair
Interest	Fair
Worth The Trip	Yes
Rating	★★+

HOLE	1	2	3	4	5	6	7	8	9	OUT
BLUE YARDAGE	343	497	380	189	436	161	391	384	556	3337
BLUE HANDICAP	8	6	2	5	1	9	3	7	4	
WHITE YARDAGE	343	497	281	189	371	161	333	293	556	3024
WHITE HANDICAP	6	2	9	4	1	8	5	7	3	
PAR	4	5	4	3	5	3	4	4	5	36
RED YARDAGE	277	415	281	117	371	83	333	293	473	2643
RED HANDICAP	4	3	8	7	1	9	2	6	5	

119

Guthrie Center Golf Club

Guthrie Center

641-747-3558

The Guthrie Center Golf Club is situated on, in, and around some very steep hills. These hills cause the fairways and greens to dry out much quicker than some flater courses leaving bare spots early in the summer. But there is hope because a new water sprinkling system was installed in 1991. There are no water hazards on the course and only two sand bunkers. Trees are small to medium in size and are scattered throughout the course. The greens are small, almost to the extent of being unfair. They are flat and have a few bare spots around the edges. The fairways are open, wide, and very hilly. Three new sand bunkers were added this year. There might not be 10 even lies on the entire course. This is a true north-south course, out and back. It is a tough course because of the hills and green size. The clubhouse is small with only candy bars and pop, they don't have any carts; walking, a great way to get into shape. The course was built in 1957. Family memberships are $275 while daily green fees are very reasonable for weekdays, $10 for all day.. With the addition of water the entire course will start to perk up over the next few years. This is really one of the hilliest courses in the central Iowa area.

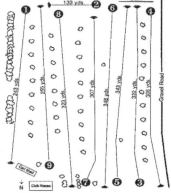

Course	9 Holes
Distance	2580 Yards
Par	35
Playability	Fair
Aesthetics	Fair
Interest	Fair
Worth The Trip	Maybe
Rating	★★

Hole	Yards	Handicap	Men's Par	Ladies Par
1	243 / 226	7	4	4
2	133	1	3	3
3*	322 / 274	6	4	4
4	306 / 286	4	4	4
5*	343 / 264	5	4	4
6	348 / 284	2	4	5
7	307	8	4	4
8	323 / 274	3	4	5
9	255	9	4	4
	2580 / 2254		35	37

Men's Total Yards 2,580

Guttenberg Golf and Country Club

Guttenberg

563-252-1423

The Guttenberg Golf and Country Club is located three miles north of Guttenberg on Highway 52. The Guttenberg course is built along the Mississippi River and benefits from its beauty. This is a long nine hole course at 3185 yards. The contour of the course is gently rolling by the clubhouse and hilly as you near the river. Holes four through six are hilly and engulfed with large trees. There are two ponds on the course that affect three holes. The trees on the remainder of the course are small to medium with new plantings made each year. The fairways are wide with a little rough standing in the ravines. Greens are medium in size; and except for number nine, rolling in nature. The Guttenberg course was built in 1962. This is an easy course to walk except for three fairways. It is challenging because of the uneven lies and three wooded holes. It is not real busy so tee times are not needed. The most outstanding feature of this course is its location and view of the river basin. This is a very scenic course in the fall; just like the rest of northeast Iowa. Golf courses are exceptionally nice if they have beautiful surroundings.

Course	9 Holes
Distance	3187 Yards
Par	36
Playability	Very Good
Aesthetics	Very Good
Interest	Good
Worth The Trip	Yes
Rating	★★★

White Tees	Par	Hdcp.	Hole	Par	Hdcp.	Red Tees
390	4	4	1	4	4	390
304	4	9	2	4	7	304
147	3	7	3	3	7	147
490	5	6	4	5	6	400
409	4	1	5	5	1	409
380	4	2	6	4	3	314
386	4	3	7	4	3	291
183	3	5	8	3	5	153
498	5	8	9	5	9	443
3187	36		OUT	37		2851

120

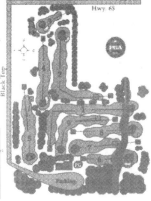

Hampton Country Club

Hampton

641-456-3256

The Hampton Country Club was voted the 9 hole course of the year in Iowa in 1984. From all observations it deserved the recognition. It is located two miles north and one mile east on Highway 65. A new clubhouse was built in 2001. One of the first things you notice about this picturesque course are the greens. Odd numbered holes have severely sloping greens and the even numbered holes have fairly flat greens. This may be a driver and wedge course but your shot to the green better be below the hole or it will be a driver, wedge, putt, putt, and putt course. There is one stream that comes into play on four holes and a pond alters play on another. The narrow fairways have a large number of wide and tall trees lining them, 30 new trees have been added to holes 2,4,& 5. The clubhouse, which has a very nice bar and serves grilled and microwave sandwiches, sits on top of a hill overlooking the course to the west. Four holes are built on the slope and the remaining five are down in the valley. Fairway watering was added in 1989. This is a fairly easy course to walk but a hard course to score well on. The course was built in the 1920's and has a membership size of 249. Yearly dues are $700 and very reasonable daily green fees of $15, any day of the week. This is a very nice course that is challenging and demands your concentration on every shot.

Course	9 Holes
Distance	3176 Yards
Par	37
Playability	Good
Aesthetics	Excell.
Interest	Very Good
Worth The Trip	Yes
Rating	★★★★

Men's Blue 70.2/114	546	552	130	356	355	252	317	300	368	3176
Men's Par	5	5	3	4	4	4	4	4	4	37
Men's Handicap	11	5	9	15	1	13	7	17	3	
Ladies' Red 74.6	534	457	130	356	321	252	240	300	284	2874
Ladies' Par	6	5	3	4	4	4	4	4	4	38
Handicap	1	3	17	9	7	15	11	13	5	
Holes	1	2	3	4	5	6	7	8	9	OUT

Harlan Golf and Country Club

Harlan

712-755-5951

The Harlan Country Club was originally built around 1910 and expanded and remodeled in 1982. The course is known for its big trees and rolling layout. A small stream runs the width of the course affecting drives on four holes. There is no sand, but the rough is cut at 2 inches on most of the holes. The size of the trees is large with many lining the fairways and located behind the greens. The greens are of average size and many are elevated with flat putting surfaces. There are also two very plush practice putting greens that are large and flat. The grass condition is good throughout the course thanks to the fairway watering system. The Harlan Golf and Country Club is a fairly long course to play but must still be considered a driver and wedge course. The clubhouse is nice with an expansive bar area. The club pro also has a full line of golf equipment including clubs and lessons. One claim to fame of this course is that Sam Snead played here in an exhibition. The Harlan Course has 250 members who pay an annual fee of $660. This is a private club, so playing with a member, except on league days, is reasonable. This is a pleasurable course located on the south edge of town.

Course	9 Holes
Distance	3232 Yards
Par	36
Playability	Fair
Aesthetics	Excell.
Interest	Good
Worth The Trip	Yes
Rating	★★★+

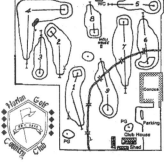

BLUE TEES	394	389	378	569	157	449	502	195	394	3471
WHITE TEES	353	375	361	531	149	424	485	187	367	3232
MEN'S HANDICAP	7	13	17	5	15	1	9	11	3	
MEN'S PAR	4	4	4	5	3	4	5	3	4	36
LADIES' PAR	4	4	4	5	3	5	5	3	4	37
RED TEES	296	365	347	413	139	470	478	159	295	2960
+/-										
HOLES	1	2	3	4	5	6	7	8	9	OUT

Rosman Glendale Farm Golf Course

Harlan

712-627-4224

The Rosman Glendale Farm Golf Course was built under unusual circumstances in 1979. As with many golf courses in Iowa, the land used to be productive farmland. Two brothers and a sister, Clara, Alvin, and Alfred Rosman, donated this farm for the purpose of building a golf course. The course is located five miles north of Harlan on old Highway 59. The contour of the land typifies valley land near a stream: flat. The course in general is still growing; trees are small and scattered throughout the course, 100 additional trees were planted in 2003. The grass condition is spotty in some places but has improved each year, and the character of the course has yet to come to the surface. The Rosman course is wide open with little rough or hazards to affect errant shots. A new lake was built on number 8 in 2001. They have also added a new fairway watering system. This is a fairly easy course to walk, although they do have carts, and an easy course to score well on, with some short par fours. The greens have been built large with flat putting surfaces. The clubhouse does have a bar and grill and a few supplies, mostly limited to balls and gloves. The 340 members pay a yearly fee of $330 for a family while green fees on this public course are very reasonable. This is a growing course that provides a nice golf course for local people who need the recreation, thanks to the Rosmans.

Course	9 Holes
Distance	3109 Yards
Par	35
Playability	Fair
Aesthetics	Fair
Interest	Fair
Worth The Trip	Yes
Rating	★★+

MEN'S TEES BLUE	401	140	280	270	380	375	558	490	215	3109
HANDICAP	1	7	8	9	3	4	5	6	2	
MEN'S PAR	4	3	4	4	4	4	5	5	3	36
LADIES TEES @ FT	301	140	280	270	265	315	497	325	218	2955
HANDICAP	1	4	6	7	8	5	3	2	9	
LADIES' PAR	5	3	4	4	4	4	5	4	4	37
HOLE	1	2	3	4	5	6	7	8	9	OUT

Meadowbrook Golf and Country Club

Hartley

712-728-2060

If you haven't played Meadowbrook Country Club in the last three years now may be a good time to discover the improved conditions on this course. This course is located three miles south of Hartley and has developed into a challenging layout. Foremost on the list of improvements are the greens. They are small in size with a little tilt and roll to them. They hold a shot much better than most small greens and are in very good condition. The entire shape of the course has taken on a greener more interesting look. A river that cuts the corner of the course comes into play on 6 holes, making pitch and run impossible on three holes. There is only one sand bunker and the fairway rough is fair and easy to contend with. Trees of all sizes are scattered throughout the course and are maturing into contention. But there is a great amount of wild flowers and natural areas scattered throughout the course. The contour of the course is generally flat but this is a deceiving course, the 3408 yards make it one of the longer 9 hole courses in the area. The clubhouse has a limited supply of golfing items, but they do have carts for rent. Members are enjoying a born again course, something they can enjoy and be proud of. This is a beautiful course with a lot of character. Green fees are average in price. Try this course, I think you'll like it, but first work on getting your driver and nine iron up in the air, otherwise it will be a wet day for you.

Course	9 Holes
Distance	3408 Yards
Par	37
Playability	Good
Aesthetics	Good
Interest	Good
Worth The Trip	Yes
Rating	★★+

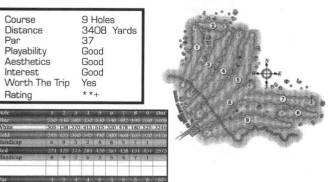

Hole	1	2	3	4	5	6	7	8	9	Out
Blue	350	146	388	150	510	340	492	125	350	5408
White	305	138	370	415	515	320	478	180	525	3246
Gold	295	126	300	395	490	300	408	165	320	3120
Handicap	6	9	3		2	4		7	1	
Red	221	125	275	281	420	265	428	151	431	2575
Handicap	8	9	2	6	3	5	4	7	1	
Par	4	3	4	4	5	4	5	3	4	37

Hawarden Golf Club

Hawarden

712-551-4444

Many courses in Iowa can be recognized by their poplar trees lining the fairways. The Hawarden Golf Club has the poplars, but in a shorter version, all their tops are cut off. There are many poplars that line the fairways, but pose little threat because you can fly over the top. This layout has a limited amount of hazard situations, the tree lined fairways, two bunkers, and a very nice bar area that might keep you entertained all afternoon. The contour of the course is flat with small valleys to keep your interest. Tees are medium in size and well maintained, the greens are also medium in size but are tilted and have a rolling putting surface, gently rolling. This is a simple course that strives to maintain a golfing atmosphere. The novice golfer would have a good experience on this course. Shoot the ball straight and you score great, push or pull a little and you still score good. The new clubhouse is very nice, a big open dining area and restaurant provide golfers and others with sandwiches and meals. Weekday green fees are reasonable for a course this size. This is a revitalized course, originally built in 1925. Hawarden is a course that lets you enjoy the game without the added pressure of thinking!

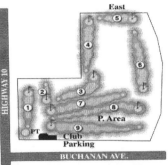

Course	9 Holes
Distance	2800 Yards
Par	35
Playability	Fair
Aesthetics	Fair
Interest	Fair
Worth The Trip	Yes
Rating	★★

HOLE	1	2	3	4	5	6	7	8	9	OUT
Men's Yardage–BLUE	358	178	318	357	133	510	307	310	329	2800
Women's Yardage–RED	257	168	298	238	123	426	297	300	240	2347
PAR	4	3	4	4	3	5	4	4	4	35

Deer Run

Hinton

712-947-GOLF

Deer Run was built in 1995 and is located south of Hinton off Hwy. 75. This is a city owned course that took advantage of rolling farmland close to town. The layout runs to the west and is basically an east west open course. The greens are generally flat but do have hidden breaks. The greens are medium in size and oval in shape. Several additional sand bunkers were added in 2002 but none really affect play. There is a creek that runs through the course coming into play on 2 holes and a small pond coming into play on 4 green. There are lots of old trees around the perimeter with several hundred new trees planted in 2002. One of the most unique features of the course is the island green, well almost, at number 4. The course is generally rolling and follows the creek valley that runs down the middle. Number 2 fairway was crowned, making the approach shot blind. Also there is a tree right in front of the tee at number 8. There are 300 members at Deer Run paying $390 for a family membership. Weekday green fees are $10.25. There were 30,000 rounds played in 2002. This is a nice course that has some unique holes and some unique shots. A very nice addition to western Iowa.

Course	9 Holes
Distance	3317 Yards
Par	36
Playability	Good
Aesthetics	Excellent
Interest	Good
Worth The Trip	Yes
Rating	★★★

HOLE		1	2	3	4	5	6	7	8	9	TOTAL
BLUE	yds	392	365	146	535	187	400	520	425	357	3317
WHITE	yds	387	345	137	525	178	390	510	415	350	3237
RED	yds	285	335	123	402	150	310	460	340	307	2712
PAR		4	4	3	5	3	4	5	4	4	36
HDCP		5	7	9	2	3	6	4	1	8	

Holstein Country Club

Holstein

712-368-2530

The Holstein Country Club has one of the strongest women's organizations is the area. The course is located on the east edge of Holstein and is built on semi-rolling country side. There is one pond on the course that comes into play on number four and three, a stream also comes into play on number nine. The course is beautifully landscaped, especially around the clubhouse and the pond area. Medium size trees are scattered throughout the course and do come into play on a few holes, they always come into play when you play your ball from the rough. The undulating greens are big and offer some innovating putts. The course was built in 1969 and is still in the growing stages. The bluegrass fairways are some of the best in the area and offer excellent iron hitting areas. The 165 members enjoy a clubhouse that offers a full line of equipment along with sandwiches and a bar area. The clubhouse was remodeled in 2000. Weekday green fees are reasonable, for all day. This is a fairly easy course that is a pleasure to play. It offers good golfing conditions, fair prices and a friendly atmosphere. The landscaping of the course is the selling point now but in a few years the entire course will sell itself.

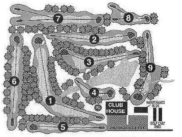

Course	9 Holes
Distance	3137 Yards
Par	35
Playability	Good
Aesthetics	Excell.
Interest	Good
Worth The Trip	Yes
Rating	★★★+

HOLE	RATING/SLOPE	1	2	3	4	5	6	7	8	9	Out
Blue	70.0/124	527	368	366	160	356	391	435	189	345	3137
White	67.4/118	507	352	354	140	346	375	333	150	300	2857
Blue/White Handicap		9/6	8/4	4/3	6/5	5/2	7/1	1/7	2/9	3/8	
Red	70.0/119	485	340	352	113	329	342	300	140	260	2661
Handicap		1	5	2	8	4	3	6	9	7	
Par		5	4	4	3	4	4	4	3	4	35

Hubbard Recreation Club

Hubbard

641-864-2647

The Hubbard Recreation Club is located on the S.E. corner of Hubbard on D55. It was a farm field before the completion of the golf course in 1962. Today the contour of the course is gently rolling, a slight change from some of the flat courses in the area. There is one pond on the course that comes into play on three holes and provides a very scenic backdrop for the clubhouse. A pond was added to hole 5 with the only other hazard a sand bunker on number 4. The trees are scattered throughout the course and additional trees are being added each year. The layout of the course is wide open with very little rough lining the fairways. The flat greens are small to medium in size but have a nice putting surface. The clubhouse sits on top of a hill on the west side of the course overlooking the pond and the rest of the course. The clubhouse has a full line of equipment plus carts for rent. There is a full kitchen for special events but normal food items are just snacks and drinks. Daily green fees are reasonable for a course this size; the 140 members pay an annual fee of $300. This is a well-kept central Iowa course that is enjoyable to walk, easy to play and a good place to enjoy some of the natural beauty of Iowa.

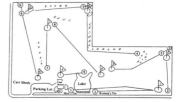

Course	9 Holes
Distance	2857 Yards
Par	35
Playability	Fair
Aesthetics	Good
Interest	Good
Worth The Trip	Yes
Rating	★★+

HOLE	1	2	3	4	5	6	7	8	9	Out
Yardage	520	182	347	396	336	352	197	358	169	2857
HANDICAP	4	6	8	9	5	3	1	2	7	
PAR	5	3	4	5	4	4	3	4	3	35
WOMEN'S PAR	5	3	4	5	4	4	4	5	3	37
Yardage	372	173	299	376	295	300	191	351	158	2515
HANDICAP	9	1	5	7	3	4	6	8	2	

Rolling Hills Country Club

Hull

712-439-2310

There was a need for a golf club in the Hull area so in 1989 the Rolling Hills Country Club was established 2 miles north of Hull on K52. This is a member owned club that came together to create recreation for the people of Hull and surrounding areas. The 250 members pay an annual family fee of $390. The contour of the course is gently rolling with the wide fairways lined with trees. There is a creek that runs through the course and effects play on 5 holes. People remarked about the size of the trees and the numbers, the softness of the greens and the unusual number 9 fairway, which is split by the creek. This is a nice course that is still young. The clubhouse serves the usual sandwiches and sells a limited supply of balls. Another example of a great Iowa course that meets the needs of local golfers.

Course	9 Holes
Distance	3325 Yards
Par	36
Playability	Good
Aesthetics	Good
Interest	Good
Worth The Trip	Yes
Rating	★★+

	HOLE	1	2	3	4	5	6	7	8	9	OUT
CHAMPIONSHIP	BLUE TEE	377	537	197	357	434	346	529	155	393	3325
MEN'S	WHITE TEE	359	485	181	337	415	328	466	145	379	3095
LADIES	RED TEE	322	431	164	322	391	301	407	133	364	2835
	PAR	4	5	3	4	4	4	5	3	4	36
	HANDICAP	15	7	11	9	1	5	13	17	3	

Deer Creek Golf Club

Humboldt

515-546-6312

Deer Creek Golf Club is a nine-hole facility on 102 acres. It opened July 18, 1992 as a public golf course and remains as such having one evening league and a limited number of outings and tournaments. The Iowa Golf Association selected Deer Creek the 1994 9-Hole Course of the Year. Back in 1973 a dairy farm was purchased by Conrad Clark. Even at the time he purchased this pasture land he felt that somewhere hidden among the hills, pond, and stream was a golf course. This 9 hole regulation course is located 6 miles north and 1/2 mile west of the Starlite Motel on the N.W. corner of Fort Dodge, or 1 mile south and 1/2 mile west of the egg plant on Highway 169. The course is laid out with a beautiful creek, which runs through and is in play on five of nine holes. Deer Creek has bent grass fairways and greens. Automatic, state of the art, watering will keep the grass condition good throughout the summer. The course spreads over 3126 yards with the general contour of the course being flat, although getting back up to the clubhouse should get the heart pumping. Greens are medium in size and boast undulating and tilted surfaces. Only one or two trees were moved as the course developed and many more have been planted. Because of the trees and their position, tee shots will be driven down narrow flyways. The clubhouse is built on top of the ridge overlooking the course.

Course	9 Holes
Distance	3126 Yards
Par	36
Playability	Good
Aesthetics	Very Good
Interest	Good
Worth the Trip	Yes
Rating	★★★

DEER CREEK
GOLF CLUB

HOLE	1	2	3	4	5	6	7	8	9	OUT	HCP	NET
BLUE TEES	339	328	314	503	200	457	157	438	390	3126		
WHITE TEES	329	318	314	490	159	439	133	369	382	2933		
RED TEES	251	264	256	413	150	385	126	329	339	2513		
PAR	4	4	4	5	3	5	3	4	4	36		
HANDICAP	5	6	7	2	4	8	9	1	3			

Humboldt Country Club

Humboldt

515-332-3364

The Humboldt Country Club has the Bermuda Triangle of north central Iowa. Holes five, six, and seven go through, over, around, under, and sometimes into a triangle shaped grove of large trees that are very threatening, no matter how many times you play the course. Humboldt is a very golf oriented club; 300 members play the daylights out of this course that was built in 1923. The course is flat with narrow fairways and a medium rough. There are no water hazards although the river can be heard running down the south side of the course. The greens are medium in size, flat and guarded by 10 bunkers. Two new greens and two new bunkers were built in 1998. The triangle has large trees but the remainder of the course has smaller trees lining the fairways, usually not coming into play. For five or six holes this is a free swinging, open course, but the middle holes cut down on your backswing drastically. This is a course blessed with fairway watering, which explains the good condition all summer long. The clubhouse has a nice bar area that serves sandwiches and a pro shop that has a full line of equipment, plus carts for rent. The course is located one mile west on Highway 4. Humboldt has a yearly family membership fee of $370 while green fees are reasonable, even less when you are a guest of a member. Humboldt is an easy course to walk, fairly easy to score on if you keep the ball in play around the woods and a has a "play till you drop" atmosphere. A fun place to experience, if you like the game, and who doesn't.

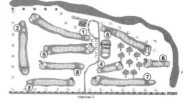

Course	9 Holes
Distance	3036 Yards
Par	36
Playability	Fair
Aesthetics	Very Good
Interest	Good
Worth The Trip	Yes
Rating	★★★+

HOLE NUMBER	1	2	3	4	5	6	7	8	9	OUT
BLUE TEES YARDAGE	454	387	353	168	388	135	475	316	360	3036
HANDICAP	5	2	6	9	1	8	3	7	4	
RED TEES YARDAGE	445	333	343	161	315	130	455	304	355	2841
HANDICAP	1	5	6	9	4	8	2	7	3	
2										
POINTS										
PAR	5	4	4	3	4	3	5	4	4	36

Humeston Golf Club

Humeston

No Phone

Humeston Golf Club, located two miles north of Humeston, is a public course built in 1966 and is surrounded on three sides by a lake. The lake or tributaries to it come into play on all but two holes. There are no bunkers and the rough is only evident along the shoreline. There are an average number of trees on the course, mostly small to medium in height. The fairway grass is in good shape and offers a nice hitting surface. The length of the course is not too long, 2660 yards, but the quality of care is high. The greens are tiny and very flat but extremely easy to hold! The course relies on a great deal of volunteer labor from his 90 members to keep the layout in top condition. These members pay only $120 a year for the privilege to play. Green fees are $10.00 anytime you want to come out; they are rarely busy. This is a fairly flat course that is picturesque, easy to walk, and easy to score well on. This is built as a "poor man's course" but there is nothing poor about the condition of the course. There is one unique feature about this course: it is one of only three in Iowa that have sand greens. The manager said they rarely have to be mowed, that's what he likes best about his job. There is no clubhouse but a down-home relaxed feeling still prevails on the course.

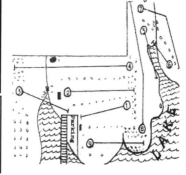

Course	9 Sand
Distance	2660 Yards
Par	35
Playability	Fair
Aesthetics	Good
Interest	Good
Worth The Trip	Yes
Rating	★★★+

Hole	Yards	Par	Handicap	Win-Lo-No	REPLACE TURF
1	308	4	8		North Star
2	365	4	3		Jupiter
3	167	3	5		Telstar
4	512	5	1		Big Dipper
5	186	3	4		Neptune
6	115	3	9		Little Dipper
7	269	4	6		Sputnick
8	452	5	2		Mars
9	290	4	7		Earth
Out	2660	35			Rating 32

Ballard Golf and Country Club

Huxley

515-597-2266

The Ballard Country Club is one of the youngest courses in central Iowa and seems to be destined for a bright future. The course is located two miles north of Huxley on Highway 69. What most people remember about this course is number 9 fairway that runs along the highway and consists of a very steep hill. But there are many more things that make this a nice golf course. There are 14 bunkers on the course and one pond. The trees are of medium to large in size and are stationed along the wide fairways. The flat fairways are also lined with rough at 3 inches. The tee boxes are landscaped nicely and in good condition, with many of them elevated. There are now 4 sets of tees with gold tee boxes added recently. The greens are medium to big in size with generally flat putting surfaces. In their short golfing history the Ballard Club has been noted for fast greens. The course was built in 1975. In 2000 a new pond was added affecting 3 holes, new grass mounds were built in several places, and 8 new bunkers were added. A new clubhouse was built recently and provides snacks and drinks to golfers throughout the day. There is a full restaurant that is open to the public at noon and members and guests in the evenings. This is a well maintained course the 300 members enjoy thoroughly.

Course	9 Holes
Distance	3228 Yards
Par	35
Playability	Good
Aesthetics	Good
Interest	Fair
Worth The Trip	Yes
Rating	★★

HOLE	1	2	3	4	5	6	7	8	9	OUT
PAR	5	4	5	3	4	4	3	4	4	36
HANDICAP	13	1	3	5	7	9	17	15	11	
WHITE	507	355	457	162	378	384	136	338	375	3092
BLUE	515	368	480	188	383	389	150	340	415	3228
GOLD	430	337	413	152	366	324	130	328	360	2840
PAR	5	3	5	3	4	4	3	4	4	35
HANDICAP	7	5	13	15	11	3	17	1	9	
RED	430	170	400	143	290	319	122	323	297	2494

Ida Grove Country Club

Ida Grove

712-364-2320

The Ida Grove Country Club located on the east side of Ida Grove is one of novelty landscaped courses in the state. Byron Godbersen designed the club and in it he has carried out a theme of castles. Over the creek he built a large drawbridge with towers; there is a lookout tower greeting the golfers on the highway; the clubhouse has castle decorations; Ida Grove is a very interesting and unique place to play golf. The course was built in 1971 and the clubhouse is a modern, spacious structure that contains a full line of equipment, a very nice bar area and elegant dining facilities. There are two ponds, one stream, and five bunkers on the course. The trees are small and scattered along the fairways and in the rough. The fairways are wide, open, flat and the grass is in excellent condition all summer thanks to the fairway watering system. Tees are large and elevated and lead to greens that are medium in size and flat. Green fees are reasonable for a course this size. This is a beautiful course to play, streams, bridges, towers, two windmills and good grass condition everywhere. The course is a little deceiving to play, though; the length may get you, or the hazards that lay in wait. Whatever the case, this is a course of interest, a course that was the vision of one man for his community.

Course	9 Holes
Distance	3004 Yards
Par	36
Playability	Good
Aesthetics	Very Good
Interest	Very Good
Worth The Trip	Yes
Rating	★★★

	HOLE	1	2	3	4	5	6	7	8	9	OUT
LADIES MEN	YARDAGE	355	309	298 / 309	407	189	357 / 375	102 / 344	413 / 469	318 / 393	2748 / 3150
LADIES MEN	HANDICAP	1 / 5	7 / 9	6 / 7	4 / 1	2 / 2	3 / 4	9 / 6	5 / 8	8 / 3	
LADIES MEN	PAR	4	4	4	5 / 4	3	4	3 / 4	5	4	36

Three Elms Club Course

Independence

319-334-4235

Three Elms was built in 1999 and is located 1/2 mile east of the baseball complex in Indepedence. The course was built on farm land and has developed into a gently rolling course. Greens are bent grass with several different sizes and shapes. The only consistent feature is the undulation of the greens and their difficulty to read and putt. There are 18 sand bunkers on the course, some in the fairways. There are also grass bunkers in landing areas. All the tree on the course have been planted and so have not matured yet. A unique feature of the course is the covered bridge between number 1 and 2, the big mounds in front of greens, especially on number 9 green. The rough is tough yet fair. There is one large pond on numbers 6 & 7, plus an overflow creek on 3 other holes. The grass condition of the course is very good. The course needs some maturity to raise to the next level of play. But the interest or the course is good with all the grass mounds and difficult greens. Three Elms has a very nice brick clubhouse that has drinks and snacks. Green fees are $10 for weekdays. Three Elms is a great course for the Independence area.

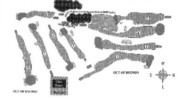

Course	9 Holes
Distance	2980 Yards
Par	35
Playability	Good
Aesthetics	Good
Interest	Very Good
Worth The Trip	Yes
Rating	★★★

Course Rating/Slope
Blue Tees - 67.2/119
White Tees - 66.2/118

HOLE	1	2	3	4	5	6	7	8	9	Out
Blue	424	370	190	297	330	501	310	179	379	2980
White	386	345	175	270	305	472	291	156	339	2739
Red	369	320	175	249	270	425	271	156	311	2546
PAR	4	4	3	4	4	5	4	3	4	35
HANDICAP	1	5	7	17	11	9	15	13	3	

Wapsipinicon Golf Club

Independence

319-334-6576

One of the toughest opening holes in N.E. Iowa is on Wapsipinicon Country Club. This 580 yard dogleg down a narrow corridor of trees may ruin many a round before they get started. The course is located two miles north of Independence on Golf Course Road. This is a private course with 150 members paying a $550 family fee. Supplies in the clubhouse are limited with a limited number of carts for rent. A full restaurant and bar are now operating out of the clubhouse. Wapsipinicon, established in 1909, is noted for its narrow fairways. This is a compact course that relies on its tree lined fairways to keep each hole separate. There is one pond on the course, five sand bunkers; with a few of the traps wrapping around one side of the green creating a major obstacle. The trees lining the fairways are full grown with new plantings filling in the gaps. The contour of the course is flat with fairways being outlined with rough, the rough is also cut in front of greens and tees. Greens are medium in size and have a varied putting surface of rolling and tilted. This is an easy course to walk but a hard course to score well on; especially if you tend to wonder out of the fairway. You have to be accurate on every shot or pay for it. If the trees don't get you the long rough will. One nice element of the area that doesn't affect the course is that the Wapsi River runs on the north side of the course, supplying some beautiful scenery. Green fees for guests are very reasonable. This is an interesting and challenging course to play; and not real busy.

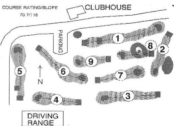

Course	9 Holes
Distance	3187 Yards
Par	36
Playability	Good
Aesthetics	Good
Interest	Good
Worth The Trip	Yes
Rating	★★★

COURSE RATING/SLOPE
70.7/116

HOLE	1	2	3	4	5	6	7	8	9	OUT
BLUE	580	190	450	314	288	408	438	198	328	3187
WHITE	560	160	438	284	270	388	420	185	315	3020
PAR	5	3	4	4	4	4	4	3	4	36
HANDICAP	7	9	13	15	17	1	5	3	11	
RED										37
PAR	5	3	5	4	4	4	5	3	4	37
HANDICAP	3	13	5	17	15	1	7	9	11	

128

Deer Run Golf Club

Indianola

515-961-5445

Deer Run golf Club offers reasonable rate daily fee play on its par 72, 6632 year course covering 200 plus acres. The scenic course includes a 16 acre lake that provides water play on the front 9, which was opened in 2001. The back 9 was built in 2000 and is a more tranquil setting. All holes are irrigated from their four tee boxes to green. The greens are undulating, medium in size and over bent grass on the landing surface. Many of the greens have grass bunkers protecting the landing area. The elevation from one hole to another provides scenic views of the course and surrounding countryside. The layout of the course has been woven into the hilly surroundings. While playing you will encounter a lot of side hill lies. This is a tough course because of the elevation change and the hilly conditions. The fairway grass is good, but again the hills come into play. A housing project now covers some of the course and divides the holes so you play one or two holes at a time. I would certainly recommend this course for fun and challenging play. The course has a range and a clubhouse with supplies. Green fees are $20 for 18 holes during the week. A weekday season pass is $520.

Course	18 Holes	Aesthetics	Good
Distance	6632 Yards	Interest	Good
Par	36-36-72	Worth The Trip	Yes
Playability	Good	Rating	***

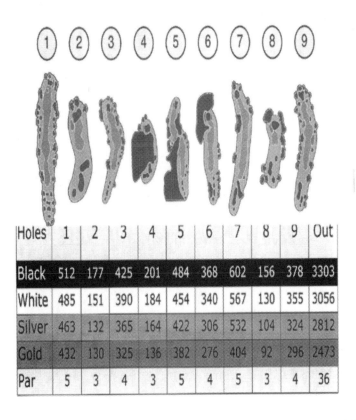

Holes	1	2	3	4	5	6	7	8	9	Out
Black	512	177	425	201	484	368	602	156	378	3303
White	485	151	390	184	454	340	567	130	355	3056
Silver	463	132	365	164	422	306	532	104	324	2812
Gold	432	130	325	136	382	276	404	92	296	2473
Par	5	3	4	3	5	4	5	3	4	36

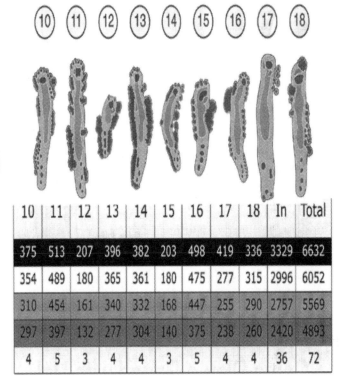

10	11	12	13	14	15	16	17	18	In	Total
375	513	207	396	382	203	498	419	336	3329	6632
354	489	180	365	361	180	475	277	315	2996	6052
310	454	161	340	332	168	447	255	290	2757	5569
297	397	132	277	304	140	375	238	260	2420	4893
4	5	3	4	4	3	5	4	4	36	72

Indianola Country Club

Indianola

515-961-2790

Indianola Country Club has one of the longest opening holes in the state. The 571 yard, par 5 hole is straight to the north but dips down over two creeks and cuts between some big trees, what a way to start a round. The contour of the entire course is rolling to hilly with tree lined fairways and two inch rough. The trees are medium to big and are the heaviest down along the two creek valleys. Small new pines have been added over the past two years. There is also two ponds that you must drive over on number 7 and 3. The course was built in 1920 and has a fairway watering system that is needed on the dry hillsides. Greens are medium in size and flat, much to the relief of someone coming off a hillside approach. The clubhouse bar and grill are located on the lower level, on the north side of the clubhouse.   It is a hard course to walk and a hard course to score well on. This is a challenging course, considered more of a placement course, and a course where you need to keep your mind on the game or be lost forever. The layout of the course is a little scrambled and it gives you an opportunity to do something other than walk out and back, out and back, it gives you a chance to do some bird watching in the woods. This hilly course is located on Country Club Road on the north side of Indianola. There is talk of adding a new 9 holes.

Course	9 Holes
Distance	3222Yards
Par	35
Playability	Good
Aesthetics	Good
Interest	Very Good
Worth The Trip	Yes
Rating	***

Hole	1	2	3	4	5	6	7	8	9	Out	Init
Blue 69.8/120	607	329	363	564	356	348	120	330	205	3222	
White 67.8/116	570	313	350	521	350	321	113	330	178	3046	
Gold	570	229	284	502	335	311	113	315	170	2829	
Par	5	4	4	5	4	4	3	4	3	36	
Red 68/112	374	210	252	432	254	297	105	272	114	2310	
Par	4	4	4	5	4	4	3	4	3	35	
Handicap	1	7	5	3	9	11	17	13	15		

Raleigh Hills

Ionia

641-394-3256

 Raleigh Hills was established in 1993 near Iona. This is a modern day Iowa course that was built on farmland close to town. In the early 1960's dozens of courses were built in Iowa with the same concept. Flat farmland was bought close to town and a golf course was built. Raleigh Hills is built on slight rolling land using some existing trees to emphasize some holes. One area has 30 acres of woods and wildlife They have planted a significant number of other trees throughout the course. The greens are medium to large in size. These are challenging greens in part to the undulation and difficulty in reading. Sand comes into play about once per hole. Four ponds and a creek and affect 4 holes.   People love to play this course. The course has the reputation of being a gently rolling course. There are lots of grassy knobs on the course, the greens are humped in the middle making them a challenge, and people say that there are no flat places on the course. Although nothing is severe there is always a hint of slope. There is a big clubhouse with meals and supplies. The 110 members pay a yearly fee of $472. Weekday green fees are $12. A nice small town course that provides a high level of playability for local golfers.

Course	9 Holes
Distance	2997 Yards
Par	36
Playability	Good
Aesthetics	Good
Interest	Good
Worth The Trip	Yes
Rating	***+

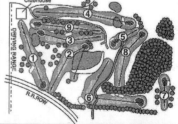

HOLE	1	2	3	4	5	6	7	8	9	Out
RED TEES	306	238	283	383	127	457	109	238	300	2441
WHITE TEES	320	307	313	470	131	527	129	303	329	2829
BLUE TEES	334	335	332	517	138	536	138	319	348	2997
PAR	4	4	4	5	3	5	3	4	4	36

Elks Country Club

Iowa City

319-351-3700

When you finish hitting the long ball on Finkbine you can tee it up at the Elks Country Club and work on your short game, especially the wedge shots. This is a private course with guest privileges, that has a membership size of 275 and requires Elk membership to join. Yearly family fees are $750 with a single member paying $525. The course is a little hard to find, tucked back into the hills on the west side of Iowa City at 637 Foster Ave. The clubhouse has a bar and grill and the dining room is open for special events. There is a limited amount of supplies and there are carts for rent. The general contour of the course is hilly; some say there isn't a flat spot on the course. It originally was cut out of the woods in 1915, so there are lots of big old trees lining the wide fairways. There is a very nice tiered cut of rough that makes the fairways much narrower than they look. The course layout was changed in 1998 with 2 totally new holes, 3 and 4. This is a hard course to walk but if you can handle your short game it is an easy course to score well on. So bring some confidence in your wedge and you will have a good time. If not, blame it on that darn rough.

Course	9 Holes
Distance	3140 Yards
Par	35
Playability	Poor
Aesthetics	Very Good
Interest	Good
Worth The Trip	Yes
Rating	★★

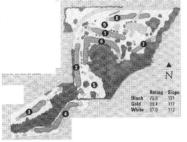

HOLE	1	2	3	4	5	6	7	8	9	OUT
BLACK TEES	300	475	385	575	150	475	255	330	195	3140
GOLD TEES	294	465	345	535	135	469	240	325	156	2964
MENS PAR	4	5	4	5	3	5	4	4	3	37
LADIES PAR	4	5	4	5	3	5	4	4	4	38
WHITE TEES	285	460	275	435	85	459	225	315	189	2728
HANDICAP	13	5	7	1	17	3	15	9	11	

Fairview Golf Course

Iowa City

319-351-9454

Fairview Golf Course, located on Muscatine Ave, is easy to play and has nice people to play with. This is definitely a placement and second shot course. If you don't leave the ball where you are supposed to, the game can become disheartening. This gently rolling course is easy to walk, but they do have carts for rent. There are three bunkers and one pond to hinder your game plan. There are two types of trees: the very young and small and the very old and large. The trees are scattered leaving the fairways wide and yielding to stray shots. The medium to large greens hold fairly well, considering that they are crowned and tilted. Several of the greens were redone in the late 90's. The course was built in 1931. A normal day has about 150 rounds with Tuesday a very busy Senior day. The clubhouse has just been remodeled and carries an ample amount of golfing supplies. The bar area has drinks and grilled sandwiches. You may be fooled by the looks of this course, it seems short, flat, and easy, but beware; more than one player has paid his $5 and come away shaking his head. The 175 members pay an annual fee of $465 for a family and $420 for a single. Weekday green fees are $10 for 9 holes. Fairview has an easy atmosphere that encourages relaxed and fun play.

Course	9 Holes
Distance	2862 Yards
Par	34
Playability	Fair
Aesthetics	Poor
Interest	Fair
Worth The Trip	Maybe
Rating	★+

Fairview Golf Course

Muscatine Avenue · Iowa City, Iowa · 351-9454

HOLE	1	2	3	4	5	6	7	8	9	IN	TOTAL
WHITE TEES	345	145	320	330	325	202	375	420/475	345	2807/2862	5614/5724
MEN'S PAR	4	3	4	4	4	4	4	4/5	4	34/35	68/70
LADIES PAR	4	3	4	4	4	3	4	5	4	35	70
RED TEES	330	138	271	315	300	180	360	400/450	315	2609/2659	5218/5318
HANDICAP	3	7	6	4	2	9	1	8	5		

131

Finkbine

Iowa City

319-335-9246

www.finkbine.com

Finkbine Field Golf Course is undoubtedly one of the best courses in the state of Iowa. It is rich in tradition, it has many of the elements found in great courses, and it is maintained by some of the most caring people around. This public course is not extremely long — 7017 yards — but is designed to challenge any golfer, even the pros. Finkbine is the home of the Ben Hogan Hawkeye Open. The course has a character all of its own, but its most outstanding feature is its landscaping and superb condition. The only pond is on number 13, a spectacular shot over the water. There is an average of three sand bunkers per hole and some ground bunkers in the fairways. The bunkers were recently changed with some expanded and some eliminated. The many trees that outline the fairways are medium to large in size. The fairways are narrow with the general contour of the course flat. Fairway rough is tiered on the sides and is cut 50 yards in front of tee and greens. The tee boxes are elevated, tiered, and plush with grass quality equal to many of the greens on other Iowa courses. The greens are generally rolling with a little tilt and medium in size. The greens were reconfigured in 1999. The pro shop handles a full line of supplies including clubs and clothes. The clubhouse also has a full line of sandwiches and drinks and a nice area to sit and view number one tee and number 18 green, which is difficult finishing hole. Finkbine also serves as the home course for the University of Iowa. There are 100 members of this course who pay a yearly fee of $1250, but green fees are a majority of the business, which is very heavy all the time. Daily green fees are a l$30 for weekdays and $37 on the weekends. The course can be found on Melrose Ave. on the west side of Iowa City. If you have an ambition to play the top courses in the state, then Finkbine Field Course would be one that you should not miss. Finkbine has been one of the best courses in the state for many years.

Course	18 Holes	Aesthetics	Excellent
Distance	7017 Yards	Interest	Very Good
Par	36-36-72	Worth The Trip	Yes
Playability	Excellent	Rating	★★★★+

Rating/Slope	Hole	1	2	3	4	5	6	7	8	9	Out
Black 74.1/134	Black	415	537	394	201/177	368	524	382	207	449	3477
Gold 72.1/131	Gold	401	511	368	163	350	504	368	185	414	3264
White 66.0/118	White	382	482	345	150	329	484	352	173	327	3024
	Hcp (M)	7	1	9	17	15	3	13	11	5	
	Hcp (W)	1	9	3	13	17	5	11	7	15	
Red 69.5/119	Red	341	406	337	137	275	399	295	129	322	2641
USGA rules govern play	Par	4	5	4	3	4	5	4	3	4	36

10	11	12	13	14	15	16	17	18	In	Tot	Hcp	Net
449	562	389	182/199	413	486	398	179/195	449	3540	7017		
420	530	357	160/177	397	462	369	158	426	3296	6560		
331	420	285	102/118	310	446	305	148	406	2769	5793		
12	2	8	14	4	16	10	18	6				
16	8	2	10	14	6	4	12	18				
328	412	277	89/102	303	409	291	114	288	2522	5163		
4	5	4	3	4	5	4	3	4	36	72		

Robert Bruce Harris
Richard Nugent
Course Architects

restrooms

Club House

Driving Range

Tee Times: (319) 335-9246
www.finkbine.com

Finkbine
UNIVERSITY OF IOWA
Home of the AEGON Advantage

132

Hi-Point

Iowa City

319-351-9434

High Point Golf Course in Iowa City added an additional 9 holes in 1999. This public course is located on Rochester Ave. east of Iowa City and has a countryside feeling. The clubhouse was built in 1964 and has a kitchen atmosphere inside: a counter, some tables, a screened-in porch, all creating a homey feeling. Green fees are $15 for 18. This is a nice relaxing course that is used a great deal late in the afternoon and early evening. There are a medium amount of trees, all about the same height, 30 feet, generally scattered. Many new trees have been added especially on the new 9 holes. The fairways are wide and the contour of the front 9 is flat. The back nine slopes down to the west and plays over a rolling surface. There are no sand bunkers and no rough to entangle yourself in. The front 9 greens are small and flat and are true to the read, mostly straight putts. The new back nine holes have larger greens and are harder to read and putt. Spraying the ball is no problem at Hi-Point; you can play just as well from the adjoining fairway. This is a popular course and maintains a steady flow of golfers. The course is popular because it is fairly short, easy and quick to walk, easy to score well on, and maintains a low pressure atmosphere. This was a nice addition to the Iowa City golfing community. It has a nice atmosphere and a hometown feeling.

Hole	1	2	3	4	5	6	7	8	9	Out
Handicap	8	1	2	14	12	4	3	17	11	
White Tees	334	361	325	283	132	292	360	221	138	2512
Red Tees	314	331	295	—	120	215	280	—	—	2227
Par	4	4	4	4	3	4	4	4	3	34

10	11	12	13	14	15	16	17	18	In	Tot	Hcp	Net
5	15	6	9	16	13	10	18	7				
356	286	340	314	270	480	279	249	158	2732	5244		
290	235	320	285	235	440	259	239	—	2471	4698		
4	4	4	4	4	5	4	4	3	36	70		

Course	18 Holes	Aesthetics	Fair
Distance	5244 Yards	Interest	Good
Par	34-36-70	Worth The Trip	Yes
Playability	Fair	Rating	**

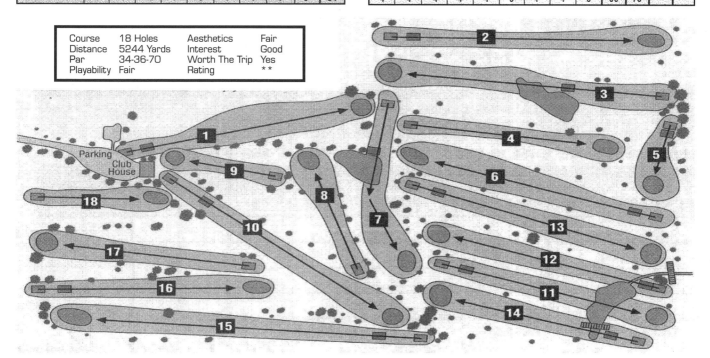

Pleasant Valley

Iowa City

319-337-2622
www.pleasantvalley-ic.com

Pleasant Valley is an eighteen hole public course that opened late in the summer of 1987. The course is located two miles south of Highway 6 on Sand Road in Iowa City. Pleasant Valley was voted the Best Golf Course in the Iowa City Area in 2002. This is an eighteen hole course that was conceived as an alternative to the other courses in Iowa City, especially Finkbine. Pleasant Valley was designed as a short and much tighter course than anything else found in the area. There are ten acres of water on the course in the form of one stream and three ponds built off this stream. The trees on the course have ten to fifteen years of growth under their roots. These have been transplanted from a nearby nursery and give the course an older look. The contour of the course is flat with narrow and tree lined fairways. Fairway watering keeps the course green and the forty-six bunkers will keep the golfer hot under the collar. The only rough is under the trees. Tees are elevated, tiered, and very large; some being one hundred feet long. Each tee has the capacity to transform the hole into a different layout just by moving the markers around. The women have a totally different set of tees that may can also be used by men for a different course layout. Greens have been built in all sizes and shapes. The size is generally large with an average of 5,500 to 6,000 square feet per green. This is a shot-makers layout that was designed by Jim Spear. It is fairly easy to walk but may be difficult for a spray hitter to score well on. Pleasant Valley is a challenging course with sand and undulating greens to contend with on every hole. The new clubhouse has a complete line of equipment and the new driving range gives you a wonderful chance to work on your game. Given some time and some TLC, Pleasant Valley might become one of the most talked about and played courses in the Iowa City area. A well thought out and designed course should be a welcome change in the Iowa City golfing community.

Course	18 Holes	Aesthetics	Good
Distance	6472 Yards	Interest	Good
Par	36-36-72	Worth The Trip	Yes
Playability	Good	Rating	★★★

HOLE	RATING/SLOPE	1	2	3	4	5	6	7	8	9	OUT
BLUE	71.6/127	380	510	422	150	330	520	352	185	380	3229
WHITE	70.5/124	365	490	405	135	320	505	340	165	370	3095
HANDICAP		13	7	3	17	15	1	11	5	9	
RED	68.4/111	285	446	358	128	244	405	245	133	300	2544
FLOW		300	416	313	120	234	390	228	134	285	2421
+/-											
PAR		4	5	4	3	4	5	4	3	4	36

10	11	12	13	14	15	16	17	18	IN	OUT	TOT	HCP	NET
410	510	328	180	400	525	360	155	375	3243	3229	6472		
395	500	315	170	385	515	345	145	360	3130	3095	6225		
4	16	18	12	2	6	8	14	10					
315	425	230	115	310	430	283	125	290	2523	2544	5067		
300	415	220	105	270	430	215	110	278	2363	2001	4354		
4	5	4	3	4	5	4	3	4	36	36	72		

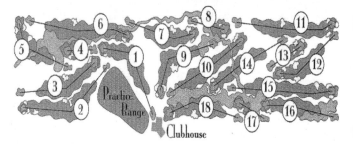

Highland Golf Course

Iowa Falls

641-648-9784

Highland Golf Course is a private course located on Highway 65 in Iowa Falls. You must live outside of the county or at least 30 miles away to pay non-member green fees. This is a fairly flat course compared to Meadow Hills east of town. Highland has gone through extensive renovation with five new hole layouts utilizing the Iowa River more. There is one pond on number 7, three sand bunkers, and a two inch rough running along the narrow fairways and in front on the tee off boxes. Most fairways are now watered. Trees are new to medium in size on the course and big and thick on the perimeter of the course. This course is located three blocks south of the downtown area along the river making it a very scenic area. Greens are medium in size and tilted. The 230 members, who pay a family membership of over $400 yearly, are privileged to play one of the oldest courses in the area, built in 1898. The original four holes were built to take advantage of the river's beauty. The renovated clubhouse sits on a hill in the middle of the course overlooking some of the natural beauty of Iowa Falls. This is an interesting course to play, easy to walk, easy to score well on, and a nice place to be in late afternoon.

Course	9 Holes
Distance	3199 Yards
Par	36
Playability	Fair
Aesthetics	Good
Interest	Fair
Worth The Trip	Yes
Rating	★★+

		1	2	3	4	5	6	7	8	9	
BLUE	70.6/116	449	388	432	140	349	164	338	486	453	3199
WHITE	69.4/113	439	379	365	132	341	150	328	471	441	3046
PAR		4	4	4	3	4	3	4	5	5	36
HANDICAP MEN B		1	5	2	8	3	7	4	6	9	
W		1	4	5	8	2	7	3	6	9	
HOLE		1	2	3	4	5	6	7	8	9	OUT
HANDICAP WOMEN SENIORS		3	4	5	8	2	9	6	1	7	
PAR		5	4	4	3	4	3	4	5	4	36
YELLOW M: 66.3 L: 70.1		424	318	300	121	297	139	252	433	292	2576

Meadow Hills Golf Course

Iowa Falls

641-648-4421

Meadow Hills is a public course located two miles east of Iowa Falls on old Highway 20. The clubhouse is located at the west end of the course and overlooks this very alpine course. A small creek runs down the middle of the course and although it does not affect play directly on any hole, it indirectly comes into play on most holes. The terrain of the course slopes toward this creek and many times you have a very uneven lie to control. There are patches of trees throughout the course but very few actually come into play. The greens are small and present a problem when contemplating your approach shot. Once you are on the greens they are flat and present no problem. This is a course that is fairly difficult to walk, but they do have carts for rent at the clubhouse. Also in the clubhouse you can buy some snacks and golf supplies. Meadow Hills has reasonable green fees for a course this size. The course was built in 1964. For most north central Iowa golfers this course presents a definite challenge: flat it isn't, easy it isn't, a good experience it is.

HOLE	1	2	3	4	5	6	7	8	9	OUT
BLUE	258	405	200	267	481	272	172	126	409	2590
WHITE	248	394	166	257	471	251	140	126	396	2449
HANDICAP	9	1	3	6	4	5	7	8	2	
PAR	4	4	3	4	5	4	3	3	5	35
HANDICAP	7	4	8	3	2	6	5	9	1	
RED	248	354	92	245	471	214	140	126	396	2286

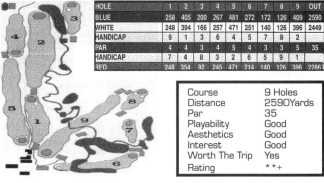

Course	9 Holes
Distance	2590 Yards
Par	35
Playability	Good
Aesthetics	Good
Interest	Good
Worth The Trip	Yes
Rating	★★+

Jackson Heights Golf Course

Jackson Junction

563-776-9181

Many Iowa rural courses were built in the early sixties. These courses were built on the edge of town on farmland, sometimes donated to the town. Many of the new courses built in the last 10 years, since 1990, have been more upscale courses, built to emulate a links style course and cater to golfers looking for an "experience". Jackson Heights Golf Course is a throw back to the "good old days' where the town comes together, buys some land and develops a nice course that local golfers can enjoy and be proud of. Jackson Heights was built in 1993 just off Hwy. 24 north of Jackson Junction. This 3169 yard, par 36 course has 180 members who pay a yearly membership of $376. Weekday green fees are $11. Hazards on the course include 6 sand bunkers, 3 ponds coming into play on 4 holes and scattered trees around a wetland region. Grass bunkers surround many of the greens. Greens are medium in size and rolling. This is a very nice, well conditioned local course. The course is not too difficult and members like the ease of play. Hats off to a new locally developed course that meets the needs of the people.

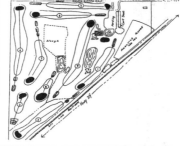

Course	9 Holes
Distance	3169 Yards
Par	36
Playability	Very Good
Aesthetics	Good
Interest	Good
Worth The Trip	Yes
Rating	★★★

HOLE	1	2	3	4	5	6	7	8	9	OUT
PAR	4	4	3	5	4	4	4	3	5	36
YARDAGE RED	286	342	120	453	328	305	323	130	426	2713
YARDAGE WHITE	301	378	143	501	345	322	366	130	485	2971
YARDAGE BLUE	333	396	188	517	360	337	390	147	501	3169

Raccoon Bend Golf Course

Jefferson

515-386-4178

The Raccoon Bend Golf Course is a private club with $8.32 green fees accepted. The course is located on Highway 4 on the south edge of town and has a membership of 174. The clubhouse contains a bar and snack area and has banquet facilities. The general contour of the course is flat although there are some side hill shots down by the river. The four bunkers are the only hazards on the course but there are some large trees that come into play on tee shots and along the fairways. The grass condition of the course is always in good shape. The greens are medium in size, flat and sloping. There is also agreement that many of the greens contain small breaks unseen by a casual observer; these subtle breaks keep the scoring average a little higher than expected. Jefferson is an easy course to walk, except for the climb back up to the clubhouse. It is situated in a scenic location by the Raccoon River, and the basic north-south layout is a long hitter's course. The course is not real busy but is played by a serious bunch of golfers. The condition of the course and its location make playing here appealing and relaxing.

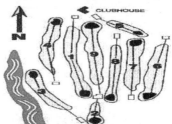

Course	9 Holes
Distance	2944 Yards
Par	36
Playability	Fair
Aesthetics	Good
Interest	Fair
Worth The Trip	Yes
Rating	★★

Hole	1	2	3	4	5	6	7	8	9	OUT
Par	5	3	4	4	3	4	4	4	5	36
Men's yardage	486	142	326	392	167	31	346	375	451	3071
Women's yardage	401	117	306	319	99	361	332	351	393	2679

Jesup Golf and Country Club

Jesup

319-827-1152

Jesup Silver Springs Golf and Country Club is a public course located on the northwest corner of Jesup on old Highway 20 West. This is a very attractive, small town course. It has a flat layout with a minimum number of hazards to upset the 200 members. There are four ponds on the course, two affecting approach shots and one stream not affecting much. There are ten sand bunkers - some being in the fairways - and a two inch rough that is tough only when neglected. Trees around the perimeter of the course are medium in size and the remainder of the trees scattered throughout the layout are 15 to 20 feet in size. 150 trees have been planted over the past two years. The greens are large and generally flat with only a four having a little roll to them. The greens also have a history of being slick and hard to hold. This course is in good shape despite the fact that it has a tendency to dry out late in the summer. Silver Springs has a new little clubhouse that has a small assortment of supplies and a nice bar area that serves drinks and all types of sandwiches. The green fees are reasonable all week; members pay $450 for a family membership. This is an easy course to walk but plays tough. It is not a very busy course and enables you to play whenever you want. Jesup Silver Springs is a family course; it is what YOU would want your small home town course to be like. Well taken care of, easy to play, and nice to look at. I hope Jesup appreciates the joys of small town living.

Course	9 Holes
Distance	3110 Yards
Par	36
Playability	Good
Aesthetics	Good
Interest	Good
Worth The Trip	Yes
Rating	★ ★ ★

HOLE	1	2	3	4	5	6	7	8	9	OUT
REGULAR	320	465	312	170	405	506	205	364	364	3111
MENS' PAR	4	5	4	3	4	5	3	4	4	36
MENS' HANDICAP	17	15	9	7	1	5	3	11	13	
LADIES'	285	430	283	100	335	448	130	327	342	2681
LADIES' PAR	4	5	4	3	4	5	3	4	4	36
LADIES' HANDICAP	17	13	9	11	1	5	15	3	7	

Jewell Golf and Country Club

Jewell

515-827-5631

The Jewell Golf and Country Club seems to be one of the greenest places in central Iowa in the summer. This course is located on Highway 69 on the north edge of Jewell and is generally a north-south course that was laid out and built in 1961. The contour of the course is flat and is very enjoyable to walk but they do have carts for rent. The clubhouse is an old structure that has the minimum amount of supplies and refreshments. Weekday green fees are very reasonable. Jewell has developed into a course that is nice to look at and entertaining to play. Some fairly large trees line the fairways but it still must be considered an open course. The greens are flat and of medium size, there are no water hazards and very few obstacles to contend with. This is an easy course to score well on and a course where you can swing freely and get away with it. A major factor of this course is the superior grass condition; for a small town course, it is of the highest caliber and gives you a good feeling just to walk on it. Another nice example of home town pride.

Course	9 Holes
Distance	3201 Yards
Par	36
Playability	Good
Aesthetics	Good
Interest	Good
Worth The Trip	Yes
Rating	★ ★ ★

Hole		1	2	3	4	5	6	7	8	9	OUT
White Tees	71.2/119	353	165	493	186	447	512	463	145	437	3201
Men's Handicap		17	11	9	7	3	5	15	13	1	
Men's Par		4	3	5	3	4	5	5	3	4	36
Red Tees	72.8/119	353	143	425	153	383	410	343	107	437	2754
Ladies' Handicap		15	11	5	9	1	17	3	13	7	
Ladies' Par		4	3	5	3	5	4	3	3	5	36

Hyperion Field Club

Johnston

515-276-1596

Course	18 Holes	Aesthetics	Excellent
Distance	6435 Yards	Interest	Very Good
Par	36-36-72	Worth The Trip	Yes
Playability	Excellent	Rating	★★★★+

Hyperion Field Club is one of the exclusive clubs in the Des Moines area. This private course has 450 members. The course is located by Camp Dodge in Johnston on Northwest Beaver. The Hyperion complex also offers six tennis courts and tennis pro, a swimming pool, a restaurant that is very elegant and private. The pro shop has a full line of golfing supplies, with an outstanding supply of clothes. There are also carts for rent to traverse the hilly back nine. The characteristics of the course include one pond on number 8 and an average of two bunkers per hole, usually guarding the front of the green. The rough is cut very distinctively along the tree line and can be quite a challenge to get out of. There is an ample assortment of trees, most being medium to large in size. The majority of trees line the narrow fairways and offer a scenic, but unwelcoming view from many tees. Greens are medium to large in size with flat contours. The layout of the course stretches down the hillside south of the clubhouse. The S.W. side of the course is much flater and has smaller and fewer trees. The condition of the grass in the fairways, on the greens, and in the rough is plush. There have been bent grass fairways since 1988. This is a control golfers course, if you can keep the ball in the middle you might find this course easy, if you spray the ball, even a little, you may find this course a little overwhelming. The greens are fast, the rough is plush and offers a significant challenge. The landscaping is typical of a top rated country club, beautiful to look at and meaningful to the layout of the course. One of the indicators of a great course is the tournaments it sponsors; one of the best ones in Iowa is the Herman Sani Open. They have also been hosting an professional women's tournament the last few years. It is held on Hyperion every year. Hyperion sets the standard that many private courses in central Iowa would like to go emulate.

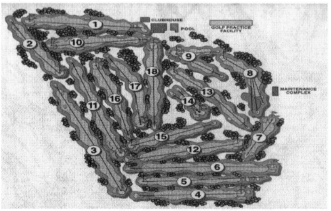

Kalona Golf Club

Kalona

319-656-3844

One of the most beautiful number one tee boxes in the state is located on the Kalona Golf course. The entire course is beautifully landscaped with flowers, shrubs, and beautifully manicured grass. This semi-private club is located two miles south of Kalona on Highway 1. This course is noted for its abundance of trees and landscaping; it was voted the Iowa 9 Hole Course of the Year in 1984. Characteristics of the course include two ponds, no sand, and a two inch rough that will create some problems. There are many trees and they come in all sizes; mostly medium to large, but there are some new plantings. The trees line all of the rolling fairways and add to the challenge of this 55 acre course. The tees are elevated and in good condition; as are the large greens. The greens are true to putt, fast, and have a sloping dimension to calculate. Kalona was first built in 1930 and rebuilt in 1982. Kalona is a rolling course that is medium to hard to score on. It is a second shot course, placement is very important. The 140 members know that there are no give-me shots on the fairways or on the greens. Kalona is a course that concentration is a must. Green fees are accepted from anyone, $10 for weekdays. Members pay annual dues of $550 for a family. The clubhouse is ordinary, one big room with a bar and sandwiches, but the supplies are quite extraordinary. This is a hard course to walk and carts are available. The beauty of this course is a real asset. Kalona offers challenging and rewarding golf for the average golfer.

Course	9 Holes
Distance	3128Yards
Par	36
Playability	Very Good
Aesthetics	Excellent
Interest	Very Good
Worth The Trip	Yes
Rating	★★★★+

BLUE TEES	370	220	308	325	337	541	505	182	340	3128
WHITE TEES	360	200	281	305	320	521	491	163	320	2961
GOLD TEES	350	180	265	300/200	300	480	475	153	300	2803/2703
MEN'S HANDICAP	12	6	10	4	14	2	8	16	18	
LADIES' HANDICAP	1	13	9	17	11	3	15	7		
RED TEES	320	130	259	141	231	416	423	115	256	2291
HOLE NUMBER	1	2	3	4	5	6	7	8	9	OUT
PAR	4	3	4	4/3	4	5	5	3	4	36/35

Elks Fairview Golf Club

Keokuk

319-524-1074

The Elks Fairview Golf Club in Keokuk is a private club owned and operated by the Elks organization. Only the 200 members and their guests can play the course. This nine hole 3076 yard course has a small pro shop that has carts for rent and a small amount of golfing supplies for sale. A separate building has the dining facilities for special occasions; a golfer can get something to drink and a sandwich in the clubhouse. There is one pond on the course, nine bunkers and no rough. Trees are medium to large in size and line most of the fairways, although they present very few problems. The contour of the course is generally flat making it an easy course to walk. The tees are flat and the greens are medium in size and flat. The grass condition on the greens is poor with bare spots showing in many places. This course has a reputation of being very friendly, everyone knowing everyone else. The Elks like the fellowship and fun the course provides. It is an easy course to score well on and lets you relax and not force you to concentrate on the game too much and still have fun and not get into trouble.

Course	9 Holes
Distance	2836Yards
Par	35
Playability	Fair
Aesthetics	Fair
Interest	Poor
Worth The Trip	Maybe
Rating	★+

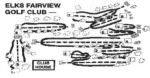

ELKS FAIRVIEW GOLF CLUB —

CLUB HOUSE

Hole	Yards	Men's Par	Ladies Par	Handicap	Ladies'
1	456	5	5	3	354
2	326	4	4	9	326
3	118	3	3	17	102
4	561	5	6	1	456
5	132	3	3	15	84
6	320	4	4	11	320
7	334	4	4	7	220
8	392	4	5	5	354
9	197	3	3	13	197
OUT	2836	35	37		2413

Keokuk Country Club

Keokuk

319-524-2002

One of the nicer country clubs in S.E. Iowa is the Keokuk Country Club. The massive white clubhouse has recently been remodeled and would rate as one of the top ten in the state and the nine hole course would rank very high too. Hole # 1 may be one of the most beautiful opening holes in the state. This private club has 250members who pay $1,500 annual dues. Green fees for anyone outside of the county are very reasonable in price. The clubhouse has an elegant restaurant that will accept reservations from non-members; the dining is exquisite. There is also a grill that offers drinks and sandwiches for the golfers during the day. The complex also offers a pool and tennis courts for members. The pro shop is located in a new small building south of the clubhouse. It offers a full line of equipment and supplies. Keokuk Country Club was built in 1899 and overlooks the Mississippi River making it one of the most scenic in the area. Being close to the river makes the contour of the course quite hilly and hard to walk. This nine hole course does offer a challenge with deep rough, overhanging trees, and dogleg layouts. This is a plush course that has the old time country club feeling, but it also has the clubhouse and course to back it up. Playing this course is like being involved in a bit of history, something special. The course is located by the river on 3318 Middle Road.

Course	9 Holes
Distance	3096 Yards
Par	36
Playability	Good
Aesthetics	Excellent
Interest	Good
Worth The Trip	Yes
Rating	★★★+

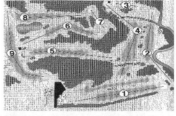

	1	2	3	4	5	6	7	8	9	
MEN'S PAR	4	4	3	5	4	4	3	4	5	36
MEN'S YDG	405	428	137	475	385	370	126	320	445	3091
MEN'S HDCP	5	3	17	1	9	11	13	15	7	
LADIES' PAR	5	4	3	5	4	4	3	4	5	37
LADIES' YDG	405	352	112	372	281	321	115	307	397	2662
LADIES' HDCP	9	3	17	1	7	11	15	13	5	
HOLE	1	2	3	4	5	6	7	8	9	OUT

River View Club

Keosauqua

319-293-3200

You will find the River View Club on the south edge of Keosauqua by the school. This is a public course that has 100 members paying $430 per year. If you live outside the county and you just want to play golf, a yearly membership is $100. The River View complex also has tennis courts and a swimming pool. The clubhouse is a nice small brick structure that has a bar and grill for drinks and sandwiches and a nice supply of balls, gloves, and clubs. They also have carts for rent but this is a nice level course to walk. This 3189 yard course has one pond, no sand, and no rough. The trees are medium to large and line many of the fairways. The trees form groves between a few fairways. The elevated greens are medium in size and tend to have a gentle roll to them. The greens have been improving over the past two years but have been labeled as "mean" in the past. This is a fairly easy course where you can spray it around in the middle a little. It is not very busy and provides a perfect place for the beginner to hone some his/her skills. This public course has an atmosphere like many others in the state, "come enjoy our course, it is the best that we have to offer." River View is also the home of the Boys 1A runner-up in 2001.

Course	9 Holes
Distance	3067 Yards
Par	36
Playability	Good
Aesthetics	Fair
Interest	Fair
Worth The Trip	Yes
Rating	★★

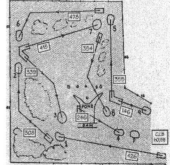

Lagos Acres Golf and Country Club

Keota

319-636-3411

The Lagos Acres Golf and Country Club is located on the east edge of Keota. This is a private club that has a 10 mile green fee radius. Fees are average in price. The 120 members enjoy a nice small town course that offers yearly memberships of $380 for families. The clubhouse is a basic one room structure that offers bar and grill items plus carts and a few supplies. The course does maintain two ponds that come into play twice but has no sand or rough. Trees on the course are medium in size and are scattered throughout the course. The fairways present a wide open hitting area with no rough guarding the edges. Tees are one of the nicer features of the course, being big and elevated. The greens are small to medium in size and generally flat with a slight tilt. The course was built in 1963. This is a wide open course that is rolling only to the degree that makes it interesting. Lagos Acres is a simple course that is easy to walk and score well on and is a drawing card for many green fees during the week and on the busy weekends. The best thing that can be said about Lagos is that it is a very nice small town course that strives to keep the members and visitors happy.

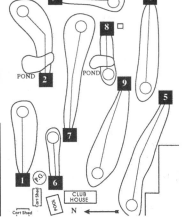

Course	9 Holes
Distance	3022 Yards
Par	36
Playability	Fair
Aesthetics	Fair
Interest	Fair
Worth The Trip	Maybe
Rating	★★

Hole	1	2	3	4	5	6	7	8	9	Out
Men's Yardage	321	347	183	380	492	161	480	209	446	3022
Men's Par	4	4	3	4	5	3	5	3	5	36
Handicap	8	6	5	2	4	7	3	1	9	
Ladies' Yardage	303	245	153	259	336	153	383	102	349	2383
Ladies' Par	4	4	3	4	4	3	5	3	4	34

Brookside Golf Course

Kingsley

712-378-2595

Brookside Golf Course in Kingsley is a course that is trying to improve. The grounds are more pleasant and in better condition than past years. About 1,200 young trees have been planted to make the future of the course most interesting. The course is located on the west edge of town on Highway 140 and supports an A-frame clubhouse that has a simple interior. The clubhouse has a nice bar area with four tables and few supplies. The proof is not in the clubhouse but out on the course. This course has a creek that runs the length of the course and comes into play on four holes. The trees are small in size, large in numbers and line all of the wide fairways. The greens are medium in size, crowned in the middle and tough to read. This is a privately owned course that is deceptively tough. It is very flat with few hazards, but it has length, lots of small trees, and greens that make you take them seriously. The 150 members pay an annual fee of $360 for a family while daily green fees are very reasonably priced $10 for 9 holes. The course was built in 1964 and is very flat yet has some future appeal to it. Try it now while you can see what's going on; in a few years you will need a saw to make the same shot.

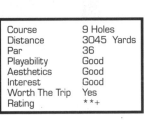

Course	9 Holes
Distance	3045 Yards
Par	36
Playability	Good
Aesthetics	Good
Interest	Good
Worth The Trip	Yes
Rating	★★★+

	1	2	3	4	5	6	7	8	9	Out
Mens Course	326	230	325	150	527	265	342	410	470	3045
Ladies Course	185	160	265	140	397	232	252	330	410	2462
Mens Par	4	3	4	3	5	4	4	4	5	36
Ladies Par	4	3	4	3	5	4	4	4	5	36

Slippery Elm Golf Course

Klemme

641-587-2670

If you are tired of playing flat courses in north central Iowa, then the course at Klemme is a must for you. A stream comes into play on 7 of the holes with water guarding 4 greens, making for tough approach shots. All the holes are rolling, sloping down to the creek, making this a tough course to walk. They do have carts to rent. This is a challenging and hard course to score on. Each shot must be placed in the correct position for the next shot. Water and tall grass eliminate any chip and run techniques that you might have perfected. The greens are small and rounded making them very difficult to hold plus they are hard to read. The course was built in 1965. The clubhouse has a supply of balls and gloves but also has the only restaurant in town, open to the public the year round at noon. The 80 members pay $200 per year and anyone else can pay green fees. If you do come to play this course make sure you bring golf balls that will float. There is also a problem with electrical lines on this course, they present a unique and shocking experience. The Slippery Elm Golf Course is located one-half mile south of Klemme.

Course	9 Holes
Distance	2645 Yards
Par	35
Playability	Good
Aesthetics	Good
Interest	Very Good
Worth The Trip	Yes
Rating	***

WHITE	242	309	448	455	145	202	292	193	359	2645
GOLD	242	257	386	351	140	195	261	194	302	2349
RED	242	252	391	386	136	135	256	129	306	2233
HOLE	1	2	3	4	5	6	7	8	9	OUT
MEN'S/LADIES PAR	4	4	5	5	3	3	4	3	4	35
MEN'S/LADIES HANDICAP	15	8	17	3	13	11	7	9	11	

Pine Knolls Country Club

Knoxville

641-842-3730

One of the older and tougher courses in south central Iowa is the Pine Knolls Country Club on Highway 5 in Knoxville. This is a private course with 200 members that will accept green fee players if you live outside the school district. The course is known for its hills, especially "Cardiac Hill" on number three. This is a very tough course to walk, but come early for carts because there aren't very many to rent. There are three holes on the course that are affected by two ponds and six bunkers that guard the greens. The trees come in all sizes and line many of the fairways. Ten new trees are replanted each year. The rough is cut at two inches and catches a lot of balls sliding off the rolling fairways. Greens are small in size and are very difficult to hit, but when you do they hold quite well. Pine Knolls was built in 1929 along a creek, which has since dried up except for a rare occasion. The entire course slopes toward the ravine, including the greens. Local members will tell you that Pine Knolls has the toughest three starting holes in the state and a very tough par 4 number eight. The clubhouse has a full line of equipment plus a bar and grill for the golfers. There is also a restaurant that serves good meals to the public on Tuesday and Saturday nights. This is basically a members course; the hills and valleys keep most of the green fees away. But if you want a little challenge try Pine Knolls. Accuracy is a must and hazards are in abundance.

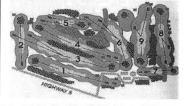

Course	9 Holes
Distance	2913 Yards
Par	35
Playability	Very Good
Aesthetics	Good
Interest	Very Good
Worth The Trip	Yes
Rating	***

HOLE	1	2	3	4	5	6	7	8	9	OUT
BLUE / WHITE YARDS	388	231	491	434	174	332	145	381	337	2913
HANDICAP										
PAR	4	3	5	5	3	4	3	4	4	35
RED YARDS	369	220	410	408	131	305	114	291	237	2485
HANDICAP										
PAR	5	4	5	5	3	4	3	4	4	37

La Porte City Golf Club

La Porte City

319-342-2249

The La Porte City Golf Club, which is located one mile east of town on Cemetery Road, also has the Wilderness Nature Bike Path winding by number 6 fairway. This 2,579 yard course stretches down to the west from the old clubhouse. This course is also built diagonally, which is quite rare for a course in Iowa. The Laporte City course is short and to the point; if you can't get the ball onto the green with your approach shot, you are in for a long day. The greens are small and elevated; they contain some small and some large breaks. The contour of the rest of the course is generally flat with the wide fairways lined with small trees. The mature trees from the original planting of 1932 are now gone and the character of the course has changed. This open course provides a variety of challenges to the average golfer; small greens, short holes that command accuracy, and open spaces that lull you into a false sense of security. Daily green fees are average in price for a course this size. The members play a course that is easy to walk and easy to score well on where you can enjoy an easy going golfing atmosphere.

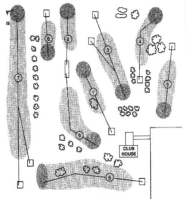

Course	9 Holes
Distance	2579 Yards
Par	35
Playability	Fair
Aesthetics	Fair
Interest	Good
Worth The Trip	Yes
Rating	★★+

HOLE	1	2	3	4	5	6	7	8	9	OUT
MEN'S YARDAGE	275	144	339	304	286	297	458	147	329	2579
MEN'S PAR	4	3	4	4	4	4	5	3	4	35
HANDICAP	9	2	1	7	3	4	8	6	5	
LADIES' PAR	4	3	4	4	4	4	5	3	4	35

Lake City Country Club

Lake City

712-464-3344

Lake City Country Club is located on Highway 175 on the east edge of Lake City. The 180 members pay an annual fee of $280 with non-members paying average green fees. The clubhouse is a new building that has a pro shop with golf supplies for sale, a large bar area that serves sandwiches and drinks, and a dining facility that is open on special occasions. Lake City is also open for Sunday brunch that is available to the public. The only water hazard on the course is a small stream that comes into play on two holes during the wet season. There are also two bunkers on numbers 3 and 8. The contour of the course is flat with small to medium size trees scattered along some of the fairways. The tees were rebuilt in '91 and are tiered and well maintained. The greens are small and flat but do have some hidden breaks that make them interesting. Lake City Country Club is usually quite busy with leagues four times a week. This course is easy to walk, easy to score well on, has few hazards to contend with and not very much tree trouble. Lake City Country Club seems to have a serious golfing atmosphere.

Course	9 Holes
Distance	2868 Yards
Par	36
Playability	Good
Aesthetics	Good
Interest	Fair
Worth The Trip	Yes
Rating	★★+

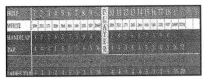

Rice Lake Golf and Country Club Course

Lake Mills

641-592-8022

Rice Lake Golf Course is a public 18 hole course that is located 2 miles south and 2 miles east of Lake Mills. The original course was built in 1922 and the additional 9 holes were added on in 1979 making it one of the more scenic and challenging courses in northern Iowa. The New clubhouse is located near Rice Lake and has a complete line of golfing supplies plus carts for rent. Green fees are very reasonable for an 18 hole course, $20 for weekdays. The 450 members pay an annual fee of $464 with an entry stock of $100. The clubhouse has a restaurant open April through November. The location of the course makes it unique. An Iowa game refuge and Rice Lake border the course on the north and east. Wildlife is in abundance and geese can be seen throughout the summer and well into the fall on and around the course. Characteristics of the course include 5 ponds, one stream that comes into play on 5 holes, a lake that comes into play on one hole, 14 sand bunkers, and a 2 inch tiered rough that is fair but can cause many problems. The contour of the wide fairways is gentle, but the size of the trees on the north side of the course makes accuracy off the tee a must. Fairway watering was added in 1990. The south side of the course has an increasing number of small evergreens plus a few replanted larger trees. The north side of the course near the clubhouse and lake support the big old original trees that come into play more often. The tee boxes are big and flat with the greens being of medium size and sloping. The greens are very true and fairly easy to putt. This is a beautiful course that is very busy for this area of Iowa but because it has 18 holes can handle a larger volume of people. It is a challenging course set in a unique back woods location. Rice Lake was voted the Iowa Course of the Year in 1999.

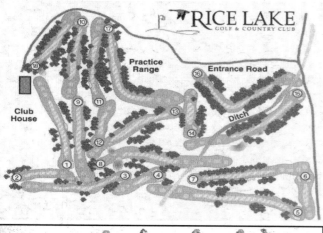

Course	18 Holes	Aesthetics	Very Good
Distance	6401 Yards	Interest	Very Good
Par	35-36-71	Worth The Trip	Yes
Playability	Good	Rating	★★★+

Hole		1	2	3	4	5	6	7	8	9	Out
Blue	70.5/122	410	178	378	193	569	135	417	530	355	3178
White	68.7/122	402	178	357	173	529	122	407	489	311	2968
Gold	66.6/115	372	157	337	158	469	122	364	390	300	2668
Handicap		3	13	1	11	7	17	5	9	15	
Par											
Red	68.6/116	327	180	320	139	412	108	322	347	269	2394

	10	11	12	13	14	15	16	17	18	In	Total	HANDICAP	NET
	324	378	162	380	174	520	447	530	280	3223	6401		
	324	348	146	360	157	500	437	490	271	3033	6001		
	302	330	146	343	142	436	347	468	271	2785	5453		
	12	6	16	4	18	14	8	2	10				
											36	71	
	287	295	133	269	134	401	323	447	213	2502	4896		

144

Silver Lake Golf and Country Club

Lake Park

712-832-3213

Silver Lake Golf and Country Club is a public course located two miles west and one mile north of Lake Park off Highway 9. A reasonable green fee is charged during the week with a slight elevation on the weekends. The 165 members pay an annual fee of $425. The clubhouse has balls and gloves plus carts for rent. There is also a full restaurant that is open six months of the year for the public. The bar area serves drinks and sandwiches during the day. The characteristics of Silver Lake include long par 4's, challenging par 3's, mowed rough, and no water hazards. There is a average number of small to medium size trees lining the fairways. But they do not contribute to the difficulty of the course. Fairways are relatively wide with a gently rolling contour. Tees are big and in average shape. Greens are large and have a rolling putting surface. This is a fairly rolling course that can be hard to walk if you are not in shape. The wide fairways allow you to spray your drives a little and the lack of rough allows you to recover without any penalty. Silver Lake is busy but tee times are not needed. The general shape of the course is better thanks to the fairway watering; the hills tend to dry out quickly in the summer. A unusual thing about the course is that number 9 is built on a bog; something of a scientific treasure.

Course	9 Holes
Distance	3220 Yards
Par	36
Playability	Fair
Aesthetics	Fair
Interest	Fair
Worth The Trip	Yes
Rating	★★

HOLE	1	2	3	4	5	6	7	8	9	OUT
Men's Par	4	4	3	5	3	4	4	4	5	36
Yards (White)	380	330	170	530	170	425	445	300	470	3220
Men's Handicap	3	7	6	4	5	2	1	9	8	
Yards (Red)	280	315	160	432	155	410	435	285	400	2872
Ladies' Handicap	3	7	6	4	5	2	1	9	8	
Ladies' Par	4	4	3	5	3	5	5	4	5	38

Sac County Golf and Country Club

Lake View-Wall Lake-Odebolt-Early

712-664-2204

The Sac County Golf and Country Club, which is also known as the Spring Lake Golf and Country Club, serves four towns in west central Iowa, Early, Lake View, Odebolt, and Wall Lake. The course is located at the intersection of Highways 71 and 175. This is a semi-private club that has 239 members paying a $100 entry certificate and $300 per year dues. The course has a adequate clubhouse that serves drinks, sandwiches, and dinners on special occasions. Supplies are limited and a few carts are available for rent. Characteristics of the course include a pond that affects two holes, a creek that comes into play four times, two bunkers, and some rough cut down the tree line. Trees on the course line many of the wide fairways and are small to medium in size. Generally the trees cause very little trouble. Greens on the layout are elevated and tilted. The only two flat greens are six and three. This is an easy course to walk but a fairly hard course to score well on. The length is long and the water does come into play if you stray too far. It is a shining example of communities getting together to form a club that will provide recreation for all. It is a picturesque country course that is enjoyed by many.

Course	9 Holes
Distance	3220 Yards
Par	36
Playability	V. Good
Aesthetics	Good
Interest	Good
Worth The Trip	Yes
Rating	★★★

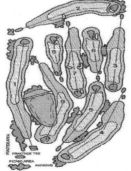

HOLE	1	2	3	4	5	6	7	8	9	OUT
White Tees	540	385	365	415	330	205	330	185	465	3220
Red Tees	447	365	345	353	310	167	310	153	420	2870
Handicap	1	3	5	2	7	4	6	9	8	
Par	5	4	4	4	4	3	4	3	5	36

Lamoni Golf and Country Club

Lamoni

515-784-6022

The Lamoni Golf and Country Club in general is quite nice but the supporting facilities are poor. There is a small clubhouse, you just pay your $11 green fees as you go. This private club has 120 members paying $360 for a family. If you live outside the city limits of Lamoni you can pay green fees. The 66 acres that this course is located on is in the S.E. corner of town and is a fairly long course at 3205 yards. There are three ponds on the course, no sand and no cut rough. The trees are medium in size and line many of the wide fairways. The trees do cause a lot of trouble for players. The grass on the course is in good shape and covers fairways that are gently rolling to the N.W. Greens are medium in size, tilted and have a gently rolling contour. The greens are easy to hold but not very easy to read. The grass greens were installed in 1977 and made this course quite nice to play on. The greens are one of the bright spots of the course. The layout of the course is good and might be considered one of the best conditioned courses in the area. The contour of the course offers up a lot of uneven lies to hit from. It is more of a long and straight hitters course, but if we could hit long and straight, we would be playing on the tour. If you want a good game of golf, easy to get on, easy to play, then try Lamoni. But don't count on a relaxing time at the bar; there is none.

Course	9 Holes
Distance	3113 Yards
Par	36
Playability	Good
Aesthetics	Good
Interest	Good
Worth The Trip	Yes
Rating	★★+

White Tee	322	524	148	375	197	336	500	355	356	3113	Total	HCP	NET
Red Tee	268	419	100	257	139	268	421	280	275	2427	Course / Slope Ratings		
Handicap Men / Women	9/9	2/2	8/6	4/4	1/1	3/3	6/5	5/6	7/7		67.8 / 109		
Hole/Par	1/4	2/5	3/3	4/4	5/3	6/4	7/5	8/4	9/4	36	72		

Meadow Acres Country Club

Larchwood

712-477-2576

Meadow Acres Country Club two miles east of Larchwood in N.W. Iowa was built in 1984. The 40 by 210 foot low slung clubhouse, not too long ago, was a chicken house. Don't let the visual image of the clubhouse turn you away. Inside they have a very nice bar and restaurant area, locker room facilities, and storage for equipment, all large areas. The course was built in 1985 and had 245 members the first year, paying $555 for a family. The course has really matured in the last 10 years. So what was a bean field three years ago is now a growing golf course. The layout includes a lake, seven sand bunkers, and tiered rough. There are very few trees on the course, and are now coming into play. The course is very open, as you would expect, and very flat. One of the outstanding features of the course is the greens. They have been built with the future in mind, big, rolling and a lot of breaks. The entire course is in good shape but the greens are in exceptional shape. Meadow Acres is a prime example of a community that had an idea, was organized by two men, investors were found, property carefully selected, and voluntary work utilized in building the course from the roots up. All of this was done so that people could go out and beat a little white ball around and have a great time doing it. All of Iowa should take notice, things can be accomplished in small communities.

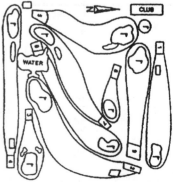

Course	9 Holes
Distance	2576 Yards
Par	36
Playability	Fair
Aesthetics	Good
Interest	Fair
Worth The Trip	Yes
Rating	★★+

HOLE	1	2	3	4	5	6	7	8	9		
WHITE	396	420	146	480	316	144	313	361	403	2979	HANDICAP / NET SCORE
RED	329	356	146	393	296	144	313	361	333	2871	
WE											
PAR	4	5	3	5		6	4	4	4	36	
THEY											
HANDICAP	1	9	5	8	4	6	7	2	3		

Latimer Golf Club

Latimer

641-579-6090

For some of the smallest greens in Iowa you don't need to go any farther than the Latimer Golf Course. They have almost a reverse bowl effect which makes the approach shot almost impossible. As for the rest of the course it is fairly easy to score on and walk. This public course was built in 1961 and has a small membership size of 110. Annual family membership fees are $260, with a $250 stock. This is an extremely short course, 2231 yards, but makes up for it in green difficulty. The small red clubhouse has very little inside. The course has a small number of trees and a majority of them are new and small. There are three bunkers, no water hazards, and no distinct rough. The tee boxes are of medium size and the grass condition is spotty. This brings us back to the unique thing about this course, its greens. They are on the verge of being unfair, extremely small, crowned, hard to hold, and tough to putt. Carts are available in the clubhouse. If you are looking for a challenge, try the greens of Latimer. The rest of the course you will enjoy.

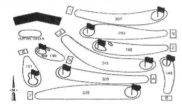

Course	9 Holes
Distance	2231 Yards
Par	33
Playability	Poor
Aesthetics	Fair
Interest	Fair
Worth The Trip	Maybe
Rating	*

Hole	Yards	Par
1	307	4
2	248	4
3	345	4
4	309	4
5	109	3
6	151	3
7	329	4
8	143	3
9	290	4
Out	2231	33

Laurens Golf and Country Club

Laurens

712-841-2287

One of the combinations that you would find in Iowa years ago was golf courses and airports. There are only a few of these left in Iowa and one of them is the Laurens Golf and Country Club. The runway for the Laurens airport runs between number 8 and 9 fairways on the golf course. The entire operation is owned by Skyways. The course has a new clubhouse that has balls, gloves, plus carts for rent. The restaurant in the clubhouse is operated as a full time venture but is only open to the 200 members. The members pay annual fees of $265 with non-members pay the average green fees. Laurens is a very flat and open course. There are five sand bunkers on the layout, two grass bunkers, a tiny number of no problem trees, and no rough. The only thing challenging about the course are the greens. They are small and rolling. Your approach shot has to be near perfect or the ball will not hold. They are a tough way to try and end a hole. The course was built in 1965. This is a small town course that tempts you by the words "swing away, hit it as hard as you can", the absence of hazards sometimes has its benefits. But you have been warned that Cessnas tend to discourage play on the runway.

Course	9 Holes
Distance	2845 Yards
Par	35
Playability	Fair
Aesthetics	Fair
Interest	Poor
Worth The Trip	Maybe
Rating	*+

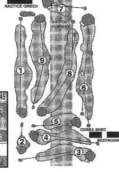

MEN'S YARDAGE	380	165	310	285	190	485	150	470	410	2845
MEN'S PAR	4	3	4	4	3	5	3	5	4	35
HANDICAP	2	5	7	3	6	8	1			
WOMEN'S PAR	4	3	4	4	3	5				36
HOLES	1	2	3	4	5	6	7	8	9	Out

Olathea Golf Course

Le Claire

563-289-GOLF

One of the outstanding attractions of many courses along the eastern edge of Iowa is that they have a view of the Mississippi River from their course. The Olathea Golf Course north of Le Claire has one of the better views, 8 holes view the Mississippi. This 3045 yard public course was once a farm near the river but was restructured into a golf course in 1983. The layout consists of one pond, one stream, five bunkers; plus a hilly disposition. The trees are small with new plantings. There are some larger trees on the fringe of the course and by the water. The condition of this family operated course is very good. The fairways are wide and green, the tees are elevated, big, and green. The greens are medium in size, rolling in nature, and green is color. This is a hard course to walk and a challenging course to play. The clubhouse is a small structure but has a nice variety of supplies inside. There is also a nice bar area, decorated in local color that serves drinks and all kinds of sandwiches. Olathea has added a driving range. There are also carts to rent to traverse the hilly country side. Yearly memberships cost $700; 100 members have taken up the cause. Weekday green fees are $9. Olathea has a splendid panoramic view of the area and the river. Olathea can be found three miles north of Le Claire on Highway 67.

Course	9 Holes
Distance	3053 Yards
Par	36
Playability	Good
Aesthetics	Excellent
Interest	Good
Worth The Trip	Yes
Rating	★★★

HOLE	1	2	3	4	5	6	7	8	9	OUT
BLUE	190	532	179	274	312	603	375	319	270	3053
WHITE	180	522	158	269	302	576	365	298	260	2930
RED	170	385	145	264	280	420	265	278	250	2457
PAR	3	5	3	4	4	5	4	4	4	36

Three Lake Municipal Golf Club

Lenox

515-333-2990

Three Lake Municipal Golf Club replaced their sand greens with green greens in 1995. When the green change occurred the size of the course doubled in size. The length of the course is 2935 which is fairly long for a 9 hole course. There is fairway watering now which helps the grass condition over the entire course. The old tradition of sand is a dying tradition in Iowa, only 3 courses remain. A small town course like this isn't out to bring in hundreds of people; members just want to relax, enjoy the outdoors, and get in a few swings. This public course has a clubhouse, that now has food and supplies. There are 140 members paying a yearly fee of $400. It is a simple course that is short and open to any type of swing. A lake comes into play four times, there is only one sand bunker, and there are very few trees on this course with 50 new trees added in 2002. The contour of the course is gently rolling and the grass is not in the best of shape. Three Lake offers the style of golf that it has known since its conception in 1925; no pressure, fun golf. But the question still remains, where are the other two lakes?

Course	Sand
Distance	2935 Yards
Par	33
Playability	Fair
Aesthetics	Poor
Interest	Very Good
Worth The Trip	Yes
Rating	★★

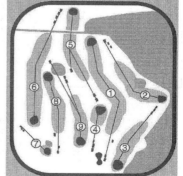

BLUE	364	385	294	170	448	535	166	350	417	3531
HANDICAP										
WHITE	520	354	274	135	418	507	124	317	286	2935
HANDICAP	5		4		6		9			
PAR	5	4	4	3	4	5	3	4	4	36
RED										
HANDICAP	3									
HOLE	1	2	3	4	5	6	7			

148

Le Mars Municipal Golf Club

Le Mars

712-546-6849

The character of the Le Mars Golf Club is shaped by the stream that meanders down the middle of the course. This hazard comes into play on eight holes and you must cross over the wet stuff eight different times. If the water doesn't get you then one of the frequent bunkers might, this a well bunkered 18 hole course. An additional 9 holes were added in September 1991. Lemars is a flat course that has a large number of trees that line many of the fairways . Because of the trees the fairways are narrow which also makes the 2 inch rough play tough. Fairway watering helps maintain that early spring look the entire summer. The original greens are medium in size and have assorted surfaces, typically flat with tiered rough around them. The new greens are larger and uniquely shaped creating more of a challenge throughout the course. The layout of the course has been changed to accommodate the holes developed farther from the clubhouse. Number 13 is an interesting par 3, surrounded by water on 3 sides and a grove of trees on the other. Number 9 has a championship tee that sets in front of a 180 yard carry over a pond, the entire hole stretches 625 yards. The original course was built in 1939 and has a lot of history and character. The clubhouse was remodeled in 1990, with the bar doubled in size and the fully stocked pro shop moved to this building. The 280 members pay the yearly family fee of $590. Non-members pay a very reasonable green fee. There is also a very active Junior Program at Lemars which is very nice for the entire community. The course does have one problem early in the golfing season, the creek has a tendency to overflow when it rains up north. But when the new 9 holes were built an assortment of grass bunkers)were placed to help protect the course from flooding. The course is located on the east side of Lemars on Highway 3.

Hole		1	2	3	4	5	6	7	8	9	Out
Champ	Slope / Rating 118 / 71.8	372	372	510	411	178	420	370	357	624	3414
Regular		367	165	489	335	167	390	360	335	424	3030
Forward	Slope / Rating	255	312	467	316	158	364	276	314	350	2828

10	11	12	13	14	15	16	17	18	IN
272	390	350	196	525	559	412	233	411	3348
267	375	345	174	493	515	402	228	400	3199
262	340	293	131	402	415	337	223	294	2674
4	4	4	3	5	5	4	3/4	4	36/37

Course	18 Holes	Aesthetics	Very Good
Distance	6750 Yards	Interest	Good
Par	36-36-72	Worth The Trip	Yes
Playability	Good	Rating	★★★+

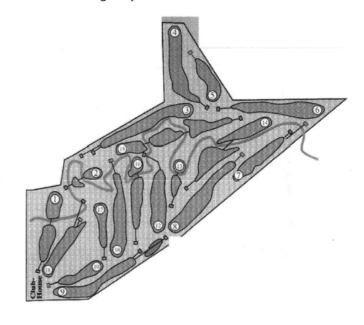

Leon Golf and Country Club

Leon

641-446-4529

The Leon Golf and Country Club is a private course that was built in 1955 and has a membership of 104 today. The unique characteristic of this course is its beauty and its fifty foot poplar trees. Poplars line most of the fairways and come into play if you stray from the beaten path. There are also evergreens that surround many of the greens, some in back and on one hole evergreens in front of the green. Forty new trees have been planted the last two years. There is one pond on the layout that comes into play, two inch rough, and one sand trap. The contour of the course is dips and valleys. Tees are small and flat and have seen better men's nights. The greens are medium in size, flat and tilted. The trees on this course make it hard to score well. They come into play on almost every hole and can cause severe damage to your score if given the opportunity. The course is located on the west edge of Leon on Highway 2. It is a pretty course that is challenging, easy to walk, and the pride of Leon and its members. If you live out of Decater county then you can pay the moderate green fee and have one heck of a time.

Course	9 Holes
Distance	3116 Yards
Par	36
Playability	Good
Aesthetics	Very Good
Interest	Fair
Worth The Trip	Yes
Rating	★★+

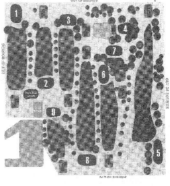

MEN'S RED	349	332	366	150	576	363	186	513	286	3116
MEN'S HDCP	13	11								
MEN'S PAR	4	4	4	3	5	4	3	5	4	36
HOLE NUMBER	1	2	3	4	5	6	7	8	9	OUT
WOMEN'S PAR	4	4	4	3	5	4	3	4	36	
WOMEN'S HDCP										
WOMEN'S RED	298	242	253	113	447	286	146	428	176	2389

3/30 Golf & Country Club

Lowden

319-944-7695

Friendly people is the name of the game at the 3/30 Golf & Country Club Course located on the east edge of Lowden. This public course has a membership size of 300 who pay $460 for a family yearly fee. Green fees are very reasonable for weekdays and a dollar more for the weekends. The clubhouse is a small house converted into a newly remodeled dining and bar area. The restaurant is open year round for guests and members. The course itself is flat; the only thing that changes the contour is the one-inch rough. There are no water hazards, but sand seems to loom on every approach shot. Trees are basically new plantings and about 430 in number, only a handful for this layout. The greens are medium in size, about 44,000 square foot each, and are flat, which makes many approach shots hard to hold. 3/30 is wide open but incorporates a lot of out-of-bounds situations if you stray too far. The contour of the course makes it easy to walk and easy to score well on, if you can hit the ball straight. With this many members it must have a lot of good things going for it; one of them has to be the people involved with the course. Try 3/30 and see what hospitality is all about.

Course	9 Holes
Distance	3175 Yards
Par	36
Playability	Fair
Aesthetics	Fair
Interest	Fair
Worth The Trip	Yes
Rating	★★+

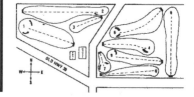

Holes	1	2	3	4	5	6	7	8	9	Out
YARDS	325	503	176	390	375	480	135	400	396	3175
MEN'S PAR	4	5	3	4	4	5	3	4	4	36
MEN'S HANDICAP	8	3	7	6	5	4	9	1	2	
YARDS	325	453	176	340	315	401	120	320	335	2785
LADIES' PAR	4	5	3	4	4	5	3	4	4	36
LADIES' HANDICAP	8	3	7	6	5	4	9	1	2	

Spring Valley Golf Club

Livermore

515-379-1259
www.springvalleygc.com

Spring Valley Golf Club came into existence only a few years ago and in that short time it has become one of the best conditioned and most talked about courses in north-central Iowa. This is a total family operation. All the design, grading of fairways, and landscaping was done by the immediate family. The 2002 season started off with 10,000 annual flowers, the place looked great! Having your own greenhouse helps with creating a beautiful course. Spring Valley Golf Course is located four miles north of Livermore and offers a country atmosphere to anyone that wants to enjoy a wide-open game of golf. The original nine holes were built in 1978 with the additional nine holes built in 1989. The new nine holes were carved out of pastureland to the south and west. The course has some flat holes near the clubhouse but the remaining layout is rolling and challenging. Creeks and ponds come into play on eleven holes making you play a position game on many of the holes. There are also one or two sand bunkers per hole and many newly created ground bunkers in some of the fairways. The grass condition of the course is really good, partially due to the fairway watering. They have even made fairway #4 Bent Grass. Rough lines all fairways and does catch an errant ball once-in-awhile. The tree size is small with many of them lining the fairways, some of the older trees are now coming into play. There are 1,500 trees on the front nine. The greens are large and rolling with many tilted. These are not member greens, they are fast and hard to read, resulting in higher scores for many. But the condition of the member's greens is very good. The emphasis on this course is condition. There is a lot of care that goes into keeping this course in excellent playing condition and making it a northern Iowa showcase of beauty. The clubhouse has a very nice eating area that overlooks the course with an accompanying bar. Oh yes, as a kicker to this great course, it was named the 9 Hole Course of the Year in Iowa in 1989!! Come to the country; it's just fine.

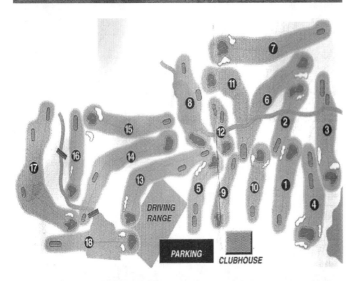

Course	18 Holes	Aesthetics	Very Good
Distance	6421 Yards	Interest	Very Good
Par	36-36-72	Worth The Trip	Yes
Playability	Very Good	Rating	★★★★

BLUE	441	192	485	302	476	380	383	165	391	3215
WHITE	424	183	480	294	466	375	373	155	383	3133
RED	404	155	445	210	394	360	358	83	375	2784
HOLE	1	2	3	4	5	6	7	8	9	OUT
PAR	4	3	5	4	5	4	4	3	4	36

374	355	140	548	529	294	351	457	158	3206	6421
364	338	130	542	518	283	342	412	123	3052	6185
353	328	115	445	130	272	333	302	105	2683	5467
10	11	12	13	14	15	16	17	18	In	Tot
4	4	3	5	5	4	4	4	3	36	72
17	13	11	4	5	18	8	2	14		

Glynns Creek Golf Course

Long Grove

563-328-3284

www.glynnscreek.com

The newest course to open in eastern Iowa is the Glynns Creek Golf Course located in Scott County Park, just north of Long Grove. This 18 hole 7,036 yard public course is set among some of the most picturesque rolling hills in this part of the state. The course will be fairly difficult to walk but will provide the average golfer with a chance to enjoy a great layout with even better scenery. The layout is designed along the lines of a Scottish course only with trees. The natural grasses and grass bunkers are incorporated into the design. The trees number in the thousands and are mature in size, which means beauty for many but hazards for a few. The trees line nine of the fairways and come into play on ten holes. There is one pond on the course and a total of 18 sand bunkers to contend with. The contour of the entire course would have to be classified as rolling and hilly with side-hill shots prevalent on many holes. Tee boxes are tiered and medium in size. The greens are medium to big in size and have been designed to challenge the average golfer. The most challenging hole on the layout would have to be number 17. A 600 yard hole, up hill, and generally into a prevailing wind. The course has a double watering system throughout so the drying hills should not be a factor as dry years come and go. The golf shop has a full range of golfing equipment and a concession area. There is also a large driving range which lessons are given by the P.G.A. Pro. Weekday green fees are $17.50. It may take a little time for the grass to mature on the hills but in a few years this may be one of the more scenic and interesting public courses in the area. Glynns Creek has a lot to offer for every type of golfer.

Clubhouse

HOLE		1	2	3	4	5	6	7	8	9	OUT
GOLD	73.5/131	429	194	365	425	400	412	505	175	499	3404
BLUE	72.1/127	413	176	343	417	377	396	490	163	485	3260
WHITE	70.4/124	394	162	321	408	349	375	473	151	467	3100
HANDICAP		6	16	14	4	2	8	12	18	10	
TIME PAR		:14	:09	:13	:15	:18	:14	:16	:09	:15	2:03
GREEN	70.6/115	357	150	283	301	313	329	414	115	428	2690
RED	68.8/110	311	150	283	301	313	302	384	115	386	2545
HANDICAP		6	16	14	12	4	8	2	18	10	
PAR		4	3	4	4	4	4	5	3	5	36

10	11	12	13	14	15	16	17	18	IN	OUT	TOT
446	207	439	403	371	546	194	600	426	3632	3404	7036
429	199	411	384	348	520	170	546	411	3440	3260	6700
401	180	380	365	321	504	158	546	398	3253	3100	6353
3	13	15	11	9	7	17	1	5			
:15	:10	:15	:14	:17	:18	:09	:18	:14	2:10		
303	165	319	320	250	468	138	454	328	2690	2690	5435
303	108	299	293	250	414	130	427	328	2552	2545	5097
3	13	11	15	9	7	1	5				
4	3	4	4	4	5	3	5	4	36	36	72

Course	18 Hole	Aesthetics	Excellent
Distance	7,036 Yards	Interest	Very Good
Par	36-36-72	Worth the Trip	Yes
Playability	Good	Rating	★★★

152

Tri-City Golf Club

Luana

319-539-4435

The Tri-City Golf Club is a semi-private course located two miles north of Luana on X-16. Non-members living outside the school district can pay green fees. The 200 members pay an initial stock of $400 with yearly fees of $160. The road leading to the clubhouse runs through the middle of the course and across three fairways. Supplies in the clubhouse include balls, gloves and a few clothes. The bar area has drinks and sandwiches. There is one stream on the course that comes into play on four holes. There is an average of one bunker per hole and a two inch rough borders the fairways. The fairways are wide and green; thanks to the fairway watering system. The fairways are also lined with evergreens and new plantings. The contour of the course is rolling to hilly. Greens are small in size. Some greens have rolling surfaces while others are crowned. The course was built in 1938 and has matured into a pleasure course. It is a short course that is hilly and hard to walk. You can spray the ball a little but a hook is penalized on four holes with out-of-bounds. The greens are getting smaller each year and tend to be too fast and too rolling. People really get involved with this course. There is excellent participation on stag night and ladies day. Like many Iowa rural course there is a mixture of age and professions; all getting along quite well.

Course	9 Holes
Distance	2821 Yards
Par	35
Playability	Fair
Aesthetics	Good
Interest	Good
Worth The Trip	Yes
Rating	★★+

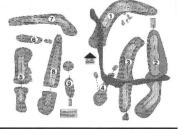

MEN'S YARDAGE	378	471	428	157	387	157	274	376	193	2821
HANDICAP	6	8	1	2	5	9	7	4	3	
MEN'S PAR	4	5	4	3	4	3	4	4	3	35
HOLE	1	2	3	4	5	6	7	8	9	Out
WOMEN'S PAR	4	5	5	3	4	3	6	5	7	35
HANDICAP	4	1	2	8	3	9	6	5	7	
WOMEN'S YARDAGE	343	438	413	113	352	148	221	369	182	2579

Diamond Trail

Lynnville

641-527-2600

Lynnville built a new course in 1999 on the SW edge of town called Diamond Trail. This 9 hole, 2997 yard course, is member owned with a 10 mile green fee radius. There is a $2500 initiation fee for the 166 members with a yearly family membership of $400. This is a fairly hilly course that is still easy to walk, 9 holes maybe not 18. The course maintained the mature trees around the edges of the course that really don't come into play. An additional 200 trees were planted over the last few years. The 6,000 square foot greens have bent grass and are easy to putt. The fairway watering keeps the course in great shape through the entire summer. A unique feature of the course is the covered bridge. The players coming off the course said Diamond Trail was the best kept secret in Iowa. It is well kept and is interesting. Water comes into play on 3 holes and average 2 sand traps per hole. Although 3 holes have 4 traps each. This is a very nice new course. I heard about this course from several other golfers on different courses as I traveled towards Lynnville, its reputation does spread across Iowa

Course	9 Holes
Distance	2997 Yards
Par	36
Playability	Good
Aesthetics	Good
Interest	Good
Worth The Trip	Yes
Rating	★★★

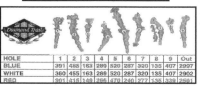

HOLE	1	2	3	4	5	6	7	8	9	Out
BLUE	391	485	163	289	520	287	320	135	407	2997
WHITE	360	455	163	289	520	287	320	135	407	2902
RED	301	415	148	266	479	240	277	135	339	2681

Spring Hills Country Club

Mallard

712-425-9582

Spring Hills Country Club is located on the east edge of Mallard and is a very nice example of a small town country club. This course has very little protection from wind or sun but has a pool to cool down members at the end of the day. The course is of medium length at 2824 yards and is quite flat, yet not real boring to look at. There is one pond on the course, three sand bunkers, and a rough that can get heavy and tough in certain places. A small quantity of trees exist on the layout and the ones that do exist are small and do not come into play. There are some medium pines that add character to the course. The Mallard course is wide open and does invite some big swinging. The greens are medium to large in size, with some elevated and some tilted. The grass condition on the greens is good while the fairway grass is a little patchy. The course was built in 1972 and has 170 members. Family memberships are $210. The clubhouse interior is very nice and carries a small line of supplies. The bar area is big and offers drinks and microwave sandwiches. Spring Hills is an easy course to walk and a fairly easy course to score well on. It is not very challenging but has the ingredients that are needed for a home grown members course.

Course	9 Holes
Distance	2757 Yards
Par	36
Playability	Fair
Aesthetics	Good
Interest	Fair
Worth The Trip	Yes
Rating	★★+

Men's Par WHITE	4	5	3	4	5	3	5	3	4	36
YARDAGE	236	469	161	245	455	167	451	170	353	2757
Handicap	⑦	⑤	②	⑨	①	⑥	④	⑧	③	Out
HOLES	1	2	3	4	5	6	7	8	9	
Women's Par RED	4	5	3	4	5	3	5	3	4	36
Women's Yardage	279	464	155	240	450	163	369	166	349	2635

Fairview Country Club

Malvern

Southwest Iowa seems to have the market on sand green courses. The Fairview Country Club in Malvern had one of the last layouts using sand. But in 1998 Malvern installed astro turf putting surfaces. You no longer have to rake the sand after play.   The course is located just on the south edge of Malvern. It is a public course with green or should I say astro fees of $8.   A new clubhouse with a kitchen was completed in 1990. The contour of the course is flat to the west, by the highway, and then builds up a hill to the east. Trees on the course line many of the medium width fairways and are medium to large in size. 106 new, fast growing trees were added in 1991. Fairview is easy to walk, easy to score on, and very easy top get on and play. Membership has increased from 50 in 1988 to 150 today. The yardage of the course is 2620 with the longest hole measuring 408 yards and the shortest 184. I am sure that astro turf is much easier to take care of but a little history has been taken away form the Iowa Golf scene.

Course	9 Holes
Distance	2620 Yards
Par	36
Playability	Fair
Aesthetics	Fair
Interest	Good
Worth The Trip	Yes
Rating	★+

HOLE	1	2	3	4	5	6	7	8	9	OUT
YARDS	297	184	307	284	296	264	268	408	312	2620
LADIES PAR	4	3	4	4	4	4	4	5	4	36
PAR	4	3	4	4	4	4	4	4	4	35
HANDICAP	3	2	9	4	5	7	8	1	6	

Manchester Country Club
Manchester
563-927-4155

Manchester Country Club is a public course that added an additional nine holes in 2001. Manchester is a challenging course layout with several tee offerings, one being up front for seniors and beginners. The uniquely designed course offers a quality 18 hole rotation intermingling the original course and the new 9 holes. The layout of the course has one water hazard guarding number 3 green. There are an average of one sand bunker per hole and a two inch rough that is very thin; allowing the ball to sink down deep creating difficult approach shots. There are clumps of big old trees throughout the course; the remainder of the trees are new plantings scattered in the rough and along the fairways. The contour of the course is rolling with wide fairways, which allows a little spraying of the ball to occur without much penalty. The new holes are more flat in nature and have new plantings. Tees are landscaped quite nicely, elevated, and a little small. Greens are also small and flat on the old holes and undulating and bigger on the new 9; but have a reputation of being easy to read and true to putt. The course was built in 1926 and operates out of a new clubhouse. There is an elegant restaurant that is open to members and guests the year round. The pro shop area has balls, gloves, and a big bar area that is relaxed. Weekday green fees are $22 for 18. This is an attractive course to play. Easy to walk, entertaining to play around and on the greens; yet has a challenge to someone who takes the game seriously. There is a little bit of everything since the additional holes have been added. The course is located South of Hwy. 20 off exit 277.

Course	18 Holes	Aesthetics	Very Good
Distance	6278 Yards	Interest	Very Good
Par	36-36-72	Worth The Trip	Yes
Playability	Good	Rating	***

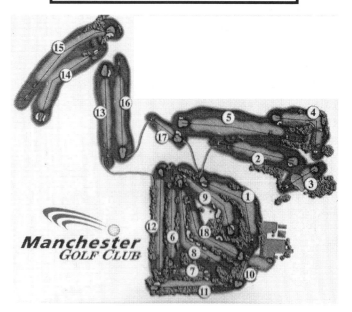

Manchester GOLF CLUB	The Walls	Gopher Hole	Water Sport	Timber Challenge	Over the Hill	Blue Spruce	Seven Steps	The Sands	Time "Team"	Out	PLAYER	The Plateau	Bunker Hill	On the Rocks	Lucky 13	Super Bowl	The Monster	Death Valley	Hide and Seek	The Oaks	In	Tot	Hcp	Net	Tee Times Recommended 563-927-4155
Hole	1	2	3	4	5	6	7	8	9	Out		10	11	12	13	14	15	16	17	18	In	Tot	Hcp	Net	
Black (Future)																									
Blue 71.0/122	387	366	165	349	503	393	173	508	310	3154		434	303	440	402	415	522	400	144	370	3124	6278			
White M: 69.6/118 W: 74.6/120	359	347	143	328	493	350	163	492	302	2977		115	291	424	384	403	503	381	128	363	2992	5969			
Blue/White HCP	1	11	17	7	5	9	15	3	13			16	14	12	6	4	2	8	18	10					
Red M: 68.9/110 W: 70.5/110	344	301	112	296	399	299	162	421	263	2587		105	256	346	313	361	438	347	93	326	2585	5172			
Red HCP	5	9	17	7	3	11	15	1	13			16	14	4	8	6	2	10	18	12					
Yellow (Youth)	129	142	74	112	170	158	84	166	121	1156		61	137	162	137	144	187	148	72	140	1188	2344			
Par	4	4	3	4	5	4	3	5	4	36		3	4	5	4	4	5	4	3	4	36	72			

Hart Ridge Golf Course

Manchester

563-927-5494

Diane and Bill Gearhart jumped into this project with both feet. Hart Ridge is a new course, opening in 1991, that is located 2 miles N.W. of Manchester on Quaker Mill Road. When you have rolling farmland with cattle sheds you do the obvious, build a golf course. In this case it might have been the right decision. Hart Ridge is a developing course that is enjoyable and friendly to play. The 2747 yard course is gently rolling until you cross the creek, all four times, then it is down and up. Almost all the existing trees, which there are quite a few in the gully, have been retained meaning that drives and approach shots do strike a branch once-in-awhile. The creek gully does provide some challenges but the general layout of the course is flat to gently rolling. Greens on the course are medium in size and challenging. There are no sand traps, no ground bunkers and no rough. There are lots of people who walk this course. This is generally an easy course to play and score well on. The remodeled clubhouse for the 250 members is found in the cattle shed, but believe me it doesn't look like there have been cattle around for a long time, a real nice Morton building with all the basics and microwave sandwiches. The course does have a driving range and has developed into a beautiful setting and excellent golfing.

Course	9 Holes
Distance	2747 Yards
Par	34
Playability	Fair
Aesthetics	Fair
Interest	Fair
Worth the Trip	Yes
Rating	★ ★

HOLE		1	2	3	4	5	6	7	8	9	IN	TOT	HCP	NET
BLUE		325	340	361	524	140	331	138	310	278	2747			
PAR	35	4	4	4	5	3	4	3	4	4	5494 4192			
RED		286	236	288	400	100	228	134	204	220	2096			

Pioneer Town and Country Club

Manly

641-454-2414

Pioneer Town and Country Club is located on the N.E. corner of Manly. This is a semi-public course that is designed for the golfer who desires a challenge. This is a difficult course to score well on because of the many hazards. There is one pond on the course affecting two holes. There is a creek that runs the length of the course and comes into play on seven holes. There are two bunkers and a large number of small trees scattered throughout the course. The fairways are of medium width but accuracy on all your shots is important because of the water. Tees are medium in size and elevated a little. Greens are medium in size also; many are slanted or banked slightly. The general contour of the course is flat except near the stream where uneven lies occur. The Manly course was built in 1969 and is still in the maturing stages. It is a tough course to score well on unless you know the positions to shot for on the layout. Green fees for this public course are reasonable in price. The cement block clubhouse has balls for sale and carts to rent. The bar has snacks and drinks; plus there is a restaurant open for special occasions. A $460 yearly fee is charged at Pioneer Town and Country. There are 150 members who enjoy a well manicured course; one that is easy to walk but tough to play. The water keeps you on your best behavior at all times.

Course	9 Holes
Distance	3053 Yards
Par	35
Playability	Good
Aesthetics	Good
Interest	Very Good
Worth The Trip	Yes
Rating	★ ★ ★

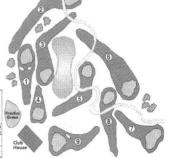

KEEP GOLF CARTS 30 ft. FROM GREENS SOFT SPIKES ONLY									
HOLE	1	2	3	4	5	6	7	8	9	Out
REGULAR	363	350	400	190	370	505	150	375	360	3053
LADIES	363	265	350	148	370	413	109	307	350	2675
PAR										

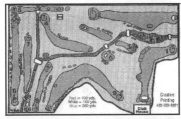

Manning-Manilla Golf Course

Highway 141 W. of Manning

712-653-3515

One of the more unusual names in Iowa golf is the M & M Country Club located half way between Manning and Manilla. The sight selection for the course is in a group of hills that has a stream running down the middle, not my idea of a nice place to chase a ball. The contour of the course is hilly, many shots are taken with the ball below or above your feet. Two ponds on the course come into play on three holes while the stream that runs the width of the course comes into play on four holes. There is no sand, but the rough narrows the fairways down to encourage straight shots. Trees line all fairways, some are larger than others but the tall poplars catch their share of drives and errant five irons. Greens are medium in size; sloping just enough to create unseen breaks. The greens are fast and are a little thin around the edges. The hills have a tendency to dry out in mid-summer leaving bare spots to hit from. The clubhouse sits on a hill to the east of the layout and has a long bar serving sandwiches and drinks. Golf supplies sold include balls, gloves, and a few clubs. They have carts for rent which come in handy the second nine holes. This is a semi-private course that has a $300 family membership fee, with a little above average green fees. The course was built in 1931 and is a true test of your climbing ability.

Course	9 Holes
Distance	2890 Yards
Par	36
Playability	Good
Aesthetics	Fair
Interest	Good
Worth The Trip	Maybe
Rating	** +

Hole	1	2	3	4	5	6	7	8	9	Total
Blue	384	482	302	375	189 174	332	293	228 189	455	3034 2986
White	372	475	295	356	154	328	287	173	450	2890
Red	314	390	287	310	141	318	260	163	370	2553
Par	4	5	4	4	3	4	4	3	5	36
HDCP	2	8	6	1	3	5	9	4	7	

Manson Golf and Country Club

Manson

712-469-3996

The Manson Golf and Country Club is located on the N.E. edge of Manson adjacent to the high school. This is a semi-private course that will accept green fees during the week and on the weekends. An initial stock of $250 was paid by the 200 members with annual fees of $250 for a family. The clubhouse is a small Morton type building that has a limited amount of supplies plus carts for rent. General bar items are available; drinks, grilled and microwaved sandwiches. In 1970 the members of the Manson Golf and Country Club purchased the golf course property from the estate that had previously owned the course. The course was completed and opened in 1979. There are very few hazards on the course. The contour of the 3041 yard layout is flat with four bunkers and no water hazards present. The trees on the course are few in number and small in stature. But new tress are added every year. Tees are elevated slightly and medium in size. Greens are medium to large in size, have flat to gently rolling putting surfaces and are easy to read. This is a wide open course with very little in your way to impede progress. A road bisects the course and causes a little confusion when driving your cart against traffic. Manson Country Club is an easy course to walk and easy to score well on. This course was conceived with local players in mind and has turned into a fun family course.

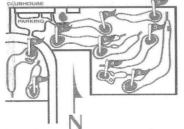

Course	9 Holes
Distance	3041 Yards
Par	36
Playability	Fair
Aesthetics	Good
Interest	Poor
Worth The Trip	Yes
Rating	++

HOLE	1	2	3	4	5	6	7	8	9	OUT
WHITE	344	358	518	136	412	304	484	177	308	3041
RED	336	350	464	129	403	295	432	163	298	2870
PAR	4	4	5	3	4	4	5	3	4	36
HANDICAP	6	4	3	9	1	7	5	2	8	

Willow Vale Golf Club

Mapleton

712-882-1002

The Willow Vale Course in Mapleton was built in 1925 but has a recently built new clubhouse that is spacious and well landscaped. The 180 members take their swings at the course located on the north edge of town on Highway 175. The contour of the course is flat with big willow trees lining some of the fairways. The fairways are narrow, making this a placement course; being in the correct position will make many of the holes much easier to control. Placement will continue to be of importance with 40 new trees added each and every year. There is one pond on the course and 21 sand bunkers, an average of two per hole. The fairway grass is in excellent condition due to fairway watering. The tees are cut nicely and are slightly elevated. The greens are small and quite undulating. This is a very well manicured course with flower beds around the clubhouse and areas between greens and tees. Because of the trees and the length of the course, this is a shot maker's layout. You get what you shoot. This is not a forgiving course. The spacious clubhouse is very nice on the inside with a big bar area that serves drinks and sandwiches. Recent changes have been expanded and moved tee boxes and more cart paths. There are also carts for rent and a full line of supplies. The daily green fees are average. The course has matured and become tighter in the last several years. Willow Vale is challenging and makes you play a thinking man's game of golf.

Course	9 Holes
Distance	3219 Yards
Par	35
Playability	Good
Aesthetics	Very Good
Interest	Good
Worth The Trip	Yes
Rating	***

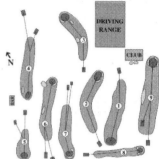

	1	2	3	4	5	6	7	8	9	OUT
BLACK	406	369	401	522	202	392	352	171	404	3219
BLUE	387	359	389	512	186	384	337	162	398	3114
PAR	4	4	4	5	3	4	4	3	4	35
HANDICAP	3	9	2	8	5	4	7	6	1	
MATCH +/-										
HOLE	1	2	3	4	5	6	7	8	9	OUT
MATCH +/-										
PAR	4	4	4	5	3	4	4	3	4	35
WHITE	357	340	367	470	152	342	316	147	380	2871
RED	340	333	343	410	141	332	295	137	292	2623

Maquoketa Country Club

Maquoketa

319-652-4515

The Maquoketa Country Club is a private club located on the west edge of Maquoketa on Highway 64. Guests must play with a member. Annual dues for the 300 members are $850 for a family; with a $450 share of stock. The clubhouse is a large modern brown structure that has an attractive restaurant available for members and their guests and a pool. The bar area has drinks and sandwiches for golfers during the day. The pro shop is located in a tiny building by the pool. Supplies are limited but they do have numerous carts for rent. The course stretches down from the clubhouse to the south. The layout has one pond affecting two holes. There are eight bunkers that are deep and molded around the greens. Trees on the course are medium in size; with some new plantings made each year. The contour of the course is rolling, especially near the clubhouse. Fairways are wide with a two inch rough separating the holes. Tee boxes are big and landscaped nicely. Greens are medium in size and flat. Two of the holes you can spray the ball without much penalty; the remaining seven requires a little more control and thought. The atmosphere is leisurely with many members taking advantage of the wonderful clubhouse facilities. Maquoketa is a well landscaped course that is young but developing into a well rounded layout.

Course	9 Holes
Distance	3095 Yards
Par	35
Playability	Very Good
Aesthetics	Very Good
Interest	Good
Worth The Trip	Yes
Rating	***+

	1	2	3	4	5	6	7	8	9	OUT
PAR	4	4	4	3	5	4	4	3	4	35
BLUE	370	338	357	209	469	381	408	375	188	3095
WHITE	353	321	343	197	458	373	396	362	175	2978
HDCP	10	18	14	4	16	6	2	8	12	
O-+WE										
HOLE	1	2	3	4	5	6	7	8	9	OUT
O-+WE										
RED	340	259	307	158	455	289	390	276	159	2780
PAR	4	4	4	3	5	4	4	3	4	36

Prairie Creek Golf Golf

Maquoketa

563-652-1833

A new 9 hole course in Maquoketa was built in 2001 on the south edge of town off 17th street. Prairie Creek Golf was farm land not too many years ago, and now it is a developing golf course and housing complex. The greens at Prairie Creek are large and uniquely shaped. Hazards on the course include sand bunkers, grass bunkers and water. There is a creek and a pond that come into play. The layout of the course is long with two par fives over 520 yards long. There are original trees on the layout and additional trees are being added every year. This is a gently rolling course that winds up through the woods making it an interesting layout. This is a new course that needs time to develop. The scenery is good, the use of the water hazards is good, and it is potentially a challenging course. But it needs time to grow into its surroundings. The clubhouse has a small amount of snacks. Green fees are $10 for weekdays. The 40 members pay an annual fee of $400 for a couple. This is a developing course that is open to the public.

Course	9 Holes
Distance	3038Yards
Par	35
Playability	Fair
Aesthetics	Fair
Interest	Fair
Worth The Trip	Yes
Rating	★★

Hole	1	2	3	4	5	6	7	8	9	Out
Red	275	425	260	135	280	230	120	455	114	
White	300	482	345	150	317	282	147	480	137	
Blue	320	502	378	160	328	314	161	507	155	
Black	345	530	405	177	365	353	177	520	166	

Marcus Community Golf Course

Marcus

712-376-4492

Marcus Golf Club is another member of the Senior League found in this part of the state. This is a good course for the senior players, the contour of the course is flat, it is a nice walking course, and there are very few difficult hazards. The course is located on the S.W. edge of Marcus along Highway 3. It's layout is fairly long at 3040 yards and lays in a diagonal direction. There are no water hazards and only two bunkers. The large poplar trees line the narrow fairways and come into play rather frequently. Numerous trees have been added over the past few years. Marcus is subject to strong winds and the effects of these gusts are only diminished by the number of trees throughout the course. The greens are medium in size and tilted. The greens are also regarded as being very fast. The course was built in 1963. Fairway irrigation was added in 1998. The clubhouse is typical of a small course with a nice bar area that serves snacks and a large dining area that is open for special occasions, there is also a new pool. This is a nice looking clubhouse that has a golfing atmosphere inside. Marcus is a very busy course, no tee times needed though. Membership size is about 260 members who pay a yearly fee of $360 for a family, green fees are very reasonable, $9 on the weekdays. This is a straight ball hitters course, off to one side on many holes and you have a 50 foot tree staring you in the face.

Course	9 Holes
Distance	3025Yards
Par	36
Playability	Fair
Aesthetics	Fair
Interest	Fair
Worth The Trip	Yes
Rating	★★

Hole	1	2	3	4	5	6	7	8	9	OUT
Men's Yards	365	495	315	200	410	320	470	295	155	3025
Men's Par	4	5	4	3	4	4	5	4	3	36
Ladies' Yards	345	475	295	180	410	300	455	280	130	2870
Ladies' Par	4	5	4	3	5	4	5	4	3	37
Handicap	3	7	5	9	1	13	11	15	17	

Marengo Country Club

Marengo

319-642-3508

The Marengo Country Club is a course of variations. No two holes play alike and no two shots are the same. The course is noted for its beautiful woodland setting. There are a medium amount of trees in which many are medium to large in size. The only major hazard is one stream that runs between the clubhouse and the course and comes into play on two holes. The tree lined fairways box in a rolling course. The tees were rebuilt in 1985 and expanded and elevated at that time. The approach shots to the small flat greens are another one of the challenges of the course. The greens have reputation of being hard to hit and hard to hold. The majority of the 165 members of Marengo Country Club are walkers although there are carts for rent. Green fees are reasonable in price with a yearly family membership of over $200. The course was first molded in 1929 and is on the upswing once again. The clubhouse has snacks and a well stocked bar plus a few golfing supplies. The Marengo Country Club, which is located two miles south of Marengo, has some fine golfing to offer. A leisurely walk and a good time would be the game of the day at Marengo.

Course	9 Holes
Distance	2809 Yards
Par	36
Playability	Very Good
Aesthetics	Excellent
Interest	Excellent
Worth The Trip	Yes
Rating	★★★+

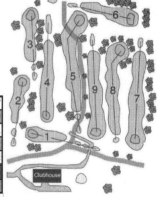

HOLE	1	2	3	4	5	6	7	8	9	OUT
BLUE TEES	165	315	291	485	411	180	346	273	343	2809
WHITE TEES	152	308	269	471	401	140	341	264	338	2684
MEN'S PAR	3	4	4	5	5	3	4	4	4	36
HANDICAP	7	4	8	2	1	9	5	6	3	
LADIES' YARDS				453	322	131	315	253	321	
LADIES' PAR	3	4	4	5	5	3	4	4	4	36

Indian Creek Country Club

Marion

319-377-4489

Indian Creek Country Club has a new modern clubhouse but still retains the old country club atmosphere. The course was built in 1925 and has a membership size of 200. These members pay an annual fee of $1500 for a family. Guests of members can pay green fees of $13, they can also eat in the fine restaurant as guests. This clubhouse dining facility has fine food and a family atmosphere. The pro shop has a full line of equipment, they also have carts for rent. This is a nine hole course that is of medium length. Indian Creek has three water hazards plus an abundance of sand. The rough is cut around tees and greens and forms a formidable barrier. The large number of trees are massive and old. A program of new plantings is being started to replace some of the oldest ones. The contour of the narrow fairways is flat. Fairway watering keeps the course in magnificent shape all during the summer. Tees are elevated and small, greens are also small and basically flat. This is an easy course to walk and easy to score well on. Trees do come into play quite a bit and the rough slows down many low rollers. This is a family club, steeped in tradition yet growing with the times. Extras include a pool on the premises. It is a busy course, but you just can't walk on and play Indian Creek any time you want a nice experience.

Course	9 Holes
Distance	2680 Yards
Par	34
Playability	Fair
Aesthetics	Excellent
Interest	Good
Worth The Trip	Yes
Rating	★★★+

MEN'S YARDS	306	200	315	283	362	132	370	300	408	2680
MEN'S PAR	4	3	4	4	4	3	4	4	4	34
MEN'S HDCP	9	3	15	11	7	17	5	13	1	
HOLE	1	2	3	4	5	6	7	8	9	OUT
LADIES' YARDS	306	200	315	283	362	132	296	300	408	2600
LADIES' PAR	4	4	4	4	4	3	4	4	5	36
LADIES' HDCP	5	15	7	11	3	17	13	9	1	

Gardner Golf Course

Marion

319-286-5586

Gardner, the old Squaw Creek Municipal Golf Course, is located at the junction of Hwy. 13 and Golf Course Road on the east side of Marion. This is a city operated 18 hole course that is located out in the country and is very scenic and tranquil. Squaw Creek has one of the biggest pro-shops in eastern Iowa. There is a tremendous selection of clothes, clubs, accessories; plus they have tables piled high with boxes of balls. The snack bar is typical for a public course with bar items and grilled sandwiches. This is not a course where you spend a lot of time in the clubhouse. People come here to play golf. The characteristics of the course include one stream that affects three holes, eleven sand bunkers, and a rough that has been mowed done to eliminate some of the frustrations and slow play of the players. Trees are small to medium in size and are generally scattered along the wide fairways. Tees are flat and big in size. Greens are medium in size and have a rolling surface. The greens have been subject to winter kill in the past and are slow to recover in the spring. The course was built in 1966 and is operated by the city. Gardner is a wide open course that has that flat, gentle roll dominating it's landscape. The course was built and is maintained with speed, durability, and heavy play in mind. This is a busy public course that requires tee-times on weekends and holidays. People travel out to this course with one purpose; play and get off. But if you do play this course make sure you spend some time in the clubhouse to browse around the many golfing items for sale. This is an easy course to walk, easy to score well on, it has some tree trouble; but basically open and hazard free. Gardner is a nice addition to the courses in the Cedar Rapids area. An exceptional public course is always a great thing to have available for all golfers.

Course	18 Holes	Aesthetics	Good
Distance	6665 Yards	Interest	Good
Par	36-36-72	Worth The Trip	Yes
Playability	Good	Rating	***

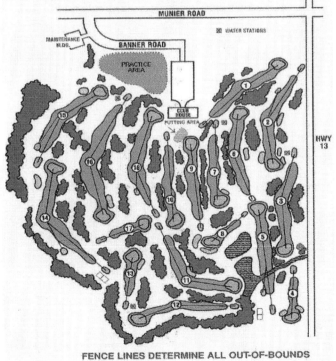

MUNIER ROAD

MAINTENANCE BLDG.

BANNER ROAD

WATER STATIONS

PRACTICE AREA

CLUB HOUSE

PUTTING AREA

HWY 13

FENCE LINES DETERMINE ALL OUT-OF-BOUNDS

PAR											P L A Y E R													
BLUE	364	504	445	138	412	453	427	218	410	3371		415	451	378	138	411	399	555	144	403	3294	6665		
WHITE	364	473	389	138	366	430	404	183	392	3139		420	416	357	138	392	383	536	144	388	3174	6313		
HANDICAP	9	15	13	11	5	17	1	7	3			6	18	12	14	10	2	8	16	4				
+/- PARTNERS																								
HOLE	1	2	3	4	5	6	7	8	9	Out		10	11	12	13	14	15	16	17	18	In	Tot	Hcp	Net
Pace of Play	:14	:31	:45	:55	1:09	1:26	1:40	1:50	2:04			2:25	2:43	2:56	3:06	3:20	3:34	3:51	4:01	4:15				
HANDICAP	13	5	11	15	9	17	1	3	7			14	18	12	10	8	4	2	16	6				
RED	332	401	343	138	302	409	371	166	361	2823		402	401	301	138	280	358	478	144	302	2804	5627		

Elmwood Country Club

Marshalltown

641-753-8111

If anyone was to rank the five best clubhouses in the state of Iowa, the Elmwood Country Club clubhouse would be near the top. The sprawling white frame structure that embodies what old style clubhouses are meant to be, has a year round restaurant that is open to members and guests and offers a very elegant atmosphere. The pro shop is located on the ground level of the clubhouse and has a full line of equipment and services. This private club located in the S.W. part of town has a total membership of 350. There is a bar and grill by the pro shop for golfers to enjoy. The character of the course is elegant. There is one pond on number 6 and two streams that come into play on seven holes. There are twenty-four bunkers on the course, all of them guarding the fronts of greens. There are some new plantings of trees on the course but the majority of the trees are old and large. All the fairways are lined with trees and two inch rough narrows the fairways down on some holes. The contour of the course is hilly, especially leading down to the streams. The greens are medium in size and have a rolling putting surface. The condition of the grass throughout the course is good, especially on the fast greens and around the tee areas. Fairway watering was installed in 1988. Elmwood has a true country club atmosphere. The members make the course thrive and families keep it alive; there are a lot of activities other than golf that go on. Elmwood is a hard course to walk but if you can keep the ball in play, an easy course to score well on. If you would like to play a course that is challenging and has a stylish club feeling and image, then Elmwood is the one you should experience. You must be a guest of a member to experience one of central Iowa's golfing treasures.

Course	18 Holes	Aesthetics	Excellent
Distance	5627 Yards	Interest	Very Good
Par	35-35-70	Worth The Trip	Yes
Playability	Very Good	Rating	★★★★

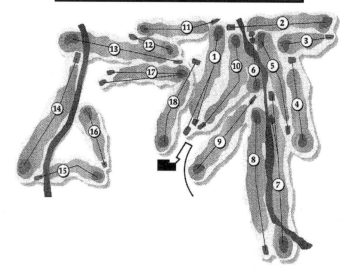

White 67.1/117	359	355	142	275	359	194 171	465	383	276	2808 2785
Par	4	4	3	4	4	3	5	4	4	35
Handicap	9	5	17	13	7	15	1	3	11	
Hole	1	2	3	4	5	6	7	8	9	OUT

383	302	119	462	419	361 336	165	319	289	2819 2794	5627 5579
4	4	3	5	4	4	3	4	4	35	70
10	12	18	2	4	6	16	8	14		
10	11	12	13	14	15	16	17	18	IN	TOT

162

Legion Memorial Golf Course
Marshalltown

515-752-1834

Marshalltown has two fine 18 hole courses. One is the Legion Memorial Golf Course located on the S.W. side of Marshalltown, 1301 So. 6th. The contour of this course is flat to gently rolling making it an enjoyable course to walk. There are carts for rent if you desire one. There are two small ponds on the course, coming into play on numbers 8,10,and 11, but they do not affect play very meh. Legion Memorial also has Linn Creek running in two directions through the course. The creek, although not very wide most of the time, comes into play on 9 holes, making it a major concern on the course. Adding to the complexity of the course are 13 bunkers, some guarding the greens, some positioned out in the middle of the fairways. All the fairways are lined with a variety of trees, mostly medium to small in size. Tees are elevated slightly and flat. Greens are medium in size, an average of 6,000 square feet per green, and have a flat to contoured putting surface. The condition of the entire course is quite good considering that there are approximately 25,000 rounds of golf played here every year. There is little league play and a junior program involves the youth of the community. The original 9 holes were built in 1957 and expanded to 18 in 1973. Today, this course would have to be considered an average players course with two tough par threes and easy par fives to make it a well-rounded and diverse course to play. There are 550 season pass holders who belong to American Legion Memorial. Cost for a yearly pass range from $350-$700. Green fees are very reasonable for weekdays $16 and a dollar more on the weekend, a nice bargain for such a nice course. The clubhouse has a full line of equipment, a PGA pro, and also provides a practice range to warm up on. The course complex has a very nice restaurant that is open to the public and has good food. This is a well-maintained course that has a lot to offer; it is busy, but many good courses are.

Yardage Discs
250 Yellow 200 Blue 150 White 100 Red

LINN CREEK

PRO SHOP

PRACTICE GREEN

DRIVING RANGE

Course	18 Holes	Aesthetics	Good
Distance	6224 Yards	Interest	Good
Par	35-35-70	Worth The Trip	Yes
Playability	Very Good	Rating	***+

HOLE	1	2	3	4	5	6	7	8	9	OUT
BLUE YARDAGES	405	616	410	391	358	400	151	334	160	3225
WHITE YARDAGES	400	603	395	366	325	385	142	315	142	3073
HANDICAP	5	1	7	11	13	3	17	9	15	
MEN'S PAR	4	5	4	4	4	4	3	4	3	35
WOMENS' PAR	4	5	5	4	4	4	3	4	3	36
RED YARDAGE	374	508	387	354	312	360	129	297	108	2829
PACE TIME	:13	:26	:39	:52	1:05	1:18	1:31	1:44	1:57	

HOLE	10	11	12	13	14	15	16	17	18	IN	TOTAL	HCP	NET
BLUE YARDAGES	349	384	487	197	344	498	171	401	168	2999	3225	6224	
WHITE YARDAGES	327	337	475	183	325	484	146	385	155	2817	3073	5890	
HANDICAP	10	4	6	14	12	8	18	2	16				
MEN'S PAR	4	4	5	3	4	5	3	4	3	35	35	70	
WOMENS' PAR	4	4	5	3	4	5	3	4	3	35	36	71	
RED YARDAGE	304	319	370	159	248	440	135	326	143	2444	2829	5273	
PACE TIME	2:10	2:23	2:36	2:49	3:02	3:15	3:28	3:41	3:54				

Highland Park Golf Course

Mason City

641-423-9693

There are 450 members of the Highland Park Public Golf Course in Mason City. With that many members there is a definite advantage to calling ahead for a tee time on this 18 hole course. There are two unique things about this course. One is the number of trees that line the fairways and that are scattered throughout the course. Wherever you look or hit there is tree trouble. The second is the fact that the front nine is divided from the back nine by a slough. The front 9 holes, built in the 1920's, can be considered a driver and wedge type of play, with a greater number of trees. The back nine, built in the 60's, is more of a long hitters' type of course, more of an open course. The pro shop is located in the old green clubhouse and has a full line of equipment. The bar area has snacks and microwave sandwiches. Although this is considered an easy course to walk there are carts for rent. The maturity of the trees is a strong characteristic of the course. Fifty foot trees line the front nine and new trees are in abundance on all 18 holes. There is approximately one sand bunker per hole with no water hazards. The fairway watering system keeps the wide fairways green all through the hot summer months. The course is basically flat which explains why the tee off boxes and greens are of the same contour. The tees are big while the greens are medium in size and about half of them tilted to catch approach shots. Highland Park Golf Course is located at 944 17 St. N.E. This is an old established course that is fun to play and beautiful at the same time. This 6202 yard course has an annual fee of $720 for a family, green fees are also quite reasonable, $15 on weekdays.

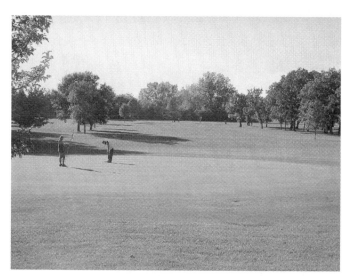

Course	18 Holes	Aesthetics	Good
Distance	6215 Yards	Interest	Good
Par	36-36-72	Worth The Trip	Yes
Playability	Good	Rating	★★+

Men's Par	5	4	3	4	4	5	3	4	4	36
Men's Tees	453	336	L 145 / R 131	331	401	422	232/180	264/252	382	2888/2966
Men's Handicap	7	13	15	17	2	9	4	18	11	
Ladies' Par	5	4	3	4	5	5	3	4	4	37
Ladies' Tees	453	329	131	331	356	422	156	239	300	2717
Ladies' Handicap	1	11	17	8	7	12	16	14	5	
Holes	1	2	3	4	5	6	7	8	9	out

4	3	5	4	4	5	4	3	4	36	72		
370	137	529	395	410	488	378	161	381	3249	6137/6215	Rtd	Slope
12	16	1	14	6	5	10	8	3			69	110
4	3	5	5	4	5	4	3.	4	37	74		
370	107	435	395	321	401	378	161	381	2949	5666	Rtd	Slope
9	15	6	4	13	3	10	18	2			70.9	110
10	11	12	13	14	15	16	17	18	In	Tot	Hcp	

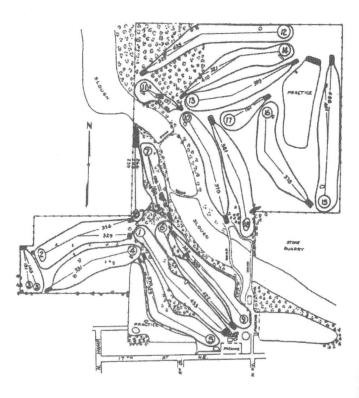

164

Mason City Country Club
Mason City
641-424-3014

Greens make the Mason City Country Club one of the more challenging clubs in northern Iowa. The size of the greens is tiny to small, the contours are flat and tilted, and the speed is fast. Combine all of these things and you have greens that are hard to stick and even tougher to get the ball in the hole. An added hazard on this 18 hole course are the 27 bunkers and the one pond. The new and medium size trees line the narrow and flat fairways. 300 new trees were planted since 2000. The fairway watering system keeps the 3 inch rough plush and difficult to find relief. Rough also surrounds the big elevated tee off boxes. Mason City Country Club is a course that is both challenging and fun. The clubhouse has a full line of equipment in the pro shop and the staff is willing to help in any way they can. The clubhouse is nice and has a full time restaurant, open nine months of the year and is available to members and guests only. This is considered one of the finer places to dine in Mason City. During the day golfers can order food and drinks from the snack bar by the pool. This private course has a membership size of 300 with a one time stock of $500 and a yearly membership fee of $1104. If you are a guest or an out of town country club member you can pay the moderate green fees and enjoy one of the finer courses in the state. This country club has a family oriented atmosphere and is located on Highway 106 west in Mason City.

Course	18 Holes	Aesthetics	Very Good
Distance	6234 Yards	Interest	Good
Par	36-36-72	Worth The Trip	Yes
Playability	Good	Rating	★★★+

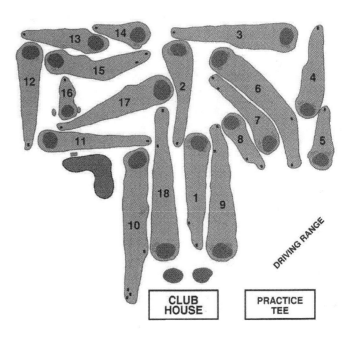

MENS	YARDAGE	379	349	362	304	112	482	404	206	517	3115
	PAR	4	4	4	4	3	5	4	3	5	36
HANDICAP MEN		7	11	9	13	17	3	5	15	1	
HOLE NO.		1	2	3	4	5	6	7	8	9	OUT
HANDICAP LADIES		13	3	1	11	17	7	5	15	9	
LADIES	YARDAGE	299	338	241	294	90	406	337	160	429	2594
	PAR	4	4	4	4	3	5	4	3	5	36

500	381	346	278	156	365	175	397	521	3119	6234			
5	4	4	4	3	4	3	4	5	36	72			
4	12	10	16	18	6	14	8	2	OUT				
10	11	12	13	14	15	16	17	18	OUT	TTL	HCP	NET
8	4	6	16	18	2	14	12	10	OUT			
435	263	339	278	150	310	166	388	423	2752	5346			
5	4	4	4	3	4	3	5	5	37	73			

165

Pine Creek Golf Course

Mason City

641-423-6831

Pine Creek Golf Course in Mason City is a short course with a length of 1856 yards and a par 32. The course is located 4 miles north of Mason City on Highway 65. Green fees are very reasonable. The course has also gone an extensive renovation with seven new holes and extended yardage. There is a small stream on the course that comes into play on seven holes and there are numerous sand bunkers with all new sand bunkers being added in 1992. There is a wide variety and size of trees on the course, and tree trouble can happen on five of the holes. The large trees are one of the highlights of this revamped course. The contour of the course is flat but a 2 inch rough along the wide fairways cuts down on the free swinging that you can do. It is considered a fairly hard course to score well on. This is a very novel little course. It is very neat and clean and easy to get on, making 9 holes of play after work a reality.

HOLES	1	2	3	4	5	6	7	8	9	OUT
Gold Tees										
Blue Tees	110	95	218	139	265	138	172	230	275	1642
Red Tees	110	95	205	134	230	96	160	201	169	1400
Par	3	3	4	3	4	3	3	4	4/3	31/30
Handicap	8	7	9	5	6	3	1	4	2	

Course	9 Holes
Distance	1741 Yards
Par	32
Playability	Very Good
Aesthetics	Good
Interest	Good
Worth The Trip	Yes
Rating	★★★

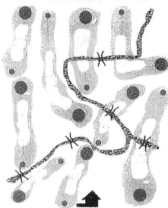

Course	9 Holes
Distance	3267 Yards
Par	36
Playability	Very Good
Aesthetics	Fair
Interest	Good
Worth The Trip	Yes
Rating	★★+

N↑

	1	2	3	4	5	6	7	8	9	OUT
BLUE	399	193	468	505	217	389	133	514	410	3208
WHITE	386	163	448	492	208	376	113	490	398	3074
(Seniors) YELLOW	370	135	437	484	200	364	107	482	387	2966
HANDICAP	5	7	9	15	3	11	17	13	1	
MENS PAR	4	3	5	5	3	4	3	5	4	36
LADIES PAR	4	3	5	5	4	4	3	5	5	38
HANDICAP	9	15	11	3	13	1	17	5	7	
RED	296	131	369	431	211	365	113	428	416	2740

5 X 80 Country Club

Menlo, Adair, Casey, Stuart, and Dexter

641-524-2345

The 5 X 80 Country Club is located at the intersection of I-80 and Highway 25. This facility serves five communities in the area; providing them with golf, swimming, tennis, and restaurant facilities. 5 X 80 has one pond that you drive across on number two, no streams, and four bunkers. There have been many new trees added since 1995. Small evergreens and new trees line some of the fairways. The contour of this course is flat with a gentle roll by the water. The tees are medium in size and the greens are also medium in size and flat. The course was built in 1965. The clubhouse is a new structure, similar to a Morton building, that has bar and snack facilities inside. There is also a full restaurant that is open to the paying golfers. Supplies include the basics; balls, gloves, carts for rent. This semi-private club has a green fees radius of outside the 5 X 80 area. The 160 members pay an annual fee of $700. Green fees are very reasonable, $13 for 9 holes on weekdays. 5 X 80 is an interesting course to play. It's fairways are open and conducive to free swinging. There are few hazards to slow your attack down, which makes playing time a little less. Overall this course is a little harder to play than first thought. It's length is a little deceiving, with a long par 3 and three par fives building up your scores.

166

Amana Colonies Golf Course

Middle Amana

319 622 6222
800 383 3636

Amana Colonies Golf Course offers one of the best, if not the best, golf setting in the state of Iowa. The course was designed and built with extra care to preserve the natural beauty of the area. This 18 hole championship course is cut out of 300 acres of rolling woods. This 6824 yard course is located one mile north of Middle Amana and provides golfers with some of the most beautiful and enchanting scenery in Iowa. The massive clubhouse offers full service for the public the year round. The pro shop has a full line of equipment along with lessons and driving range facilities. The layout of the course ranges from gently rolling to severe hills, there are basically no flat lies. The narrow bent grass fairways wind their way up, down, around, and over the countryside. Bulldozing the layout took a few trees but many of the 150 year old hardwoods are still lining the fairways and creating a forest between green and the next tee box. There is an average of 3 sand bunkers per hole, generally surrounding the green, but the slope of the fairways will give you much more anguish than the sand. Although there is really no need for rough, there is a unmistakable 2 inch cut down the sides and in front of greens and tees. A few yards of many holes are left uncut and natural, a real hazard, but a very nice touch in keeping with nature. There are 5 sets of elevated tees with yardages ranging from 5228 to 6824. The greens are large in size, tilted and generally rolling. They have the reputation of being hard to read and with deceiving putting lines. This is definitely a cart course with 6 1/2 miles of walking, all up hill. Carts are required before 2:00 p.m. each day. Amana is a challenging course for a number of reasons, but I think the one that strikes you first is that the natural beauty has been incorporated in the course, and this natural beauty means natural hazards. Amana has been left as natural as possible. It is a beautiful course that embraces all the best things about golf in Iowa. The Amana Colonies Golf Course is one of the five best courses in the state and you must play it if you call yourself an Iowa Golfer.

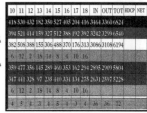

HOLE	1	2	3	4	5	6	7	8	9	OUT
BLACK	420	522	412	179	372	548	348	191	368	3360
BLUE	403	511	407	166	360	521	338	174	361	3241
WHITE	388	491	391	149	341	504	331	155	358	3108
MEN'S HDCP	7	1	3	17	9	5	11	15	13	
GOLD	375	456	365	120	328	489	298	131	344	2909
RED	348	431	343	119	236	450	261	96	313	2597
LADIES' HDCP	7	1	3	17	9	5	11	15	13	
PAR	4	5	4	3	4	5	4	3	4	36

10	11	12	13	14	15	16	17	18	IN	OUT	TOT	HDCP	NET
418	530	432	182	350	527	405	204	416	3464	3360	6824		
394	521	414	159	327	512	388	192	392	3242	3299	6540		
382	508	388	155	306	488	370	176	313	3086	3108	6194		
6	12	2	18	14	8	4	10	16					
359	477	356	145	289	360	353	162	294	2809	2909	5801		
347	441	328	97	235	440	334	134	275	2631	2597	5228		
6	12	2	18	14	8	4	10	16					
4	5	4	3	4	5	4	3	4	36	36	72		

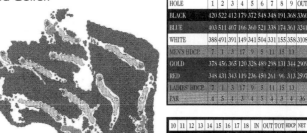

Course	18 Holes	Aesthetics	The Best
Distance	6824 Yards	Interest	Excellent
Par	36-36-72	Worth the Trip	Yes
Playability	Excellent	Rating	★★★★★

Woodlyn Hills Golf Course

Milford

712-338-9898

Course	18 Holes	Aesthetics	Very Good
Distance	2660 Yards	Interest	Good
Par	35	Worth The Trip	Yes
Playability	Fair	Rating	★★+

Woodlyn Hills Golf Course, located 1 1/2 miles east of Milford, has about 200 members but plays like 300 due to the tourist population in the summer. Green fees on this public course are $11 for all day; any day. Memberships are also available at $250 for a family. The clubhouse has a snack bar and newly added pro shop. They have clubs and carts for rent, plus a nice selection of merchandise for sale. Visiting golfers are attracted to Woodlyn Hills for a number of reasons. It is an excellent golf value, especially for families on vacation. Woodlyn Hills expanded to 18 holes in the summer of 2003. The additional 9 holes were laid out to the north and bring in some more rolling fairways and marsh land. Woodlyn Hills is challenging without being too long. Five holes border the pond with a variety of wildlife. There are no sand traps and a minimum amount of rough runs the length of the fairways. Many new trees have been planted over the years with several added each year. The contour of the course is generally flat with some slope coming near the water. Tees are small, greens are also small on the old nine with sloping surfaces but are easy to hold on approach shots. The new 9 have larger greens with much more challenging reads. Woodlyn Hills is an easy course to walk and an easy course to score well on. It is a relaxed, laid back course helped along by the surrounding beauty. The expansion to 18 was done in part to help the summer tourist crowd. If you are in the lakes area and you want to play some golf that is relaxing and worth the money, Woodlyn Hills is the place; it may require a little wait at the first tee, but it will be worth it.

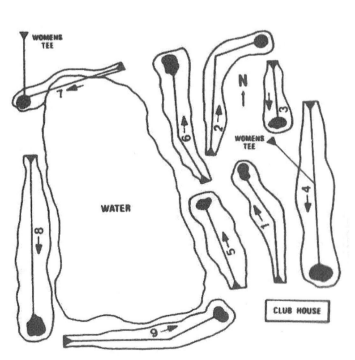

HOLE	1	2	3	4	5	6	7	8	9	OUT
MEN'S YARDAGE	360	315	165	505	160	445	120	290	300	2660
HANDICAP	1	6	3	2	4	8	7	9	5	
MEN'S PAR	4	4	3	5	3	5	3	4	4	35
WOMEN'S PAR	4	4	3	5	3	5	3	4	4	35
WOMEN'S YARDAGE	345	290	155	415	155	405	100	285	300	2450

Logan-Missouri Valley Country Club

Missouri Valley-Logan

712-642-2124

The Logan-Missouri Valley Country Club is a shared course located on Highway 30 between Logan and Missouri Valley. This is a private course which will accept green fees from outside of Harrison county. Weekday green fees are a little above average for a course this size. There are 225 members each paying an annual family membership of $550. L-MV has a stylish clubhouse that has a full time restaurant open Tuesday through Saturday. The clubhouse also has a spacious bar area that serves drinks, sandwiches, and sells a small amount of golfing supplies. There are no water hazards on the course, three bunkers, and very little rough to contend with. Trees come in all sizes and line many of the narrow fairways. The contour of the course is flat to the east and hilly to the west with a bank of trees throwing balls back down onto the course. The tees are medium in size and elevated slightly. The greens are small in size and hard to hold. L-MV was built in 1946 and is a mature course with tree and hill trouble. The landscaping on the course makes it stand out. The grass is in great condition. The course is interesting and somewhat of a challenge to play.

Course	9 Holes
Distance	3008 Yards
Par	35
Playability	Good
Aesthetics	Good
Interest	Fair
Worth The Trip	Yes
Rating	★★+

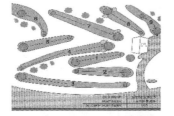

HOLE	1	2	3	4	5	6	7	8	9	OUT
MENS YARDS	266	151	398	461	161	403	372	307	325	2844
LADIES YARDS	258	129	357	444	142	397	351	280	294	2652
MENS PAR	4	3	4	5	3	4	4	4	4	35
LADIES PAR	4	3	4	5	3	4	4	4	4	35

Monroe Gateway Recreation

Monroe

641-259-3246

The Monroe Gateway Recreation Golf Course is another fine small town golf course. This 9 hole semi-private course, having a ten mile greens fee radius, is located on the west edge of Monroe. The 400 members purchase an initial stock of $100 then pay an annual fee of $350. Green fees are average for a course this size, $10.50 for 9 holes. The clubhouse is a new brick building that has been remodeled with additional supplies now available. There are carts for rent to traverse this gently rolling course. The characteristics of the course include one stream that comes into play on three holes, plus there is one pond that you drive over on number 5. The pond was extended in 2000. The new fairway watering keeps the course in good shape. Several additional sand bunkers have been added making this course a little more interesting. There have been over 100 trees planted in the last 5 years with a few medium size ones by the stream. The fairways are wide on this open course with very little rough to contend with. The greens are medium in size and flat in surface contour, which lends itself to a lot of putting speed. The greens are elevated which makes it very difficult to roll your approach shot on. The Monroe course was built in 1968 and has a pool by number 7 green. This is a good course to try if you want to work on your uphill and downhill lies.

Course	9 Holes
Distance	2871 Yards
Par	36
Playability	Poor
Aesthetics	Fair
Interest	Poor
Worth The Trip	No
Rating	★+

HOLE	1	2	3	4	5	6	7	8	9	IN
YARDAGE	324	428	152	376	330	463	140	325	333	2871
MEN'S PAR	4	5	3	4	4	5	3	4	4	36
WOMEN'S PAR	4	5	3	5	4	5	3	4	4	37
HANDICAP	11	13	15	1	3	9	7	17	5	

Montezuma Country Club

Montezuma

641-623-5714

The Montezuma Country Club is located 1 mile west of Montezuma on county road F57. The clubhouse is located on the northeast corner of the course and only serves food for special events. There is no snack bar, no beverages, no supplies, and no one to take your money, although course policing is in effect at all times— pay on tee box #1. There is a pool located by the clubhouse which is used by the town. The courses contour is quite hilly; in fact there doesn't seem to be a level lie on the course. Very few hazards exist, only two bunkers to catch an errant shot. There are a medium amount of trees on the course, mostly in the 10 to 20 foot range. The fairways are wide with no distinct rough cut. Tees are flat and small in size, greens are medium to large in size and flat with a little slope to some of them. A lake has been added to the layout and a fairway irrigation system helps with the condition of the course. The Montezuma course is not very busy, waiting to tee off is no problem. This is an easy course to score well on but fairly hard to walk. Montezuma is another small town course that is maintained quite well but played very little. A hidden treasure for the members.

Course	9 Holes
Distance	2933 Yards
Par	35
Playability	Good
Aesthetics	Good
Interest	Fair
Worth The Trip	Yes
Rating	★★

HOLES	1	2	3	4	5	6	7	8	9	OUT
MEN'S YARDS	365	340	240	305	164	366	422	573	158	2933
MEN'S PAR	4	4	4	4	3	4	4	5	3	35
LADIES' YARDS	350	300	200	287	147	326	377	533	110	2630
LADIES' PAR	4	4	4	4	3	4	5	6	3	37

Monticello Golf Club

Monticello

319-465-5225

There is one unique thing about the Monticello Golf Course and that is the racetrack that runs parallel to number nine fairway. It is very possible to slice your drive onto the track which makes retrieval a little difficult during a race. The course is located on the fairgrounds of Monticello, in the 600 block of N. Maple. There are 240 members of this private club who pay a family fee of $350. Weekday green fees are reasonable and even less when playing with a member. The clubhouse has a nice bar area but a limited amount of supplies. There is a short order menu available during the day in the clubhouse. The course was built in the 1930's and has developed into a small compact golf course that is flat and easy to walk. There is one pond on the course and a small amount of sand. The trees are medium in size, with a few new plantings. At this time they are of no threat to the golfer. The fairways are narrow and flat with very little rough to hinder a stray ball. Tees are spotty in some instances but elevated and big. The greens are small, a few flat, a few sloping and all fairly hard to read and putt. This is a family and couples oriented course that is easy to play and easy to get on.

Course	9 Holes
Distance	3026 Yards
Par	34
Playability	Fair
Aesthetics	Fair
Interest	Fair
Worth The Trip	Yes
Rating	★★

MEN'S YDG.	303	361	508	360	295	220	342	130	490	3009
MEN'S PAR	4	4	5	4	4	3	4	3	5	36
HANDICAP	17	1	9	3	13	5	11	15	7	
LADIES' YDG.	271	346	410	306	281	210	315	120	370	2629
LADIES' PAR	4	4	5	4	4	4	4	3	5	37
HANDICAP	13	1	5	3	15	17	7	11	9	
HOLES	1	2	3	4	5	6	7	8	9	Out

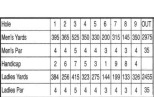

Mount Ayr Golf and Country Club

Mount Ayr

515-464-2430

The Mount Ayr Golf and Country Club is located on the S.E. corner of Mount Ayr and offers a golfing atmosphere that is relaxed, fun, and bordering easy. Hazards on the course include two ponds that affect three holes during the rainy season, no sand and no rough unless you really get off the beaten path. The trees range from new plantings to twenty foot poplars to mature leafy trees. There are some new plantings that line some of the fairways and are definitely coming into play. The condition of the grass throughout the layout is good. One of the nicer features of the course are the tee boxes. They are landscaped nicely, in plush condition, elevated and of medium size. The greens are small to medium in size and tend to have flat putting surfaces. The contour of the course is gently rolling, a nice walking course. This layout would be considered more of a driver and five iron course. The clubhouse was remodeled in 1993 and has a nice bar and sandwich area. Mount Ayr has 196 members paying an annual fee of $240. There is a limited amount of supplies and a few carts for rent. Mount Ayr is an easy course to walk and play. It is a course that only asks that you have a good time and leave the turf the way you found it.

Course	9 Holes
Distance	2975Yards
Par	35
Playability	Good
Aesthetics	Good
Interest	Fair
Worth The Trip	Yes
Rating	★★

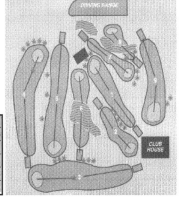

Hole	1	2	3	4	5	6	7	8	9	OUT
Men's Yards	395	365	525	350	330	200	315	145	350	2975
Men's Par	4	4	5	4	4	3	4	3	4	35
Handicap	2	6	7	5	3	1	9	8	4	
Ladies Yards	384	256	415	323	275	144	199	133	326	2455
Ladies Par	4	4	5	4	4	3	4	3	4	35

Mount Pleasant Golf and Country Club

Mount Pleasant

319-986-6157

Mount Pleasant Golf and Country Club is a private course located just north of the Blue Bird Bus buildings in Mount Pleasant. The 230 members pay a family fee of $1250 while green fees are accepted from anyone living outside the Henry county area. A new clubhouse provides drinks and sandwiches. Supplies include balls, gloves and carts. The 2833 yard layout has one pond, one stream, no sand, and no rough. 96 trees have been added during the past five years and come medium to small in size. The contour of the watered fairways is gently rolling with many of them lined with assorted trees, but posing no real threat to the golfer. Something that you may find difficult in traversing are the ravines that run through the course. One ravine affects play on four holes. A new pond was built in 99 and comes into play on #2 and #9. Tees are elevated and in good shape. One of the most outstanding characteristics of Mount Pleasant are the greens. They are small in size and rolling with some tilt in surface contour. They make the course much more difficult to score well on, and the placement of the pins is a good thing to know before you tee off on number one. This is a busy course that is easy to walk and can be easy if you play with authority. Attack the greens and don't let them scare you into submission.

Course	9 Holes
Distance	2833 Yards
Par	36
Playability	Fair
Aesthetics	Good
Interest	Fair
Worth The Trip	Yes
Rating	★★+

HOLE	1	2	3	4	5	6	7	8	9	OUT
MEN	273	354	140	450	150	433	367	310	356	2833
PAR	4	4	3	5	3	5	4	4	4	36
HANDICAP	9	4	7	3	8	6	2	5	1	

Hillcrest Country Club

Mount Vernon

319-895-8193

The condition of the greens can form the character of a course. The Hillcrest Country Club, located one mile east of Mt. Vernon, is a course where the talk in the clubhouse is based around the greens. They're too small, they're too fast, too many breaks, very deceptive. The greens are a little small and flat but they still have a lot of character, they bring life to the layout. The contour of the course is flat with a two inch rough guarding the narrow fairways and tiered around the greens. Trees on the course are of every size and are scattered throughout the 2521 yard course. Hillcrest, which was built in 1953, is a couples oriented course. There is a nice bar area that overlooks the course to the east. This is a fun and sporty course that has 190 members paying a family fee of $500 per year. This is also a deceptively tough course that is hard to walk and generally considered a cart course. Try the greens and then plead your case in the clubhouse! I'm sure they have heard it all before.

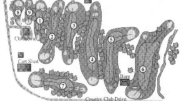

Course	9 Holes
Distance	2521 Yards
Par	35
Playability	Fair
Aesthetics	Fair
Interest	Good
Worth The Trip	Yes
Rating	★★

Hole	1	2	3	4	5	6	7	8	9	Out
Black	255	304	331	481	256	299	290	155	176	2521
Gold	243	285	325	469	251	286	275	143	169	2482
Men's Handicap	17	7	5	15	13	3	11	9	1	
Women's Handicap	15	7	5	3	9	13	11	17	1	
Red	237	279	286	410	251	260	257	133	169	2282
Par	4	4	4	5	4	4	4	3	3	35

The Meadows Country Club

Moville

712-873-3184

The Meadows Country Club on the north side of Moville has a little bit of history built in. The course was built in 1968 on 78 acres of farm land that had a big white barn. The barn, which was built in 1917, was converted into a spacious clubhouse. Inside there is a nice bar area and a very nice special occasions dining facility. There is a full line of equipment on hand and the green fees are very reasonably priced at $11. This is a busy course that has a gently rolling layout. There are three ponds that come into play on four holes and two bunkers, at one and three. Trees are small in stature and medium in number and do not play much of a part on this course. The grass throughout the course is watered daily and maintains its plush condition all summer. The greens are big and rolling and have a history of being some of the best in the area. Meadows has a family atmosphere. A youth program lasts ten weeks in the summer and is a start for their high school teams that have been to state many times in the past. They like their golf in Moville, and I like their course, a well kept small town course that originated from the basics and has developed into a fine recreation facility. This is a very interesting course that is in good shape. It is traditionally mentioned as one of the toughest 9 hole courses in Iowa.

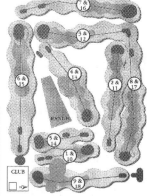

Course	9 Holes
Distance	3388 Yards
Par	36
Playability	Good
Aesthetics	Very Good
Interest	Good
Worth The Trip	Yes
Rating	★★★+

MEN'S HCP	6	4	2	3	8	1	5	7	9	
BLUE TEES	208	451	290	432	220	515	402	537	333	3388
WHITE TEES	200	441	280	420	185	505	390	528	267	3216
PAR	3	5	4	4	3	5	4	5	4	36
HOLE	1	2	3	4	5	6	7	8	9	OUT
PAR	3	5	4	4	3	5	4	5	4	36
RED TEES	172	432	219	407	157	449	290	437	256	2819
LADIES HCP	5	3	8	2	9	1	6	4	7	

Geneva Golf and Country Club
Muscatine
319-262-8894

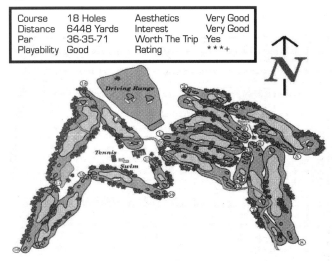

The Geneva Golf and Country Club was rebuilt in 1980 and offers the golfers of eastern Iowa a chance to play a narrow and short course. This private 18 hole course is 6448 yards long and carries a par of 71. The layout of the course has been completely re-arranged. The new layout is fairly difficult and relies on past experience to guide your choices. There is now hidden trouble and blind shots. The characteristics of the course include one pond, one stream that comes into play on five holes, an average of three sand bunkers per hole, and a two inch rough that makes the fairways play even narrower. The contour of the course is rolling with many uneven lies confronting the golfer. There are a large number of trees lining many of the fairways. These trees are either old and large or new plantings. The back nine has more new plantings since it was first laid out in 1980. The condition of the grass throughout the course is helped by the fairway watering system. Tees do tend to be a little spotty from the heavy traffic. Geneva makes up for it's below average grass condition by constructing tees large, tiered, and beautifully landscaped. The greens are tilted and rolling, medium in size; which carries over the basic contour of the fairways. A new expansive clubhouse was built last year and has a pro shop that offers a full line of supplies and lessons on the driving range. The clubhouse offers a year round restaurant that has a relaxed atmosphere - plus good food - and is open to members and their guests. Members also enjoy a pool that is located by the clubhouse. During the day snacks and drinks can be found on the lower level of the clubhouse. Green fees for guests are very reasonable. Geneva is a cart course that is short but rewards accuracy off the tees and on approach shots; a long ball is not helpful on Geneva. It is an entertaining course to play, full of challenges and hazards. Geneva has a relaxed country club feeling with some of the perks from the old style country club. The course can be found on bypass 61 in Muscatine.

Course	18 Holes	Aesthetics	Very Good
Distance	6448 Yards	Interest	Very Good
Par	36-35-71	Worth The Trip	Yes
Playability	Good	Rating	***+

HOLE	1	2	3	4	5	6	7	8	9	OUT		10	11	12	13	14	15	16	17	18	IN	TOT	Rated/Slope
BLUE	357	377	171	503	204	380	174	586	360	3112		341	188	410	170	375	512	350	560	430	3336	6448	70.5/128
WHITE	342	361	150	480	185	358	158	560	350	2944		328	149	365	155	353	490	336	538	410	3144	6088	69.3/123
GOLD	294	320	145	440	155	338	140	484	310	2626		275	132	298	134	278	440	329	464	379	2729	5355	66.0/114
HANDICAP	7	5	17	9	11	3	15	1	13			8	18	4	16	14	10	12	2	6		HCP	NET
PAR	4	4	3	5	3	4	3	5	4	35		4	3	4	3	4	5	4	5	4	36	71	
MBR#																							
MBR#																							
HANDICAP	11	7	15	3	17	5	13	1	9	1		14	18	8	16	12	4	10	2	6			Rated/Slope
RED	288	308	128	419	142	298	140	474	203	2480		263	102	284	129	268	426	320	450	365	2607	5087	68.8/118

(PLAYER)

173

Muscatine Municipal Golf Course

Muscatine

319-263-4735

The other selection of 18 hole courses in Muscatine is the Muscatine Municipal Golf Course on Highway 38 north. This is a public course that has 450 members who pay a yearly fee of $450. Green fees of $11 are very reasonable for an 18 hole course. The municipal course was built in 1967 and is still in the maturing stage. Trees consist of new plantings, small in size and scattered throughout the course. Plus some mature trees that are now just coming into play. Water hazards include one pond and one stream. Muscatine Municipal does have an average of one bunker per hole to make things interesting along the flat fairways. There is a short rough lining the wide fairways but does not take away from the expansive fairways. Tees are very large, flat, with a few tiered. Greens are medium in size and generally flat. Muscatine Muni is a course that is wide open and an intriguing place to play. It is also an easy course to score well on once you know the layout and the placement of hazards. There is very little tree trouble yet and all the other hazards are fair and easy to avoid. This is another one of the young courses that mature trees will change the character of the course drastically. The clubhouse is a metal building that is basic inside. There is a full line of equipment, including clubs and clothes. Food consists of hot dogs and brats with a drinks also available. This 18 hole course also sports a driving range and big shaded parking area. The staff has done a fine job keeping this course in above-average condition considering the traffic that it handles. If you are looking for a course that offers wide open swinging with few penalties, and one that brings some fun back into your game, then Muscatine Municipal might be a course to try. Call ahead for tee times and bring your gorilla swing with you; just don't hurt yourself.

Course	18 Holes	Aesthetics	Good
Distance	6520 Yards	Interest	Good
Par	36-36-72	Worth The Trip	Yes
Playability	Good	Rating	★★+

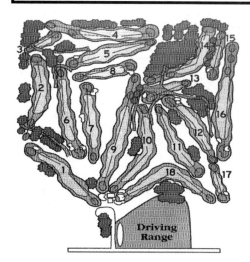

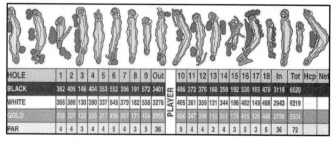

HOLE	1	2	3	4	5	6	7	8	9	Out		10	11	12	13	14	15	16	17	18	In	Tot	Hcp	Net
BLACK	382	405	146	404	353	552	396	191	572	3401		486	372	376	160	359	192	530	165	479	3119	6520		
WHITE	366	389	130	390	337	545	379	182	558	3276		465	361	359	131	344	186	482	149	466	2943	6219		
GOLD	758	307	120	336	317	435	367	171	484	2966		456	347	348	110	311	174	410	135	445	2738	5604		
PAR	4	4	3	4	4	5	4	3	5	36		5	4	4	3	4	3	5	3	5	36	72		

Whispering Pines Golf Course
Muscatine
563-288-4324

Whispering Pines Golf Course is a new 9 hole public course in the Muscatine area. The 3038 yard par 36 course was built in 2000 on local farm land and is located just off bypass 61. Like many new courses being built around the state Whispering Pines is laid out within a housing development. "You are just about as likely to hit a house as a tree out there," said a player in the clubhouse. The greens are medium in size and generally rolling in nature. There are an average of one sand bunker per hole mainly guarding the fronts of the greens. A tiered rough lines the fairways. Yardage ranges from 168 to 525 yards, with three holes being fairly severe doglegs. Even though Whispering Pines is young the trees are medium in size. Two ponds do come into play on 2 holes. This is a likeable course, easy to get on, inexpensive and fun to play. The clubhouse as sandwiches and a small pro shop. Daily green fees are $15 that includes a cart. The big pond in front of the clubhouse welcomes you to Whispering Pines.

Course	9 Holes
Distance	3038 Yards
Par	36
Playability	Good
Aesthetics	Very Good
Interest	Good
Worth The Trip	Yes
Rating	★ ★ ★

Nashua Town and Country Club
Nashua
641-435-4466

The Town and Country Club in Nashua is located south of town on Asherton Ave. . This private course was built in 1962 and is just starting to mature into a challenging course. The large greens are the most unique feature on the course. Pin placement is very important in the way you attack this course. Greens can become almost impossible if the pins are put in a difficult spot. As for the remainder of the course there are no water hazards and five sand bunkers guarding the greens. Trees are small to medium in size and generally line the fairway. The maturing trees have made the par 5's play closer to their rating. The contour of the course is hilly and it's difficult to walk but the wide fairways do provide a chance to go for the long drive. The clubhouse has an adequate supply of balls and gloves and also has carts for rent for the non-walker. The bar area offers drinks and microwave sandwiches. If putting is the thorn in your side then the course in Nashua may be a pain in your lower back. Town and Country drains very well and is usually one of the first courses open in the spring or after a heavy rain in the summer. Town and Country is a thinking person's course. The saying that golf is 90 % mental can be documented on this course, if you forget what you are doing your game can get out of hand.

Course	9 Holes
Distance	2956 Yards
Par	35
Playability	Fair
Aesthetics	Good
Interest	Good
Worth The Trip	Yes
Rating	★ ★ ★

HOLE	1	2	3	4	5	6	7	8	9	OUT
Distance	387	165	331	179	372	470	411	196	445	2956
Men's Par	4	3	4	3	4	5	4	3	5	35
Ladies' Par	4	3	4	3	4	5	5	3	5	36
Handicap	13	17	7	15	9	1	5	11	3	

Quail Run Country club

Neola

712-485-2266

A new course in western Iowa is Quail Run in Neola. This is a course with a layout that benefits senior players and high handicappers. It is a wide-open course that lets you play out of hazards. There are no bunkers and the rough is easy to get out of. It is a quiet course, meaning that nothing jumps out at you and ruins your day. One of the unique features of the course is the pond on number 6 that surrounds the green, not quite an island green but close. Quail Run was built in 1995 and is located 2 miles west of Neola. This is another current example of a local association securing the money and building a course that fits the needs of the local interest. Greens are medium in size and flat. The course sprang out of a farm field so all the trees have been planted. The clubhouse sits on a hill overlooking the course. The 150 members pay a yearly fee of $540 with green fees of $10 for a weekday. There is also a driving range to the west of the course. This is a nice developing course, one that has some interesting characteristics. I would certainly recommend this course for anyone that would like a nice walk, not ruined by the game of golf.

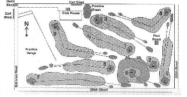

Course	9 Holes
Distance	3277 Yards
Par	36
Playability	Good
Aesthetics	Good
Interest	Good
Worth The Trip	Yes
Rating	★★

	1	2	3	4	5	6	7	8	9	OUT
Blue Tees	367	190	472	405	330	175	539	400	399	3277
White Tees	331	169	441	371	303	146	506	373	385	3025
Red Tees	288	102	390	290	236	117	444	318	339	2524
PAR	4	3	5	4	4	3	5	4	4	36
Hole	1	2	3	4	5	6	7	8	9	OUT

Indian Creek Country Club

Nevada

515-382-2528

One of the most tree laden courses in central Iowa is Indian Creek Country Club in Nevada. The course was renumbered in 2000 and fairway watering was added. The contour of the course is hilly with trees lining every fairway and occupying some of the middles too. The trees are not prohibitive though, they are big enough that you can go under them in most cases. There are no water hazards on the course, but the twelve bunkers and two inch rough provide other diversions to your game. Tees are small and greens are small to medium with some flat surfaces; but others tilted with a little roll. The grass condition of the greens is fair to good. The members enjoy a course that is difficult to walk, especially on the back 3 holes. It is a challenging course that has hills and trees to contend with on every hole. Indian Creek is a private course located two miles south of Nevada. They accept green fees from people 40 or more miles away . There is also has a full time restaurant that is open nine months of the year, evenings for members and guests; lunches are also served to the public. There are carts to rent to traverse the hills, but this is a great place to walk. This is truly a beautiful course. The immense trees add an unmistakable grandeur to the course. The trees and rolling hills make this a must course to play in central Iowa.

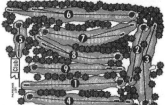

Course	9 Holes
Distance	2971 Yards
Par	35
Playability	Good
Aesthetics	Very Good
Interest	Very Good
Worth The Trip	Yes
Rating	★★★★

	1	2	3	4	5	6	7	8	9	OUT
WHITE	336	197	307	377	185	487	326	309	337	2861
BLUE	343	205	319	400	190	510	335	319	350	2971
HANDICAP	7	8	9	2	6	1	3	4	5	
HOLE	1	2	3	4	5	6	7	8	9	OUT
PAR	4	3	4	4	3	5	4	4	4	35

New Hampton Country Club

New Hampton

641-394-4340

The New Hampton Country Club is a family oriented course. They are a close knit group of people where everyone knows everyone else. A lot of family golf is played on this course that is located 4 miles east of New Hampton on Highway 24. There is a creek that runs through the middle of the course in which six holes are affected. During normal play, four bridges are used to cross at different points. Most of the trees on the course are located by the river and the rest of the course has new and 15 foot trees scattered about. The fairways are narrow and demand accuracy off the tees. The tees are elevated and medium in size, the greens range through all the sizes with most of them tilted to hold approach shots. A new pond was built by holes 7 & 3. It is an easy 9 holes to walk and an average course to score well on. New Hampton has a very nice clubhouse that has a full line of supplies in the basement pro shop. A bar area serves sandwiches and pizza. The dining area is spacious and has a nice view of the course but is only used for special occasions. Annual membership fees are $530 for 180 members and daily green fees are reasonable, at $15 for all day. This course was built in the 30's and maintains a family golfing atmosphere for everyone to enjoy. New Hampton is a very beautiful course that adds a lot of class to the golfing community.

Course	9 Holes
Distance	2974 Yards
Par	36
Playability	Good
Aesthetics	Very Good
Interest	Very Good
Worth The Trip	Yes
Rating	****

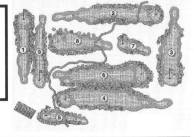

HOLE		1	2	3	4	5	6	7	8	9	OUT
BLUE TEES	68.8/119	297	529	333	414	171	463	155	312	300	2974
WHITE TEES	67.2/114	286	513	316	401	150	447	140	293	286	2832
RED TEES	68.4/114	269	467	216	297	137	396	128	275	274	2459
PAR		4	5	4	4	3	5	3	4	4	36

Deerwood Golf Club

New London

319-367-5216

Deerwood Golf Club is a semi-private club located less than three miles south of New London on X-23. The 185 members pay a family membership of $325. The clubhouse has a full line of equipment including a very nice selection of clubs. The bar area is set up more as a snack bar serving drinks and a few grilled sandwiches. The layout of the course has three ponds and six bunkers. Trees around the perimeter of the course are big, catching many balls heading out of bounds. Inside on the course the trees are small and scattered. The grass condition is healthy thanks to the fairway watering. Tees are big and elevated and are one of the nicer features of the course. Greens are medium in size, flat and sloping. The greens also have a reputation of being fast. This is a flat and open course that is easy to walk and easy to score well on. It is a fairly lengthy course and but can be negotiated quite easily. In recent years the fairways have been redesigned with more tiered rough. Deerwood is easy to get on with no tee times required. It is a good course for the beginner; few hazards, good grass to hit off of. It is also short which helps in case a bad game is getting out of hand.

Course	9 Holes
Distance	3015 Yards
Par	36
Playability	Good
Aesthetics	Very Good
Interest	Good
Worth The Trip	Yes
Rating	**+

Hole	1	2	3	4	5	6	7	8	9	Out
Blue	350	175	515	305	315	320	485	350	200	3015
White	335	161	496	305	315	466	342	185	2910	
Red	315	155	430	285	305	310	401	335	165	2701
Handicap	8	4	1	7	9	5	6	2	3	
Par	4	3	5	4	4	4	5	4	3	36

Prairie Knolls Golf Course

New Sharon

641-637-4200

If you have difficulty finding Prairie Knolls Golf Course in New Sharon just set your direction for the city water tower and you will find the clubhouse underneath. This is a public course that is located on the N.E. side of New Sharon and is a typical course for Iowa, except for the swimming pool. It is just an average course for the average golfer to have an average time. The 2806 yards is nothing to complain about, the one pond doesn't catch many balls, the two bunkers don't cause much trouble. There are a medium number of trees of medium size, with a few new plantings added to the layout every year. The contour of the course is gently rolling with wide fairways and no rough to get hung up in. The grass condition is good unless there is a long dry spell. The greens are of medium size and basically flat which accounts for the minimum number of breaks that a golfer must read and interpret. The New Sharon course is one that all the members love — easy to walk, easy to score well on, very little tree or hazard trouble, plus they have good greens. What more could a person ask of a course? This is a nice course in a nice small town. Try something that asks nothing in return but only for you to have a good time. Yearly memberships are $350. Small town golf in Iowa. What could be better?

Course	9 Holes
Distance	2806 Yards
Par	35
Playability	Poor
Aesthetics	Fair
Interest	Poor
Worth The Trip	Maybe
Rating	*+

WOMEN'S PAR	6	4	3	4	4	4	3	4	5	37
MEN'S PAR	5	4	3	4	4	4	3	4	4	35
DISTANCE YARDS	502	362	117	346	305	292	143	349	390	2806
HANDICAP	1	5	9	3	6	7	8	4	2	OUT
HOLE	1	2	3	4	5	6	7	8	9	

Newell Golf Park

Newell

712-272-4424

The Newell Golf Course is another small town course that is maintained to the specifications of the members, which is the way we all should be enjoying golf. There are very few hazards, only one sand trap and some 2 inch rough along the fairways. The trees vary in size from new plantings to big and old. The greens are small in size and have a variety of putting surfaces, most being flat in contour. Fairways are wide and encourage free swinging. Fairway watering was added in 1990. This is also an easy course to walk being fairly compact and flat. This is a well maintained course for a small town environment. The 250 members pay an annual fee of $320 but if you would like to pay green fees you can play all day for $11. The course, which is located on the N.E. side of Newell and was built in the 1930's and still has that basic golfing atmosphere. This public course is based on the golfing principal that golf should be fun, not something that brings out the worst in people. It should be played to relax and played fairly cheaply. The Newell course abides by these rules. It is a simple game — get the little white ball in the hole.

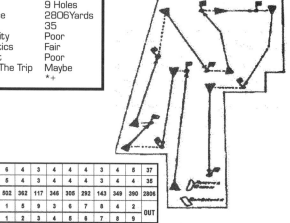

Course	9 Holes
Distance	2868 Yards
Par	36
Playability	Good
Aesthetics	Good
Interest	Fair
Worth The Trip	Maybe
Rating	**

Men's Handicap	9	4	3	8	5	2	7	6	1	
Yardage	251	325	330	285	470	209	305	179	515	2868
Men's Par	4	4	4	4	5	3	4	3	5	36
Ladies' Par	4	4	4	4	5	3	4	3	5	36
Yardage	251	325	292	285	433	143	305	112	477	2603
Ladies' Handicap	8	5	2	3	7	6	4	9	1	
HOLES	1	2	3	4	5	6	7	8	9	OUT

Course	18 Holes	Aesthetics	Very Good
Distance	6221 Yards	Interest	Very Good
Par	36-35-71	Worth The Trip	Yes
Playability	Excellent	Rating	★★★+

Westwood Golf Club

Newton

641-791-7561

Newton's public golf course, Westwood, is located on 1st Ave. West. The 400 members pay an annual fee of $781 for a family and $617 for a single. Green fees are very reasonable for an 18 hole public course, $13 for 18 weekdays. Like many 18 hole courses the front side has a different character than the back side. The front nine was built in 1927 and is very hilly. The greens are medium in size and offer a rolling putting surface. The front side greens also seem to hold your approach shot better. The back nine, built in 1966, is more of an even layout. The greens are firmer, it is much easier to walk, and the grass condition is usually much better. The back nine fairways are also watered. But the backside also holds the challenge of accuracy. On the front nine you are able to spray the ball around a little without affecting your score too much; coming home putting the ball in the right place is the name of the game. This holds especially true of number eleven where a creek runs the length of the fairway. The entire course has an ample supply of trees, many large in size. There have been 200 trees added in the last few years. The wide fairways are lined with these trees, which come into play especially on the backside. There is very little fairway rough but it does come into play on the border holes. There course is always in good shape. There is a full line of equipment in the clubhouse, including carts, which you might need on the front nine. There is an especially good line of clubs and bags. The clubhouse also has a bar and microwave sandwiches. The back nine demands accuracy and precision, especially after playing the front nine. Westwood is an attractive course but different looking depending on where your ball is at the time. This might be a course that you would want to try, a good price, some interesting terrain, and a course that you can use all of your clubs in the bag hopefully not too many times.

HOLE	1	2	3	4	5	6	7	8	9	OUT
CHAMPION	418	360	145	390	365	170	370	508	470	3196
MEN	418	360	145	345	365	170	370	508	470	3151
LADIES	418	250	125	345	365	125	300	450	470	2848
HOLE HANDICAPS	3	12	15	4	9	18	8	13	11	
PAR	4	4	3	4	4	3	4	5	5	36

10	11	12	13	14	15	16	17	18	IN	TOT	HCP	NET
215	380	395	380	365	170	525	360	355	3125	6321		
195	360	355	360	345	150	500	340	335	2940	6091		
195	245	355	330	345	150	475	340	335	2770	5618		
14	1	5	7	2	17	6	16	10				
3	4	4	4	4	3	5	4	4	35	71		

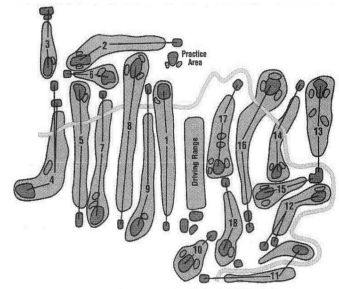

Newton Country Club

Newton

641-792-6619

Newton Country Club is one of the true old style country clubs in the state. It is a private club of 300 members who pay an annual fee of $1,700. Only members and guests of members are allowed to play the course. They are also the only ones that are able to eat in the country club's restaurant, which is too bad because they have some of the best food in town, served in an elegant environment. The pro shop is in a separate building that has a full line of equipment packed into a fairly small space. As a side benefit the course has a pool and tennis courts available to the members. This 3112 yard course is trapped very well with 33 sand bunkers. The trees are large and old on most fairways with new plantings in sparse areas. The trees are scattered throughout the layout with only a few fairways lined. The fairway grass is in excellent condition, thanks mainly to the fairway watering system. The rough along the fairways is tiered but does not present much trouble. The contour of the course is rolling which also applies to the medium size greens. The greens are in good condition as might be expected. This is a hard course to walk but an average course to score well on. The rough and density of trees make it a challenging course that requires accuracy especially on the approach shots; unless you are a terrific bunker player. If you want the atmosphere of country club living then the Newton Country Club has the course for you.

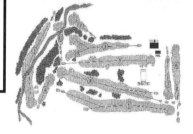

Course	9 Holes
Distance	3009 Yards
Par	35
Playability	Good
Aesthetics	Very Good
Interest	Good
Worth The Trip	Yes
Rating	★★★+

MEN'S TEES	337	132	403	148	568	278	183	533	427	3009
MEN'S PAR	4	3	4	3	5	4	3	5	4	35
MEN'S HDCP	14	18	2	13	4	17	9	10	7	
HOLE	1	2	3	4	5	6	7	8	9	OUT
LADIE'S HDCP	9	17	11	7	15	5	3	13		
LADIE'S PAR	4	3	5	3	5	4	3	5	5	37
LADIE'S TEES	322	110	401	134	463	263	153	426	417	2689

West Hills Golf and Country Club

Nora Springs

641-749-5522

West Hills Golf and Country Club, located west of Nora Springs on Highway 18, has been a community project pulling the people of the community toward a common goal. This was a new course built in 1992 that magnifies the pride of small communities and the interest in Iowa golf. This par 36 layout is spread over 3170 yards of rolling pasture land. There is one pond that comes into play on numbers 1 & 9, catching you going out and coming back in. Other hazards include 6 sand bunkers and approximately 30 ground bunkers scattered throughout the layout. A five year tree planting plan will begin next fall and eventually spread 400 trees along fairways and around greens. The contour of the course is rolling but the course is laid out so there are very few side-hill shots. Although number nine fairway can funnel your ball down the hill and far-far-away. This will be a placement course when fully developed. It is fairly long and you have to put the ball in play for your final approach shot. The tee boxes are medium to big in size with a three tiered blasting area. The greens average 5,000 sq. feet in size with a few double tiered greens and some undulating surfaces. The toughest hole may turn out to be #4; a long par 5 uphill extending almost 530 yards. This is an easy course to walk despite the hills and has developed into a beautiful place to play.

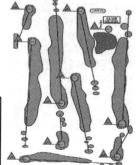

Course	9 Holes
Distance	3170 Yards
Par	36
Playability	Good
Aesthetics	Good
Interest	Good
Worth the Trip	Yes
Rating	★★★

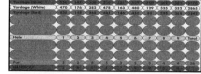

180

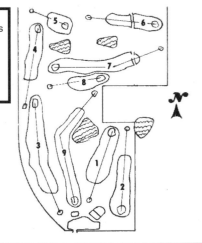

Knoll Ridge

North English

319-664-3700

Knoll Ridge is a public course located on the N.W. side of North English. The 110 members enjoy a pool and golf course for a yearly fee of $370. Daily green fees are average in price for a small 9 hole course. This is a moderately hilly course that compensates by being very open. But you do need to drive straight to score well on Knoll Ridge. This 2891 yard course has four ponds and one stream that affect five holes all together. Hazards are very limited, no sand, and no rough. The trees vary in size from large to new plantings; the trees do not effect play very much. Greens are medium in size and have a reputation of being very quick. The course was built in 1967 and was laid out over some hilly land that members can honestly state that there are no flat holes on the course. Knoll Ridge is not very busy and you can tee off number one almost any time during the week. The clubhouse is one of the weaker points of the course. It is a ranch style structure that has a bare cupboard, very few supplies and next to nothing in terms of food. This is a hard course to walk; carts are available to rent. Another example of a small town course that is fairly well maintained, but not used much.

Course	9 Holes
Distance	2849 Yards
Par	36
Playability	Fair
Aesthetics	Good
Interest	Fair
Worth The Trip	Yes
Rating	★★

HANDICAP	HOLE	YARDS		PAR
		MENS	LADIES	
8	1	288	288	4
3	2	343	233	4
4	3	460	390	5
5	4	305	305	4
9	5	119	105	3
6	6	288	201	4
1	7	379	327	4
7	8	141	141	3
2	9	526	374	5
	Totals	2849	2364	36

Quail Creek Golf Course

North Liberty

319-626-2281

Quail Creek Golf Course is located one mile south of North Liberty and was voted the top 9 hole course in Iowa in 1985. It was also listed as one of the top 50 courses in the nation. The honor was received because of the excellent condition of the course and the active membership. This course has quite a reputation. It is a flat course that is spread over 3523 yards from the back tees. There are three ponds that come into play on three holes, one stream that leaves it mark on two holes, no sand but some fairway grass bunkers, especially down # 9 fairway. "Amen Corner", numbers 6 & 7 are probably the toughest on the course. Number 6 has been lengthened and fitted with a new green behind a creek and a pond. Number 7 is one of the Register's toughest holes in the state. The trees have now matured and become a definite hazard to deal with. The greens are nice and big with a rolling putting surface. They are noted for being very firm, very fast, and possessing a lot of little hidden breaks. The clubhouse has a full line of equipment but a limited amount of food and bar items. It is a nice clubhouse to relax and get ready to attack the course again. This is a public course with an annual fee of $590 for a family. Weekday green fees are $12 for 9 and $19 on the weekend. Quail Creek also has a large driving range. This is an outstanding young course, a course that is becoming much better as it matures.

Course	9 Holes
Distance	3523 Yards
Par	36
Playability	Good
Aesthetics	Very Good
Interest	Very Good
Worth The Trip	Yes
Rating	★★★+

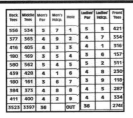

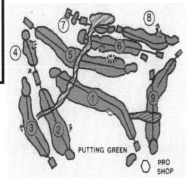

Back Tees	Middle Tees	Men's Par	Men's Hdcp.	Hole	Ladies' Par	Ladies' Hdcp.	Front Tees
556	534	5	7	1	5	3	421
377	365	4	9	2	4	7	354
416	405	4	3	3	4	1	316
180	169	3	5	4	3	8	157
580	562	5	4	5	5	2	511
459	428	4	1	6	4	8	230
180	161	3	6	7	3	9	118
384	375	4	8	8	4	5	287
411	400	4	2	9	4		334
3523	3597	36		OUT	36		2746

PUTTING GREEN

PRO SHOP

181

Northwood Country Club

Northwood

641-324-1662

The Northwood Country Club has the distinction of being one of the closest courses to Minnesota. The course is located one mile north of town on Highway 65 and one mile west. This location puts it about three miles from the border. This is a private club with green fees accepted from anyone outside the Northwest Kensett district. The 120 members pay a family membership of $410 with an initial stock of $200. The clubhouse has a limited amount of supplies. The bar has drinks and snacks for golfers and the restaurant operation is open to the public on every night during the summer. A large pond bisects fairways seven and eight. There is sand on two holes and a two inch rough runs the length of five holes. Twenty foot trees and evergreens line many of the wide fairways. New plantings are added to the layout each year. The contour of the course is flat around the clubhouse but has a few depressions as you move to the south. Tees are generally flat and small. Greens are medium in size and flat. Northwood was built in the early 1900's. It has maintained that small course feeling throughout the years and is enjoyed by everyone. It is an open course with a little length; just enough challenging situations to make you feel like you accomplished something when you walk back to the clubhouse.

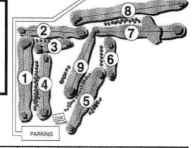

Course	9 Holes
Distance	3002 Yards
Par	36
Playability	Fair
Aesthetics	Good
Interest	Fair
Worth The Trip	Yes
Rating	★★+

HOLE		1	2	3	4	5	6	7	8	9	OUT
BLUE TEES		395	307	153	286	382	160	454	522	343	3002
HANDICAP		7	15	13	11	9	5	3	1	17	
PAR	Men/Ladies	4	4	3	4	4	3	5/4	5	4	36/35

Oakland Country Club

Oakland

712-482-6614

The Oakland Country Club is a course located in Pottawattamie county in S.W. Iowa. The course is located north of Oakland on Highway 6. The course was built in 1952 and was laid out on and around a hillside. There is one pond that really does not come into play unless you slice a great deal, there are no sand bunkers, and the medium size trees are scattered throughout the rough except for a large grove of trees in the middle of the course which come into play if you hook a great deal. The contour of the course is hilly; in fact, you may have trouble finding a level shot during your round of golf. The greens are medium to small in size and are rolling to a small degree. Oakland does have an Iowa Hall of Fame hole in number 2. This is a severe dogleg to the right in which cutting the corner adds two strokes for out-of-bounds. The Oakland course is quite short, 2383 yards, with an above average number of trees and an above average number of hills. The 200 members claim that it is S.W. Iowa's most beautiful course. The new Ladies tees make it more accessible to the women playing the course. The course is a challenge but good placement of drives and chips brings it to its knees. The old clubhouse has a limited supply of balls and gloves plus a bar and grill. Dues are $380 for a family per year and green fees are reasonable for a small town course. An interesting course with some character - building shots.

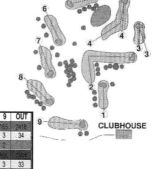

Course	9 Holes
Distance	2418 Yards
Par	33
Playability	Fair
Aesthetics	Good
Interest	Fair
Worth The Trip	Yes
Rating	★★+

HOLE		1	2	3	4	5	6	7	8	9	OUT
MEN'S BLUE TEES		242	280	189	460	156	342	300	284	165	2418
PAR	HCP LD#	4	4	3	5	3	4	4	4	3	34
HANDICAP		9	6	7	3	5	1	8	4	2	
LADIES' TEES		242	280	175	375	156	342	275	275	165	2291
PAR		4	4	3	4	3	4	4	4	3	33

182

Countryside Golf Course

Norwalk
515-981-0266

Countryside Golf Course opened in June of 2000 with the first nine holes ready for play. The 2nd nine was opened in 2002 and the new clubhouse is now under construction. The course is located 1 mile east of Norwalk, Hwy. G14, on the north side of the road. Countryside has 145 acres of rolling land that embraces the natural lay of the land. The course has approximately 7 acres of lakes and ponds and ten acres of native prairie grass areas. The course offers bent grass fairways and greens and many challenging holes. There are water hazards on six of the first nine holes. Countryside is a par 72 regulation size that measures 4611 yards form the front tees and 6345 from the Black back tees. There are three sets of tees to accommodate all golfers from beginners to the low handicappers. The greens are medium to large measuring five to seven thousand square feet. A characteristic of the course is the rolling fairways and the number of difficult pin placements. This is a public golf course that everyone in the community can enjoy. This is a very nice course that is in the development stage. The layout of the course makes it one of the emerging courses in central Iowa.

Course	18 Holes	Aesthetics	Good
Distance	6345 Yards	Interest	Very Good
Par	36-36-72	Worth The Trip	Yes
Playability	Good	Rating	* * *

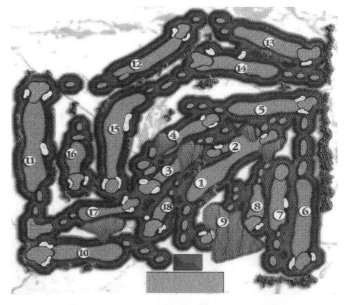

Hole	1	2	3	4	5	6	7	8	9	Out	P L A Y E R	10	11	12	13	14	15	16	17	18	In	Tot	Hcp	Net
Black	574	222	455	324	429	530	327	306	176	3222		281	488	416	366	392	491	221	283	185	3123	6345		
White	538	185	294	281	400	488	288	268	154	2896		251	452	377	321	351	455	191	228	169	2795	5691		
Handicap																								
Par	5	3	4	4	4	5	4	4	3	36		4	5/4	4	4	4	5	3	1/3	3	36/34	72/70		
Red	479	167	252	185	290	356	224	223	123	2299		202	323	342	292	289	402	155	169	138	2312	4611		

Legacy Golf Club

Norwalk

515-287-7885
www.thelegacygolfclub.com

The Legacy golf Club is a new golf club that includes an 18-holoe par 72 golf course located just north of Norwalk on Hwy. 28. The Legacy has global positioning technology on all cart rentals. The practice range usage is included in green fees. Green fees are $43 with a cart during the week. The challenge of this course will be the precision required for approach shots and the undulating putting surfaces. The par-35 front nine features many bunkers (40) and several water hazards that come into play on five of the holes. There are six par fours on the front nine that give you a variety of required shots. Putting greens are strategically sized to accept the approach for the particular hole. The second hole, a par 4, is a beautiful downhill driving hole with a spectacular approach over a five acre lake. The par 37 back nine will be a stern test with water hazards coming into play on all the holes. The par fours on the back nine require pinpoint tee shots through the hilliest part of the course. The back nine have some large greenside bunkers and several holes have hazards to catch errant tee shots. The par 5 eighteenth is a brutal 611 yards from the back tee, finally hitting into a bowl green area. The course opened in June 2002 and will be developing its unique personality for the net few years. The clubhouse seats 180 people for golf related outings. They have a typical grill items. The condition is very good for such a young course. The 1,100 watering heads keep the course green. The course has lots of mounds, rolling fairways, and a premium of flat lies. I would certainly recommend this course to anyone in central Iowa.

Course	18 Holes
Distance	7089 Yards
Par	36-36-72
Playability	Good
Aesthetics	Excellent
Interest	Very Good
Worth The Trip	Yes
Rating	★★★+

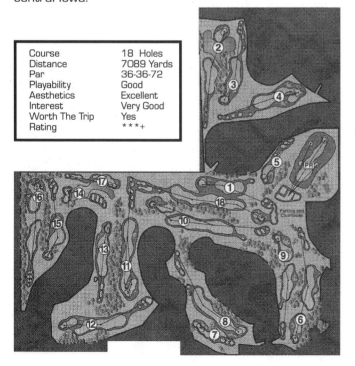

HOLE	1	2	3	4	5	6	7	8	9	OUT		10	11	12	13	14	15	16	17	18	IN	TOT
BLACK	368	434	408	389	214	517	168	469	466	3433	I N I T I A L S	561	525	442 428	305	189	350	463	210	611	3656 3642	7089 7075
GOLD	348	386	386	361	196	493	145	437	437	3189		542	497	427 400	286	170	327	447	166	602	3464 3437	6653 6626
SILVER	322	362	360	331	173	443	120	398	402	2911		521	470	379	259	151	297	547	135	585 554	3224 3193	6135 6104
STROKE INDEX	18	6	14	10	12	8	16	2	4			5	9	7	17	11	13	1	15	3		
PAR	4	4	4	4	3	5	3	4	4	35		5	5	4	4	3	4	4	3	5	37	72

Rolling Hills Golf Course
Norwalk
515-981-0419

Opening Spring 2005 is the new revised, revamped, redirected Rolling Hills Golf Course 3 miles south of Norwalk on Hwy. 28. This is truly a rebirth story. Old Rolling Hills was a par 3 course that fell into disrepair a few years back. With the basic land there Rolling Hills has been turned into a nine hole regulation course and a par 3 course built into the interior of the course. The par 3 course has LIGHTS!! This is one of only 3 courses in the state with lights. A unique concept. The regulation course is 2885 yards long. This is a very challenging course for many reasons. The layout of the course is built on very hilly terrain. The course is totally irrigated so the grass was in good shape at the end of 2004. There are no straight holes on the regulation layout and the signature hole #7 is 175 yards down hill to the left over water. There are lots of ponds on the course and comes into play on 4 holes. Other hazards include the timber surrounding the course and lining a few fairways. The fairways are bluegrass with the 3 sets of tees being pencross and bent grass. The greens average 4,000 square feet on the regulation layout and 5,000 on the par 3 course. Both the regulation and par 3 course are similar in features. There are no flat lies on wither course and the different elevations on the course affect almost every shot. The par 3 course is 1060 yards long with holes ranging from 65 to 165 yards long. I commend the builders of this course. They saved an old golf layout and have given it new life. The regulation course is unique with the rolling terrain and use of elevation to make holes interesting. The par 3 course will be a must play next year under the lights. Thanks to people who care about saving existing courses and making them live again. A nice addition to the Norwalk area.

REGULAR COURSE

HOLE	1	2	3	4	5	6	7	8	9	TOT
BLUE	315	345	460	130	335	375	175	300	450	2885
WHITE	300	330	435	120	300	335	160	268	435	2683
PAR	4	4	5	3	4	4	3	4	5	36
HANDICAP	7	6	4	9	8	1	2	5	3	
RED	275	320	410	105	290	312	90	220	385	2407
PAR	4	4	5	3	4	4	3	4	5	36

FAMILY COURSE

HOLE	1	2	3	4	5	6	7	8	9	TOT
BLUE	110	105	105	100	75	95	135	185	150	1060
WHITE	95	90	95	90	65	80	120	165	130	930
PAR	3	3	3	3	3	3	3	3	3	27
HANDICAP	6	5	8	4	9	2	7	1	3	
RED	75	75	85	80	55	80	100	150	115	815
PAR	3	3	3	3	3	3	3	3	3	27

Course	9/Par 3	Aesthetics	Good
Distance	2885/1060	Interest	Good
Par	36/27	Worth Trip	Yes
Playability	Good (next Spring)	Rating	★★+

Hickory Grove Country Club

Oelwein

319-283-2674

Oelwein has two nine hole courses, one is the Hickory Grove Country club located on Hickory Grove Road in the S.E. part of Oelwein. This is a public course that is noted for its large greens and supper club. The pro shop for Hickory Grove is located next to the supper club and has a nice assortment of supplies. There is also a bar area for drinks and sandwiches in the pro shop. The course has one water hazard, few bunkers, and a rough that is cut along the tree line. The trees are scattered throughout the course and range from medium size shade trees to new plantings; there are also some ten foot evergreens. Fairways are flat and wide; the trees on the course are of little concern to the average golfer. Greens are large and undulating. They also have the reputation of being hard to read and putt. Hickory Grove was named the best nine-hole course in Iowa in 1978. This is an easy course to walk and an easy course to score well on. It is a long hitter's course stretching over 3485 yards. Hickory Grove has a lot to offer its members; when you have food and golf, what more do you need.

Course	9 Holes
Distance	3485 Yards
Par	36
Playability	Good
Aesthetics	Good
Interest	Very Good
Worth The Trip	Yes
Rating	★ ★ ★ +

CHAMPIONSHIP	461	191	449	376	489	165	405	573	374	3485
MEN'S	438	179	426	355	471	156	401	548	357	3331
GOLD	395	165	350	333	431	110	340	501	345	2970
MEN'S PAR	4	3	4	4	5	3	4	5	4	36
HANDICAP	1	11	3	9	13	15	5	7	17	
LADIES'	415	165	403	333	432	105	401	523	341	3129
LADIES' PAR	5	3	5	4	5	3	5	5	4	39
HANDICAP	11	7	13	5	9	17	15	1	3	
HOLE	1	2	3	4	5	6	7	8	9	Out

Lakeview Golf Course

Oelwein

319-283-3258

The Lakeview Golf Course in the S.W. corner of Oelwein at 1432 Q Ave. is considered a beginners course. It is relaxing to play, easy to walk, easy to score, and has a very friendly atmosphere. Another plus for the beginner is that the course is not very busy so they won't feel rushed or watched. Lakeview is a semi-private course with 150 members paying a $325 family fee. There is a nice range of golfing supplies in the clubhouse; including carts. Lakeshore Resorts has been incorporated with the course providing 96 campsites. Lakeside Course is a 2nde shot course. Being accurate into the green is the ticket to a low score. The course is bordered on one side by Lake Oelwein, which comes into play on three holes. There is an average of two bunkers per hole and large areas of rough come into play along the tree lines and between some fairways. Medium sized trees line many fairways with larger trees around the perimeter of the course. The tees are big and landscaped very nicely. The greens are medium to large in size, flat with a few surfaces tilted and conditioned to catch approach shots. Over the past few years the tee boxes have been changed and additional landscaping added to the course. Lakeview was built in the 1950's and has a friendly atmosphere that is initiated by the operators and members. This is a fun course to play; easy, scenic, and not too busy so you can enjoy a leisurely round of golf.

Course	9 Holes
Distance	2932 Yards
Par	35
Playability	Good
Aesthetics	Good
Interest	Fair
Worth The Trip	Yes
Rating	★ ★

HOLE		1	2	3	4	5	6	7	8	9	Out
BLUE TEES	68.1/109	240	429	433	561	202	151	310	316	290	2932
HANDICAP		17	3	1	5	7	13	11	9	15	
PAR		4	4	4	5	3	3	4	4	4	35

Boone County Golf Course

Ogden - Don Williams Park

515-353-9225

The Boone County Golf Course, better also known as the Don Williams Course, is located six miles north of Ogden in the Don Williams Recreational Area. This course is built on the hillsides around the lake. As you can imagine there is not a level fairway shot on the course, or perhaps it just seems that way. The lake comes into play on three holes and the stream on one. There are no bunkers but the rough is cut along the tree lines at three inches. The medium number of trees are medium to large and are scattered throughout the course. The trees are generally poplar and evergreen. Greens are small to medium in size and have a sloping characteristic. The condition of the grass throughout the course is good considering the fact it has to grow on a hillside. The clubhouse is small but offers very good grilled sandwiches and dinner items that are available all the time. A few clubs are available along with balls and gloves, plus carts for rent. Green fees are very reasonable on weekdays and a dollar more on the weekends. This is a scenic course which can be challenging and frustrating at times. Don Williams also seems to have its share of strong winds blowing shots even farther down the hill towards the lake. There are no tee times but the course is one of the busiest in the area; come early and leave a ball in the rack.

Course	9 Holes
Distance	3045 Yards
Par	36
Playability	Good
Aesthetics	Good
Interest	Very Good
Worth The Trip	Yes
Rating	★ ★ ★

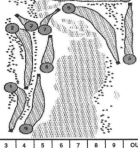

HOLES	1	2	3	4	5	6	7	8	9	OUT
YARDS	410	475	115	370	390	465	150	280	390	3045
MEN'S PAR	4	5	3	4	4	5	3	4	4	36
LADY PAR	5	5	3	4	4	5	3	4	5	38

The Inn at Okoboji

Okoboji

712-332-2113

The New Inn Motel on Lake Okoboji is the site of a miniature golf course, a driving range, and a par 3 golf course. The public par 3 course is 1225 yards long and is located across the street from the motel, north side of West Okoboji. There are no yearly memberships but there are very reasonable green fees. If you are a guest at the New Inn Motel you can play the course for $2. The clubhouse is a small structure whose only purpose is the collection of money for the golfing activities. They have pull carts to rent and club rental. It should be mandatory to walk a short, flat course such as the Inn. There are three bunkers and very little rough; in fact the only rough that does exist is where the mower missed around the trees. The few number of trees are small to medium in size and rarely come into play. This is a flat course that is wide open but long errant drives may find a cornfield. Greens are tiny and flat giving this par 3 course a bit of a challenge. The New Inn is a good learning course, for beginners and someone toning up their iron game. The one bad thing about the course is the condition of the greens, they are burned and very spotty. Greens on a par 3 course are the most important element. Otherwise it is a enjoyable place to spend an afternoon while in the Lakes region.

Course	9 Holes
Distance	1225 Yards
Par	27
Playability	Good
Aesthetics	Poor
Interest	Poor
Worth The Trip	No
Rating	★ ★

THE INN AT OKOBOJI
SCORE CARD

HOLE	1	2	3	4	5	6	7	8	9	FINAL
YARDS	160	150	130	115	100	155	120	175	120	

Brooks Golf Course

Okoboji

712-332-5011
www.brooksgolfclub.com

One of the more famous golf complexes in the Iowa Lakes region is Brooks Golf Course, located along Highway 71, just north of the lake. This is a public 27 hole course that added 9 additional holes in 2000. This 9 hole layout is called the Mounds and is a Scottish Links design. The maturity of the classic parkland course is intermixed with new challenging links style holes. Bent grass tees, fairways and greens have been updated to provide excellent playing conditions. The Brooks complex includes a motel, convention center, pool, indoor tennis courts, and access to all of the Iowa Lakes activities. The pro shop has a full line of equipment for sale and is located in a new clubhouse. Brooks is well know throughout the state and is played by a variety of people; members, vacationers, convention goers, and area leagues. The course was originally built in 1934 and was the premier course in the Lakes area. The revamped greens are much larger than the old, faster, and have a variety of putting surfaces. Hazards on the course include numerous ponds, an average of one bunker per hole, and tiered rough that extends from in front of the tee boxes along the fairways to the front of the greens. It is kept short in height but is long in quantity. There are a great number of trees on the course, mainly large, but new plantings are being introduced each year. This is an easy course to walk and an easy course to score well on too. The front nine holes demand accuracy while the back nine is a little longer and wide open. From the back tees you play a fairly long course at 6798 yards. Brooks is the site of the state husband and wife tournament each year. Brooks is once again developing into one of the finest courses in the area. The course has been rated "4 stars" by golf Digest "places to play". A full driving range with multiple tiers and targets offer the golfer ample area to improve shot making skills. It has a feeling of country club golf on a public course.

Course	27 Holes
Distance	6798 Yards
Par	36-36-72
Playability	Excellent
Aesthetics	Excellent
Interest	Good
Worth The Trip	Yes
Rating	★★★★

Val Brooks to

HOLE	1	2	3	4	5	6	7	8	9	Totals	
PAR	4	4	4	5	3	5	4	3	4	36	71
Blue	405	355	444	522	176	470	430	168	394	3364	6566
White	382	318	427	498	170	460	405	153	373	3186	6095
HANDICAP	5	7	2	3	8	4	1	9	6	Fill fairway divots with sand.	
Yellow	326	244	411	421	141	380	320	121	317	2681	5123
PAR	4	4	5	5	3	5	4	3	4	37	72

Scots' Links to Val Brooks

HOLE	1	2	3	4	5	6	7	8	9	Totals	
PAR	4	4	5	4	3	5	5	3	4	36	72
Blue	396	365	558	385	150	425	535	195	425	3434	6798
White	379	342	534	360	133	401	505	155	375	3184	6370
HANDICAP	5	7	2	6	8	4	1	9	3	Rake sand bunkers & fix ball marks.	
Yellow	336	284	476	280	112	324	400	130	290	2632	5313
PAR	4	4	5	4	3	4	5	3	4	36	73

Mounds to Scots' Links

HOLE	1	2	3	4	5	6	7	8	9	Totals	
PAR	4	4	4	5	4	4	4	3	4	35	72
Blue	324	370	337	508	435	400	293	352	201	3202	6638
White	302	355	277	508	399	391	180	323	158	2909	6093
HANDICAP	5	3	7	1	2	4	8	6	9	Replace rough divots please.	
Yellow	255	295	217	499	315	326	159	251	135	2442	5074
PAR	4	4	4	5	4	4	3	4	3	35	71

188

Onawa Country Club

Onawa

712-423-1712

A course that is making a comeback after losing 500 trees to Dutch Elm disease is the Onawa Country Club located one mile S.W. of town off 15th St. This is a very flat course, the new trees line the narrow fairways with some larger trees scattered throughout the course. A creek runs across the southwest corner coming into play on three holes. The greens are medium in size and flat, with a few tilted towards the approach shot. Other hazards include four sand bunkers and a little rough. This course was built in 1922 and claims to be the third oldest course in western Iowa. The course was reorganized in 1949 and that is when the clubhouse was built. It still stands as a remembrance of that era. The clubhouse has balls for sale plus a bar and grill offering refreshments. But don't come to Onawa to see the clubhouse, come here to play a flat, nice course and to see one of the oddest things in Iowa. The airport runway runs between the clubhouse and the course, thus making it a little difficult to get to the first tee during landing traffic. The 210 members pay $404 per year to have a Cessna land during their back-swing, something unusual like this can only be found in Iowa.

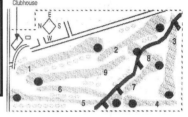

Course	9 Holes
Distance	3056 Yards
Par	36
Playability	Good
Aesthetics	Good
Interest	Fair
Worth The Trip	Yes
Rating	★★+

HOLE	1	2	3	4	5	6	7	8	9	Total
YARDS	467	369	299	270	420	379	230	114	508	3056
PAR	5	4	4	4	4	4	3	3	5	36
HANDICAP	8	4	7	6	3	2	1	9	5	

Course	9 Holes
Distance	2638 Yards
Par	36
Playability	Good
Aesthetics	Excellent
Interest	Excellent
Worth The Trip	Yes
Rating	★★★+

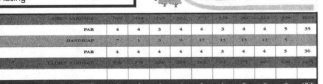

		1	2	3	4	5	6	7	8	9	
PAR		4	4	3	4	4	3	4	4	5	35
HANDICAP		7	1	3	9	17	15	13	11	5	
PAR		4	4	4	4	4	3	4	4	5	36
HOLE		1	2	3	4	5	6	7	8	9	OUT

Sunny Brae Golf and Country Club

Osage

515-732-3435

The Sunny Brae Golf and Country Club is a unique course. The layout of the course was created by the natural surroundings. The hills, trees, and river were used to shape this into a tight, challenging course. The course was built in 1916. This is a hard course to walk. Lugging clubs up and down the hills, along and over the river, luckily they do have carts to rent. There are 200 members who pay the $400 annual fee with an optional $100 stock. Green fees are reasonable. Fairway and automatic green watering was added in 1990. Other characteristics of the course include the river which comes into play on three holes, five bunkers, very little rough, and one large hill, nicknamed cardiac hill, that you have to go up once. The greens are small and flat and traditionally have been fast. The clubhouse is built into the side of the hill and has only a small bar and the basic golf supplies. But if you want a real challenge and a variety of golfing situations, then you need to drive two miles south of Osage then west along the river and determine the best technique to use for traversing the floating bridge on number six. Hole number 2 has been recognized as one of the best in the state, This course really is one of the more interesting in northern Iowa.

Landsmeer Golf Club

Orange City

712-737-3429

Course	18 Holes	Aesthetics	Very Good
Distance	6370 Yards	Interest	Good
Par	35-36-71	Worth The Trip	Yes
Playability	Good	Rating	* * *

Landsmeer which means "Lake of the Land" is a new 18 hole course in the far corner of NW Iowa in Orange City. The course was opened in 1995 and is built on a former corn field with a housing development sprouting up around it now. Wind has been an important factor in playing this course. There are very few trees to block the gusts coming in from the south in the summer. Landsmeer is a difficult course when the wind blows, and so it shall be. This is a fully irrigated course that relies on natural grasses to give it a links course atmosphere. The front side nine has more trees and water hazards. The back nine has more of links style layout, few trees open fairways and a variety of holes. Overall the course is open. The greens average 4,500 square feet in area and have a variety of breaks. Other hazards include an average of 2 sand bunkers per hole and a massive number of grass bunkers throughout the layout. The clubhouse is a massive new structure that has a full line of equipment and a variety of sandwiches. Approximately 300 members belong to Landsmeer paying $580 for a family golf pass. Weekday green fees are $20. This is a very nice course, with a lot of thought going into the layout design.

Hole	1	2	3	4	5	6	7	8	9	OUT	PLAYER	10	11	12	13	14	15	16	17	18	IN	TOT	HCP	NET
Navy 70.6/120	526	179	334	150	379	361	140	423	517	3009		507	191	512	173	380	483	426	232	457	3361	6370		
Oak 69.2/117	506	155	326	147	366	341	136	398	487	2862		489	169	480	153	355	469	394	206	431	3146	6008		
Wine	459	125	283	113	304	306	115	379	446	2530		436	133	422	113	319	433	351	155	360	2722	5252		
Handicap	7	5	11	17	3	15	13	1	9			10	8	12	14	16	18	2	6	4				
Par	5	3	4	3	4	4	3	4	5	35		5	3	5	3	4	5	4	3	4	36	71		

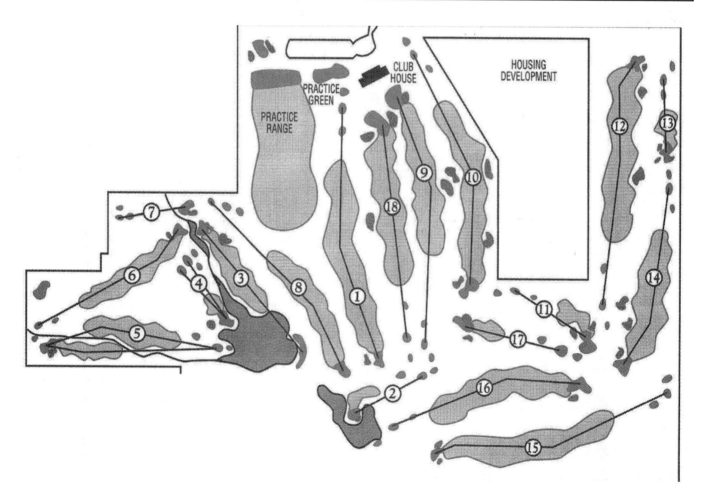

190

Osceola Country Club

Osceola

641-342-3717

One of the hillier courses found in south central Iowa is the Osceola Country Club. This private club is very hard to walk and has a scarcity of flat lies. The course is built on a hillside leading down from the clubhouse and flattens out near a stream. This stream runs the width of the course and comes into play on six holes, two new ponds have also been added. The medium number of trees line the fairways but are no trouble and range in size from new plantings to medium in height. The fairways stay in good shape throughout the summer, thanks to watering; there is no rough guarding the edges of the fairways. The course relies on hills to complicate your game. Tees are in fair shape and lay flat to the ground with no distinction. The greens are tiny to small with flat, quick putting surfaces. This is a hard course to walk and a challenging course to play. The hills and small greens make approach shots very delicate. Inside there is a year round restaurant that is quite nice and serves good food. The brick structure has three bars and two spacious dining rooms. Golf supplies are limited in the clubhouse. If you live outside of Clarke county you can pay the green fees and enjoy a rolling tour of the immediate area. The 200 members pay $580 a year. This is a course that lives by its hills and suffers by them too. They add to the beauty and challenge of the course but the hills also contribute to the drying process and cause this course to be on the brink of brown links often, too.

Course	9 Holes
Distance	2742 Yards
Par	35
Playability	Good
Aesthetics	Good
Interest	Good
Worth The Trip	Yes
Rating	**+

	1	2	3	4	5	6	7	8	9	Out
Par	4	4	4	5	4	3	4	3	4	35
Women's Yardage	239	247	250	461	235	142	259	120 160	295	2348 2388
Men's Yardage	301	338	255	501	351	150	348	120 160	338	2702 2742
Local Handicap	9	13	17	15	1	11	5	3	7	

Harvest Point

Oskaloosa

641-673-3100
www.geocities.com/harvestpoint.com

A new nine hole course has taken shape in Oskaloosa. Jeff Smith, PGA Pro, wanted a course he could call his own and laid out a course on some rolling farmland just to the west of Edmundson. The native grasses are a big part of the layout of this course. An interesting fact is that a large number of artifacts were dug up when this course was being shaped. Greens average 5,000 square feet and have a little bit of everything included in them. There are eleven sand bunkers and lots of grass mounds on the sides of the fairways throughout the course. Six greens have grass bunkers protecting the approach shot. Most of the trees are original and appear in the valleys. One of the unique features of Harvest Point is a double green for holes two and seven. This green covers 9,000 square feet and has some troublesome putting areas. There are four sets of tees so you really have two different courses if you take advantage of them on consecutive rounds. Most golfers find that they use every club in their bag. There are lots of birdie opportunities yet challenging if you are not paying attention. The clubhouse has a full line of equipment. The weekday green fees are $8. Harvest Point is a very nice addition to the area, a course that is quite different form the other two.

Course	9 Holes
Distance	3051 Yards
Par	35
Playability	Good
Aesthetics	Good
Interest	Very Good
Worth The Trip	Yes
Rating	**+

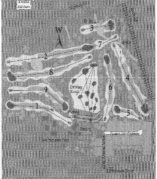

Tee/Hole	1	2	3	4	5	6	7	8	9	Out
Blue 68.8/113	390	460	188	502	160	320	140	504	387	3051
White 66.6/109	356	410	150	430	146	290	135	481	365	2763
Black 63.0/102	329	340	114	395	126	266	120	394	330	2414
Red	264	310	100	348	105	250	113	363	309	2164
Par	4	4	3	5	3	4	3	5	4	35

Edmundson Golf Course

Oskaloosa

641-673-5120

The Edmundson Golf Course is a public course located on Edmundson Drive in Oskaloosa. The original nine holes was built in the 1930's with the additional nine holes built in 1965. The characteristics of the course include a stream that runs through the middle of the course and comes into play on five holes. Bunkers are very scarce with only six on the layout, and the rough is cut about the same length as the fairways and possesses very few problems. There are an above average number of trees that range from medium to large in size. Many trees are scattered but some line the regulation fairways. Tees are being enlarged to accommodate increased play. The greens are medium in size and have rolling and sloping putting surfaces. Three greens and five tees were replaced in 1985 and have added additional challenge and character to the course. The 400 members of this course pay an annual fee of $590 for a family. Green fees are very reasonable. The old brick clubhouse was built in the 1880's with an additional 2100 sq. ft. of shop space added in 1988. The overall picture of this course is that it is hard to walk but exciting to play. There exists on the layout all types of different shots; some will be easy and many will be difficult. There are not a great many of hazards on the course except for the trees that will come into play unless you stay down the middle. Because this course is run by a family it has a kind of family atmosphere. The old brick farmhouse helps, too. This is a nice 18 hole course that has no flat lies and keeps your uphill and downhill stroke in tune most of the round. It is a scenic course that is there to dispense golf with very few frills, just the way I like it.

Course	18 Holes
Distance	6031 Yards
Par	35-35-70
Playability	Excellent
Aesthetics	Very Good
Interest	Very Good
Worth The Trip	Yes
Rating	★★★★

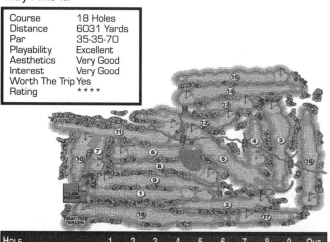

Hole		1	2	3	4	5	6	7	8	9	Out
Blue Tees	68.6/116	348	339	379	217	362	371	126	419	467	3028
White Tees	66.9/113	347	319	348	192	348	351	119	402	447	2873
Handicap		13	15	5	9	3	7	17	1	11	
Par		4	4	4	4	4	4	3	4	5	35
Black Tees	63.0/102	322	300	281	147	317	240	106	335	382	2430
Red Tees	66.9/112	320	288	256	147	307	240	100	335	382	2375
Handicap		11	9	7	15	3	13	17	1	5	

10	11	12	13	14	15	16	17	18	In	Tot	Hcp	Net
184	498	383	158	378	337	353	211	501	3003	6031		
178	488	319	143	342	328	348	206	443	2795	5668		
16	2	12	18	6	14	4	8	10				
3	5	4	3	4	4	4	3	5	35	70		
164	387	268	120	314	292	272	162	425	2404	4834		
157	387	262	116	309	292	230	162	411	2326	4701		
16	2	10	18	6	8	12	14	4				

Elmhurst Country Club
Oskaloosa
641-673-5234

Oskaloosa has three fine golf courses, one is the Country Club located on the S.E. side of town. This course is laid out over some gently rolling terrain. An additional nine holes were added in 1996. The front nine remains the same, the back nine is rolling with tough holes and hills. The course has one water hazard that comes into play on five holes. There are eleven bunkers and a two inch rough that is fair and easy to recover from. The trees are medium to large in size and are scattered throughout the course. The back nine has new trees spread out over a longer layout. The trees become larger and thicker as you near the edges of the water. The fairways vary in width from narrow to wide. The greens are medium in size with some flat surfaces and some rolling. The grass throughout the course is in good condition. The clubhouse is very nice with a full time restaurant open to members and their guests. There is also a tennis court and pool for members. This is a private course, but non-members can pay green fees if they live outside Mahaska County. The 160 members pay an annual membership of $1495. The clubhouse has a pro shop that sells balls and gloves plus four carts for rent. This is a cart course but all privately owned. Elmhurst is an easy course to walk and an average course to score well on. It can be a challenging course if you spray the ball a great deal and play out of the trees a lot. Elmhurst has one of the toughest par 5's in Iowa. This is an old style country club that relies on membership participation to maintain it's excellent facilities. Elmhurst has an interesting layout that brings golfers back; it may also be the fine condition of the course that makes people like it so much. Friday's are open to the public to play.

Course	18 Holes	Aesthetics	Very Good
Distance	6382 Yards	Interest	Very Good
Par	36-36-72	Worth The Trip	Yes
Playability	Good	Rating	★★★+

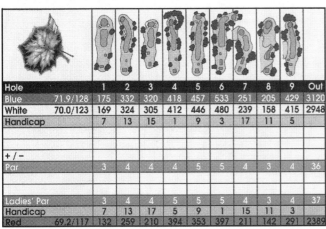

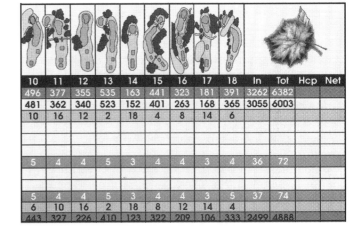

Hole		1	2	3	4	5	6	7	8	9	Out
Blue	71.9/128	175	332	320	418	457	533	251	205	429	3120
White	70.0/123	169	324	305	412	446	480	239	158	415	2948
Handicap		7	13	15	1	9	3	17	11	5	
+/-											
Par		3	4	4	4	5	5	4	3	4	36
Ladies' Par		3	4	4	5	5	5	4	3	4	37
Handicap		7	13	17	5	9	1	15	11	3	
Red	69.2/117	132	259	210	394	353	397	211	142	291	2389

	10	11	12	13	14	15	16	17	18	In	Tot	Hcp	Net
	496	377	355	535	163	441	323	181	391	3262	6382		
	481	362	340	523	152	401	263	168	365	3055	6003		
	10	16	12	2	18	4	8	14	6				
	5	4	4	5	3	4	4	3	4	36	72		
	5	4	4	5	3	4	4	3	4	37	74		
	6	10	16	2	18	8	12	14	4				
	443	327	226	410	123	322	209	106	333	2499	4888		

193

Silver Springs Golf & CC

Ossian

563-532-8904

A big lake in front of the clubhouse dominates the Silver Springs Golf and Country Club in Ossian. This course was built in 1993 on a rolling piece of pasture land south of town. The general contour of the course is rolling with many of the fairways having more hilly challenges. The greens generally are medium in size and generally flat, a relieve from the approach shot. The fairways do have some grass bunkers. Once of the original designs of the course was to plant trees lining the fairways. After 10 years there are 20 foot trees just now coming into play. This hilly course has a unique number 8 where you hit up a hill the entire way. There are water hazards on 3 holes. The course is in good shape. Players say that they like the greens and the course is easy to get on. The clubhouse serves sandwiches and has a small pro shop. The 192 members pay $535 yearly dues. Weekday green fees are $10. This is a nice course that is gaining maturity over the years.

Course	9 Holes
Distance	3067 Yards
Par	36
Playability	Good
Aesthetics	Good
Interest	Fair
Worth The Trip	Yes
Rating	★★+

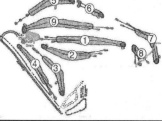

BLUE TEES	481	376	310	382	349	165	376	128	500	3067
WHITE TEES	453	348	298	350	321	156	336	118	476	2856
HANDICAP	9	2	6	1	4	7	3	5	8	36
MEN'S PAR	5	4	4	4	4	3	4	3	5	
WOMEN'S PAR	5	4	4	4	4	3	4	3	5	36
HANDICAP	9	2	6	1	4	7	3	5	8	
RED TEES	426	291	274	307	273	151	299	94	421	2535
Hole	1	2	3	4	5	6	7	8	9	OUT

Lake Panorama West

Panora

641-755-2250

One of the harder courses to find in the state is the Par 3 course in Panora. It is located on the west side of Lake Panorama two miles north of Highway 44. This private course does accept green fees of $10. The 170 members pay a family fee of $240. The clubhouse is small with little food and less to drink. There are no water hazards on the course, but the lake is only a few hundred yards away. There are four bunkers that guard the large greens, large greens for a par 3 course, medium for regulation. The greens are rolling and offer some challenges. The course is laid out around a swamp and has a deep rough in the middle. This is a fairly nice par three course and gives the people of the area a choice between this and the 18 hole championship course on the other side of the lake. The par 3 has lush tee boxes and is well taken care of. The one flaw of the course is that it is located on back roads and there are very few signs to indicate the direction to the course. The course was built in 1970. In 1999 the course added some length so you can now play some holes as par 4's. This adds an extra 400 yards to the course. Like many other short courses or par 3 courses, playing time is relatively short and playing pressure is minimum.

Course	Par 3
Distance	1378/1749 Yards
Par	27
Playability	Good
Aesthetics	Good
Interest	Fair
Worth The Trip	Yes
Rating	★★+

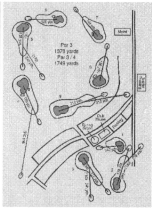

GOLF COURSE		Par 3 Par 4
Hole	Distance	Hdcp
1	140 yds	7
2	170 yds / 278 yds	4
3	177 yds / 241 yds	6
4	150 yds / 380 yds	3
5	139 yds / 240 yds	9
6	120 yds	5
7	144 yds	6
8	126 yds	8
9	212 yds / 310 yds	1
TOTALS	1378 yds / 1749 yds	

Cedar Creek Golf Course

Ottumwa

641-683-0646

The golfers in Ottumwa are lucky to have two fine 18 hole courses in their city. Besides the country club there is Cedar Creek golf Course, formally, Ottumwa Municipal, two miles north of town on Highway 63. This is a mature course, built in 1931. The trees are medium to large in size and are in great numbers along the fairways and scattered in the rough. There is one stream on the course and eighteen bunkers, mostly guarding greens. The fairways are forty yards wide, which creates a tight landing area. The nice feature about this course is the cutting done on the course. It provides a very nice visual effect with patterns and the layered look. Tees are in good shape with a little elevation. The 1992 season will see 4 sets of tee boxes on every hole. Greens are medium in size and generally are gently rolling and tilted. Three greens were recently reconstructed making approach shots easier. The new tee to green irrigation has helped the beauty and durability of the course. This municipal course has 450 members. Green fees are very reasonable for an 18 hole course. The clubhouse is the weakest part of the course. They do have a full line of supplies and also a full service snack bar. There are carts for rent but this would be a nice easy course to walk. This is a harder course than first appears. The trees come into play on many holes, it is challenging around the greens, and rough also comes into play around the greens. There is nothing better than a town that supports a public golf course, both with play and spirit. This is a scenic course that can be enjoyed by everyone. Try it out once: keep it straight and don't over swing and success will be yours.

Course	18 Holes	Aesthetics	Very Good
Distance	6335 Yards	Interest	Very Good
Par	35-37-72	Worth the Trip	Yes
Playability	Very Good	Rating	★★★★

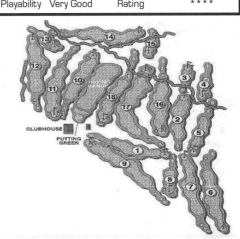

HOLES		1	2	3	4	5	6	7	8	9	OUT
Blue Tees	70.4/122	370	337	155	179	347	492	434	218	564	3096
White Tees	69.8/119	357	323	146	172	337	480	409	191	542	2957
Gold Tees	68.0/115	345	309	136	165	328	460	398	176	459	2776
Handicap		13	17	11	15	9	5	1	7	3	
Par		4	4	3	3	4	5	4	3	5	35

10	11	12	13	14	15	16	17	18	IN	TOT	HCP	NET
394	403	411	158	369	143	414	523	424	3239	6335		
384	367	399	149	358	143	386	504	383	3073	6030		
355	350	347	139	335	127	332	458	279	2722	5498		
14	10	4	12	8	18	16	2	6				
4	4	4	3	4	3	4	5	4	35	70		

Ottumwa Country Club

Ottumwa

515-684-4471

The Ottumwa Country Club is truly one of the finer 18 hole courses in the state. It is based on the philosophy that a good course must look the part to be of championship caliber. This is a private course that allows guests of members to pay the reasonable green fees. The course has an ample supply of hazards scattered throughout the 18 holes. There are two ponds that you must cross, a creek valley that you come in contact with four times, 32 bunkers arranged in various spots on the course, and a high rough that tends to be a little tough if you get into it. The trees are medium to large in size and line many of the wide fairways. Tees are constructed of bent grass, small and have a nice hitting surface. The medium size greens are in top quality condition and have sloping surfaces. This is an easy course to walk despite the evidence of hills. It is also harder to play than first indications. You must be accurate off the tees to avoid trees and rough; anything that strays will cause scores to soar upward. If you keep the ball in play the course will become one of your favorites. The front nine holes was built in 1900 and has a hillier contour with larger and flatter greens. The front nine is flat all over. The front nine, because of its age has larger trees. The back nine was built in 1961. The pro shop has a complete line of clothing and equipment, a very complete area. The staff is available to give lessons on the driving range and are very willing to help in any way. The clubhouse is nearby and has a full restaurant, for members and guests only, that has good food and a country club atmosphere. This is what a course is supposed to look like.

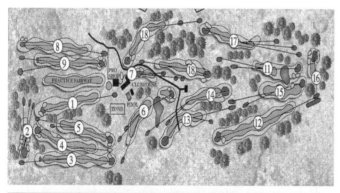

Hole	Rating/Slope	1	2	3	4	5	6	7	8	9	Out
Championship	71.6/124	356	166	436	361	357	368	208	405	387	3044
Men's	70.6/119	336	166	436	361	357	320	177	405	387	2965
Handicap		13	15	17	11	7	9	1	3	5	
Ladies'	71.2/115	349	159	348	349	293	263	108	398	303	2570
Handicap		1	9	3	5	15	11	17	13	7	
Par		4	3	5	4	4	4	3	4	4	35

10	11	12	13	14	15	16	17	18	In	Tot	Hcp	Net
313	390	480	357	409	365	148	469	388	3319	6363		
302	412	456	340	396	350	139	441	294	3030	5995		
218												
294	296	434	265	295	292	130	351	284	2641	5211		
12	4	8	16	14	10	18	2	6				
4	4	5	4	4	4	3	5	4	37	72		

Course	18 Holes	Aesthetics	Excellent
Distance	6363 Yards	Interest	Very Good
Par	37-35-72	Worth The Trip	Yes
Playability	Excellent	Rating	★★★★+

196

Lake Panorama National Golf Course

Panora

641-755-2024
1-800-879-1917

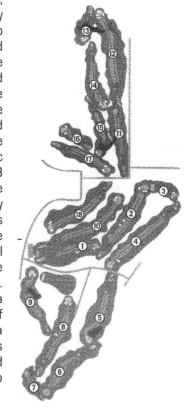

One of the best conditioned courses anywhere in the state is the Lake Panorama National Golf and Tennis Club located on the north edge of Lake Panorama in Panora. This is the only course listed in the top ten in the state that is a public course. This is a very busy course and tee times can be made one week in advance. Green fees are reasonable for an 18 hole course especially one of this caliber. There are 220 members of Lake Panorama who pay a family membership fee. The clubhouse is located in the Clover ridge complex in the middle of the course. They have a full line of supplies, a bar and menu items to eat. The course also has three full time pros and a driving range. Also in this complex is the Clover Ridge Condominiums and Restaurant. This is a very nice restaurant and convention center that has added extra golfers to the course. The course has a championship golfing atmosphere. There are five ponds included in the layout in which six holes are affected. The contour of the course is flat on the front side and rolling on the back side. There are 30 bunkers on the course, many being large and guarding fronts of greens. The rough is cut to a height of 3 inches and comes into play a great deal but is fair and easy to recover from. The front 9 has small new trees that line the fairways, the back 9 has large old trees scattered throughout the valleys. The greens on the front side are medium in size and gently rolling, coming back in the greens are large, tiered and rolling. It may sound like they have two different courses rolled into one, but the course fits together very well and affords you the opportunity to experience many situations and conditions all in one afternoon. This public course was built in 1973 is a championship course that gets better every year; The Iowa Open has been played here since 1985. A lot of additional landscaping was done during the spring of 98. Lake Panorama is a beautiful course, a stiff challenge to many, and a course that brings together all the good things that golf has to offer.

Course	18 Holes	Aesthetics	Excellent
Distance	7010 Yards	Interest	Very Good
Par	36-36-72	Worth the Trip	Yes
Playability	Excellent	Rating	★★★★+

	1	2	3	4	5	6	7	8	9	OUT	10	11	12	13	14	15	16	17	18	IN	TOT
BLUE	375	489	161	576	394	423	191	458	365	3432	592	414	585	171 185	391	389	179	386	471	3578 3592	7010 7024
WHITE	352	475	152	560	386	412	186	442	355	3320	568	380	558	156	380	367	170	372	458	3409	6729
YELLOW	345	462	152	545	368	334	165	388	346	3105	473	370	462	147	370	354	167	358	376	3077	6182
RED	280	381	140	432	298	312	120	334	337	2634	411	309	399	117	331	300	151	293	320	2631	5265
MEN'S HCP	13	18	17	4	9	8	12	3	11		5	7	2	10	15	6	16	14	1		
LADIES' HCP	4	8	18	12	14	6	16	10	2		3	15	5	7	11	1	17	9	13		
HOLE	1	2	3	4	5	6	7	8	9	OUT	10	11	12	13	14	15	16	17	18	IN	TOT
PAR	4	5	3	5	4	4	3	4	4	36	5	4	5	3	4	4	3	4	4	36	72

Beaver Meadows Golf Course

Parkersburg

319-346-1870

Beaver Meadows Golf Course in Parkersburg has an intense population of trees, everywhere. The narrow fairways are lined with sixty foot trees making tree trouble a real danger. This can be considered a placement course, short, straight, and narrow, with second shots very important. It might be wise to leave your driving wood in the bag and use a more controlled iron shot. There is no sand on the course and only one water hazard coming in play on one hole. The contour of the course is flat with little or no rough along the fairways. Tees are small and flat and the greens possess a lot of hidden breaks but are basically flat with a little tilt. The course was built in 1955. The 150 members pay an annual family membership of $360. Daily green fees are very reasonable. The little brown clubhouse has a minimum of golf supplies and the bar has sandwiches. There is a restaurant that is open for 6 months of the year to the public. This semi-private course can be found north west of Parkersburg on Highway 14. Beaver Meadows is a scenic course to encounter and a friendly place to play.

Course	9 Holes
Distance	2554 Yards
Par	34
Playability	Good
Aesthetics	Good
Interest	Fair
Worth The Trip	Yes
Rating	★★+

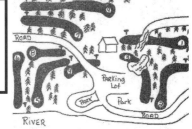

PAR	4	4	4	3	4	4	4	3	4	34
YARDAGE	370	329	307	130	303	253	335	159	420	2606
	314	314	307	130	303	253	335	159	420	2535
HANDICAP	3	5	2	9	6	8	4	7	1	

Paullina Golf Club

Paullina

712-448-3477

The Paullina Golf Club is a public course located on the east edge of Paullina on Highway 10. This is a member owned club that encourages daily green fee play. The character of this course is dominated by the creek that runs down the middle. Seven holes cross this creek and you have five wooden bridges to keep you dry. There are two bunkers on the course and a rough cut along the wide fairways and around the back of the greens. The course is bordered by large trees, but the trees along the fairways are small to medium and are randomly scattered. The contour of the course is flat with only a little variance as the land approaches the stream. The course is known for it's small but well manicured greens. Some are rolling, some flat. In the past two years there has been noticeable improvement on the course. The watering system has helped the grass condition on the course. The clubhouse is a small structure that includes a full line of supplies, but in small amounts. There are carts to rent but this is level course and requires very little effort to walk it. Refreshments consist of drinks and sandwiches. This is an easy course to walk and easy to score well on. The atmosphere is small town golf club, which relies heavily on playing a fun game of par golf. The challenge on this course are the water crossings.

Course	9 Holes
Distance	2784 Yards
Par	35
Playability	Good
Aesthetics	Fair
Interest	Fair
Worth The Trip	Maybe
Rating	★★

HOLE	1	2	3	4	5	6	7	8	9	OUT
MEN'S WHITE TEES	130	264	506	380	337	300	216	213	438	2,784
MEN'S PAR	3	4	5	4	4	4	3	3	5	35
MEN'S HANDICAP	9	8	3	1	6	7	2	5	4	
LADIES' PAR	3	4	5	4	4	4	4	4	4	36
LADIES' RED TEES	130	230	425	289	328	232	216	213	345	2,378
LADIES HANDICAP	9	7	2	4	3	6	5	8	1	

Bos Landen

Pella

641-628-4625

The Bos Landen Golf Club opened for operation in the Spring of 1994. This public 18 hole course is located 1 mile S.W. of Pella on County T-15. The back tees stretch the course to 6932 yards while the front tees have 5155 yards to negotiate. Tee boxes are tiered and have 3 to 5 different blasting areas. This is a carefully designed 340 acre tract of land that offers a par 72 golf course and a 75% occupied housing development. The designer is Dick Phillips, a senior consultant for Hale Irwin designed courses. The Bos Landen complex has an abundance of native Iowa Oak and the beauty of the timber has been woven into the layout of the course. Each of the nine holes has three fairways that are cut right through the timber, with as few trees taken as possible. Another three holes weave in and out of the timber and the remaining three holes on each nine leads the golfer into open areas. The natural beauty and the variety of the terrain will be the drawing card for the course. The 90 feet of elevation change throughout the course creates some moderate slopes, but it will still be a fairly easy course to walk. There is a large lake that runs along Fairway #12 and #13. There are a number of streams that meander beside and through a number of the rolling fairways. Approximately 30 fairway sand and ground bunkers will greet the golfer on every turn. Generally there are flat landing areas with fringes banked like the Amana course. Greens are undulating and big with some tilt. Number 18 may be the toughest hole with a 418 yard dogleg cut out of the timber with two creek crossings thrown in. This is a fully irrigated course that will get a lot of green fee traffic from the Red Rock area and Des Moines area. The huge clubhouse has a full line of equipment and has a new dining room for sandwiches. This is a beautiful course that takes advantage of the existing terrain and natural woods and grasses.

Course	18 Holes	Aesthetics	Excellent
Distance	6932 Yards	Interest	Excellent
Par	36-36-72	Worth the Trip	Yes
Playability	Excellent	Rating	★★★★+

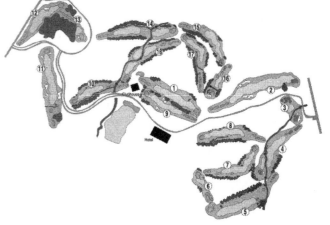

TEE	YARDAGE	PAR	MEN slope/rating	LADIES' slope/rating
● Black	6932	72	131/73.5	
● Blue	6480	72	130/71.5	
○ White	5900	72	126/70.2	
○ Gold	5790	72	121/69.0	140/76.0
● Red	5155	72		125/71.0

Pella Golf and Country Club

Pella

641-628-4564

In keeping with the Dutch tradition the Pella Golf and Country Club marks its tees with wooden shoes and each hole is named after Dutch towns and events. This is a course that rewards a good placement shot. There are only four sand bunkers and no water, but the lush deep rough that seems to be everywhere makes the course difficult to play and to score well on. The trees are small to large and line many of the narrow fairways. The courses contour is flat which makes it easy to walk. Tees are elevated and of medium size plus the greens are medium in size with flat and sloping areas. This course was built in 1946 and has grown to have a personality of its own. The clubhouse is very nice with a full restaurant that is only open to members and their guests year round. A limited quantity of golfing supplies are available to the 315 members. If you live outside the school district you can pay the reasonable green fees without being a guest. If you would like to join, the annual fee is $820with an initial payment of $500. The Pella course has very active league play but is not real busy other times considering the size of the area it draws from. This is a course that is suited for the placement player, more of a thinkers course. This course is located on Elm Street in northern Pella.

Course	9 Holes
Distance	2981 Yards
Par	36
Playability	Good
Aesthetics	Good
Interest	Fair
Worth The Trip	Yes
Rating	**

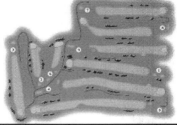

Hole	1	2	3	4	5	6	7	8	9	Out
White Tees	375	145	257	488	513	149	329	355	370	2981
Red Tees	347	145	257	411	452	149	329	355	287	2732
Par	4	3	4	5	5	3	4	4	4	36

Course	9 Holes
Distance	3102 Yards
Par	36
Playability	Good
Aesthetics	Good
Interest	Fair
Worth The Trip	Yes
Rating	**+

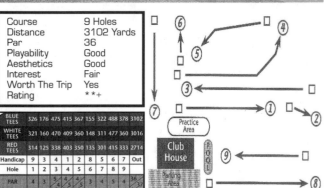

BLUE TEES	326	176	475	415	367	155	322	488	378	3102
WHITE TEES	321	160	470	409	360	148	311	477	360	3016
RED TEES	314	125	338	403	350	135	301	415	333	2714
Handicap	9	3	4	1	2	8	5	6	7	Out
Hole	1	2	3	4	5	6	7	8	9	
PAR	4	3	5/4	5	4/5	3	4	5	4	36/37

Perry Golf and Country Club

Perry

515-465-3852

The Perry Golf and Country Club was built in 1916 and is considered by the members as a sporty course. The members believe this because the course is in good shape and is a fairly easy course for the members to play. Some hazards include four bunkers, and some fairway rough that impedes progress at times. A new pond was built and comes into play on holes 2,3, & 9. There are some new plantings of trees but many are of medium size and leafy in nature. Greens are flat and small to medium in size. The contour of the course is generally flat with a few rolling areas. This is a placement course, putting the ball in the right place for your next shot can save many other shots. This is a private course with a 20 mile green fee radius. The interior of the clubhouse verges on elegance. There is a spacious rounded bar, a big dining area for the year round restaurant, plus the food is good. The 288 members pay an annual fee of $655 for a family while green fees are very reasonable while playing with a member. This north-south course can be very tough in spots but over all is fun to play. Perry Country Club has the reputation of being one of the most challenging in the area. Best of all you can enjoy clubhouse dining at its finest when you are done.

200

Thunder Hills Country Club

Peosta

563-556-3256

Thunder Hills Country Club is a private club that was built in 1971 and has a growing membership of 315 today. The course is located about eight miles west of Dubuque, turn north at mile marker 307. Green fees are only available to guests of members and out-of-town guests. This is a beautifully landscaped course with plantings around the tees and drives and also around the clubhouse. Thunder Hills has fine dining and is open to members and guests. The lower level of the clubhouse has a pro shop stocked with a full line of golf equipment along with professional staff to assist members with their needs. Thunder Hills has matured into a beautiful course that combines country atmosphere with fine golf. The recent addition of an automatic double row fairway irrigation system makes the grass condition even nicer. The sand, the grass bunkers, the rolling hills, along with the two water hazards make Thunder Hills a true test of golf. The two inch rough borders narrow fairways, but will allow an errant shot to be played. The contour of the course is semi-hilly; it is easy to walk but is still considered a cart course. The greens are some of the biggest in the area; average square footage is 8,000. Not only are they huge, but they are undulating. Greens 16 and 17 have severe breaks and can cause a good round to fall apart. The putting surface is quick and very true, so when you line up a putt, what you see is what you get. The course is surrounded by a housing development which is also an added attraction to the facility. Inside the clubhouse is a large collection of club and event tags from Iowa and around the country. You could spend an hour just looking at this rare collection. Thunder Hills is becoming one of the finest country clubs in the eastern part of the state. It has matured and has become a very beautiful course. It seems to get harder every time you play it.

Course	18 Holes	Aesthetics	Very Good
Distance	6365 Yards	Interest	Good
Par	35-36-71	Worth The Trip	Yes
Playability	Good	Rating	****

HOLE	1	2	3	4	5	6	7	8	9	Out		10	11	12	13	14	15	16	17	18	In	Tot
BLACK 71.2/127	316	551	194	335	162	403	342	372	488	3163		410	143	403	532	175	344	560	188	447	3202	6365
BLUE 69.8/124	290	534	166	318	144	390	327	351	472	2992		402	129	385	525	154	331	549	156	432	3063	6055
GOLD M 67.4/118 L 71.5/123	280	482	143	241	118	367	315	305	452	2703		385	124	360	515	150	320	515	123	355	2847	5550
BLACK HANDICAP	12	4	6	18	16	2	8	10	14			5	17	9	15	13	11	3	7	1		
BLUE HANDICAP	16	2	6	14	18	12	4	8	10			5	17	7	11	15	9	1	13	3		
RED 69.3/116	275	479	97	226	106	297	307	288	443	2518		301	120	320	453	144	314	508	123	350	2633	5151
RED HANDICAP	14	4	18	16	12	10	6	8	2			11	17	9	3	13	7	1	15	5		
PAR	4	5	3	4	3	4	4	4	5	36		4	3	4	5	3	4	5	3	4	35	71

Timberline Golf Course

Peosta

563-876-3422

Timberline is a unique course. When the course was built in 1979 they cleared a small path right through the timber. In 1989 they fired up the same bulldozer and cleared out another 9 holes, more challenging than the last, out of adjacent hills and woods. There are four ponds on the course affecting six holes, one stream that alters play slightly on three holes. You might even say the course was dominated by water if it wasn't for all those darn trees and hills. There are 5 holes on the course that are basically flat, to the north by the stream. The remaining holes have large trees lining the fairways, although the wooded areas don't seem to close in on you as you walk the course. The greens are medium in size and generally flat, although there is a display of all types of putting surfaces throughout the course. The greens are getting faster as the grass develops over the years. The addition of the back nine has added additional character to Timberline. This nine is more challenging, harder greens to read, tougher to score well on, and narrower for drives and approaches. There are only 2 holes on the backside that you should feel comfortable using a driver off the tee. Demon's Run, 15,16,17, &18, on the backside are some of the toughest finishing holes in eastern Iowa. The course is hard to walk, but they do have carts. A new clubhouse was built in 1995 and has a beautiful view over one of the ponds and up a hill. Inside there is a very nice bar that has all the necessities plus clothing. Weekday green fees are $14. There has also been an addition of a driving range across the road. This is a unique setting, one of the most interesting in the state. It might be worth your green fee to drive four miles south and two miles west of Peosta to play this one, turn south on exit 308.

Course	18 Holes	Aesthetics	Very Good
Distance	6572 Yards	Interest	Very Good
Par	36-36-72	Worth The Trip	Yes
Playability	Good	Rating	***+

HOLE		1	2	3	4	5	6	7	8	9	Out
BLACK	71.4/119	341	488	168	392	200	485	419	352	369	3214
SILVER	70.8/116	324	468	160	365	180	470	372	340	333	3012
PAR		4	5	3	4	3	5	4	4	4	36
RED	73.5/113	309	410	139	301	152	393	305	318	273	2600
PAR		4	5	3	4	3	5	4	4	4	36
HANDICAPS		14	17	12	7	11	18	3	10	13	

10	11	12	13	14	15	16	17	18	IN	TOT
320	530	147	350	184	384	400	439	604	3358	6572
299	511	129	329	161	364	356	419	564	3132	6144
4	5	3	4	3	4	4	4	5	36	72
270	412	118	280	142	312	289	361	534	2718	5318
4	5	3	4	3	4	4	5	5	37	73
15	16	8	5	9	1	2	4	6		

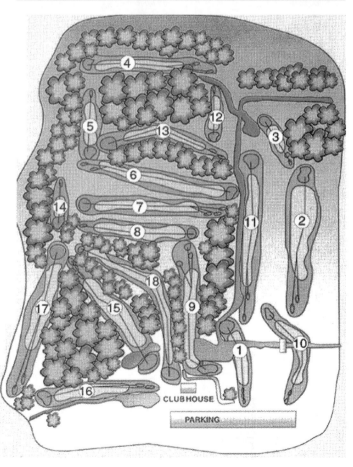

202

Pierson Golf Club
Pierson

There is only one thing to say about the new nine hole course in Pierson, it is sand. Iowa lost 2 sand green courses over the last 10 years, so it is with great enthusiasm that I report to you that another one has been added in NW Iowa The course is laid out in a former pasture on the west edge of Pierson. There are a few trees scattered throughout. There is nothing fantastic about the course. Interest in the course would not be very high. The clubhouse is not much bigger than the 3rd grade boys clubhouse in the middle of town. But it doesn't matter, Pierson golf Club has sands greens, that is all that matters. Travel the distance to play this course.

Course	Sand
Distance	2347 Yards
Par	36
Playability	Good
Aesthetics	Fair
Interest	Historical
Worth The Trip	Yes
Rating	**

DISTANCE YARDS	407	290	357	236	256	276	85	225	243	2347
PAR (Men's)	5	4	4	4	4	4	3	4	4	36
Handicap	1	5	2	6	4	3	9	7	8	
Women's Par	5	4	5	4	4	4	3	4	4	37
HOLES	1	2	3	4	5	6	7	8	9	Out

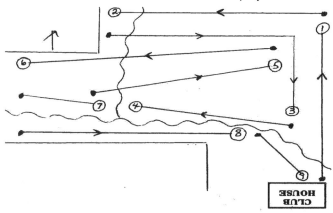

Pleasantville Golf and Country Club
Pleasantville
515-848-5716

A course should reflect what the membership expects it's course to play like; the Pleasantville Golf and Country Club offers members something that will not get boring or send them home never wanting to return. This course is very open. The contour of the layout is flat which makes for easy walking. This is also an easy course to score well on. There are 310 members who pay yearly fees but green fees keep the course busy much of the time, green fees of $9 are accepted on the days. Pleasantville Golf Course was built in 1966 and is a typical small town course. There is one pond on the course, no streams, four sand bunkers, and rough cut along the fairways. There are not many trees on the course, although more trees are planted each year; the few that are there line the fairways but present few problems. The greens are medium to large in size and flat. The course is located south of Pleasantville. The overall character of this course is laid back and easy going. There are many senior players on this course and many others that enjoy the exercise and easy golfing. The clubhouse does have snacks and a few golfing supplies.

Course	9 Holes
Distance	2962 Yards
Par	35
Playability	Fair
Aesthetics	Fair
Interest	Poor
Worth The Trip	Maybe
Rating	*+

BLUE TEES	470	395	190	412	295	500	145	370	185	2962
WHITE TEES	449	375	158	361	281	466	131	358	173	2752
HANDICAP	9	2	3	6	5	7	8	4	1	
PAR	5	4	3	4	4	5	3	4	3	35
HOLE	1	2	3	4	5	6	7	8	9	OUT
RED TEES	428	320	135	290	262	405	112	312	158	2422
LADIES HCP	5	1	4	9	2	7	6	8	3	

Copper Creek Golf Course

Pleasant Hill

515-263-1600

Copper Creek golf Course was opened in 1997 off E. University in Pleasant Hill. This 18 hole course was built on a gently rolling wooded track of land. This is a public course that offers yearly dues of $1440. Weekday green fees are $18. The most unique feature of the course are the abundance of trees. Thick trees are found lining the fairways on all but 4 holes. A creek runs the length of the back nine and comes into play on four holes. A pond affects errant shots on number 11. There are fairway bunkers and green side bunkers throughout the course. Grass condition is very good and has matured nicely in the last two years. Greens are undulating and vary in size and shape. The landscape of Copper Creek sells the course. Many of the holes stand by themselves making it a personal experience. The 5 finishing holes are tight and provide a real driving challenge. The clubhouse provides the essentials. This is a very nice addition to the east side of metro area. Part of the Copper Creek experience is the housing development that line 6 of the holes. A beautiful setting that is well worth the trip.

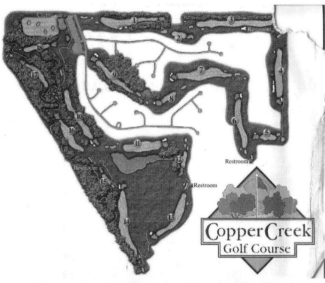

Blue	497	181	572	422	171	381	446	189	422	3281
White	494	163	545	412	143	350	415	176	367	3065
Handicap	11	15	1	3	17	9	7	13	5	
Par	5	3	5	4	3	4	4	3	4	35
Red	400	110	462	298	106	315	321	123	296	2431
Par	5	3	5	4	3	4	4	3	4	35
Hole	1	2	3	4	5	6	7	8	9	Out

490	355	196	394	524	128	352	317	301	3057	3281	6338	
483	327	157	386	510	118	349	314	299	2943	3065	6008	
4	8	16	2	14	18	6	10	12				
5	4	3	4	5	3	4	4	4	36	35	71	
389	289	142	290	436	98	246	258	211	2359	2431	4790	
5	4	3	4	5	3	4	4	4	36	35	71	
10	11	12	13	14	15	16	17	18	In		Tot	Hcp Net

Course	18 Holes	Distance	6338 Yards
Par	36-35-71	Interest	Very Good
Playability	Good	Worth The Trip	Yes
Aesthetics	Very Good	Rating	★★★+

Pocahontas Golf Club

Pocahontas

712-335-4375

Pocahontas Golf Club was built in 1931 and is located on the eastern edge of Pocahontas. The clubhouse has a roomy bar area that is in visual contact with number one tee. The clubhouse has balls and gloves for sale. There are carts for rent. There isn't a restaurant but snacks and drinks are available. Green fees are normal in price for this size of course. The 250 members pay an annual fee of over $300. A new pond was built on hole on number 4 and 6 new sand traps were put in. The rough does exist, sometimes a little higher than wanted. The medium size trees line many of the narrow fairways but are not very restrictive. The contour of the course is flat and compact but still has a yardage of 3131 yards. The grass condition throughout the course is good with the rough being a little too good in spots. The greens are small and flat, something to think about as you make your approach shots, hopefully the thought will come before you roll your ball across the green. This is an easy course to walk and a fairly easy course to score well on. It is moderately busy but waiting to tee off is not very common. The course is played by many loyal members and people from outside the community. This is almost another airport course, the runway is about 300 yards north of the course.

Course	9 Holes
Distance	3051 Yards
Par	36
Playability	Good
Aesthetics	Fair
Interest	Poor
Worth The Trip	Maybe
Rating	★★

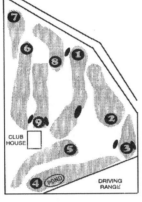

HOLE	1	2	3	4	5	6	7	8	9	OUT
MEN'S YARDAGE	485	346	139	475	355	392	176	357	326	3051
HANDICAP	5	3	8	7	6	1	2	4	9	
MEN'S PAR	5	4	3	5	4	4	3	4	4	36
WOMEN'S PAR	5	4	3	5	4	5	3	4	4	37
WOMEN'S YARDAGE	437	336	129	409	345	382	166	347	316	2867

Plum River Golf Course

Preston

563-689-4653

Plum River Golf Course is located 2 miles north of Preston on Hwy. Z34 in Jackson County. This is a new course which still utilizes a farmhouse as its clubhouse. The natural setting has been preserved as much as possible. There are a number of large trees that do come into play if you let them. When the course was built a irrigation system was installed and so the condition of the course is good. Each hole has at least two sets of tees to choose form. Tees are elevated and give a good look at the hole ahead. This is an open course and missing the fairway is not the end of the world. Greens are large in size and vary in shape. The layout of the course is good with 5 holes either stating or ending at the clubhouse area. This could be called a walking course. The layout of the course is generally flat but still is interesting. A family membership is $525, weekday green fees are $11. The only other hazard is a pond that comes into play on 2 holes. This is a nice new rural course. A laid back atmosphere and an interesting place to play.

Course	9 Holes
Distance	2742 Yards
Par	35
Playability	Good
Aesthetics	Good
Interest	Good
Worth the Trip	Yes
Rating	★★+

Hole	1	2	3	4	5	6	7	8	9	Out
Blue										
White	312	322	489	161	388	155	273	155	487	2742
Red	233	256	407	108	282	134	204	139	440	2203
Par	4	4	5	3	4	3	4	3	5	35
Handicap	13	17	5	3	1	9	15	11	7	

Tournament of Iowa

Polk City

515-984-9440
www.tcofiowa.com

Arnold Palmer designed The tournament of Iowa course in Polk City. TCI is located on the west edge of Polk City and opened in 2003. The general layout of the course was designed in a wooded area that is hilly. Fifteen holes have wooded areas that come into play. A rule of thumb is, if you hit a ball into the woods, let it go, don't waste your time looking for it. Three holes have been designed with stadium seating for possible future tournament seating. Each holes has four sets of tees. Yardage ranges from 4990 to 7043 yards. Greens average 7,000 square feet and have A1-A4 Bent grass. Fairways also have bent grass surfaces and are in fantastic shape for being in the first year of operation. There is a first cut rough that intermingle with some natural areas along the fairways. There is an average of two sand bunkers per hole, some being very big. There is approximately 5 acres of sand on TCI. The layout of the course was generally cut out of the woods so the trees are mature and there is no long-range plan to plant more. The look of the course is already mature. Water hazards include a creek that runs through the front 9. Water comes into play on seven holes. TCI is a great addition to Iowa golf. There are generous target areas for drives but tightens up significantly on the approach shot. The spacious clubhouse has all the amenities of a country club. Collared shirts and no jeans are allowed on the course. There is a full line of clubs and clothes in the pro shop. There is a driving range with an abundance of balls. Green fees are $67, which include a cart and balls for the range. This is a great course that will only get better.

Course	18 Holes	Aesthetics	Very Good
Distance	7108 Yards	Interest	Very Good
Par	335-36-71	Worth the Trip	Yes
Playability	Very Good	Rating	****

HOLE	1	2	3	4	5	6	7	8	9	OUT		10	11	12	13	14	15	16	17	18	IN	TTL
KING	553	420	186	593	185	480	386	234	456	3493		356	376	442	526	325	195	231	640	459	3550	7043
PALMER	527	386	170	578	164	448	359	170	395	3197		347	369	427	504	301	182	188	595	441	3354	6551
DEACON	495	349	140	536	154	420	341	138	355	2928		323	351	375	469	229	157	171	560	399	3034	5962
MEN'S HANDICAP	4	6	14	8	12	2	10	18	16			15	7	1	11	13	17	9	5	3		
LEGEND	396	270	113	478	100	393	253	107	305	2415		273	308	348	445	140	90	117	516	338	2575	4990
LADIES' HANDICAP	6	8	16	2	18	10	4	12	14			15	11	1	5	13	17	9	3	7		
PAR	5	4	3	5	3	4/5	4	3	4	35/36		4	4	5	4/3	3	3	5	4	36/35	71	

Primghar Golf and County Club

Primghar

712-757-6781

Primghar Golf & Country Club was named the Iowa 9 Hole Course of the Year in 1990 after only 3 years of play!!! This 72 acre tract of land was given to Primghar by Harold Metcalf for the express purpose of developing a unique golf course that the community could enjoy. Unlike many courses in Iowa, Primghar does not have a long range plan of covering the course with trees. This is and will forever be a wide open course that lets the natural landscape and man-made ground bunkers take their toll on the golfer. Primghar has let natural areas flourish, making it a new preservation area. Every fairway is lined and interwoven with ground bunkers. They are beautiful to look at but do create a great many side hill shots. Fairway watering keeps the entire course in immaculate shape, definitely one of THE best in western Iowa. The tees are elevated slightly and small to medium in size. Greens are medium to large in size but have characters of their own. Some combine rolling and tilted surfaces to make this ancient game a real challenge, nothing too severe though. The green's surfaces putt true and are in excellent shape. There are 5 holes that are affected by water, one creek runs through the course and 2 ponds catch a few balls also. There are 5 sand bunkers to go along with the grass bunkers. This is not a tree course but it is already a tough course because of the landscape and water hazards. There are very few gimmicks built into the course. It is well taken care of and offers the members a chance to play a clean game of golf. The clubhouse is very nice with lots of seating and dining and has a limited range of supplies. This is a family course that requires no tee times. The driving range adds some hitting alternatives. Primghar Golf and Country Club is one the best facilities in the entire state. It is really a thing of beauty from opening morning to closing evening. If you get the chance, play it.

Course	9 Holes
Distance	2550Yards
Par	36
Playability	Excellent
Aesthetics	Excellent
Interest	Good
Worth the Trip	Yes
Rating	★★★★★

Hole No.	1	2	3	4	5	6	7	8	9	OUT
Ladies' Red Tees	415	290	120	340	420	240	325	120	280	2550
Ladies' Handicap	2	6	7	3	1	4	5	8	9	
Ladies' Par	5	4	3	4	5	4	4	3	4	36
Men's Par	5	4	3	4	5	4	4	3	4	36
Men's Handicap	3	4	9	5	2	1	6	8	7	
Men's White Tees	485	345	150	395	485	305	380	155	340	3040
Men's Blue Tees	510	365	160	405	520	315	390	185	390	3240

Quimby Golf Club

Quimby

712-445-2236

The Quimby golf Club started out as a town project years ago and turned into a fine nine hole golf course in 1997. The layout of the course is set on some gently rolling farmland. The course maintains some of the natural settings and grasslands. Each hole has a set of three tees With total layout yardage of 2807 from the blue tees. Green size varies, but most are quite large. The speed of greens also vary according to players coming off 9. Quimby has a big grove of trees around the outside and a few plantings on the course. Quimby is unique in the aspect that they have incorporated all the natural settings of the area. There are natural grasses and use of the rolling terrain plays well on the layout. This is a fun course to play with the big greens helping out to make it a good experience. Number 2 green is 13,000 square feet, a monster. The Little Sioux River runs beside Quimby Golf but does not come into play. The 167 members pay a yearly fee of $385. Weekday green fees are $9. In 2002 there were six hole-in-ones on # 4., a 143 yard par 3.

Course	9 Holes
Distance	2807 Yards
Par	36
Playability	Good
Aesthetics	Good
Interest	Good
Worth The Trip	Yes
Rating	★★★

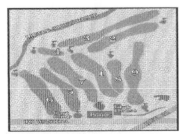

HOLE	1	2	3	4	5	6	7	8	9	OUT	TOTALS
HANDICAP	7	6	9	5	4	3	1	2	8		
BLUE TEES	286	295	420	143	350	300	375	208	430		2807
WHITE TEES	250	237	365	143	324	272	337	208	375		2511
RED TEES	230	195	300	123	304	225	305	180	300		2162
PAR	4	4	5	3	4	4	4	3	5	36	

Radcliffe Friendly Fairways

Radcliffe

515-899-7969

If you are tired of crowds and tee times and you want a golf course that is flat and easy to walk, then Radcliffe Friendly Fairways is a course that you can contend with. Green fees are very reasonable. Friendly Fairways was built in 1971 and is still in the developing stages. This is a wide open course that has a very flat contour. Trees are generally small and do line some of the fairways but seldom come into play. Greens are medium in size and also have flat putting surfaces. The clubhouse has a limited amount of supplies and snacks. Many people come from the Ames and Story City areas to play this course because it is easy to get on and play. This is an easy course to score well on. There are very few hazards, you can go out and have some fun just hitting the ball around. The atmosphere seems to be laid back and easy, a typical central Iowa small town course. Radcliffe is another fine example of a small town course that was developed for the enjoyment of local residents. It doesn't claim to be of championship caliber, just a place to come and enjoy the game.

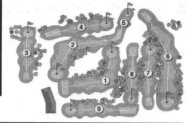

Course	9 Holes
Distance	3125 Yards
Par	36
Playability	Fair
Aesthetics	Fair
Interest	Poor
Worth The Trip	No
Rating	*+

HOLE	1	2	3	4	5	6	7	8	9	OUT
WHITE	520	397	226	308	160	486	352	326	350	3125
PAR	5	4	3	4	3	5	4	4	4	36

Oak Leaf Country Club

Reinbeck

319-345-2079

Jack Jones designed the Oak Leaf Country Club that is located two miles west of Reinbeck. Prior to World War II this course was the Grundy County Golf Club owned by the American Legion Club. During the war money became scarce and the course was plowed under and used as a corn field. In 1956 two men, Paul Tschrigi and Leroy Moser decided to build a new course on this original site. Most of the rebuilding was done by these two men and the course officially opened again in 1960. Today this private course has a spacious clubhouse that is moderately elegant on the inside with very comfortable dining facilities. The outside is surrounded by giant oak trees and presents a country club atmosphere. These big Oaks are also scattered throughout the course, making it a beautiful place to play. There are no sand bunkers but a stream comes into play on six of the holes. The general contour of the fairways is gently rolling, with greens flat and tilted slightly. The beauty of this course attracts the 250 members who pay a yearly fee of $445. If you are a guest of a member you are able to pay a nominal green fee and enjoy the oaks plus have an enjoyable game of golf.

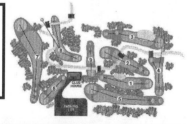

Course	9 Holes
Distance	2999 Yards
Par	35
Playability	Good
Aesthetics	Very Good
Interest	Good
Worth The Trip	Yes
Rating	***

	1	2	3	4	5	6	7	8	9	OUT
PAR	4	4	4	3	5	3	5	4	3	35
CHAMPIONSHIP	345	370	385	202	520	152	490	370	165	2999
HANDICAP	17	7	5	3	1	15	11	9	13	
REGULAR	335	360	375	192	510	142	480	360	155	2909
HANDICAP	17	5	3	15	1	13	7	9	11	
RED	325	340	355	170	480	137	470	330	112	2719
PAR	4	4	4	4	5	3	5	4	3	36
HOLE	1	2	3	4	5	6	7	8	9	OUT

Red Oak Country Club
Red Oak
712-623-4281

Red Oak Country Club has one of the most bizarre holes in the state. Their number four is called the Bull Pen. It is 145 years long, down hill, and is surrounded by grass bunkers. Your drive either makes it on the green or you spend some time getting up, over, or around the bunkers, a real masterpiece of a hole. The course added an additional 9 holes a couple of years ago and now the expanded 6231 yard course is nicer than ever. There is one stream that comes into play two times on the back 9, plus if you are really wild there is the pool by the clubhouse. Bunkers guard a few of the large greens. Greens are flat on the front side and rolling and undulating on the new back side. The contour of the course is semi-rolling with wide fairways and a two-inch rough. There are many side-hill lies that are very challenging. The placement of your tee-shot may create some blind approach shots that can become quite aggravating. The front nine has a great number of big, old trees that line all the fairways and come into play quite often. The back-side has very few trees, just wide open spaces. The original course was built in 1922 and is located two miles east of Red Oak on old Highway 34. The large clubhouse has a big bar and snack area plus dinner facilities. This is an outstanding course that offers beauty and $820 for a family while daily green fees are reasonable. The new nine holes has added a great deal to the course and in time will make this one of the nicer courses in S.W. Iowa. If for no other reason, travel to Red Oak to play in the Bull Pen. Or to look over the new nine from a hill. That is what golfing is all about.

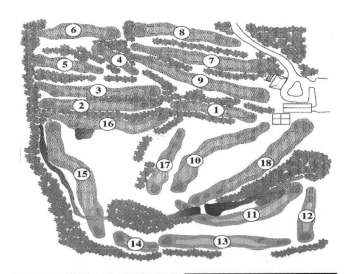

Hole	1	2	3	4	5	6	7	8	9	Out	10	11	12	13	14	15	16	17	18	In	Tot	Hcp	Net
Blue Tees																							
White Tees	299	372	342	148	210	272	453	342	453	2891	359	460	159	344	111	453	323	146	508	2863	5754		
Par	4	4	4	3	3	4	5	4	5	36	4	5	3	4	3	5	4	3	5	36	72		
Handicap	7	5	3	17	1	15	11	9	13		14	10	6	8	18	16	2	12	4				
Gold Tees	299	372	290	148	195	272	405	296	405	2682	327	410	159	344	111	443	250	146	472	2662	5344		
Red Tees	289	358	290	140	195	228	401	296	401	2898	327	400	124	323	100	443	222	111	409	2459	5057		
Par	4	4	4	3	3	4	5	4	5	36	4	3	3	4	3	5	4	3	5	36	72		
Handicap	13	5	9	17	1	15	7	11	3		6	2	14	12	18	8	10	16	4				

Course	18 Holes	Aesthetics	Very Good
Distance	6231 Yards	Interest	Good
Par	36-36-72	Worth The Trip	Yes
Playability	Good	Rating	★★★

Remsen Country Club

Remsen

712-786-2266

The Remsen Country Club was built in the middle 70's and is still developing and growing. This is another one of N.W. Iowa's flat courses built out of a cornfield. The course is located on the west edge of Remsen along Highway 3. There are two ponds on the course that affect three holes. The fairways are open and wide allowing some free swinging without much penalty. The south end of the course has small trees and not many of them, the north end has a few more and a little larger in size. New trees are being planted each year increasing the difficulty of the course. Tees are marginal and the greens are medium in size and elevated. There are two sand bunkers in the layout. The course is in good condition and provides flat fairways for landing areas. The installation of fairway watering has improved the overall grass condition. The clubhouse is basic small town with a bar area that serves snacks and tables overlooking the course. Membership to Remsen Golf Club is $325 for a family per year. Greens fees are reasonable on the weekends and holidays. Remsen is another course that has that small town, welcome to our club feeling. Friendly people on and off the course and fun to play to boot.

Course	9 Holes
Distance	3165 Yards
Par	36
Playability	Good
Aesthetics	Good
Interest	Fair
Worth The Trip	Maybe
Rating	★★

HOLE	1	2	3	4	5	6	7	8	9	TOT
MEN	355	470	135	525	425	170	335	365	385	3165
LADIES	345	445	125	475	365	160	325	355	375	2970
PAR	4	5	3	5	4	3	4	4	4	36
Handicap	3	9	6	7	1	5	8	4	2	

Riceville Country Club

Riceville

641-985-2447

The Riceville Country Club is located on the east edge of Riceville on Highway 9. The remodeled clubhouse has a nice supply of golfing equipment and there are carts for rent. The contour of this course is generally flat and fairly easy to walk. The layout of the course has been changed to speed up player traffic. A small stream runs down the west side of the course and comes into play on number 7. Many of the trees line the fairways and are in the 20 to 30 foot range. Accuracy off the tee is very beneficial and should be strongly considered before teeing up your first drive. Any push or draw can bring you in contact with the trees, not a pleasant experience. The fairways are fairly wide, with no rough to contend with. The greens are of medium size with a variety of surfaces, some flat, some rolling, and some tilted. This is a nice, small-town course with a relaxed golfing atmosphere. Almost any time you can tee off number one without any delay. Even with the trees, Riceville Country Club is an easy course to score well on and a low tension course to play.

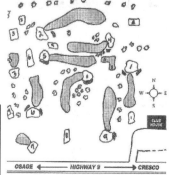

Course	9 Holes
Distance	2677 Yards
Par	35
Playability	Poor
Aesthetics	Fair
Interest	Poor
Worth The Trip	No
Rating	★+

	1	2	3	4	5	6	7	8	9	
Blue Tee Yardage	356	490	160	332	337	246	148	333	355	
White Tee Yardage	343	460	136	340	330	228	141	322	345	
MEN'S PAR	4	5	3	4	4	4	3	4	4	35
WOMEN'S PAR	4	5	3	4	4	4	3	4	4	35
Red Tee Yardage	330	400	128	333	323	210	118	272	335	
HOLE	1	2	3	4	5	6	7	8	9	OUT

OSAGE ← HIGHWAY 9 → CRESCO

The Harvester Golf Club
Rhodes

877-963-GOLF

www.harvestergolf.com

The Harvester Golf Club is located 30 minutes NE of Des Moines near Rhodes on Hwy. 330. The design of the course takes its inspiration from the slopes, long ridges, and sweeping valleys. Very little dirt was moved when shaping the course. Instead the owners opted to carve fairways, bunkers, and greens into the landscape to accentuate existing features. A shotmaker's course with risk-reward options, the 7,240 yard, par 72 layout, home of the Iowa State's men and women's golf teams, has a 60 acre lake, smaller ponds. Wetlands, creeks, and an 80 foot elevation change. The second hole, a short uphill par 4 plays over a cavernous trench cut into the side of a hill with the green above it, a decision to go over the trench or play it safe to the side. The par-three third drops from an elevated tee over a pond to a natural peninsula green the size of a skating rink. A possibility of three putt is a reality. Coming home is thrilling. The short par-three 17th is a pretty piece of poison, its slim green flanked by water and a pair of deep bunkers. The par-five 18th is a gamblers delight, a hairpin-shaped hole where players who drive close to the water's edge on the right side can go for the green. The green fee, $48 for walkers, $60 with a cart. The course built in 2000 has already won several awards. Golf Magazines top 10 to play in U.S. Ranked number 2 best new affordable public courses in the U.S. Ranked #7 America's 100 Best Courses for less than $100. Ranked the Best Public Course in Iowa. A must course to play for any golfer in Iowa.

Course	18 Holes	Aesthetics	Excellent
Distance	7340 Yards	Interest	Excellent
Par	36-36-72	Worth The Trip	Yes
Playability	Excellent	Rating	★★★★★

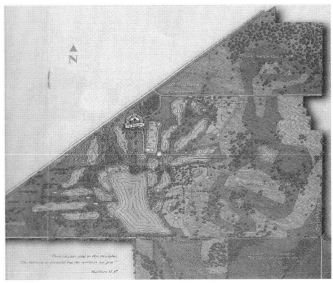

HOLE	1	2	3	4	5	6	7	8	9	OUT		10	11	12	13	14	15	16	17	18	IN	TOT	HCP	NET
BLACK	425	360	195	575	370	560	405	225	465	3580	P	470	385	410	390	230	650	480	180	565	3760	7340		
BLUE	390	345	180	545	320	530	370	200	430	3310	L	450	355	390	355	205	600	440	165	540	3500	6810		
WHITE	375	330	165	490	300	515	350	180	410	3115	A	435	340	380	335	195	550	415	155	490	3295	6410		
YELLOW	340	300	149	480	235	495	330	165	380	2870	Y	400	280	355	280	185	515	345	145	415	2920	5790		
RED	335	265	135	465	230	430	250	100	370	2580	E R	306	240	260	275	135	480	340	90	410	2535	5115		
PAR	4	4	3	5	4	5	4	3	4	36		4	4	4	4	3	5	4	3	5	36	72		

Rock River Golf & Country Club

Rock Rapids

712-472-3168

Another fine course found in extreme N.W. Iowa is the Rock River Club located one mile north of Rock Rapids. This course was built in 1924 with a new clubhouse reconstructed in 1966. The clubhouse has a solid wall of north side windows looking over the course. The bar area is small and has meals and snacks for golfers. The clubhouse has few supplies but has a golfing, relaxed atmosphere. The contour of the course is very flat, as are most courses in this part of the state. A new double row watering system was installed in 1990. The Rock River comes into play on two holes and the medium size trees come into play on some of the narrower fairways. One of the most unique things about this course are the old greens. They have lasted through all the years and are noted for being small, hard to hold, and just plain hard to hit on your approach shot. The 250 members enjoy a course that is not too busy and still survives the financial pinch. Fairway watering and a top grounds keeper can be credited with keeping these members happy with the condition of the course. Tom Vinson was voted the IGA grounds keeper of 1984 and in 1988 and he seems to have lived up to his credentials. Green fees are reasonable for a 9 hole course. This is a course for the calm at heart though, read the greens with a clear and logical mind and you might have a decent round, if not; have you heard of the game Annie-Annie-Over?

Course	9 Holes
Distance	2737 Yards
Par	35
Playability	Good
Aesthetics	Good
Interest	Fair
Worth The Trip	Yes
Rating	**+

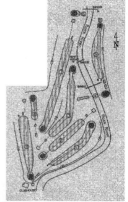

Welcome to Rock River Golf & Country Club										
Hole	1	2	3	4	5	6	7	8	9	Out
White	367	326	435	131	285	142	520	176	355	2737
Red	298	283	393	92	247	133	444	148	296	2334
Handicap	2	4	5	9	7	8	1	6	3	
Par	4	4	5	3	4	3	5	3	4	35

Rock Valley Golf Club

Rock Valley

712-476-2427

One of the nicer landscaped courses in N.W. Iowa is Rock Valley Golf Club. Split rail fence lines the driveway, small trees surround the clubhouse area along with shrubs and bushes. The extras out on the course make it more of a relaxed and pleasant atmosphere to play in.   Members enjoy a small town course that has some length and diversity. There are three holes that come in contact with a piece of the pond, there are also five sand bunkers that lie in wait for your ball. The course is fairly young, demonstrated by the height of the trees. 300 trees have been planted in the last 5 years. The entire course was reseeded in 2002. Fairway watering has also been added giving the course a new fresh look. The greens are surrounded by a low cut of rough and green size would be classified as big with sloping surfaces. The Rock Valley course is quite busy, with green fees being reasonably priced, $12 for 9 holes. The clubhouse has a full line of equipment, carts, and bar items. If you would like a flat course with a few dips, one that offers somewhat of a challenge, yet is still fairly easy to play, then locate the Rock Valley course on the S.W. side of town and give it your best. Make sure you bring your heavy putter, some putts are short drives.

Course	9 Holes
Distance	3253 Yards
Par	36
Playability	Good
Aesthetics	Good
Interest	Good
Worth The Trip	Yes
Rating	***

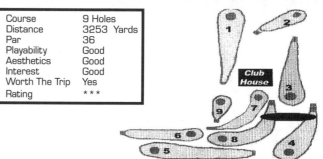

Hole	1	2	3	4	5	6	7	8	9	OUT
Championship - Blue	403	189	384	379	527	368	365	464	174	3253
Men's Yardage-White	378	163	368	364	504	356	343	432	160	3068
Ladies Yardage -Red	290	141	316	324	460	268	261	397	150	2607
Par	4	3	4	4	5	4	4	5	3	36

Rockford Golf and Country Club

Rockford

641-756-3314

If you like to use every club that you have in the bag, then you need to attack the Rockford Golf and Country Club located on B47 southwest of Rockford. This is a very flat course that can be challenging, especially if there is any amount of breeze coming out of the southwest. There are four sand bunkers and water comes into play on one hole. Recently 500 trees were planted throughout the course plus there are some medium size trees and evergreens that come into play if you wander from the wide fairways. The tees were recently rebuilt. The greens are basically oval and of medium size. The course was built in 1963. This is an easy course to walk and maintains a clean and well-groomed feeling. The 250 members pay an annual family membership of $350. The clubhouse is a very nice new brick structure that has a nice southern view of the course and serves beverages and sandwiches from the bar. They also have a swimming pool for members. A nice course to play but also a course that may force you to use all the tricks that you have in your repertoire of shots.

Course	9 Holes
Distance	3186 Yards
Par	36
Playability	Very Good
Aesthetics	Good
Interest	Good
Worth The Trip	Yes
Rating	★★★

HOLE	1	2	3	4	5	6	7	8	9	OUT
YARDAGE	312	132	385	399	187	374	466	398	533	3186
HANDICAP	17	15	11	1	5	9	13	3	7	
MEN'S PAR	4	3	4	4	3	4	5	4	5	36
LADIES PAR	4	3	4	4	3	4	5	5	6	38
YARDAGE	295	120	372	325	177	289	421	389	521	2909
HANDICAP	17	15	11	1	5	9	13	3	7	

Linn Grove Country Club

Rockwell

641-822-4990

Linn Grove Country Club is located on the west edge of Rockwell and is dominated by a small stream that runs through the course and comes into play on seven holes. Not only is the water a problem but there are ten bunkers and medium to large size trees lining the stream. This is an easy course to walk, but you must be accurate off the tees or you will do a lot of extra walking and swinging. The tee boxes are flat and have improved over the past few years. The greens are large, flat, fast, and some are tilted. The course was built in 1979 and has a new clubhouse that has adequate seating and party facilities. The deck is a perfect place to sit and watch the trees grab flying Top Flights. This is a public course that has a length of 2801 yards and a par of 35. Green fees are average for a course this size. The 170 members pay $350 per year . For a short course this has every hazard that you could possibly want, making it a interesting and challenging course. This is a beautiful course that brings natural calm to your game.

Course	9 Holes
Distance	2801 Yards
Par	35
Playability	V. Good
Aesthetics	Good
Interest	Fair
Worth The Trip	Yes
Rating	★★+

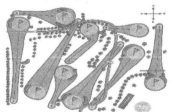

HOLE	1	2	3	4	5	6	7	8	9	OUT
WHITE COURSE	299	350	543	155	555	120	333	145	301	2801
HANDICAP	2	3	1	8	5	9	7	6	4	
PAR	4	4	5	3	5	3	4	3	4	35
RED COURSE	255	287	543	155	456	120	333	145	287	2541
HANDICAP	5	4	1	8	2	9	3	7	6	

Twin Lakes Country Club

Rockwell City

712-297-8712

The course that my father taught me the game of golf on is Twin Lakes Country Club. The course is located five miles north of Rockwell City on South Twin Lake. This is a public course with 170 members with annual fees of $425 for a family. Daily green fees are reasonable for a course this size. The course is a picturesque, well maintained, easy, home town course. There are three small bunkers in the layout and a little rough that rarely comes into play. Trees are medium to large in size and line portions of all the fairways. There are some large trees on the perimeter of the course that supply wind breaks from South Twin Lake, these trees also have the ability to catch your drive from going into the lake on occasions. The greens are medium in size and basically flat with one crowned and a few tilted. The greens have the reputation of being easy to read and putt; plus are always in good shape. This is a short course that is easy to walk, easy to score well on, and has a friendly golfing atmosphere. The course was built in 1927 and is designed as a drive and pitch course. I know of a few people who have worn out their seven irons on this course. Twin Lakes is a relaxing and fun course to come home to.

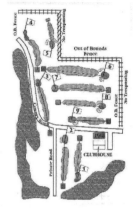

Course	9 Holes
Distance	2447 Yards
Par	34
Playability	Good
Aesthetics	Very Good
Interest	Fair
Worth The Trip	Yes
Rating	★★+

HOLES	1	2	3	4	5	6	7	8	9	OUT
BLUE	270	300	280	210	136	458	343	261	189	2447
WHITE	258	287	264	204	126	446	331	253	179	2348
PAR	4	4	4	3	3	5	4	4	3	34
HANDICAP	6	2	7	4	9	1	3	8	5	

Rolfe Golf Club

Rolfe

712-848-3662

The Rolfe Golf Club is a public course located on the south edge of Rolfe, this course has a park atmosphere. There is an old racetrack that was once a part of the course but has now grown over. Part of the original track rises from the ground on some of the fairways; interesting hazards. The entire course used to be a park and still retains many of the big trees throughout the layout. There are no water or sand hazards on the course but there are many ground bunkers in the fairways. The contour of the course is flat with very few rises except for the ground bunkers. The large trees line the fairways and block a few shots to a green. Greens are small and crowned. This would have to be labeled a placement course. The tree location and green size make it very important to put the ball in the right place for the approach shot. Distance is not so important on this 2551 yard course. The clubhouse is located in the middle of the course and is surrounded by large old Oak trees. Inside the facilities are small but do remind you of a golfing facility. The only supplies in the clubhouse are balls. Refreshments include drinks and sandwiches. The 150 members pay a yearly fee of $150 for a family, while green fees are very reasonable. If you want a scenic place to play, without worrying about crowds and the pressure of big time golf, Rolfe is the place, and it is priced right too.

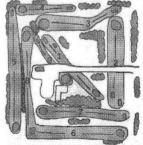

Course	9 Holes
Distance	2551 Yards
Par	34
Playability	Fair
Aesthetics	Good
Interest	Fair
Worth The Trip	Yes
Rating	★★

HOLE	1	2	3	4	5	6	7	8	9	OUT
MEN'S YARDAGE	300	277	315	210	352	342	330	270	155	2551
HANDICAP	6	7	5	4	1	2	3	9	8	
MEN'S PAR	4	4	4	3	4	4	4	4	3	34
WOMEN'S PAR	4	4	4	3	5	5	4	4	3	36
WOMEN'S YARDAGE	300	277	315	147	352	342	330	270	155	2488

Toad Valley Public Golf Course
Runnells

515-967-9575

Toad Valley Public Golf Course is located just off N.E. 80th St., one mile south of the Southeast Polk High School. This public course has a reputation of being windy. The contour of the course is gently rolling but it sits out in the country and catches winds from every direction. There is one pond on the course that you cross twice, a stream that runs along three holes, no sand, and a two inch rough that is fair and easy to get out of. There are new plantings of trees every year and all the trees are still small. The greens are medium to large and members boast of having some of the best greens in the Des Moines area. The layout of Toad Valley is wide open; the course designer had free swinging in mind. It is a fairly easy course to walk, short and gently rolling. The greens are in very good shape and are easy to hold. They do present a problem when reading angles on putts; they rely on some deception. The course was built in 1973. The 6170 yard course has 250 members that pay $425 for a Monday through Friday pass. Anyone can pay the very reasonable green fees. The newly enlarged clubhouse is a nice structure that has a full line of equipment plus carts. The bar area is average in size and has drinks and grilled sandwiches. Toad Valley is a clean course that has a nice layout and plays on the easy side. It is more of a straight away placement course, relying more on your finesse than power. The atmosphere is one of average, fun-loving golfing. It is fairly easy to get on, although tee times are needed 7 days a week. Toad Valley should provide you with some interesting and rewarding golf.

Course	18 Holes	Aesthetics	Good
Distance	6170 Yards	Interest	Good
Par	36-35-71	Worth The Trip	Yes
Playability	Good	Rating	**+

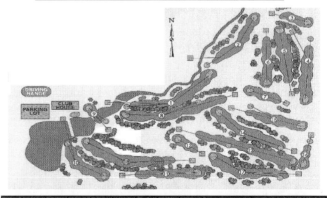

HOLE	1	2	3	4	5	6	7	8	9	OUT
YELLOW/BLUE TEES	535	410	150	375	355	330	170	530	135	2990
HANDICAP	5	1	15	7	11	9	3	13	17	
RED TEES	430	360	145	345	350	325	165	450	75	2645
PAR	5	4	3	4	4	4	3	5	3	35

10	11	12	13	14	15	16	17	18	IN	OUT	TOT	HCP	NET
345	350	140	530	405	375	185	355	495	3180	2990	6170		
6	8	16	10	2	12	4	14	18					
230	345	135	360	350	285	185	270	490	2650	2645	5295		
4	4	3	5	4	4	3	4	5	36	35	71		

Lost Island Golf Club

Ruthven

712-837-4800

Another golf course that could come under the heading of wildlife refuge is the Lost Island Golf , located five miles north of Ruthven near Lost Island Lake. The course is surrounded by natural marshes and lakes can be seen in the distance. Geese were a problem in the past but do not seem to be involved with the course any more. The club has 140 members who pay $345 a year for this privilege; and to play golf. Green fees are very reasonable for a 9 hole course. The course is built near the lake on the edge of a slough. The layout contains one pond, one stream, and some sand bunkers. The contour of the course has a gentle roll and is easy to walk. There is light rough and the fairways are wide open. But don't let the tranquility of the course lull you to sleep because the small greens and water will bring you back to your senses. Tee boxes have been completely redone in 1998 and are slightly elevated; the greens are small and contain a variety of putting surfaces, sometimes on the same green. The course was built in 1970. The atmosphere of Lost Island is laid back and relaxed. The course is not very difficult, not very long, not very busy, but very unique and beautiful. The clubhouse does have carts to rent along with a few supplies, with a lounge and restaurant.

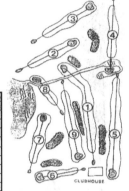

Course	9 Holes
Distance	2809 Yards
Par	34
Playability	Fair
Aesthetics	Good
Interest	Good
Worth The Trip	Yes
Rating	★★+

Blues' Yards	481	157	308	367	460	220	327	159	330	2809
Men's Yards	468	147	273	354	415	207	316	148	297	2638
Men's Hdcp.	3	4	8	1	7	9	5	2	6	
HOLE	1	2	3	4	5	6	7	8	9	Out
PAR	5	3	4	4	5	4	4	3	4	36
Women's Hdcp.	2	5	8	1	3	9	7	4	6	
Reds' Yards	434	140	235	337	384	183	290	122	220	2345

Sac Country Club

Sac City

712-662-7342

The Sac Country Club in Sac City is located in the S.W. corner of town and is built on flat land except for one enormous dip that stretches across three holes. This gully has dense trees growing around it and come into play on numbers one and two. The remainder of the course is void of any big trees; a yearly planting plan of 30 trees is being carried out each year. The watered fairways are in good shape and are fairly narrow, guarded on the edges by two inch rough. The greens come in a variety of sizes, most are in good shape and many having unseen breaks that members are very vocal about. Five greens have been rebuilt and enlarged. The redecorated clubhouse has a nice stock of equipment for sale and is nestled among the big oaks and offers a cool place in the summer to think about what might have been. The bar area inside has a large seating capacity which also serves as the dining area for special events. The Sac course is a member of the N.W. Iowa Senior Citizen League and maintains a friendly and social atmosphere. An odd highlight of the course occurred in 1979 when Wayne Hasek, as a 19 year old, aced number 2, two days in a row, something for all of us to shoot for.

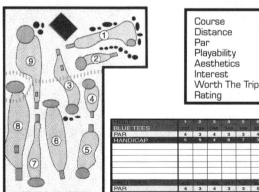

Course	9 Holes
Distance	2621 Yards
Par	34
Playability	Good
Aesthetics	Good
Interest	Fair
Worth The Trip	Yes
Rating	★★+

HOLE	1	2	3	4	5	6	7	8	9	OUT
BLUE TEES	237	126	340	143	198	302	380	450	259	2575
PAR	4	3	4	3	3	4	4	5	4	34
HANDICAP	5	9	4	8	7	3	2	1	6	
RED TEES										
PAR	4	3	4	3	3	5	5	5	4	36
HANDICAP										

Sanborn Golf and Country Club

Sanborn

712-729-5600

One of the best new courses in N.W. Iowa is the Sanborn Golf and Country Club located in Miller Park in Sanborn. The park complex was built in 1980 and includes a golf course, walking paths, tennis courts, softball fields, and picnic areas. The clubhouse on the course has a spacious dining room and an excellent restaurant that is open to the public. There is also a very nice bar and snack area that overlooks much of the course to the south. The clubhouse offers a complete line of equipment and carts. The contour of the course is very flat with new trees lining the fairways, although they will not become a factor for several years. What is a factor is the sand, there are 17 bunkers that are large in size and shaped to fit the circumference of the green. The greens are also above average in size and contain some odd shaped borders with sloping putting surfaces. The greens do hold well but are not easy to read. The greens are in good shape along with the rest of the course. The park has an irrigation system that maintains the entire complex. The Sanborn Golf & Country Club technically is a nine-hole course, but you can drive the ball off 18 different tees. The innovative feature of the course is that each hole has two tee boxes. After playing nine holes, the golfer has the option of playing another nine using a second set of tee boxes to get a different perspective of the course.

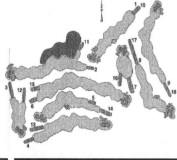

Course	9 Holes
Distance	3089 Yards
Par	36
Playability	Good
Aesthetics	Good
Interest	Fair
Worth The Trip	Yes
Rating	★★+

HOLE	1	2	3	4	5	6	7	8	9	OUT	10	11	12	13	14	15	16	17	18	IN	TOTAL
BLUE	317	465	206	415	346	502	147	332	393	3123	333	454	159	377	395	454	127	369	421	3089	6212
WHITE	310	454	195	405	335	491	131	320	384	3025	326	443	149	369	385	441	117	357	412	2999	6024
MEN'S PAR	4	5	3	4	4	5	3	4	4	36	4	4	3	4	4	5	3	4	4	35	71
HANDICAP	15	5	13	3	9	1	17	11	7		14	2	16	10	8	4	18	12	6		
RED	290	432	174	382	314	380	95	295	366	2728	298	415	130	353	365	389	95	332	393	2770	5498
LADIES PAR	4	5	3	4	4	5	3	4	4	36	4	4	5	4	4	5	3	4	5	36	72

Schleswig Community Golf Course

Schleswig

712-676-3343

The Schleswig Golf Course was built in 1966 and is located on the S.W. edge of Schleswig on Highway 59. The clubhouse sits overlooking the course from the west. They have a small amount of supplies and a nice snack bar in the basement. The layout of the course is built on the side of a hill. There are no flat lies on this course; you either address the ball above or below your feet. There are two ponds on the course that come into play on three holes plus there are three bunkers to include on the hazard list. There are a medium number of trees that are scattered along the fairways and in the rough. The trees are a factor during play because of their height and their position on the course; of course they will not bother anyone who plays down the middle. The greens are medium in size and possess some sloping qualities because the remainder of the course is sloping. This is a fairly difficult course to walk. They do have carts for rent, and it is an average course to score well on. The length of the course is offset by the contour. The 200 members pay $397 a year while daily green fees are reasonable for 9 holes. This is definitely a placement course. Being at the bottom of a hill behind a tree can make a hole very long and difficult. Getting on the course to play is no problem; the problem seems to be trying to get back up the hills to the clubhouse.

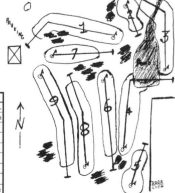

Course	9 Holes
Distance	2708 Yards
Par	35
Playability	Good
Aesthetics	Good
Interest	Fair
Worth The Trip	Yes
Rating	★★+

Mens' Course Rating 65.3

Hole	1	2	3	4	5	6	7	8	9	Tot.
Mens' Yards	481	160	269	376	171	290	272	325	364	2708
Mens' Par	5	3	4	4	3	4	4	4	4	35
1										
2										
3										
4										
Ladies' Par	5	3	3	4	3	4	4	4	4	34
Ladies' Yards	448	160	156	310	171	290	272	325	320	2452

217

Ridge Stone Golf Club

Sheffield

641-892-8040

www.ridgestonegolfclub.com

Ridge Stone is a new public golf course that opened in 2002, just southwest of town. Ridge Stone offers a unique challenge to North Iowa golfers with its 9 hole links style course and special feature of a 9 hole par 3 and driving range on the south side of the clubhouse. The #1 hole starts you out on a 582 yard dog leg left. The course features 5 little ponds, a stream that runs alongside #1 and #7, fescue and both sand and grass bunkers. The number 4 hole will have you driving to the green through the Smith Brick and Tile structures that were once a business in Sheffield. The fairway leads you through the remains of the plant. Hole #7 is the signature hole playing along Bailey's Creek on the left and a pond on the right. Green size average 7,500 and are undulating. The course is open to the public with $7 green fees for 9. The 135 members pay an annual fee of $495. The spacious clubhouse overlooks the course with a dining room and pro-shop. This is a tough course that introduces the players to a links layout.

Course	9 Holes	Aesthetics	Good
Distance	3427 Yards	Interest	Good
Par	36	Worth The Trip	Yes
Playability	Good	Rating	★★★

To the Middle of the Green:
RED plates in fairway 100 Yds.
WHITE plates in fairway 150 Yds.
BLUE plates in fairway 200 Yds.

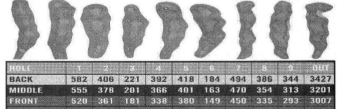

HOLE	1	2	3	4	5	6	7	8	9	OUT
BACK	582	406	221	392	418	184	494	386	344	3427
MIDDLE	555	378	201	366	401	163	470	354	313	3201
FRONT	520	361	181	338	380	149	450	335	293	3007
FORWARD	387	314	139	289	298	105	393	260	252	2437
PAR	5	4	3	4	4	3	5	4	4	36

218

Sheldon Golf and Country Club

Sheldon

712-324-4275

The most unique feature about the Sheldon Golf and Country Club is the presence of the Floyd River running through the course. The river sets the mood for the course, coming into play on six holes, but more than that it is visually present on all nine holes. Six bridges have been built to traverse the river and these become part of your game plan while you are playing. Do you lay up, go over, play close to the bridge so you won't have so far to walk, they are definitely part of the course. The fairways are lined with medium size trees, just enough to give you some trouble. The greens are medium in size, flat in most cases, and elevated. The 200 members pay $400 for a family membership while green fees are reasonable for a 9 hole course. The clubhouse has a small bar area on the lower level with dining and kitchen facilities for special occasions above. There is a nice screened in area where you can enjoy the river and watch players go down one and up nine. This flat course is not for beginning golfers. You must get the ball in the air to clear the creek, it is a tough 9 hole course and takes pleasure in causing many lost golf balls. For many it is a hard course to score well on and a tough course to play. But we all need a challenge to keep our game growing. Sheldon Golf and Country club is located two miles N.E. of Sheldon.

Course	9 Holes
Distance	3189 Yards
Par	36
Playability	Good
Aesthetics	Good
Interest	Good
Worth The Trip	Yes
Rating	***

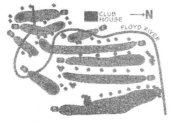

Hole	1	2	3	4	5	6	7	8	9	OUT
Blue	156	385	149	207	563	468	385	511	365	3189
White	137	375	142	164	553	455	371	503	354	3054
Yellow	126	294	127	148	489	444	300	444	295	2667
Handicap	15	5	13	7	1	17	9	3	11	
Par	3	4	3	3	5	5	4	5	4	36

Sibley Country Club

Sibley

712-754-2729
www.sibleygolf.com

Sibley Golf & Country club was completely redesigned in 1996. The greens are now more undulating and provide a great challenge. Hazards include four ponds, a waterway, 16 bunkers and lush rough. The layout offers the best of traditional American and links-style play. In 1998, Stephen Roseberry was named IGA Superintendent of the year, and Sibley was named the IGA Course of the Year in 1999. The new layout begins with a dogleg right stretching 385 yards toa challenging two-tiered green and continues to wind its way through three more holes lined with mature shade trees before moving on to the links-style holes 5 through 8. These holes contain three, fescue lined ponds and long, yet reachable par 5's. This 3,429 yard course finishes up on a par 4, 9th that is guarded by dense rough on moguls left, Maples right, and a waterway dissecting the fairway, making it the number 1 handicap hole on the course. The recently renovated clubhouse has a fully equipped snack bar, banquet area and a pro shop offering a wide variety of golf equipment. Sibley should be proud of this pristine gem, which provides an arduous, but fair test of both the ball-striking and short game of golfers at all skill levels.

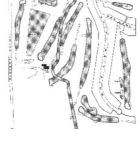

Course	9 Holes
Distance	3345 Yards
Par	35
Playability	Fair
Aesthetics	Good
Interest	Fair
Worth The Trip	Yes
Rating	**+

Hole	1	2	3	4	5	6	7	8	9	OUT
Blue	377	151	391	391	200	490	340	590	415	3345
White	350	138	363	351	184	485	325	505	377	3078
Gold	293	120	334	328	148	451	310	447	327	2758
Handicap	2	9	4	7	6	5	3	8	1	
Par	4	3	4	4	3	5	4	5	4	36

American Legion Country Club

Shenandoah

712-246-2067

Shenandoah is a lovely town in S.W. Iowa that has a lot of nice trees and nice houses. The golf course fits right into the community. The American Legion Country Club was built in 1925 in the southern part of Shenandoah among large wooded hills and around a stream. This is an 18 hole course that has water on seven holes and sand on about six. The contour of the course is gently rolling and seems to be an open course despite the number of trees that line the fairways. The size of the trees ranges from medium to large and many are full shade trees that restrict some tee shots. Tees are big and the greens are also quite large and in many cases tilted and sloping. The grass condition is good throughout the course and the landscaping is also nice around the tees and greens. The clubhouse is big and is suited for a country club atmosphere. Inside there is a full line of equipment including carts for rent. There is also a restaurant that is open to members and guests, which includes most of the town. The membership includes 300 people who pay $1000 a year. This is a private American Legion Club but if you live outside of a twelve mile radius, you can pay the moderate green fees and enjoy one of the finer courses in S.W. Iowa. The use of existing tees and landscaping has made this one of the better small town, 18 hole courses in the state. The town should be proud to have such a facility in the community. One of the most unique features of the course are the 6 bridges on the course. They are privately owned, custom designed, and built by the community. The atmosphere of the course is leisurely country club. The course is stimulating to play and displays some true Iowa golf surroundings.

Course	18 Holes	Aesthetics	Excellent
Distance	5803 Yards	Interest	Very Good
Par	35-35-70	Worth The Trip	Yes
Playability	Good	Rating	★★★+

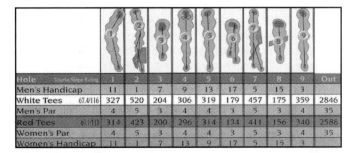

Hole	Course Slope Rating	1	2	3	4	5	6	7	8	9	Out
Men's Handicap		11	1	7	9	13	17	5	15	3	
White Tees	67.4/116	327	520	204	306	319	179	457	175	359	2846
Men's Par		4	5	3	4	4	3	5	3	4	35
Red Tees	69.7/113	314	423	200	296	314	134	411	156	340	2588
Women's Par		4	5	3	4	4	3	5	3	4	35
Women's Handicap		11	1	7	13	9	17	5	15	3	

Hole	10	11	12	13	14	15	16	17	18	In	Tot	Hcp	Net
	6	8	18	14	10	2	4	16	12				
White Tees	360	478	122	362	315	419	408	150	343	2957	5803		
	4	5	3	4	4	4	4	3	4	35	70		
Red Tees	353	382	105	359	245	390	391	128	260	2613	5201		
	4	5	3	4	4	5	5	3	4	37	72		
	2	8	18	16	10	4	6	14	12				

Freemont County Golf Course

Sidney

712-374-2347

If you are looking for a course in the extreme corner of the state then you must travel three miles south of Sidney in S.W. Iowa to the Freemont County Course. This is a very nice course, well taken care of, a recently remodeled clubhouse that is well supplied, challenging, and quite scenic. The course slopes down to the creek that runs east and west through the course. The perimeter of the course is lined with large trees, the fairway trees have now become large enough to become a definite factor in play. The contour of the course is very hilly and the layout contains four dogleg holes. The course stays green the entire summer thanks to fairway watering. The extra water also helps the greens and the beautiful tee boxes. The Freemont Course was built in 1966 and is located in a conservation recreation area that is owned by the county; the first course to be county owned in the state. The 300 members enjoy a very green and hilly course. The clubhouse is small but has a very nice pro shop. The facility also has tennis courts available to the public.

Course	9 Holes
Distance	3012 Yards
Par	35
Playability	Very Good
Aesthetics	Very Good
Interest	Good
Worth The Trip	Yes
Rating	★★★+

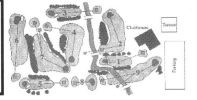

PAR		4	4	3	5	4	4	4	3	4	35
Blue	68.5	287	400	212	455	327	395	440	128	368	3012
Handicap		8	3	2	6	7	4	1	9	5	
White	68.5	297	410	222	465	335	408	452	148	375	3112
PAR		4	4	4	5	4	4	5	3	4	37
Handicap		7	2	8	1	6	3	5	9	4	
Red	68.8	265	365	210	420	310	385	340	110	295	2700
HOLE		1	2	3	4	5	6	7	8	9	Out

Sigourney Golf and Country Club

Sigourney

515-622-3400

The Sigourney Golf and Country Club is a public course located on the west edge of Sigourney and a mile north. There are two ponds on the course and one stream that effects two holes. There is no sand and the two-inch rough does not present many challenges. The trees on the course are scattered along the wide fairways and come in all sizes. The contour of the course is gently rolling and provides golfers with opportunities to commit to a full swing. Tees are small and close to the ground but have fairly good grass, as do the fairways. The greens are one of the weaker points of the course. They are small, flat and have poor grass. The clubhouse is comprised of one big room that has an old bar with drinks and grilled sandwiches. Golf supplies consist of the usual, but there are no carts for rent. Sigourney Country Club would have to be considered an open course that is easy to walk and easy to play. There are very few dangers to impede your game. A nice local course to play for the pleasure of it.

Course	9 Holes
Distance	2602 Yards
Par	35
Playability	Fair
Aesthetics	Fair
Interest	Fair
Worth The Trip	Maybe
Rating	★★

HOLE	1	2	3	4	5	6	7	8	9	OUT
BLUE	426	424	381	297	168	191	284	254	177	2602
RED	426	385	294	232	168	150	284	228	177	2344
HANDICAP	17	15	3	7	9	1	11	13	5	
PAR	5	5	4	4	3	3	4	4	3	35

Sandy Hollow Golf Course

Sioux Center

712-722-4866

Sandy Hollow Golf Course is located three miles east of Sioux Center on B-40. This is a traditional north-south course that is a little longer than most at 3239 yards. Because of its location out in the country the winds play an important part in how you attack each hole and how well you score on this course. The contour of the course is flat with seven sand bunkers and a few ground bunkers in the fairways. A new pond was built by #8 green and #6 as a hazard and water supply for the new watering system. Plus three large mounds were built to catch errant drives. There are lots of small (300 new plantings) and medium size trees lining the fairways and scattered in the rough. A stream comes into play on five holes and the local swimming hole comes into play once. The greens are medium to large and are generally flat, like the rest of the course. The course was built by all volunteer work in 1962 and has a total membership of near 500. A new nine holes is being considered. Yearly fees are $400 with an initial stock of $100. Green fees are a little above average for a 9 hole course. The clubhouse has a large sitting area with drinks and grilled sandwiches. The area around the clubhouse is landscaped very nicely. Supplies include balls, clubs, and gloves, plus there are carts for rent. This is a fairly easy course to walk but looks easier to play than it really is. The water hazards can be avoided but are there to catch the errant shot. Sandy Hollow is a wide-open course that is left open for winds to take control. With the swimming beach, campground, and course, this is one busy place in the summer.

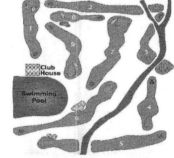

Course	9 Holes
Distance	3124 Yards
Par	36
Playability	Fair
Aesthetics	Fair
Interest	Good
Worth The Trip	Yes
Rating	★★+

HOLE	1	2	3	4	5	6	7	8	9	OUT
MEN'S YARDS	392	346	478	182	333	330	515	152	396	3124
LADIES' YARDS	350	296	410	155	293	267	461	125	343	2700
PAR	4	4	5	3	4	4	5	3	4	36

Hidden Acres Golf Club

Sioux City

712-239-9942

Hidden Acres Golf Club, north of Sioux City on Hamilton Blvd., is another example of a hilly course in northwest Iowa. The course is young, built in 1968, and has not matured into a fine tuned course yet. There are two big ponds on the course, both coming into play on your drives on the par 3's. Other hazards include five bunkers and all the difficult ball positions you could want. The layout is designed around a hill with the fairways mainly in the valleys. The trees are scattered or at the base of the valleys and do not come into play unless you stray from the beaten path. The highlight of the course are the large greens. They are hard to read, tough to get on and hold, plus they are rolling in most cases. This is a pitch and putt course; if you have those two aspects of the game mastered you can play here. But then, if you have those two things mastered, you can play in the PGA. The A-frame clubhouse has a small bar and snack area, but does have a full line of equipment, including carts. An individual will pay $400 for a year membership while daily green fees are very reasonable. This is a nice country course that has used some pastureland and put it to good use. A course that has an entertaining atmosphere and is fun to play.

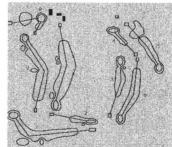

Course	9 Holes
Distance	3104 Yards
Par	35
Playability	Fair
Aesthetics	Fair
Interest	Good
Worth the Trip	Yes
Rating	★★

HOLE		1	2	3	4	5	6	7	8	9	OUT
PAR		5	3	4	3	4/3	4	4	5	3	35/34
YARDS	Blue	560	150	371	173	335	405	370	570	170	3104
	White	515	140	334	151	275	390	348	550	135	2838
	Red	455	125	303	141	165	365	328	490	115	2487

Dakota Dunes Country Club
Sioux City (Dakota Dunes S.D.)
605-232-3080

Just mention the name Arnold Palmer and most golfers come to attention immediately. Dakota Dunes Country Club commands the attention of anyone passing by or through. This is a Palmer designed and managed course that lies just outside the reach of the Iowa border (but it is within a good 3 wood of the river so I included it in the book. This is a private club located off exit 1 leaving Sioux City to the NW. A long drive winding between/among the fairways leads you through a massive stone gate and eventually up to the impressive clubhouse and separate pro shop. The clubhouse has a full restaurant with seating for 350 members and guests. The 225 members pay one of the 34 different membership fees. The pro shop has a full line of equipment and is connected to the clubhouse by a walkway. A driving range is on the grounds and head pro Steven David will help you with your game. As you pick up your cart you head off to the first tee, a 585 yard dogleg left, 5 sand bunkers, many grass bunkers, and tons of trees, have a nice round!!! This course is spectacular. The grass condition the summer of 2004 was fantastic, the look of the course was very good. Dakota Dunes measures 7165 yards from the gold tees, one of the longer courses around. There are 22 sand bunkers and numerous grass dunes throughout the course. Every green is guarded by these dunes, which makes the course look very graceful. Palmer carved this layout out of the trees that are prevalent along the Missouri River, Lewis and Clark may have played this course, maybe not. There have been hundreds of trees planted along the fairways making it a very striking layout. The fairways are narrow and you can get in trouble with the trees, there is out-of-bounds almost on every hole. The Bent Grass fairways are watered and have lots of knolls rising out of the earth, some are gentle some are quite undulating. The rough is distinctively cut along fairways and in front of greens and tees and is tough to negotiate. Tee boxes are big, plush, and tiered. Greens are also large with 150 foot putts possible on several greens. The majority of greens are also undulating and fast, what a course. Dakota Dunes is almost 7 miles long to walk after you go through the trees from green to tee, 300 yards in some cases. Accuracy off the tree is important because of narrow fairways and trees. Water comes into play 5 times with an island green on 18. Dakota Dunes is a fantastic golfing experience. This is a very well conceived and built golf course that adds to the already find gathering of courses in the western Iowa area.. The beauty that surrounds you is well worth the effort.

223

Floyd Golf Course

Sioux City

712-274-1059

Floyd Golf Course is another city golf course in Sioux City. Unlike Green Valley, this course is built in the city and is quite short — 4067 yards. There are seven holes 110 yards or less making this a true short iron course. This is a popular course for many; it is located in town, it has low green fees, it offers a challenge, and it is a short walk. I might add that it might be short, but yards may add up when you are going up and down the hills. Water hazards come into play on four holes, sand on twelve. This is a tough, short course with some of the more interesting par threes in the area. The contour of the course is hilly and trees are scattered throughout the course and are few in number. Fairways are watered and stay green most of the summer. The rough is only found under trees along the narrow fairways. Tees are elevated and landscaped nicely, greens are medium in size and have an assortment of sloping, tilted, rolling, and flat surfaces. The clubhouse is a new brick structure that has a few snacks and all the basic supplies. Green fees at Floyd are $$7 weekdays. Floyd has initiated a new style of golf to accommodate this short course. Floyd plays 4091 yards but only takes about three hours to play. The balls are hard to lose because the farthest you can hit them is 120 yards and they float if you land in the water. So try Floyd Municipal, either for a regular game or a new challenge, Cayman Golf.

Course	18 Holes	Aesthetics	Good
Distance	4091 Yards	Interest	Good
Par	31-32-63	Worth The Trip	Yes
Playability	Fair	Rating	★★+

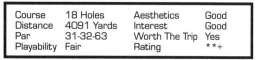

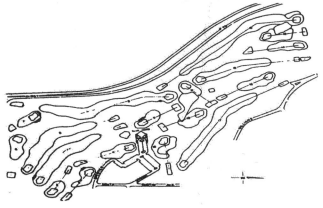

KEY:
— 200 Yards from the Tee
..... 150 Yards from Green
Water Hazards
Sand Trap

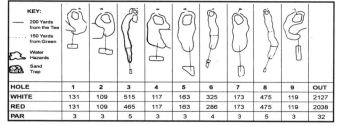

HOLE	1	2	3	4	5	6	7	8	9	OUT
WHITE	131	109	515	117	163	325	173	475	119	2127
RED	131	109	465	117	163	286	173	475	119	2038
PAR	3	3	5	3	3	4	3	5	3	32

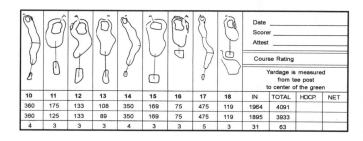

	10	11	12	13	14	15	16	17	18	IN	TOTAL	HDCP.	NET
WHITE	360	175	133	108	350	169	75	475	119	1964	4091		
RED	360	125	133	89	350	169	75	475	119	1895	3933		
PAR	4	3	3	3	4	3	3	5	3	31	63		

Date _____
Scorer _____
Attest _____

Course Rating

Yardage is measured from tee post to center of the green

Course	18 Holes	Aesthetics	Good
Distance	7085 Yards	Interest	Very Good
Par	36-36-72	Worth The Trip	Yes
Playability	Excellent	Rating	★★★+

Green Valley Municipal Golf Course

Sioux City

712-252-2025

Green Valley Municipal Golf Course is a city owned course that has 225 members who pay $695 for a family and $475 for a single. Green fees are reasonable for 9 or 18 holes, but come early or call ahead; this is a very busy course. The course is located in South Sioux City at 4300 Donner Ave. and is built up against the bluffs. Three holes are entrenched in a pocket of the bluffs. The general contour of the course is flat once you get away from the bluffs. The fairways are wide open and invite the long hitter to beat them. There are lots of trees, mostly small to medium in size, and they line some of the fairways but many are scattered. There are three ponds on the course that affect play on six holes. The rough is left uncut only to save mowing some of the long layout. For western Iowa the grass on this course remains very green in the summer, thanks to a watering system. The tees are elevated, big, and long thus avoiding any worn spots that may occur. The greens are big, elevated and have some noticeable depressions in the putting surface. A new spacious clubhouse was built and has all golfer needs. The course looks used from the clubhouse on out. It is really a scenic course. Views of the bluffs and almost of the river, what more could you ask for? Carts are available and I suggest you use them for the 7095 yard course. Cart paths go almost anywhere that you hit the ball. The course was built in 1963 and is developing into a very challenging course. The course layout is very diversified with many doglegs and odd-shaped fairways. This is a driver's course and there is a driving range by the clubhouse to warm up your gorilla swing. A great public course for the Sioux City area.

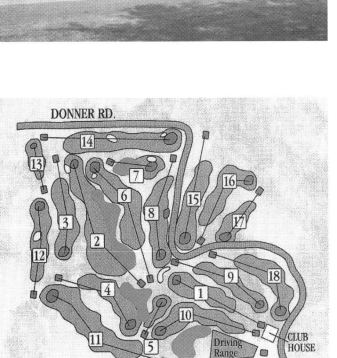

	Gold Tees	Blue Tees	White Tees	Red Tees	Par	Handicap
1	406	388	365	360	4	11
2	576	560	545	433	5	13
3	428	409	389	310	4	5
4	405	390	320	281	4	7
5	189	162	152	145	3	15
6	524	509	495	410	5	17
7	235	215	200	160	3	1
8	422	407	380	310	4	3
9	399	379	365	300	4	9
Out	3584	3419	3211	2709	36	
						Initial:
10	413	393	375	365	4	8
11	565	545	520	425	5	14
12	400	382	367	275	4	12
13	189	157	157	150	3	18
14	528	510	480	430	5	16
15	425	407	380	295	4	2
16	393	374	354	300	4	4
17	223	200	170	150	3	10
18	365	346	326	210	4	6
In	3501	3314	3129	2600	36	
Total	7085	6733	6340	5309	72	

Sioux City Country Club

Sioux City

712-277-4612

The Sioux City Country Club is a northwest Iowa experience. The majestic red brick clubhouse is one of the top five in size and elegance in the state. The interior of the clubhouse has just gone through remodeling and has two large dining rooms, a fitness center, three bars, a locker room for members, a caddy room, and a pro-shop that is ready to equip champions. The complex also has a pool and tennis courts. Sioux City Country Club has that old style country club feeling. The restaurant serves two grand dining areas. Golfers can order from the men's grill on the lower level during the day. This private club has a membership of 350. There are three ponds on the layout affecting three holes. There is also one stream running through five fairways. Sand is abundant with twenty-two bunkers present. Trees are medium to large in size and line all fairways; sometimes creeping out into the fairways. Much of the beauty associated with the course comes from the abundance of trees and rolling contour of the layout. The watering system keeps the two inch tiered rough and regulation fairways in great shape all summer. Tees are small but tiered to create diversified driving situations. Greens are also small and sloping. Greens have been quickened in the last few years and now present a challenge. This is definitely a placement layout; good iron play is rewarded. The front nine holes are hilly with the back nine much flatter. The back nine are located across Hamilton Street to the west. The clubhouse is located at Jackson and 40th. The course was built in 1906 and has the trees, terrain, and greens to make it one of the biggest challenges in northwest Iowa. Only a personal trip to the Sioux City Country Club can show you what a beautiful and divergent course this is. This is truly a fine-tuned championship course.

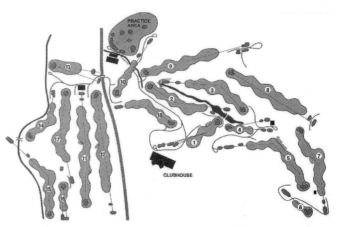

Course	18 Holes	Aesthetics	Excellent
Distance	6400 Yards	Interest	Excellent
Par	36-36-72	Worth The Trip	Yes
Playability	Excellent	Rating	★★★★+

HOLE	1	2	3	4	5	6	7	8	9	OUT	10	11	12	13	14	15	16	17	18	IN	Total
HANDICAP	17	1	3	13	5	15	11	7	9		6	8	10	16	14	12	18	2	4		
BLUE	260	399	387	400	517	160	371	515	399	3208	367	518	505	160	314	370	157	424	377	3192	6400
WHITE	239	393	379	175	500	140	365	512	394	3097	359	512	504	157	302	351	153	418	363	3119	6216
RED	217	315	313	152	414	122	322	458	359	2672	286	470	459	129	202	278	130	402	342	2768	5440
HANDICAP	17	5	11	15	1	13	9	3	7		14	2	4	18	10	12	16	8	6		
PAR	4	4	4	3	5	3	4	5	4	36	4	5	5	3	4	4	3	4	4	36	72

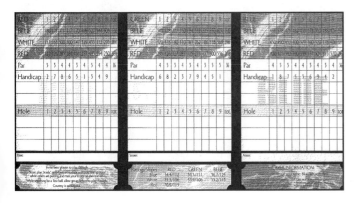

Twenty-Seven Flags
Sioux City (Sergeant Bluff)
712-943-2299

Twenty-Seven Flags is a nice addition to the greater Sioux City area. This course is the Sergeant Bluff High School home course. The course was built in 1996 over farmland just west of Sergeant Bluff and just south of the Sioux City Airport. This privately owned course is really 3 courses spread out over some gently rolling farmland, previously farmland. This is not a links layout and could be called partial to slicers, my kind of course. Fairways are wide making this a wide open course. Players said it was hard to loose a ball. This course is advertised as "fun for the whole family." They have a flourishing Junior PGA program and promote a quicker round. Flags is a course for the whole family. Different 9's offer somewhat of a different challenge. One thing that is consistent throughout the course are the water hazards. There are ponds on every hole and come into play almost on every hole. There are only 2 sand bunkers and no grass bunkers in the fairways. The 2" rough provides another hazard throughout the layouts. The bent grass greens average about 7,000 in area. There is 188,000 square feet of greens in the layout. The greens are domed, rolling and fast. The 3 courses are generally flat and can be walked. Trees have been planted throughout the course and 100 additional ones were planted in 2004. This is a friendly, family oriented course. There are no age restrictions for play and no tee times. This is a good course for the beginner. The clubhouse has a full sandwich menu and some equipment. There is a full driving range also . Twenty-Seven Flags is open year round, dependent on the daily weather. A duel sprinkler system keeps all holes green, there are 1,000 sprinkler heads. A final note is that the course provides great sunsets.

Course	18 Holes	Aesthetics	Good
Distance	6857 Yards	Interest	Good
Par	36-36-36	Worth The Trip	Yes
Playability	Very Good	Rating	***

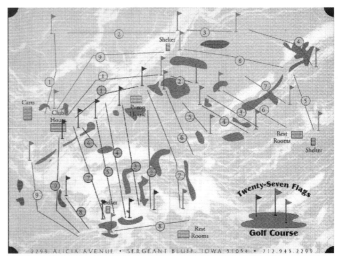

227

Two Rivers Golf Club
Sioux City
605-232-3241

Two Rivers Golf Club, formally SC Boat Club, has been in the middle of the Dakota Dunes development for the past two years. Two Rivers is managed by Arnold Palmer Golf Management Company. It recently became a public facility, August 1991, and carries green fees of $19. You can now enter Two Rivers off Exit 1 when leaving Sioux City. The clubhouse handles fees with a few supplies. This clubhouse was built 98 years ago. At that time there were only 9 holes; the second nine was added in 1931. Two Rivers is the oldest course in the Siouxland. The characteristics of the course include three ponds that affect five holes. The river runs the length of 9 and 18, and there are sand bunkers on many of the holes. In the early 60's Dutch Elm disease wiped out a large percentage of the trees but many did survive and some new plantings are starting to mature now. The contour of the course is flat with landscaping on every hole. There is fairway watering so the grass is in excellent shape all summer. The greens are of medium size with a majority of them tilted. This is a very well kept course and one of the most scenic in the area. It is not an easy course to score well on and might be considered a championship course; it certainly was prior to the 60's. A highlight would have to be the Sioux City Open of 1954 when Ben Hogan and Sam Snead played here.

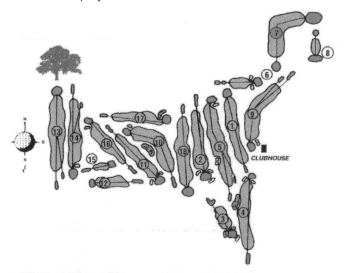

Course	18 Holes	Aesthetics	Excellent
Distance	6181 Yards	Interest	Very Good
Par	36-36-72	Worth The Trip	Yes
Playability	Good	Rating	★ ★ ★ +

HOLE	1	2	3	4	5	6	7	8	9	OUT	10	11	12	13	14	15	16	17	18	IN	Total	Hcp	Net
Back Tees	375	457	177	354	500	144	417	154	510	3088	339	337	214	406	358	153	353	356	406	2922	6010		
Par	4	5	3	4	5	3	4	3	5	36	4	4	3	4	4	3	4	4	4	34	70		
Handicap	11	9	13	7	5	15	3	17	1		14	16	8	2	12	18	6	10	4				
Handicap	11	9	13	7	5	15	3	17	1		14	16	6	2	12	18	8	10	4				
Par	4	5	3	4	5	3	5	3	5	37	4	4	3	4	4	5	4	4	5	35	72		
Forward Tees	342	421	148	330	359	131	398	132	402	2663	312	327	190	311	258	115	327	335	386	2561	5224		

Whispering Creek Golf Club

Sioux City

712-276-3678

A fantastic new 18 hole course in the Sioux City area is Whispering Creek Golf Club off I29 exit 144A. First off a unique feature of this course is that the existing clubhouse, an old barn type structure, is the birthplace of Gateway Computer. The first Gateway was conceived and built in this structure. This structure was the barn for the cattle ranch that Whispering Creek is now laid out on. The tee boxes at Whispering Creek have been positioned as to how you want that hole to challenge you. The tees are not by gender, but by ability. If you choose to play the gold and black tees, the holes will be longer, but the landing areas narrower and more difficult shots into the greens. Greens are bent grass and come in all shapes and sizes. The greens have severe contours that make putting a unique expe3rience. There are 40 sand traps on the course. Many of them deep and sod faced. The course has a prairie links look with natural areas shaping the look of the course. The back nine has a lot of elevation change and so there are blind approach shots for errant drives. This is a challenging course that has a lot to offer. Whispering Creek has very few wind breaks and so the course is noted for windy conditions. A creek running through the course shapes many of the holes. Opposite the creek is high grass and deep bunkers. All of these features certainly shape the character of the course. The 240 members pay an annual fee of $1,200. Weekday green fees are $20. A must play when you are on the west side of Iowa.

Course	18 Holes	Aesthetics	Excellent
Distance	7113 Yards	Interest	Very Good
Par	36-36-72	Worth The Trip	Yes
Playability	Excellent	Rating	★★★★+

HOLE	1	2	3	4	5	6	7	8	9	OUT	PLAYER	10	11	12	13	14	15	16	17	18	IN	TOT	HCP	NET
BLACK	416	189	405	395	396	185	555	565	436	3587		434	171	557	184	403	490	611	161	515	3526	7113		
GOLD	383	177	397	365	349	155	508	542	416	3292		412	151	541	161	385	378	516	148	551	3243	6535		
SILVER	353	160	365	351	291	139	470	507	377	3013		394	143	526	137	346	360	488	133	499	3026	6039		
COPPER	261	122	307	251	255	116	412	418	340	2482		324	111	465	117	324	325	403	123	442	2634	5116		
PAR	4	3	4	4	4	3	5	5	4	36		4	3	5	3	4	4	5	3	5	36	72		

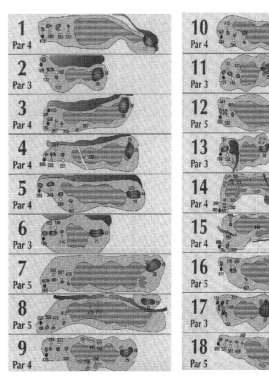

Sun Valley Golf Course

Sioux City

712-258-9770

Sun Valley Golf Course is a very interesting par 3 course or should I say one of the more unique regulation courses. The par 3 course is laid out on flat ground and a regulation size course is laid out around the outside of the par 3 course on rolling ground. This is a very busy set of courses. The clubhouse is small and is not the place to sit around discussing the day's round — no chairs. There is one pond in the complex, an average of one sand bunker per hole, and a large number of trees, both medium and small scattered throughout both courses. The greens are flat and medium in size. Many of them just appear out of the fairway. The course was built in 1960 and supports a large league membership. The daily green fees are $3.00 for the regulation and $2.75 for the par 3. The clubhouse will rent you clubs, rent you a cart for your bag, sell you snacks or drinks, and direct you to the first tee. The course is located at 2101 Military on the west side of Sioux City. This is a unique layout. Try your hand at the par 3 and if you feel an urge to swing a little harder, try the regulation course. Both courses have a great deal of rough and are a little more challenging than they first appear.

Course	Par 3
Distance	944/2037Yards
Par	27/33
Playability	Fair
Aesthetics	Good
Interest	Good
Worth The Trip	Yes
Rating	★★+

PAR 3 COURSE

HOLE	YARDAGE	PAR
1	118	3
2	107	3
3	87	3
4	90	3
5	92	3
6	146	3
7	84	3
8	105	3
9	115	3
Total	944	27

REGULATION COURSE

HOLE	YARDAGE	PAR	LADIES PAR
1	219	4	5
2	114	3	3
3	246	4	5
4	281	4	5
5	402	4	5
6	238	4	5
7	259	4	5
8	122	3	3
9	156	3	3
Total	2037	33	39

Little Sioux Golf and Country Club

Sioux Rapids

712-283-2162

Little Sioux Golf and Country Club is another example of a short course that can be a little testy if you don't treat it with respect. It is a second shot course that requires straight shots off the tees for good approaches to the greens. This is a public course with 200 members. Green fees are average for a course this size. The clubhouse offers a small number of supplies, carts to rent, and a bar that serves drinks and a full menu of club food. The character of the course is molded by the valleys and hills that run through the course. Old Oak trees surround the course and the interior trees are medium to large in size and line many of the fairways. The contour of the course is hilly with five of the nine holes intersecting hills. Number seven is nothing but a tee box, a big ravine, and a green; you are either on in one or lost. Greens are of medium size and flat. The grass condition on the course is a little below average but that seems due to the hills and shade covering most of the fairways fringes. The course was built in 1961 with conversion to grass greens coming in 1981. The course is located one mile north of town on Highway 71. Little Sioux is built on top of a hill, does that give you a clue as to the terrain of the course and the problems you will be facing?

Course	9 Holes
Distance	2492 Yards
Par	35
Playability	Fair
Aesthetics	Good
Interest	Fair
Worth The Trip	Yes
Rating	★★+

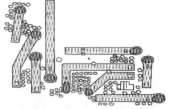

HOLES	1	2	3	4	5	6	7	8	9	OUT
MEN'S YARDS	278	260	125	408	160	275	157	466	363	2492
MEN'S PAR	4	4	3	5	3	4	3	5	4	35
LADIES' PAR	4	4	3	6	3	4	3	5	4	36
LADIES' YARDS	260	230	125	400	150	255	115	386	283	2204

Sloan Golf Course

Sloan

712-428-9993

In western Iowa you can find hilly courses and some very flat ones. One of the flattest is the Sloan Golf Course located on the north side of Sloan on old ûK45. This is a wide-open course made for the person who can drive long and pitch it short onto the green. The few hazards that you have to maneuver around include a pond that comes into play on one hole along with about six sand bunkers. The small number of trees line the wide fairways. A fairway watering system keeps the course green throughout the summer. The tees are cut with distinction and elevated slightly like the greens. The fairways may be level but the greens are big and rolling making the approach shot very important. The course was built in 1970 and obviously is still growing. The 145 members enjoy a nice clubhouse that has the essentials: food, drink, and a few supplies. Weekday green fees are $7. This is a very easy course to walk, void of any dips, plus it is a fairly easy course to score well on. It is not very busy so tee times are not necessary; just come to enjoy a relaxed atmosphere of average golfers. People seem to like the greens; it must be because it gives them a chance to walk up and down hills a little.

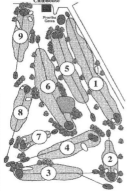

Course	9 Holes
Distance	3144 Yards
Par	36
Playability	Poor
Aesthetics	Fair
Interest	Poor
Worth The Trip	Maybe
Rating	★ ★

HOLE	1	2	3	4	5	6	7	8	9	OUT
BLUE	505	210	380	383	440	515	172	316	311	3144
WHITE	498	196	370	328	431	492	162	263	300	3040
RED	442	180	360	311	413	448	144	251	281	2840
MEN'S PAR	5	3	4	4	4	5	3	4	4	36
LADIES' PAR	5	3	4	4	5	5	3	4	4	37

Lake MacBride Golf Course

Solon

319-624-2500

One of the shortest highways in the state leads up to Lake MacBride Golf Course. Highway 382 runs 4 miles from Solon west to the golf course. The course is nestled in a housing development by the lake. It is a generally flat course that can become a day of anguish for a slicer. Many holes are built so that a slight drift to the right will cause a home wner to inquire about your insurance policy. The course has six bunkers and one pond to put a cramp in your game. What few trees there are on the course are new to medium in size and line the narrow fairways, but are not much of a hazard. The bent grass greens are large in size and have a sloping contour. Lake MacBride is an easy course to walk, although they do have carts for rent. It is also an easy course to score well on if you can keep the ball in the fairway. Green fees for the public are reasonable. The club has a membership of 125 that pay an annual fee of $260 for a family. The clubhouse is a small structure, but carries a full line of golfing supplies and has a restaurant that is open to the public on Fridays only. Otherwise there are sandwiches and bar items. The atmosphere of this course is easy going and relaxed.

Course	9 Holes
Distance	3133 Yards
Par	36
Playability	Good
Aesthetics	Good
Interest	Good
Worth The Trip	Yes
Rating	★ ★ ★

HOLE	1	2	3	4	5	6	7	8	9	OUT
CHAMPIONSHIP TEES	382	349	125	399	370	182	499	338	489	3133
MEN'S TEES	364	333	116	393	358	168	475	324	469	3000
MEN'S PAR	4	4	3	4	4	3	5	4	5	36
WOMEN'S TEES	351	321	108	331	358	157	463	312	424	2825
WOMEN'S PAR	4	4	3	4	4	3	5	4	5	36
HANDICAP	11	7	17	5	13	15	1	9	3	

231

Saddleback Ridge

Solon

319-624-1477

Saddleback Golf Course was conceived about 12 years ago when the owner bought a track of land from his Aunts, anticipating building a golf course. Saddleback is located at 4646 - 180th St. in NE Solon. The layout of the land is flat but the layout of the holes is good. The entire course is irrigated. The greens are medium in size with a variety of shapes. Other hazards include one sand bunker and several fairway bunkers. I would also list the island green as a hazard. There are some new tree plantings, but most of the trees are big and have a history on the course. This is a good layout that the average golfer can play. Saddleback is a fast playing course that golfers can have fun with. The new clubhouse has a limited amount of equipment and food at the grill. Weekday green fees are $12. This is an interesting course that is worth the effort.

Course	9 Holes
Distance	3225 Yards
Par	36
Playability	Good
Aesthetics	Good
Interest	Good
Worth The Trip	Yes
Rating	**+

Club House: 319-624-1477					H O L E
CHAMP TEES	BACK TEES	MIDDLE TEES	**PAR**	HCP	
385	365	337	4	9	1
185	167	145	3	17	2
330	300	280	4	13	3
204	178	170	3	15	4
504	489	455	5	5	5
361	342	305	4	7	6
539	509	498	5	1	7
172	148	140	3	11	8
545	514	480	5	3	9
3225	3012	2810	36		

Indian Hills Golf Club

Spirit Lake

712-336-4768

One of the most unique courses in the Iowa Lakes region is Indian Hills Golf Club; located west of Spirit Lake on Highway 9. The course was originally built in 1921 but remodeled and redesigned in 1976. This course is laid out over 91 acres that includes a fourteen acre lake. Indian Burial grounds can also be seen on the course. Indian Hills claims to be the oldest course in the area. This nine hole public course has 225 members each paying $340 for a family. Weekday green fees are reasonable for this area. The clubhouse is made of logs and features a 30 foot bar with pine ceilings. A modest amount of supplies can be bought along with carts to rent. The bar area serves drinks and microwave sandwiches. Indian Hills is a Scottish type course, play out and then play back. The bass lake comes into play on five holes, there are twelve bunkers, some fairway rough, and a fairway watering system that keeps the course green throughout the summer. Trees are medium in size and are scattered, tees are elevated and cut in moderation. The greens are large, averaging over 5,000 square feet each. This is a placement course that is tough on hookers. Big hits and shots to the left are penalized. Indian Hills is a casual course directed at the average golfer. It is a moderately challenging course that has beauty and history to back its reputation.

Course	9 Holes
Distance	2872 Yards
Par	35
Playability	Fair
Aesthetics	Fair
Interest	Fair
Worth The Trip	Yes
Rating	**+

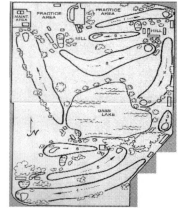

Spencer Golf and Country Club

Spencer
712-262-2028

Spencer Golf and Country Club is the home of the Northwest Iowa Amateur Golf Tournament and has been called one of the nicest - if not thee nicest - 18 hole course in N.W. Iowa. This is a private club with a five mile green fee radius that has 250 members who enjoy one of the best conditioned courses in the area. Green fees may be paid if you live outside the five miles or playing as a guest of a member. The clubhouse is located at 2200 W. 18th and has a full line of equipment with a nice selection of clothes and clubs. The restaurant, which is in a separate building, is open year round for members and guests. They also offer golfers drinks and grilled sandwiches during the day. The layout has two ponds affecting four holes. There is an average of three sand bunkers per hole and a three inch rough that is cut and tiered everywhere. There are many medium size trees lining all the fairways. The contour of the course is flat with ground bunkers located in many of the fairways. Tees are composed of bent grass and are cut distinctively and cover a large area. Greens are medium in size, flat, and have a tradition of being fast. The greens are also cross cut and maintain a very true putting surface. The course was built in 1963 and is a very busy course. This is a long course that rewards straight shots off the tees. The rough is tough and can create great havoc during a round. This is an easy course to walk, but is generally considered a cart course. It is also considered a casual family course; but when tournament time comes it is anything but casual. The course is blessed with beautiful landscaping and fine conditioning. One of the comments I heard from almost everyone was " it is one of the finest conditioned courses in the state." It is one of the finest layouts and conditioned courses anywhere, well worth your effort to play. Make sure you bring your good golfing attitude and your gorilla stick.

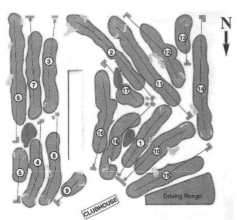

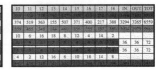

Course	18 Holes	Aesthetics	Excell.
Distance	6888 Yards	Interest	Good
Par	36-36-72	Worth The Trip	Yes
Playability	Very Good	Rating	****

Hole	1	2	3	4	5	6	7	8	9	OUT
Blue Tees - Rated 71.4 / 124										
White Tees - Rated 71.4 / 124	359	493	393	353	197	525	419	382	144	3265
Gold Tees - Rated 68.4 / 116	354	475	369	351	187	460	360	351	149	
B-W-G Handicap Check Tees Played	Hdcp	11	5	7	13	15	1	3	9	17
Red Tees										
Red Tees Handicap	5	3	7	11	17	1	13	9	15

10	11	12	13	14	15	16	17	18	IN	OUT	TOT
374	519	363	155	507	371	400	217	388	3294	3265	6559
355	345	344	460	356	351	187	389		3476	3279	5699
10	6	16	18	8	12	4	14	2			
									36	36	72
									36	36	72
4	2	12	16	6	10	18	14	8			

Spencer Municipal Golf Course

Spencer

712-580-7280

Spencer Municipal Golf Course is a public course that was rebuilt in 1973 and expanded to 18 holes in 2000. The course is located on the south edge of Spencer on 4th Ave. S.W. The course four water hazards on the new layout, the layout also averages 2 sand bunkers per hole. There is also a two inch rough located in front of tees, along fairways, and around greens. The medium number of trees come in all sizes; including some new plantings. Fairways are wide and gently rolling, some are lined with trees. Tees are large and elevated, greens are large in size and rolling with a little tilt to some of them. The greens also have a reputation of being very fast and difficult to read; with a lot of hidden breaks. The over 500 members pay $550 per year while green fees are reasonable $16.50 an 18 hole course. The clubhouse features a lounge and sandwich shop, along with a pro shop. This municipal course is a challenging course that looks easy but plays hard. The out-of-bounds are easy to find and the rough is nice but a struggle to cope with. The course is busy most of the time but is in good shape despite the heavy use. A full length driving range is a new feature at Spencer Municipal.

Course	18 Holes	Aesthetics	Good
Distance	6809 Yards	Interest	Good
Par	36-36-72	Worth The Trip	Yes
Playability	Very Good	Rating	***+

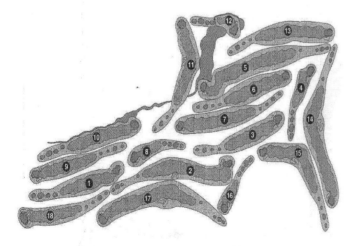

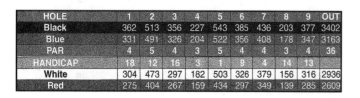

HOLE	1	2	3	4	5	6	7	8	9	OUT
Black	362	513	356	227	543	385	436	203	377	3402
Blue	331	491	326	204	522	356	408	178	347	3163
PAR	4	5	4	3	5	4	4	3	4	36
HANDICAP	18	12	16	3	1	9	4	14	13	
White	304	473	297	182	503	326	379	156	316	2936
Red	275	404	267	159	434	297	349	139	285	2609

	10	11	12	13	14	15	16	17	18	IN	OUT	TOT	HCP	NET
	401	395	167	428	518	405	188	548	357	3407	3402	6809		
	372	364	143	400	496	374	167	528	327	3171	3163	6334		
	4	4	3	4	5	4	3	5	4	36	36	72		
	2	7	10	6	11	8	15	5	17					
	341	337	117	369	477	344	143	507	300	2935	2936	5871		
	310	309	97	340	408	315	123	439	268	2609	2609	5218		

Okoboji View

Spirit Lake

712-337-3372
www.okobojiview.net

Another 18 hole public course that can be played in the lakes area of N.W. Iowa is Okoboji Vu. The course was built in 1962 and is located west of Spirit Lake on Highway 86. This 6151 yard course has 250 local members who pay an annual fee of $636. Green fees are $22 for this 18 hole course in the Lakes area. The clubhouse has a full line of supplies; plus carts for rent. It is a typical public course clubhouse with a few snacks and a small area to sit and relax. The atmosphere is very friendly, due mainly to the fact that this is a tourist course in the summer and green fees are the base for survival. The course is located on the west side of Lake Okoboji and has one pond that affects three holes. There are two streams that run beside eight additional holes and an average of two bunkers per hole. There are 400 Evergreens, of small and medium size, scattered in the rough and lining some of the fairways. The rough is two inches high and lies in front of tees and greens as well as along the rolling fairways. Tees are big, elevated, and cut very professionally. The medium size greens are flat and have a very good putting surface. The trees on the course are just starting to become an important factor in shot selection. Right now you can spray the ball around a little without much penalty, soon accuracy will be at a premium. In years past the rough was much higher but has been cut down recently and has helped speed up play. This is a course used by many vacationers in the area, tee times are preferred by the manager. It could also be classified as a family course; it is easy to walk and easy to play. Okoboji View plays hard enough to keep you interested but easy enough to score well on. This even balance makes you feel good about the game and eager to return. A delicate balance for a course to maintain. This is a beautifully cut course; greens, tees, and fairways are cut to look like tour courses. New fairway watering was added and has greatly increase the beauty of the course.

Course	18 Holes	Aesthetics	Excellent
Distance	6151 Yards	Interest	Good
Par	35-35-70	Worth The Trip	Yes
Playability	Good	Rating	***+

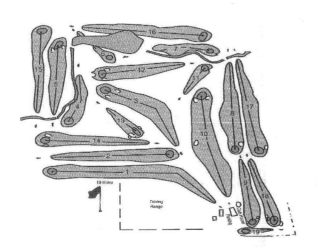

HOLE	1	2	3	4	5	6	7	8	9	OUT	10	11	12	13	14	15	16	17	18	IN	Total	HDCP	NET
BLUE YARDAGE	555	414	388	231	367	176	276	421	318	3158	470	158	317	173	357	364	425	435	292	2993	6151		
WHITE YARDAGE	521	381	368	212	337	155	257	393	303	2927	465	150	300	163	341	349	367	427	282	2844	5771		
HANDICAP	2	7	5	8	12	18	14	6	15		13	17	10	3	11	9	4	1	16				
MEN'S PAR	5	4	4	3	4	3	4	4	4	35	5	3	4	3	4	4	4	4	4	35	70		
Women's Par	5	4	4	3	4	3	4	4	4	37	5	3	4	3	4	4	5	4	4	36	73		
Handicap	2	7	5	8	12	18	14	6	15		13	17	10	3	11	9	4	1	16				
Red Yardage	427	371	348	189	248	123	202	364	290	2610	458	142	161	161	314	338	406	406	262	2662	5308		

235

Acorn Park Golf Course

St. Ansgar

515-736-4450

Acorn Park Golf Course is one of the shorter 9 hole courses in the state. Before being built in 1980 the fairways were used for farming. Some of the woods were cleared, the farming stopped and there is now a very nice golf course. This public course is located one mile west of St. Ansgar on Highway 105 and is built along the Cedar River which comes into play on two holes and anew pond has been built on hole three. The fairways of Acorn Park are narrow and are dominated by big trees that make accuracy a must off many of the tees. The first four holes are fairly open and the last five closed in by trees. The thick three inch rough can also present a problem on this flat course. The large sloping and tilted greens are tough to hold and tougher to putt. This is a very busy course that sports a very nice modern clubhouse, selling basic golf supplies plus microwave sandwiches and bar items. Generally this is an easy course to walk and an easy course to score on, but you can be lulled to sleep by the beauty of the surroundings. This is a fine example of how marginal farmland can be converted into a very useful and beautiful recreation area.

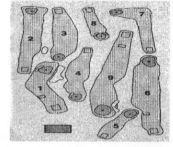

Course	9 Holes
Distance	2490 Yards
Par	35
Playability	Fair
Aesthetics	Very Good
Interest	Good
Worth The Trip	Yes
Rating	***

Holes	1	2	3	4	5	6	7	8	9	OUT
Distance, White	261	329	289	268	133	376	262	130	442	2490
Distance, Red	206	315	274	256	122	333	248	118	390	2262
Par	4	4	4	4	3	4	4	3	5	35

Storm Lake Municipal Golf Course

Storm Lake

712-732-8025

Storm Lake Municipal Golf Course was built in 1915 along Storm Lake and benefits from the view even today. The lake does not actually touch the course but can be seen from almost anywhere on the course, creating a very tranquil and scenic atmosphere to play in. The course is over 2,980 yards long and is very flat. There are eight bunkers that come into play along with a large number of medium size trees that line many of the wide fairways. The greens are flat, medium in size and have a true putting surface, which is nice to encounter once in awhile. The overall shape of the course is good and is busiest on the weekends. Green fees are a little above average for a 9 hole course. The clubhouse is located on the west end of the course and has balls and bags, plus a bar and sandwich area. There is no need for tee times, especially during the week, although there were 30,000 rounds played in 1999 on this municipal course. Storm Lake Municipal was initially a private course but became a public course in the 80's. Today there are 250 members who enjoy easy par 5's and beautiful lakeside scenery.

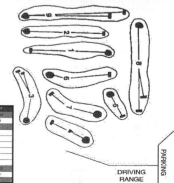

Course	9 Holes
Distance	3094 Yards
Par	36
Playability	Fair
Aesthetics	Fair
Interest	Fair
Worth The Trip	Yes
Rating	**

Lincoln Valley Golf Course

State Center

641-483-2054

State Center is the home for Lincoln Valley Golf Course, located 2 miles east of town. This is a semi-private course that added nine holes in 1993 and created a rolling golfing challenge. Lincoln Valley has 266 members paying an initial stock of $390 and a yearly membership of $545. Green fees for people outside of the radius are reasonably priced for a small town course. The clubhouse is a modern brick structure that has a L shaped bar and about 20 tables. Refreshments on hand in the clubhouse include drinks and microwave sandwiches. Very few supplies are available; but they do have balls, gloves, and carts for rent. The characteristics of the course include one pond, one stream that divides the course and comes into play on seven of the eighteen holes, fourteen bunkers, and a tough rough that guards the tees, greens, and edges of the fairways. The original course was built in 1977 and has medium size trees scattered throughout the course. The contour of the course is hilly; comments were made about having lies above or below your feet, never on an even plain. Tees are elevated and small, greens are medium with rolling and sloping putting surfaces. This is not a slicers course nor a course for a weak putter. It is a challenging course with no waiting, but a lot of pleasure. Additional landscape has made this a developing course. The layout of the course is challenging and keeps the members on their toes. A nice course in the central Iowa area.

Course	18 Holes	Aesthetics	Very Good
Distance	6432 Yards	Interest	Good
Par	37-35-72	Worth The Trip	Yes
Playability	Good	Rating	* * *

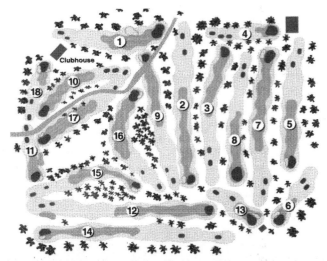

Hole		1	2	3	4	5	6	7	8	9	Out
Black Tees	69.7/112	323	526	429	182	419	169	491	403	451	3393
Gold Tees	67.1/110	310	518	352	167	387	143	463	363	440	3143
White Tees	67.5/113	257	431	322	155	345	127	429	314	344	2724
Par		4	5	4	3	4	3	5	4	5	37
Handicap		13	3	5	11	1	17	9	7	15	

10	11	12	13	14	15	16	17	18	In	Tot	Hcp	Net
337	187	555	153	584	333	370	344	176	3039	6432		
322	173	533	141	549	312	350	332	154	2866	6009		
273	137	421	112	433	263	301	286	129	2355	5079		
4	3	5	3	5	4	4	4	3	35	72		
6	10	12	18	2	14	16	4	8				

237

Lake Creek Country Club

Storm Lake

712-732-1548

Lake Creek Country Club, located on Highway 7 west of Storm Lake, is a long ball course, but rewards are only reaped if the big dog is straight. This is a well designed course that utilizes many of the natural hazards in the area. There are four ponds on this 18 hole course that come into play, drastically on five holes. A creek which is not very wide affects your golf thinking on 9 holes. Plus there are 14 bunkers. The course was built in 1964 and has now matured to full championship size. The medium number of trees do line the narrow, flat fairways. Lake Creek does have fairway watering and maintains a high degree of heavy rough during the summer. The entire course is landscaped very effectively, especially the tees and around the clubhouse. The greens are some of the best in the area, if not the state, and are best described as big, rolling, fast, and challenging. The beauty of the course can be traced to Dave Sherman who was the Superintendent of the Year in Iowa in 1984. This is a semi-private club that is blessed with a modern clubhouse that has a fine restaurant and bar area. The dining room has some tasteful eating with seating overlooking the back nine. The pro shop has a full line of equipment, plus many carts for rent. This course hosts one of the major tournaments in Iowa each year, the Lake Creek Open. It is a difficult course that is well suited for the long ball and thinking player. The 300 members enjoy a country club golfing atmosphere, that is backed by one of the best courses in the state and is still maturing. The weekend green fees of $30 are reasonable for a good 18 hole course. If you would like to join, a family membership is $990, with an initial stock of $1,000. Lake Creek is a challenging course that will make you play and score the old fashioned way, you earn it.

Course	18 Holes	Aesthetics	Excellent
Distance	6813 Yards	Interest	Very Good
Par	36-35-71	Worth The Trip	Yes
Playability	Good	Rating	****

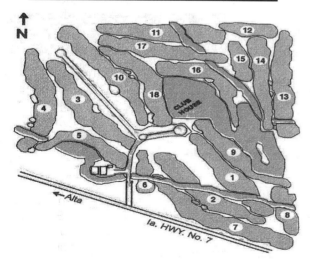

HOLE	1	2	3	4	5	6	7	8	9	OUT
PAR	4	4	4	5	4	3	5	3	4	36
BLUE	405	445	400	535	350	150	540	180	395	3400
WHITE	390	420	385	500	330	140	520	165	385	3235
GOLD	375	410	375	475	320	130	510	120	375	3090
MEN'S HDCP	5	1	11	7	13	17	3	15	9	
RED	315	385	328	440	290	125	470	115	330	2798
WOMEN'S HDCP	3	1	11	9	13	15	5	17	7	

10	11	12	13	14	15	16	17	18	IN	TOT
5	4	3	5	4	3	4	4	4	36	72
500	420	222	465	395	180	420	397	414	3413	6813
485	400	210	460	380	165	385	383	396	3264	6499
465	390	155	450	375	140	375	370	345	3065	6155
4	2	16	6	14	18	12	10	8		
460	323	150	428	320	135	300	310	340	2766	5564
12	4	18	14	6	16	10	8	2		

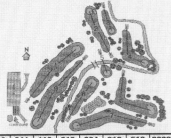

River Bend Golf Course

Story City

515-733-2611

River Bend Golf Course is located on the east edge of Story City and has 320 active members who take pride in their course. This wide open course is beautiful and well kept thanks to a program initiated by the members. Each member is assigned a hole that is their responsibility to look after and repair as they play their round, so each hole gets a little tender loving care during each day. Members pay $170 per year while green fees are very reasonable. This is a municipal 9 hole course that is busy much of the time with. The clubhouse has a full line of equipment plus sandwiches and bar items for sale. The characteristics of the course include a pond on two holes, a river that you cross just once, seven bunkers, and a three inch rough that outlines the fairways. Five holes have new trees while the remaining four have medium size trees. The greens are medium in size with putting surfaces ranging from flat to a rolling. River Bend is an easy, wide open course that is well taken care of and survives on a lot of community pride. It is not difficult to play and is accented by a river on one side, a housing development on the north and an artisian well to the south, something not every course can lay claim to.

Course	9 Holes
Distance	2980 Yards
Par	37
Playability	Fair
Aesthetics	Good
Interest	Good
Worth The Trip	Yes
Rating	★★+

MEN'S YARDAGE	465	472	138	341	110	310	324	310	510	2980
LADIES' YARDAGE	423	424	138	341	94	293	324	310	471	2818
PAR	5	5	3	4	3	4	4	4	5	37
HOLE	1	2	3	4	5	6	7	8	9	OUT

Backbone Golf and Country Club

Strawberry Point

319-933-4545

Backbone Golf and Country Club is located south of Strawberry Point on Highway 410; adjacent to Backbone State Park. The parks beauty extends out onto the course, also the parks wildlife extends onto the course at times. This is a public course that has 150 members paying $357 for a family. Inside the clubhouse is a full line of golfing supplies, including carts for rent. The clubhouse eating area includes drinks and grilled sandwiches. The characteristics of the course include three bunkers, no water, a two inch rough, and beautiful surroundings. The trees were large around the perimeter but new on the interior; many lining the fairways. The contour of the land was gently rolling with a few gullies to cause troublesome lies. Greens were medium in size and tilted, plus they were in very good shape. The course is best known for being the course next to Backbone State Park. But it has some true merits of its own. This layout is harder than it looks. You can spray the ball a little but the rough and dips in the fairways may cause you some trouble. What separates this course from many is that deer appear almost nightly during the summer; something quite special. Backbone is an interesting, relaxing course that is not very busy; but is building its reputation on beauty and conditions.

Course	9 Holes
Distance	3039 Yards
Par	36
Playability	Fair
Aesthetics	Good
Interest	Fair
Worth The Trip	Yes
Rating	★★+

HOLE	1	2	3	4	5	6	7	8	9	OUT
MEN'S YARDS	370	401	510	260	330	251	190	407	320	3039
MEN'S PAR	4	4	5	4	4	4	3	4	4	36
HANDICAP	5	4	6	7	3	8	9	1	2	
LADIES' PAR	4	5	5	3	4	4	3	5	4	37
HANDICAP	5	3	2	4	6	7	8	1	9	

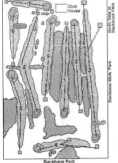

Backbone Park

Meadowbrook Country Club

Sumner

563-578-8123

The Sumner High School parking lot doubles as the parking lot for Meadowbrook Country Club in Sumner. This par 35, 2529 yard course, has a membership size of 250 with annual fees of $125 and with a stock option of $200. Daily green fees are very reasonable for a small town course. The clubhouse has carts for rent and has a limited supply of golf supplies on hand. There is a small bar area that has snacks for sale. Characteristics of the course include one stream that comes into play on six holes, eight bunkers, and no rough. The fairways are lined with 30 foot trees with fairways that are narrow and tight to drive through. Tees are flat and small much like the greens, which are also flat and small, making them very hard to hold. There is nothing really unique about this course; it is a typical small town course that is well taken care of, easy to walk, and easy to score. A course that was built out of need by the people in Sumner who wanted a local golf course to play on.

Course	9 Holes
Distance	2529 Yards
Par	35
Playability	Fair
Aesthetics	Good
Interest	Fair
Worth The Trip	Yes
Rating	★★

HOLE	1	2	3	4	5	6	7	8	9	OUT
HANDICAP	9	1	15	3	7	17	13	5	11	
YARDAGE	483	381	257	205	290	258	261	144	282	2529
MEN'S PAR	5	4	4	3	4	4	4	3	4	35
WOMEN'S PAR	6	5	4	4	4	4	4	3	4	38

Tama-Toledo Country Club

Tama

515-484-2027

The Tama-Toledo Country Club was voted the IGA Golf Course of the Year in 1981. It is a challenging 9 hole course that was built in 1946 with changes made in 1975 and most recently a new course layout. A new watering system along with improving greens will make this a better course in 1992. The clubhouse sits east of the course on a hill with the layout of the course running down to the flat valley to the west. The course is located 5 blocks south of the Tama-Toledo High School on 13th St. , which is on highway 63 south. The course does have three ponds and an average of one bunker per hole, usually guarding the green. The contour of the course is flat with some two inch rough, but would have to be considered an open course. Tree size ranges from new plantings to some medium in size, 75 new 6 foot pines were planted in 1991. The landscaping of the course is pleasing with nicely cut greens and fairways, tees that are elevated and medium in size. Greens are big and sloping in most cases with grass condition good. The 250 members pay an annual fee of $485. This is a fairly long course with the par 4's being long driving holes. This is a nice representation of a typical Iowa nine hole golf course that is excellent shape. This is an easy course to walk once you get down into the valley and moderately easy to score well on.

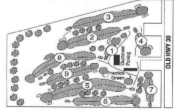

Course	9 Holes
Distance	3013 Yards
Par	35
Playability	Good
Aesthetics	Good
Interest	Good
Worth The Trip	Yes
Rating	★★★

	1	2	3	4	5	6	7	8	9	OUT
MEN'S TEES	141	388	409	138	512	378	199	476	372	3013
MEN'S PAR	3	4	4	3	5	4	3	5	4	35
MEN'S HDCP	13	11	1	17	9	3	7	15	5	
LADIES' HDCP	17	11	3	15	5	1	13	7	9	
LADIES' PAR	3	4	4	3	5	4	3	5	4	35
LADIES' TEES	141	343	359	138	442	362	140	426	332	2683
+/-										
HOLE	1	2	3	4	5	6	7	8	9	OUT

Pleasant Valley Golf Club

Thornton

515-998-2117

Most courses in central and north central Iowa are flat. The Pleasant Valley Golf Course at Thornton is certainly no exception. The contour of the course is very flat, even the greens are flat. This public course lies on the N.E. edge of Thornton. The green fees are moderate in price, and there are presently 140 members who pay an optional $100 stock and $192 annual membership fee, which is not optional. The little white clubhouse has a supply of balls and gloves inside and will rent you a cart, even though the 3063 yard course is long, it is still easy to walk because of the general contour. The bar area has grilled sandwiches and assorted beverages. The course layout has one stream that comes into play on three holes, three bunkers, and no rough. The fairways are wide but are all lined with new and medium size trees and bushes. The tees are elevated slightly and the greens are of medium size and flat. The opening hole gives you a little hint of what to expect the rest of the day; 520 yard dogleg. Pleasant Valley was built in 1966. This course is an easy course to score on, easy to hold the greens, and has true putting surfaces. With business not real brisk during the week it is an easy course to get on. If you want to lower your handicap a few strokes, Pleasant Valley is the place you want to be.

Course	9 Holes
Distance	3094 Yards
Par	36
Playability	Good
Aesthetics	Fair
Interest	Poor
Worth The Trip	Maybe
Rating	*+

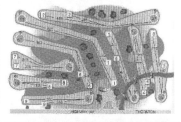

HOLE	1	2	3	4	5	6	7	8	9	OUT
WHITE COURSE	520	418	220	277	343	453	343	190	330	3094
RED COURSE	402	284	140	207	247	348	315	128	243	2314
MEN'S PAR	5	4	3	4	4	5	4	3	4	36
HANDICAP	7	1	5	17	3	15	11	9	13	
LADIES' PAR	5	4	3	4	4	5	4	3	4	36
HANDICAP	5	13	11	17	1	7	15	3	9	

Tipton Golf and Country Club

Tipton

319-886-2848

The Tipton Golf and Country Club is one of the many courses in the state that the ball is either above or below your feet on your second shot, never a level lie to hit from. Two of the holes are entirely uphill making it a hard course to walk. Hazards consist of two sand bunkers and one stream that comes into play on holes 1 and 2. There are some new plantings of trees but the majority are of the big old variety. There are also some new tees and green configurations. Most fairways are wide, allowing you to spray the ball around a little. The fairways are protected on the sides by two and three inch rough. You drive from elevated tees to medium size greens that have a variety of surface contour, basically flat in nature though. The greens have a history of being fast with a few subtle breaks, usually when you least expect them. The course was built in 1940 and contains no sharp dogleg holes but is considered a challenging course to play. In the clubhouse you can rent carts and buy supplies including clubs. There is also a restaurant open year round for members and their guests. The course is located S.W. of Tipton on South St.

Course	9 Holes
Distance	2938 Yards
Par	36
Playability	Good
Aesthetics	Good
Interest	Fair
Worth The Trip	Yes
Rating	**+

HOLES	1	2	3	4	5	6	7	8	9	OUT
Men's Yards	495	161	296	467	143	395	130	365	486	2938
Men's Handicap	2	10	13	8	11	1	18	15	9	
Men's Par	5	3	4	5	3	4	3	4	5	36
Ladies' Yards	458	144	274	387	128	385	101	341	433	2651
Ladies' Handicap	1	5	7	9	15	11	17	3	13	
Ladies' Par	5	3	4	5	3	5	3	4	5	37

Cedar Valley Golf Club

Tipton

563-886-0218

Cedar Valley Golf Club, affectionately know as the Badlands was built in 2001 SE of Tipton on 265th St. The course is still in a rough stage. But that is what it makes it interesting. Standing at the clubhouse and looking out, you see rolling hills, one pond and two greens. But that view is deceiving. There is water trouble on every hole except two. Thirteen holes surrounded by water and 9 holes, some of the same, that you have to carry the water. Those two holes come back over a deep valley. This is a very interesting course. Not a course for the light hearted. It is certainly a cart course, unless you are an expert climber, I mean walker. The layout covers 120 acres, 40 of the acres have been turned into fairways, the remaining 80 have remained woods that reach out and grab your ball. The bent grass greens average about 5,000 square feet. This is a very scenic course, I really like the layout, but it is young and still developing. This is a shot selection course where position on every shot makes the next one much easier. The clubhouse is big with a bar and 5 big screen TV's. There are 100 members that pay a single membership of $425. I certainly would recommend this course to anyone with a little adventure in their swing.

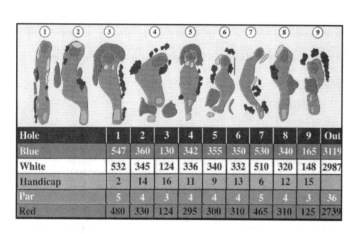

Hole	1	2	3	4	5	6	7	8	9	Out
Blue	547	360	130	342	355	350	530	340	165	3119
White	532	345	124	336	340	332	510	320	148	2987
Handicap	2	14	16	11	9	13	6	12	15	
Par	5	4	3	4	4	4	5	4	3	36
Red	480	330	124	295	300	310	465	310	125	2739

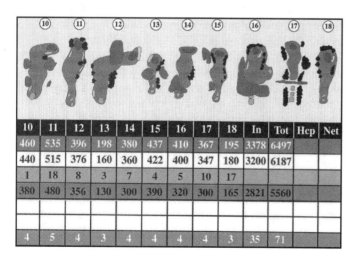

10	11	12	13	14	15	16	17	18	In	Tot	Hcp	Net
460	535	396	198	380	437	410	367	195	3378	6497		
440	515	376	160	360	422	400	347	180	3200	6187		
1	18	8	3	7	4	5	10	17				
380	480	356	130	300	390	320	300	165	2821	5560		
4	5	4	3	4	4	4	4	3	35	71		

Course	18 Holes	Aesthetics	Good
Distance	6497 Yards	Interest	Very Good
Par	36-35-71	Worth The Trip	Yes
Playability	Good	Rating	***+

242

Traer Golf and Country Club

Traer

319-478-2700

The Traer Golf and Country Club has a unique history. The course was built in 1922 and had grass greens up until World War II broke out. At that time there wasn't enough money to maintain them so the members converted the greens to sand. The sand greens were used until 1972 when grass was installed again. The condition of the course is very good, and considered by many to have some of the finest greens in the area. The character of the course is shaped by the water hazards — there are four ponds that come into play on six holes. There is no sand but the difficulty of the course is increased by the number of large trees that line some of the tight fairways. The greens are in excellent shape and are medium to large in size. The contour of the course and greens is flat, making it an easy course to walk. The course is located on highway 63 on the north edge of Traer and still operates out of a remodeled clubhouse that has a lot of character . The 180 members have a limited selection of balls and gloves and the bar area just has snacks and drinks. The members pay $425 for a family membership while the daily green fees include play for all day.

Course	9 Holes
Distance	2978 Yards
Par	35
Playability	Fair
Aesthetics	Good
Interest	Fair
Worth The Trip	Yes
Rating	* * +

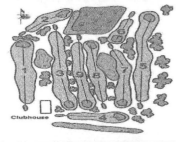

Clubhouse

MEN'S TEES	392	155	482	153	520	196	360	350	370	2978
MEN'S PAR	4	3	5	3	5	3	4	4	4	35
MEN'S HDCP	1	8	6	9	4	5	2	7	3	
LADIES' TEES	392	155	482	153	500	196	360	330	370	2938
LADIES' PAR	4	3	5	3	5	3	4	4	4	35
LADIES' HDCP	1	8	6	9	4	5	2	7	3	
HOLE	1	2	3	4	5	6	7	8	9	OUT

Treynor Recreation Area

Treynor

712-487-3302

Treynor Recreation Area in Treynor can claim the title of good will ambassadors of local golf. Nothing but high praise came from members, players, and employees. This is a course that was built in 1964 on the east edge of town. It not only includes a 2966 yard golf course but a swimming pool, small park, and picnic area. The layout of the course could be classified as hilly with a medium number of small and medium size trees. Treynor is on a tree planting rotation so new trees are added every few years These trees are scattered along the creek bed and throughout the course. Greens are large in size with flat elevated putting surfaces. Water comes into play on every hole, some by ponds and some by a ditch area. This is a very popular course in this area, it pulls a lot of people out of the Council Bluffs area and is busy most of the summer. Fairway watering was added in 90. Green fees are quite reasonable for a small town course. The 300 members pay $570 for a yearly membership. The clubhouse sits on a hill overlooking the course and offers sandwiches and drinks plus a small amount of golfing supplies. This is a challenging course that features many sand bunkers, large greens, and an upbeat atmosphere that makes it fun to play. If you want to know how good this course really is, just ask someone in the clubhouse; they will be proud to tell you.

Course	9 Holes
Distance	2966 Yards
Par	36
Playability	Good
Aesthetics	Good
Interest	Good
Worth The Trip	Yes
Rating	* * *

HOLE	1	2	3	4	5	6	7	8	9	OUT
MEN'S YARDS	486	204	387	295	490	165	293	333	313	2966
LADIES' YARDS	387	128	320	283	408	128	282	269	335	2540
PAR	5	3	4	4	5	3	4	4	4	36
HANDICAP	15	5	1	17	3	13	9	7	11	

Maple Hills Country Club

Tripoli

319-882-4229

The Maple Hills Country Club, located 1 mile east of Tripoli, is considered a long hitter's course. This 3161 yard course is fairly wide open and condusive to the big free swing with 2 1/2 inch rough throughout the course. It has very few hazards: only three bunkers and no water. The trees are young, small in size and should not come into play in a few years. The general contour of the course is flat with a few gently rolls on some of the wide fairways. The tees are flat and not cut any differently than the fairways. The greens are of medium size, fast, flat, but hold fairly well. This is an easy course to walk but because of its length a moderately hard course to score well on. The course was established in 1969 and is not very busy any time during the week. There are 200 members that pay an initial $100 stock and a yearly membership of $340. Daily green fees are average for a small town course. The clubhouse supports a small amount of supplies and a bar that serves sandwiches and snacks. This private course is for members and their guests unless you live outside Bremer County. If you are in a hurry to play, go to Tripoli, rent a cart, and swing as hard as you can.

Course	9 Holes
Distance	3161 Yards
Par	36
Playability	Fair
Aesthetics	Fair
Interest	Poor
Worth The Trip	Maybe
Rating	★★

Hole (Front Nine)	1	2	3	4	5	6	7	8	9	OUT
White Yardage	527	336	184	330	428	138	320	474	424	3161
Men's Par	5	4	3	4	4	3	4	5	4	36
Men's Handicap	5	11	9	15	3	17	13	7	1	
Women's Handicap	1	9	11	7	15	17	13	3	5	
Women's Par	5	4	3	4	5	3	4	5	4	37
Women's Yardage	506	322	162	320	412	126	305	456	331	2940

South Hardin Recreation Area

Union

641-486-2335

The South Hardin Recreation Golf Course, located on the north edge of Union. This flat farm site was purchased in 1968 and built by a golf course contractor. Because this is a young course it is still wide open and void of any medium or large size trees. One-hundred new trees have been planted in the past few years. There is a stream that comes into play on four holes and becomes more of a problem during the wet season. The fairways are wide with very little rough to contend with. The medium size greens are undulating and have been known to bring people to their knees, literally, while they are looking for all the breaks in the putting surface. The clubhouse has a limited full line of supplies and sandwiches to go with the bar items. A bar and lounge area were added to the clubhouse recently. The 275 members pay an annual fee of $170. The Union course can be considered a drive and chip course, very open with a limited amount of hazards. New tile and watering has improved the playability of the course. It is an easy course to walk but they do have carts. It is a nice example of what determined people can do to provide themselves with recreation. Although the course is not a thing of beauty, the pride and success of the community is.

Course	9 Holes
Distance	2700 Yards
Par	35
Playability	Better
Aesthetics	Fair
Interest	Poor
Worth The Trip	No
Rating	★

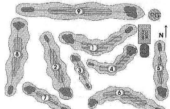

HOLE	1	2	3	4	5	6	7	8	9	OUT
White Tees	365	320	150	330	185	430	160	260	500	2700
Handicap	3	5	7	4	1	9	6	8	2	
Par	4	4	3	4	3	5	3	4	5	35

Urbandale Golf and Country Club

Urbandale

515-276-5496

The Urbandale Country Club is a private club located at 86th and Clive in Urbandale. The address is 4000 86th St. This is a tough course because of the terrain, the length, and the crowned greens. The contour of the course is flat by the clubhouse but much hillier by the stream on the west side of the layout. There is one pond on number nine and one stream that you must cross six times. There are six bunkers and a two inch rough along the fairways. The medium number of trees come in all sizes and line many of the rolling fairways. Urbandale Golf has a program for planting new years on a regular basis. One of the outstanding features of the course are the greens. They are in excellent condition, small to medium in size, and crowned in most cases. The greens are true to putt and have a nice smooth surface. This is a tough course to walk and a tough course to find a flat lie once you get into the heart of the layout. The Urbandale course was built in 1965. The clubhouse has a pool and a full restaurant that is only open to the public during noon lunch. You must be with one of the 250 members to play or eat at this course. Yearly family memberships cost $3,525. Green fees for guests are very reasonable at $22. This course was laid out and constructed in the middle of town on some rolling creek land. It is in good shape and has a close knit country club atmosphere. It is a finesse course that allows you few errors once you get around the green.

Course	9 Holes
Distance	3119 Yards
Par	36
Playability	Very Good
Aesthetics	Very Good
Interest	Good
Worth The Trip	Yes
Rating	★★★+

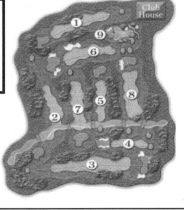

Hole	White	Gold	Hcp	Par	Red	Hcp
1	345	268	9	4	263	9
2	547	464	1	5	466	1
3	382	305	5	4	298	5
4	169	157	11	3	152	15
5	374	284	7	4	279	13
6	330	265	13	4	260	17
7	397	354	3	4/5	348	3
8	445	375	15	5	368	7
9	130	84	17	3	89	11
Out	3119	2556		86/37	2523	

Tara Hills Country Club

Van Horne

319-228-8771

One of the most glamorous and unique clubhouses can be found in Van Horne at the Tara Hills Country Club. The course is located two miles west of Van Horne. The course was built in 1985 and is still short on maturity. There are two ponds and one stream on the course, an average of one bunker per hole, and three inch fairway rough. A scant amount of new trees dot the course and are now just beginning to come into play. The contour of the course is very flat. Tees are big in square footage. Greens are medium to large in size and are rolling in nature. The greens and fairways need a few years to mature. The fabulous thing about this course is the clubhouse. It was an old barn moved from across the road, remodeled, and added on to. It has become the best small course clubhouse in the state. A full restaurant is open the year round with dining for hundreds. Vaulted ceilings and great views makes this clubhouse a place to enjoy and linger. A luxurious bar area serves drinks and sandwiches to golfers; offering a very comfortable and relaxed area. The persons responsible for this complex are the late John and Betty Lou Barry. The course is now leased by the members from the Barry family. John Barry wanted to put something back into the community of Van Horne so he built a recreation facility and dining area that standards are set by. Tara Hills is now enjoyed by the 400 members, 300 are golfing members. Golfing dues are $490 per year, social membership is $50. A trip to this young course is a must just to tour the clubhouse. It offers much more than I can list here. Hats off to the Barry family and Van Horne.

Course	9 Holes
Distance	3083 Yards
Par	36
Playability	Good
Aesthetics	Good
Interest	Fair
Worth The Trip	Yes
Rating	★★★

WHITE TEES	387	382	121	500	416	333	481	138	325	3083
MEN'S PAR	4	4	3	5	4	4	5	3	4	36
MEN'S HCP	3	1	8	5	2	7	4	9	6	
LADIES' PAR	4	5	3	5	4	5	5	3	4	37
RED TEES	267	327	121	307	416	333	400	138	325	2634
LADIES' HCP	3	5	9	1	2	7	4	8	6	
HOLE	1	2	3	4	5	6	7	8	9	OUT

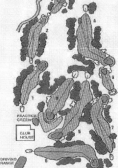

245

Villisca Golf Club

Villisca

712-826-5322

Villisca Golf Club is a very short, par 32 course that is a nice outlet for local golfers. This course is an iron course, the longest hole being 372 yards with the shortest 100 yards. The course is built around a hillside giving it some uneven lies, like many other courses in the area. Trees are medium in size and line some of the fairways but are also scattered throughout the dips in the course. The tees are flat on the ground and offer very little change from fairway grass. The greens were rebuilt in 2001 and are small to medium in size and sloping in many cases. The expanded clubhouse is open with supplies, drinks and food. Weekday green fees are $15 for all day. The 170 members pay an annual fee of $265. Villisca is a good course to sharpen your iron game on. It is also a course where the atmosphere of the club is to have a friendly, relaxing game of golf. Villisca is not a course to take very seriously, but maybe that is what the game is all about. The course has become much more playable and interesting since 1995. The course is located one mile north of Villisca and will be waiting for you when you drive up the lane; no waiting line to tee off.

Course	9 Holes
Distance	2063 Yards
Par	32
Playability	Good
Aesthetics	Good
Interest	Good
Worth The Trip	Yes
Rating	★★+

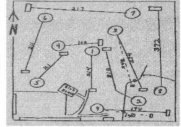

Hole	1	2	3	4	5	6	7	8	9	Out
Yards	214	310	284	100	161	211	217	372	194	2063
Mens par	3	4	4	3	3	4	4	4	3	32
Hcp	1	3	4	9	8	6	7	2	5	
Womens par	4	4	4	3	3	4	4	5	3	34
Yards	214	310	240	100	161	211	217	372	140	1975
Hcp	4	1	2	9	8	6	6	3	7	

Vinton Country Club

Vinton

319-472-4052

The greetings will be warm when you visit and play the Vinton Country Club. The Vinton course includes a big, spacious clubhouse. Inside there is a roomy bar area, and dining facilities for special occasions. An annual family fee of $737 is paid by the 300 members. The course was built in 1916 and has developed into a distinctive golfing layout. There are no water hazards on the course and only three bunkers. There are a large number of trees that are scattered throughout the majority of the course, although number two fairway is a lined dogleg to the left. The contour of the course is rolling with a small amount of rough guarding the fairways. The small greens are one of the bigger challenges on the course, but the overall play of the course is fun and easy. This course has a friendly golfing atmosphere, and the biggest asset of the course might well be the members that play the game. No tee times are needed, just stop by and I'm sure someone will invite you to play along. Weekday green fees are $15. The course is located on the east side of Vinton by the hospital.

Course	9 Holes
Distance	2803 Yards
Par	35
Playability	Fair
Aesthetics	Good
Interest	Fair
Worth The Trip	Yes
Rating	★★+

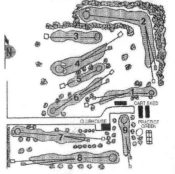

PAR	4	5	3	4	3	4	4	4	4	35
WHITE TEES	357	465	155	354	149	316	331	392	284	2803
HANDICAP	3	4	5	2	9	8	7	1	6	
HOLE	1	2	3	4	5	6	7	8	9	OUT
PAR	4	5	3	4	3	4	4	4	4	35
RED TEES	302	380	155	301	136	252	276	346	245	2395

Indian Hills Golf and Country Club

Wapello

319-868-7747

www.ihgcc.com

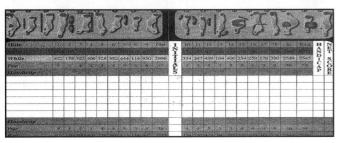

The Indian Hills Golf Course is located between Morning Sun and Wapello. This public course charges annual fees of $600 for its 225 members. Green fees for this 6311 yard course are $12 for 18 on a weekday. A back nine was added to Indian Hills in 1998. It is not a very busy course, mainly due to its location. Weekdays are usually the easiest time to play. The clubhouse is typical for a small course; large dining area upstairs for special occasions and a small bar area below with drinks and snacks. What is not very typical for a course this size is the pool and driving range included in the facilities. There is a large selection of supplies; including clubs, clothes, and carts for rent in the clubhouse. This is an open course that has a country setting with natural timber and water shaping the courses character. Three of the new nine holes were built on some surrounding farmland. They have incorporated grass bunkers for your enjoyment. There are several holes cut out of the woods. The reconfigured layout has much more elevation change on the course. There are five ponds on the course affecting 9 holes, three bunkers, and two inch rough along the wide fairways. Large trees surround the course and create a small grove in the middle, but a much smaller number of new trees are scattered throughout the remainder of the course. Greens are medium in size and are sloping, plus the greens have a reputation of being easy to hold. Indian Hills was built in 1965 and is still a developing course. This course has a variety of terrain changes but is easy to walk and fairly easy to score well on. It offers the golfer a chance to enjoy the game without trying to beat it to death. With the addition of the nine new holes, Indian Hills has become more challenging and interesting to play. The scenery is good and the golfing relaxing. Country golf sometimes has its advantages.

Course	18 Holes	Aesthetics	Very Good
Distance	6311 Yards	Interest	Good
Par	37-36-73	Worth The Trip	Yes
Playability	Good	Rating	***

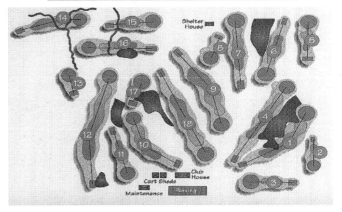

247

Gates Park Golf Course

Waterloo

319-291-4485

Gates Park is an 18 hole public course on 820 E. McDonald in Waterloo. Green fees are reasonable or you can buy a city pass for $550 that is good on all the Waterloo public courses. This is a very busy course averaging 35,000 rounds per year; it might be wise to call ahead for a tee time. Gates Park is noted for its large Oak trees that are found throughout the course and create chaos on many holes. There are also two ponds that come into play on three holes, one stream that has to be dealt with on five holes and an average of one sand bunker per hole. The fairways are wide and lined with big oaks and where there are no oaks they have planted new trees to replace fallen ones. The tees are large and tiered. The course rebuilt five tee boxes in 2000, incorporating several tee box alternatives. Greens are large and basically flat. A very slight rolling effect does appear in some of the larger ones. The rough is cut to 3 inches and runs the length of the fairways and in front of some tee boxes. The layout of the course tends to favor the big hitters; it is by no means a chip and putt course. Gates Park is a nice municipal golf course that is easy to walk, fairly hard to score well on, and possesses a golfing atmosphere. Full irrigation was added in the late 90's. The clubhouse has a large pro shop that has a full line of supplies, including clothing and clubs. There is a large selection of snacks, drinks, and sandwiches that can be eaten in a roomy dining area. It might also be added that this was, as many courses were, a 9 hole sand green course until the mid 50's. Weekday green fees are $15. Gates Park is one of the finer public courses in the area.

Course	18 Holes	Aesthetics	Very Good
Distance	6839 Yards	Interest	Good
Par	36-36-72	Worth The Trip	Yes
Playability	Very Good	Rating	***+

Hole	1	2	3	4	5	6	7	8	9	Out
Blue Tees	384	536	395	196	435	526	392	185	401	3450
Yellow Tees	371	478	362	141	422	506	370	174	380	3204
Red Tees	279	422	299	119	375	408	323	154	316	2695
Par	4	5	4	3	4	5	4	3	4	36

10	11	12	13	14	15	16	17	18	IN	TOT	HCP	NET
493	373	189	424	440	523	367	182	398	3389	6839		
483	336	166	405	402	506	346	162	372	3178	6382		
452	299	151	375	334	457	317	145	343	2873	5568		
5	4	3	4	4	5	4	3	4	36	72		

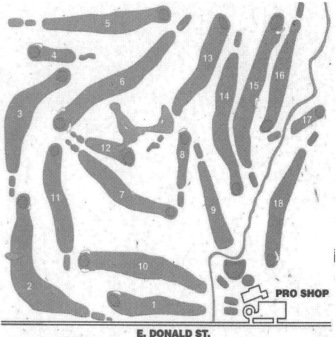

Irv Warren Memorial Golf Course

Waterloo
319-234-9271

The Irv Warren Memorial Golf Course, formally Byrnes Park, pro and club manager was very enthused about this course. He stated that Irv Warren is the best kept public course in the nation. It is a very nice and well manicured course and is located on 1000 Fletcher Ave. in Waterloo. This 18 hole course is part of the Waterloo public course program in which there are about 900 season ticket holders. Annual membership is $550, and daily green fees are very reasonable for an 18 hole course, $15 for 18 holes. The pro shop is located in the sprawling white clubhouse and has a full line of equipment. It is also located right next to the snack bar area, causing a little confusion. This course is groomed to attract all ability levels of golfers. Irv Warren is an entertaining course to play, not too difficult, and is in very good condition, fully irrigated. This is a short course at 6194 yards and so puts emphasis on the driver and wedge when playing it. Some of the characteristics of the course are four ponds that come into play on four holes, ten bunkers, and a two inch manicured rough that tends to be very tough on the golfers that spray their balls into it. There is a medium amount of trees, many of them very old and big, and many more that are new, which means that there is some tree trouble that you can get into. The contour of the course is flat. The fairways have a variety of widths with most of them tree lined. The tee boxes are flat to the ground but are landscaped nicely. The greens are small to medium in size and shift from rolling to flat. They are fast and true to putt. Irv Warren Memorial Golf Course was built in 1906 and has been the site of the Waterloo Open many times. This public course has a little bit of everything. It is also an easy course to walk if you don't rent one of the pro shops carts, and can be easy to score well on if you can keep it out of the trees and rough. This course is usually busy so it might be wise to call ahead if you want to play on the best-kept public course in the nation, at least in North East Iowa.

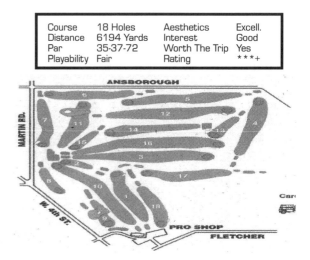

Course	18 Holes	Aesthetics	Excell.
Distance	6194 Yards	Interest	Good
Par	35-37-72	Worth The Trip	Yes
Playability	Fair	Rating	***+

Hole	1	2	3	4	5	6	7	8	9	Out
Blue Tees	346	156	511	386	452	369	320	207	189	2936
Yellow Tees	339	153	504	374	447	334	300	205	179	2835
Red Tees	322	140	440	310	362	282	284	174	132	2446
Par	4	3	5	4	5	4	4	3	3	35

10	11	12	13	14	15	16	17	18	IN	TOT	HCP	NET
496	314	477	166	375	157	557	361	355	3258	6194		
489	303	471	157	350	148	550	315	336	3119	5954		
475	268	404	133	325	125	496	260	262	2748	5194		
5	4	5	3	4	3	5	4	4	37	72		

Red Carpet Golf Club

Waterloo

319-235-1242

The Red Carpet Golf Club is one of the oldest clubs in north-east Iowa, founded in 1919. This public course has a membership size of 300 with yearly dues of over $600. Weekday green fees are moderately priced for a public course. Of course there are carts for rent but none should be needed for this gently rolling course. The Red Carpet complex has a separate pro shop and restaurant. The pro shop is stocked with a full line of equipment, especially a nice line of clothes and clubs. The snack area for the golf course is found at the 19th hole. This course has a lot of tradition. The foundation of this tradition are the greens. Many are original greens built around 1919 and have been molded into some of the most challenging putting surfaces in the area. There are subtle breaks that even the veteran member has trouble reading. The greens are large rolling surfaces and are fairly hard to hold on the approach shot. There are approximately forty sand bunkers guarding the greens and one pond that comes into play on three holes. Some of the wide fairways are lined with trees but many of the forty foot trees are scattered in the three to four inch rough. Tee boxes are very plush. Many of them are elevated, big in size and landscaped with flower beds and bushes making it a very scenic area. Irrigation has been added in recent years making tees and fairways better than ever. This is a gently rolling course that makes it easy to walk. It is also a good course to score well on if you play a smart game. There is also a driving range that is part of the course. The Red Carpet Golf Club Course is located at 1409 Newell Street in Waterloo and can be a real golfing challenge. If you are looking for a course that has tradition and is well taken care of, then this is a good place to play when in the Waterloo area.

Course	18 Holes	Aesthetics	Very Good
Distance	6672 Yards	Interest	Good
Par	36-36-72	Worth the Trip	Yes
Playability	Very Good	Rating	***+

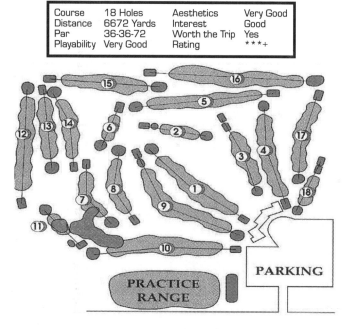

HOLE		1	2	3	4	5	6	7	8	9	OUT
BLUE	71.0/122	422	222	371	471	395	182	346	370	470	3249
WHITE	69.6/119	411	192	350	441	388	163	329	355	447	3076
HANDICAP		1	17	11	5	9	15	3	7	13	
RED	72.1/106	397	143	333	428	381	154	259	348	432	2875
HANDICAP		5	17	13	9	3	15	11	1	7	
PAR		4	3	4	5	4	3	4	4	5	36

10	11	12	13	14	15	16	17	18	IN	TOT	HCP	NET
410	155	561	357	344	371	508	415	202	3323	6572		
400	130	536	347	330	361	496	404	186	3190	6266		
2	16	4	12	14	10	6	8	18				
389	101	481	338	317	340	447	339	127	2879	5754		
10	16	4	6	14	8	2	12	18				
4	3	5	4	4	4	5	4	3	36	72		

PRACTICE RANGE

PARKING

South Hills Golf Course

Waterloo

319-291- 4268

The golfers in the southern part of Waterloo can enjoy a fairly new course to the Waterloo area, South Hills, located at 1830 E. Shaulis Rd. This course was built in 1972 and is developing at a nice rate. This is a public course that measures 6653 yards long with a par of 72. The pro shop carries a complete line of equipment and has a rather large supply of clubs and bags. The snack area has tables to sit and enjoy a drink and microwave sandwiches, along with the usual snacks. The clubhouse area is clean and sunny and gives a feeling of being in a golf course setting. The course is only about 15 years old but has an ample supply of medium size trees that line many of the fairways. There are two ponds on the course that affect play on two holes; there are no other water hazards but eight bunkers are scattered throughout the course to add to the stress of play. The contour of the course consists of gently rolling hills, making it a rather hard course to walk. The tees are elevated and big, giving an abundance of good grass to tee off from. The greens are medium in size and have a rolling and sloping effect, plus they are noted for being fast, especially in late summer. This seems to be the hardest of the municipals in Waterloo. The trees are in locations that prevent you from cutting the corner, the greens can bring you to your knees if your placement shot is not right, and you have to be accurate off the tees or the two inch rough will make the trees even bigger. This is a fairly busy course on the weekends, so you will need tee times, but during the week you can play almost any time. Green fees are very reasonable for an 18 hole course. This is a very challenging course, especially for its young age.

Course	18 Holes	Aesthetics	Good
Distance	6653 Yards	Interest	Good
Par	36-36-72	Worth The Trip	Yes
Playability	V. Good	Rating	***

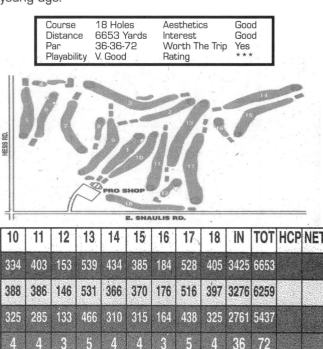

Hole	1	2	3	4	5	6	7	8	9	Out
Blue Tees	341	355	593	165	388	322	362	191	511	3228
Yellow Tees	331	309	493	156	338	316	354	184	502	2983
Red Tees	323	291	433	131	285	307	305	174	427	2676
Par	4	4	5	3	4	4	4	3	5	36

10	11	12	13	14	15	16	17	18	IN	TOT	HCP	NET
334	403	153	539	434	385	184	528	405	3425	6653		
388	386	146	531	366	370	176	516	397	3276	6259		
325	285	133	466	310	315	164	438	325	2761	5437		
4	4	3	5	4	4	3	5	4	36	72		

Sunnyside Country Club
Waterloo

319-234-1707

This private 18 hole course was built in 1974 and was designed to compete as a championship course. Sunnyside was rebuilt in 1999. The fifteenth tee was moved. Grass mounds were added around the greens and fairway bunkers were added. The changes have been good. There is an average of six bunkers per hole, five ponds that affect shots on eight holes and plush rough that is tiered along the fairways and thick around the greens and tee boxes. The trees are small and are starting to define the fairways. An additional 500 trees have been planted in the past few years. The fairways are cut narrow with thick rough to catch the errant shot. The contour of the front nine is flat and the back nine tends to be a bit more rolling, still making it an easy course to walk. The greens at Sunnyside are large and have individual character to them. The greens are framed better now with the changes done to the layout. Since the conception of the course the greens have had a reputation of being rolling, quick, and always in good shape. All greens are bunkered but approach shots will hold. This may be considered a wide open course because there is very little tree trouble, but the rough and narrow cut fairways will close the door on your free swing quickly. The pro shop is open for lessons and advice. It also has a complete line of equipment and is located near the tennis courts. There is a very nice brick clubhouse that has a year round restaurant and spacious areas for meeting and relaxing. Both the lower and upper areas have been remodeled recently. Sunnyside is a spectacular complex, which includes a pool, tennis courts, luxurious clubhouse, complete pro shop, and a challenging golf course to complete the package. There is one catch to this course; you must be a member or a guest of a member to play or eat in the restaurant. The green fees for guests are reasonable for a private 18 hole course. Carts are available with approximately 75% of the players using them. The initiation fee for the 350 Sunnyside members is $7,500, with a yearly dues fee of $2,400. If you haven't been on Sunnyside for a few years, it has a different look. This should be considered one of the best new and developing championship courses in the state.

Course	18 Holes	Aesthetics	Excell.
Distance	6756 Yards	Interest	Excell.
Par	36-36-72	Worth The Trip	Yes
Playability	Good	Rating	****

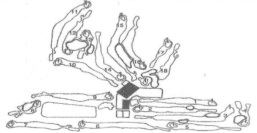

Hole	1	2	3	4	5	6	7	8	9	Out
Black 72.6/130	405	425	557	172	365	489	361	155	419	3368
Blue 71.1/127	386	412	546	147	354	478	376	145	407	3251
White 68.0/120	368	351	499	126	311	437	345	126	373	2936
Men's Hdcp	9	3	1	17	13	5	11	15	7	
Ladies' Hdcp	9	5	1	15	13	3	11	17	7	
Red 71.6/126	296	344	420	109	305	433	339	102	326	2674
Par	4	4	5	3	4	5	4	3	4	36

Hole	10	11	12	13	14	15	16	17	18	In	Total	Hcp	Net
Black	375	507	365	157	399	533	422	202	368	3368	6756		
Blue	366	497	345	157	389	522	394	192	358	3200	6471		
White	339	446	317	155	380	456	332	182	290	2897	5833		
Men's Hdcp	14	4	8	18	6	2	12	16	10				
Ladies' Hdcp	14	2	8	18	10	4	12	16	6				
Red	355	401	269	129	321	406	327	138	284	2610	5284		
Par	4	5	4	3	4	5	4	3	4	36	72		

Washington Golf and Country Club

Washington

319-653-2080

One of the more active ladies courses in S.E. Iowa is the Washington Golf and Country Club in Washington. This course was built in 1924 and is located 1/2 mile south of town on W55. Non-member green fees can be paid before 4:00 p.m. each day if you live at least seven miles from the course. There are no green fees accepted on the weekend, except guests of members. The 250 members pay an initial stock of $300 and an annual fee of $640 for a family. Members and their guests also have the use of the restaurant that is open six months of the year. Food during the day for golfers includes bar items and grilled sandwiches. This country club is known for good food all the time. The clubhouse is spacious inside with a panoramic view of the course. This is another hilly course; but it is easier to play and score well on than it looks. There is one pond, one stream that affects four holes. In 2000 sand bunkers were added and all the greens were rebuilt. Many medium to large trees are scattered along the wide fairways. The tees are tiered and in good shape. The greens are small to medium in size and have a tilted and sloping aspect to them. Washington has a lot of down hill lies and tree trouble on three holes. One trait of the course is it dries out in the summer and leaves the greens hard to hold and the fairways spotty in some areas. Despite the hills this is an easy course to walk and a confidence builder for many golfers.

Course	9 Holes
Distance	2942 Yards
Par	35
Playability	Very Good
Aesthetics	Good
Interest	Good
Worth The Trip	Yes
Rating	★★★+

HOLE	1	2	3	4	5	6	7	8	9	OUT
BLUE	330	162	389	335	177	260	552	395	342	2942
WHITE	323	146	320	326	145	254	541	383	336	2774
HANDICAP	7	13	11	9	15	17	3	1	5	
RED	316	108	239	321	137	247	401	374	325	2468
HANDICAP	3	15	11	1	13	17	5	7	9	
PAR	4	3	4	4	3	4	5	4/5	4	35/36

Green Valley Golf

Waukon

563-568-4866

Green Valley Golf Course is a public course located one mile north of Waukon on Highway 9. This is a short compact course of only 1434 yards that offers a plain and simple course for beginners to build a little confidence. Green Valley is basically a green fees course with only 100 members. Fees are $6.50 for 9 holes and $11 for 18. Members pay $275 for a family membership. The clubhouse has been remodeled recently. The only supplies are balls but there is a bar selling drinks. The course has one pond, one stream, no sand, and a rough that is deep in some places and very tough. Trees on the course are medium in size and average in number. The contour of the wide fairways is flat. Tees are medium in size, elevated and in below average shape. Greens are medium in size, have a variety of surfaces, and are very hard to hold. The greens also have the reputation of hiding a lot of little breaks. The course was built in 1978. This is an easy course to walk and an easy course to score well on; due to the short length and lack of hazards. Green Valley is a simple course intended only as a place to learn and enjoy the game. The condition of the course has improved over the past few years. It is not very busy so you can play almost any time. If you need to improve your iron game try this one.

Course	9 Holes
Distance	1434 Yards
Par	30
Playability	Poor
Aesthetics	Fair
Interest	Fair
Worth The Trip	Maybe
Rating	*+

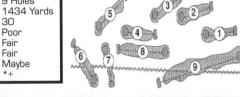

HOLE	1	2	3	4	5	6	7	8	9	OUT
YARDAGE	133	105	118	133	107	103	84	251	400	1434
PAR	3	3	3	3	3	3	3	4	5	30

Waukon Golf and Country Club

Waukon

563-568-9939

The Waukon Golf and Country Club is a public course located in the S.E. section of Waukon on 3rd Ave. S.E. Weekday green fees are $14 for 9 and $19 for 18. The clubhouse has a small bridge leading from the parking lot to the bar area. Inside there is a selection of balls, gloves, and clubs. The bar area has drinks and a few snacks. The sitting area facing the course has lots of glass so you can relax and watch others struggle around the course. There are no water hazards on the layout but 13 sand and many grass bunkers do exist. All the fairways are lined with trees. Most of the trees are the twenty to fifty foot evergreen and shade tree variety. Many new trees have been planted on the outside boundary. There has also been a flower planting spree around tees and the clubhouse. You can spray the ball a little on the course but trees become a real problem if you stray too far. The contour of the course is gently sloping, especially as you move to the south. Tees are medium in size with a few elevated. The sloping, medium size greens are in excellent condition. Many of the greens have little, unseen breaks; pin placement can make or break a good approach shot. Waukon Golf and Country Club was built in the 1930's. It is a predictable course; there are always twenty to fifty foot trees to your right and left as you move down the fairways. Something to think about as you start that full swing.

Course	9 Holes
Distance	3017 Yards
Par	35
Playability	Good
Aesthetics	Good
Interest	Good
Worth The Trip	Yes
Rating	★★★+

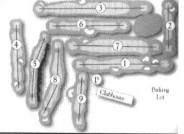

BACK TEE	430	200	520	280	280	410	432	330	135	3017
MIDDLE TEE	410	167	500	275	277	397	408	300	130	2864
HANDICAP	2	8	4	7	5	3	1	6	9	
PAR	4	3	5	4	4	4	4	4	3	35
PAR	5	3	5	4	4	5	5	4	3	38
LADIES' TEE	400	135	486	260	260	390	375	290	120	2716
HOLE	1	2	3	4	5	6	7	8	9	OUT

Webster City Country Club

Webster City

515-832-1533

The Webster City Country Club was built in 1915, one-half mile north of Highway 20 on Des Moines Street in Webster City. This course is surrounded by trees and a large number of the twenty year old leafy variety line the fairways. The contour of the course is basically flat with two inch rough along the fairways and around the greens. Seven sand bunkers were added a couple of years ago. The tees are slightly elevated and small. The greens are also small with a few on the verge of tiny. Greens are flat and possess hidden breaks making them tough to read. One of the unique things about the course is that you will not have a flat, straight putt all round. This is a fairly fun and easy nine hole course to play. Many would consider it a driver and wedge course. It is an easy course to walk, easy to score well on, offers a limited amount of tree trouble, and is a well manicured course. It is a lovely course to play. The spacious brown clubhouse has a big bar area and a very nice dining area. The full restaurant is open four nights a week during the summer and two nights during the winter. A new public driving range was added in 1998. The 300 members pay an annual fee of $685. A unique feature of this course is a large Oak tree in the middle of Number 1 fairway, about 80 yards off the tee.

Course	9 Holes
Distance	3047 Yards
Par	36
Playability	Fair
Aesthetics	Fair
Interest	Fair
Worth The Trip	Yes
Rating	★★

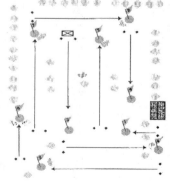

Hole	1	2	3	4	5	6	7	8	9	Out
Ladies	99	437	469	248	245	144	494	149	360	2645
Mens	112	449	484	294	309	162	528	171	377	2886
Blue	155	492	491	311	319	170	540	184	385	3047
Handicap	5	9	7	4	8	2	6	3	1	
Par	3	5	5	4	4	3	5	3	4	36

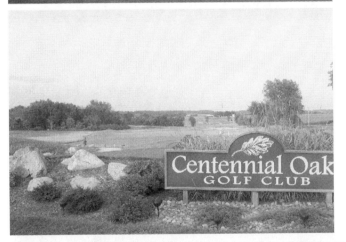

Centennial Oaks Golf Club

Waverly

319-483-1765

www.centennialoaks.com

The newly developed Centennial Oaks Golf Club offers 18 holes of spacious watered fairways and large elevated greens. The course has 5 tee boxes stretching from 4728 yards to the Black tees 6614 yards. The original nine holes was built in 2001 with the second nine following a year later. The greens average 6,000 square feet, are fast and putt very true. There are mounds and other forms of grass bunkers on every hole. Grass bunkers on the side of the fairways are one of the real hazards on this course. Centennial was built on farmland but many of the trees that are on the course are originally from the gullies and wooded areas of the farm. Much of the original prairie grass still remains also, a large portion of the rough is not mowed in the summer so this becomes a hazard also. As with most courses built in the last 5 years, this course takes on the layout of a links course. Lots of natural grasses, grass bunkers, and a layout of out and back. Players coming off the course said they lover the greens, they are true and fast. It is a course you can walk but carts are available. Daily green fees are $15 with a monthly family fee of $80. The massive clubhouse offers golfers and guests a great place to relax after a fun round of golf. You'll also be able to experience a delicious menu and cool drinks at the Oaks Club. This is a very nice developing new course. The landscaping is very nice and highlights the existing terrain. I certainly would recommend play on Centennial Oaks

Course	18 Holes	Aesthetics	Good
Distance	6614 Yards	Interest	Very Good
Par	34-38-72	Worth The Trip	Yes
Playability	Very Good	Rating	★★★+

Hole	1	2	3	4	5	6	7	8	9	Out	10	11	12	13	14	15	16	17	18	Back	Tot	Hcp	Net
Black	369	326	515	484	167	526	148	380	352	3267	378	511	411	182	529	470	350	152	364	3347	6614		
Blue	348	311	486	455	145	498	131	360	334	3068	357	483	383	157	505	437	325	131	341	3119	6187		
White	322	298	457	425	134	472	122	338	316	2884	330	456	357	136	475	408	304	111	313	2890	5774		
Yellow	297	280	419	384	114	433	103	316	290	2636	307	430	316	117	437	364	285	94	292	2642	5278		
Red	273	259	379	350	93	356	81	285	265	2341	278	397	284	99	391	341	256	85	256	2387	4728		
Par	4	4	5	4	3	5	3	4	4	36	4	5	4	3	5	4	4	3	4	36	72		

Waverly Municipal Golf Course

Waverly

319-352-1530

The Waverly Municipal Golf Course has a great deal of variety for the typical north Iowa golfer. The 18 holes are stretched over 5888 yards with some interesting individual holes. The entire course was rebuilt from 2000-2002. The new design makes Waverly a safer course, fewer hazards, the tees are higher and the fairways are lower. There are five par 3's, three of them being around two hundred yards each. Five new ponds were added to the layout coming into play on 8 holes. There is an average of two sand bunkers per hole. The trees lining the fairways basically consist of pines, approximately 735 of them, and they are of medium to large in size. The contour of the course is rolling, which is also the shape of the greens, medium in size and rolling. Waverly Municipal is located on the south edge of Waverly on highway 218, turn on 5th avenue. The clubhouse includes a full restaurant with two bars that is open 10 months of the year to everyone. The pro shop for the course has a small amount of supplies, balls and gloves, plus a large quantity of carts for rent. There were 16,000 rounds of golf played in 2002 by the 350 members and green fee players. Green fees are very reasonable for an 18 hole course. The members pay $645 for a family membership. The original nine holes in Waverly were built in 1930 and the additional nine were added in 1965. The 18 holes now cover 80 acres and also sport a driving range. This is pleasure type of course: easy to walk, fairly easy to score well on and yet very challenging because of the different situations. The three inch rough can be difficult in places and the pine trees can make some holes longer than listed. If you like a little variety in your game the Waverly course may be to your liking. The changes in the course have made a good course better. Players now seem to be coming from different areas around Waverly to play the new layout.

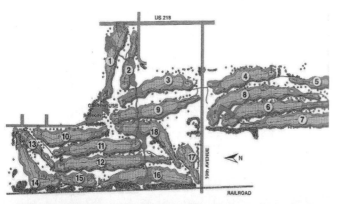

Course	18 Holes	Aesthetics	Good
Distance	5888 Yards	Interest	Very Good
Par	36-34-70	Worth The Trip	Yes
Playability	Very Good	Rating	★★★+

HOLE	1	2	3	4	5	6	7	8	9	OUT
YARDAGE - BLUE	297	206	331	292	196	496	433	517	387	3155
YARDAGE - WHITE	281	193	317	278	182	483	420	505	377	3036
YARDAGE - RED	263	144	244	269	131	410	360	402	321	2544
Blue/White HANDICAP	11	15	9	13	17	3	5	1	7	
PAR	4	3	4	4	3	5	4	5	4	36

10	11	12	13	14	15	16	17	18	IN	TOT	HCP	NET
319	380	507	180	309	154	392	144	348	2733	5888		
308	367	472	164	285	134	378	124	331	2563	5599		
276	347	414	138	249	112	342	110	290	2278	4822		
10	6	2	14	12	16	4	18	8				
4	4	5	3	4	3	4	3	4	34	70		

Briggs Woods Golf Course

Webster City

515-832-9572

Briggs Woods Golf Course is located 3 miles south of Webster City on Highway 17. The course is operated by the Hamilton County Conservation Department. The original 9 holes opened in 1971, and an additional 9 holes opened for play in August 1991. The front 9 can most easily be described as being rolling and fairly wide-open. The fairways are moderately narrow and lined with smaller trees. The greens are large but basically flat, with subtle undulations. The longer hitter has an advantage, as long tee shots take the hills out of play. The back nine is a mixture of long and open, and very tight. Holes 13 through 16 put the premium on accuracy. These four holes are among the most scenic in the state. The course is an excellent example of the blending of conservation and recreation. Deer, wild turkey, coyote, and various water fowl can be seen from time to time on the back nine. The back nine has been described as the "beauty with a bite". A wide variance in tee positions allows players of all different skill levels to enjoy Briggs Woods. In the spring of 1991, a new clubhouse opened. It includes a full service restaurant, a bar, and a well stocked pro shop. Briggs Woods is a very interesting golf course, and from the blue tees can be one of the tougher tests of golf around. Briggs Woods received the 1990 National Golf Foundation Golf Achievement Award, one of only two courses in the state to be recognized. Season pass holders pay $546 for a family membership. Weekday green fees are $19, very reasonable for an 18 hole course. If you are looking for some good golf, or just pleasant surroundings, Briggs Woods Golf Course is the place.

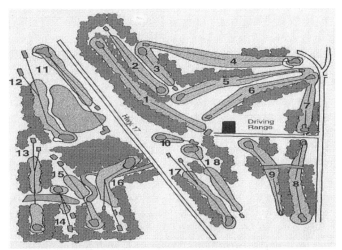

Course	18 Holes	Aesthetics	Very Good
Distance	6502 Yards	Interest	Very Good
Par	36-36-72	Worth the Trip	Yes
Playability	Good	Rating	* * * +

HOLE	1	2	3	4	5	6	7	8	9	OUT
Championship	539	293	179	451	439	393	216	379	410	3299
White	517	274	169	442	428	377	211	357	400	3175
Handicap	9	17	13	15	1	3	5	11	7	
Men's Par	5	4	3	5	4	4	3	4	4	36
Red	300	261	157	340	412	309	144	297	387	2607
Handicap	17	11	9	3	5	7	15	13	1	
Par	4	4	3	5	5	4	3	4	4	36

10	11	12	13	14	15	16	17	18	IN	TOT	HCP	NET
158	463	481	421	206	330	365	386	393	3203	6502		
146	456	464	336 391	168	316	309	373	373	2941	6116		
18	10	16	4	14	12	8	2	6				
3	5	5	4	3	4	4	4	4	36	72		
118	296	349	292	117	299	239	293	253	2256	4863		
18	14	6	8	16	12	10	2	4				
3	4	5	4	3	4	4	4	4	35	71		

257

Wellman Golf Club

Wellman

One of the few sand greens courses left in the state is located in Wellman. Evergreens are prevalent throughout the course and a few shade trees can be found along the stream. The course does have a tiny stream running through it; coming into play on three holes. There are no sand bunkers and no rough. The lay of the course is a little hilly but is still easy to maneuver around on. Grass condition on the fairways and tees has improved. The sand greens are typical, small, round, flat, but very easy to hold! The 2593 yards presents a nice challenge for a course of this type. The Wellman course is located on the east edge of town on Highway 22. The clubhouse is one big room that has a pop machine and tables for special events. Green fees can be paid at the first tee, with the cost being $5 for everyone, everyday; children can play free through the eighth grade. The membership has grown to 65. This public course is one of the rare treats left in Iowa. Only a few sand courses are left, if you have a chance play a sand green course do it and experience a part of Iowa golf history that is becoming extinct.

Course	Sand
Distance	2593 Yards
Par	36
Playability	Good
Aesthetics	Fair
Interest	Fair
Worth The Trip	Yes
Rating	**+

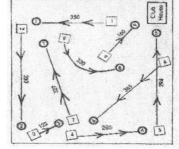

HOLE	1	2	3	4	5	6	7	8	9	OUT
YARDAGE	350	350	122	295	294	365	327	330	160	2593
LADIES' PAR	4	5	3	4	4	4	5	4	4	37
MEN'S PAR	4	4	3	4	4	4	4	4	3	34
HANDICAP HOLES	1	5	9	7	3	4	6	8	2	

Meadowbrook Golf Course

Wellsburg

641-869-3766

There are still a few courses in Iowa that have put their trust in fellow golfers, pay as you play, Meadowbrook Golf Course is such a course. The clubhouse is a small structure that is not open except for special functions. Refreshments include the pop machine by the front door, there are no supplies available. Your daily green fee of $5 can be dropped in a small box by the door where you can also pick up a score card. The 2671 yard course is part of a park complex located in the southern part of Wellsburg. This complex also includes a park, a pool, and the high school football field. The course can be described as flat with young trees lining the wide fairways. The grass condition on the course is very good especially on the small, flat greens. The entire complex, including the course, was built in 1963 and is still in the growing and molding stages. This is a north-south course that is very easy to walk and relatively easy to score well on. Of course the atmosphere is very relaxed and friendly, it is a place that you can go and enjoy a little exercise and the experience of small town golf. Meadowbrook is not very busy so come any time and take number one on.

Course	9 Holes
Distance	2671 Yards
Par	35
Playability	Fair
Aesthetics	Good
Interest	Fair
Worth The Trip	Maybe
Rating	**

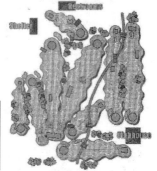

BLUE TEES	292	260	174	407	132	384	137	469	416	2671
MEN'S PAR	4	4	3	5	3	4	3	5	4	35
WHITE TEES	292	260	174	361	132	301	137	365	349	2374
LADIES' PAR	4	4	3	5	3	4	3	5	4	36
MEN'S HDCP	5	6	4	9	8	3	7	2	1	
HOLE	1	2	3	4	5	6	7	8	9	OUT
LADIES' HDCP	5	6	4	9	8	3	7	2	1	

Hillside Golf Club
Wesley
515-679-4262

The Hillside Golf Club was built on a hillside three miles east of Wesley in 1962. The contour of the course is a little hilly but nothing to shy away from. There are no water hazards on the course and only one bunker. The medium size poplars line many of the fairways and offer a form of obstacle if you spray the ball too much. The medium size trees and new plantings are still in the medium number range. Greens are medium in size and flat. The grass condition on the course is good with cart paths being worn on the edges. One of the better features of the course is the clubhouse. It is comfortable inside and offers a full menu of food to the general public. The food is good and attracts many of the 91 members out for an evening meal. A yearly membership costs $295, while daily green fees are reasonable for a 9 hole course. The big bar area is comfortable and offers a cool place to relax after a hard round. Hillside is a moderate course to walk and an easy course to score well on. A lot of people play this course because it is a smaller course located in the country and is not very busy. You can spray the ball on this course without much penalty, but when the wind is blowing out of the north this can be a very difficult course to maneuver around.

Course	9 Holes
Distance	3110 Yards
Par	36
Playability	Fair
Aesthetics	Fair
Interest	Fair
Worth The Trip	Yes
Rating	**+

Men's	YARDAGE	363	150	303	533	316	296	463	166	520	3110
	PAR	4	3	4	5	4	4	4	3	5	36
Ladies	YARDAGE	318	129	275	463	266	270	453	138	468	2780
	PAR	4	3	4	5	4	4	5	3	5	
HOLE NO.		1	2	3	4	5	6	7	8	9	OUT
HANDICAP		5	9	6	3	4	8	1	7	2	

Men's	YARDAGE	363	150	303	533	316	296	463	166	520	3110
	PAR	4	3	4	5	4	4	4	3	5	36
Ladies	YARDAGE	318	129	275	463	266	270	453	138	468	2780
	PAR	4	3	4	5	4	4	5	3	5	
HOLE NO.		1	2	3	4	5	6	7	8	9	OUT
HANDICAP		5	9	6	3	4	8	1	7	2	

West Bend Country Club
West Bend
515-887-6217

One of the most hospitable groups of people associated with golf can be found at the West Bend Golf & country Club. They are friendly, helpful and interested in everyone and everything. The course can be found south of West Bend on Hwy. 15. the 160 members have built a new clubhouse that is very spacious and attractive inside. There are snacks and drinks for golfers during the day and a kitchen that serves special occasions with "Country Cooking" when needed. They serve breakfast and lunch 6 days a week. With a Brunch on Sunday. Supplies are limited but do include carts for rent. Green fees are average for a rural course. The contour of the layout is flat with only a few swales in the surface towards the west end of the course. There are very few medium size trees but small trees line many of the fairways. The greens are medium in size and maintain an above average surface. This is a wide-open course that has a few doglegs. It is fairly easy to score well at West Bend and easier to get on and play. This is a bright spot on the West Bend southern skyline. It has given the local golfers an attractive and interesting place to play golf. It also gives a visitor a place to take in some of that rural Iowa hospitality and friendship.

Course	9 Holes
Distance	3022 Yards
Par	36
Playability	Fair
Aesthetics	Good
Interest	Fair
Worth The Trip	Yes
Rating	**

Men's Par	4	5	4	3	4	5	4	3	4	36
White	286	526	334	177	309	516	349	185	340	3022
Blue	300	567	350	195	333	535	370	210	375	3235
Men's Handicap	17	1	3	13	7	11	5	15	9	
Hole	1	2	3	4	5	6	7	8	9	Out
Ladies' Par	4	5	4	3	4	5	4	3	4	36
Red	276	434	324	157	294	455	329	155	325	2749

Fox Run Golf & Country Club

West Branch

319-643-2100

The 3027 yard course in West Branch is located one mile west and one-half mile north of town. This is a long hitter's course laid out over 83 acres. A stream that runs down the middle of the course comes into play on four of the holes but can be driven over on three of the holes. There is also one pond that comes into play on one hole if you really push your drive to the right. The two inch rough that lines the wide rolling fairways can become nasty if it is not kept cut down to the proper height. There are a medium number of trees that range from 15 to 20 feet tall. New trees are being added each year. Poplars line the driveway leading to the clubhouse making a very inviting entrance. In general the entire course has a hilly contour which includes the rolling greens. The greens are of medium size and are tilted to improve the impact of the approach shot. The course was built in 1965 and is now maturing into a respectable course. The trees are becoming more of a factor each year and grass conditions are becoming more even and solid. Weekday green fees are $10, very reasonable for a 9 hole course. The 200 members pay an annual fee of $550 for a family and have a clubhouse that offers supplies, carts, with bar and snack items in the dining area. There is also a pool available for members and guests.

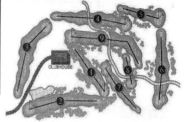

Course	9 Holes
Distance	3237 Yards
Par	36
Playability	Good
Aesthetics	Good
Interest	Fair
Worth The Trip	Yes
Rating	★★+

HOLE	1	2	3	4	5	6	7	8	9	Out
White/ Blue	315	451	335	560	160	433	386	181	416	3237
Handicap	8	7	5	3	9	2	4	6	1	
Par	4	5	4	5	3	4	4	3	4	36
Red	303	370	295	458	142	310	288	135	253	2554
Ladies' Handicap	5	3	4	1	7	2	9	8	6	

Ponderosa Public Golf Course

West Des Moines

515-225-1766

One of the 9 hole public courses in Des Moines is the Ponderosa Course located on 60th Street in West Des Moines. This is a long layout that is flat to gently rolling and is easy to walk. It is a course that was designed and built for the average golfer. The layout is designed for the slicer, a controlled slice will be your best shot on most holes. This public course has reasonable green fees. This is generally a green fees course with weekends at $13. Golf supplies in the small clubhouse include balls, gloves, and putters. Snacks and drinks are also available at the counter. Water hazards are located on five holes; one pond and one creek. There are two bunkers on the course and no rough, grass is cut evenly throughout the course. Trees are medium in size and scattered along fairways and around greens. Greens are medium in size, averaging around 5,000 square feet per green. The contour of the greens is flat and are cut quite long and are easy to read and putt. This is a wide open and easy course. It is a long hitters course that allows a little error in direction without much punishment. The course was built in 1966. Ponderosa is more of a relaxed, fun atmosphere course, a change from some of the other courses in the area. The condition of this course has greatly improved in the new millennium.

Course	9 Holes
Distance	3169 Yards
Par	35
Playability	Fair
Aesthetics	Fair
Interest	Fair
Worth The Trip	Yes
Rating	★★

Des Moines Golf and Country Club
West Des Moines
515-440-7575

Pete Dye is the architect for the Des Moines Golf and Country Club. This is the home of the 1999 U.S. Senior Open. DMGCC is a private course that has two championship courses, both rated in the top ten in the state. Both courses are adjacent to a luxurious clubhouse. The club operates a full time restaurant that is one of the finer establishments in Des Moines. It would take too long to describe the characteristics of both courses, so I will try to give an overview of both. There are four ponds on the site, one creek that comes into play eight times on the north course and six times on the south. There is an abundant supply of sand bunkers on both, a total of 90. The fairways are regulation PGA width, 40 to 50 yards. They have bent grass with blue grass in the roughs. The course is thick with small and medium size trees, some lining the fairways and some scattered. The greens are typical Pete Dye style, large and undulating. The tees are some of the best around. Surfaces are bent grass, they are elevated and tiered. The course was built in 1968 and has developed into a high class complex, just as it was designed to do. The front nine was reconfigured prior to the 99 Open. There are 950 members who enjoy the two courses and the other advantages of the club. Non-members can play DMGCC if they play with a member as a guest or are a member of another private club, the fees would be $80. The pro shop is large and carries a complete line of golfing supplies, in mass quantities. This is a nice course to walk but there are a large number of carts to rent. DMCC is a very busy complex so tee times are a necessity. Future growth of the trees and maturing fairways and greens can only make this course better and more challenging. For now it can be rated as one of the best in the region, something to admire and attack. The course has a new country club atmosphere. The Des Moines Country Club is located two miles west of the interstate on University. DMCC is a true championship course, a real asset to Iowa golf. DMCC was the site of the 1999 US Senior Open.

Course	36 Holes	Aesthetics	Excell.
Distance	7103 Yards	Interest	Excell.
Par	37-36-73	Worth The Trip	Yes
Playability	Excell.	Rating	*****

North Course

Hole	1	2	3	4	5	6	7	8	9	Out	10	11	12	13	14	15	16	17	18	In	Tot	Rating/Slope
Black	389	618	197	410	199	454	393	392	521	3573	356	418	179	552	481	454	360	190	637	3627	7200	74.9/139
Green	362	584	166	377	166	409	367	365	497	3293	332	402	157	516	466	427	350	173	590	3413	6706	72.3/137
Blue	346	558	145	334	137	387	327	346	454	3034	293	376	127	427	447	381	336	152	525	3064	6098	M-70.0/129 W-74.7/137
Handicap	13	5	17	3	15	1	7	11	9		18	10	16	4	8	2	12	14	6			Hcp Net
+/-																						
Par	4	5	3	4	3	4	4	4	5	36	4	4	3	5/4	5	4	4	3	5	37/36	73/72	
+/-																						
Bronze	302	443	121	298	113	339	291	289	395	2591	268	304	110	365	423	326	289	103	470	2658	5249	M-65.8/121 W-68.6/113
Bronze Hcp	13	7	15	5	17	1	3	11	9		10	12	18	6	8	14	2	16	4			

South Course

Hole	1	2	3	4	5	6	7	8	9	Out	10	11	12	13	14	15	16	17	18	In	Tot	Rating/Slope
Black	387	487	389	460	191	552	384	537	163	3550	410	396	386	522	449	199	558	194	439	3553	7103	75.4/140
Green	371	469	368	439	173	540	373	523	155	3411	396	374	364	498	429	185	539	184	424	3393	6804	73.7/128
Blue	327	388	331	392	131	494	359	463	142	3027	344	342	335	467	405	167	510	170	363	3103	6130	
Handicap	5	9	11	1	15	7	3	13	17		6	14	12	8	2	16	4	18	10			Hcp Net
+/-																						
Par	4	5/4	4	4	3	5	4	5	3	37/36	4	4	4	5	4/5	3	5	3	4	36/37	73	
+/-																						
Bronze	269	310	307	311	96	452	349	410	129	2633	298	306	311	436	365	141	447	160	308	2772	5405	M-66.6/111 W-68.6/111
Bronze Hcp	5	3	1	13	15	11	9	7	17		4	12	6	8	10	18	2	16	14			

261

Glen Oaks Country Club

West Des Moines

515-221-9500

Glen Oaks Country Club was established in 1994. All golfers playing Glen Oaks are in for a special and unique experience. The quality of the course is outstanding and golfers will be compare Glen Oaks with the best courses they have played. To do this course justice I would need to describe every hole. The layout is gently rolling with some severe hills. The back nine is hilly and about 120 yards longer. The course was initially designed with the abundant wooded areas in mind. Greens are tiered, fast and undulated. The layout has almost 80 sand bunkers designed to catch errant shots. There are many natural areas throughout the course with fescue grass beginning after the first cut of rough. The 419 yard 1st hole requires two long shots to reach the green, you need to add one club to allow for uphill slope. From the highest point on the golf course the par 5, #4 has the greatest change in elevation of any hole. On number 9 club selection is critical on this long narrow green. Shots to the right will have to deal with waterfalls and a bunker. From front to back this par 3 green is a two to three club difference. One of the most difficult tee shots on the course will start off the back nine. A narrow landing area that slopes from left to right makes positioning vital. The approach to this deep green requires an extra club due to the uphill approach. Water comes into play on 8 hoes. The most intimidating is the 14th where the 206 yard shot is totally over water. Every holes can be described as one-of-a-kind and beautiful. The entire course is in tremendous shape and can be touted as the top course in the state. Green fees are $90 with a member. You can play if you area member of another country club. Glen Oaks is the home of the Seniors Alliance tournament in late summer. This is a tremendous course that can takes its place as one of the great courses in the Midwest.

Course	18 Holes	Aesthetics	Excellent
Distance	7000	Interest	Excellent
Par	35-36-71	Worth The Trip	Yes
Playability	Excellent	Rating	★ ★ ★ ★ ★

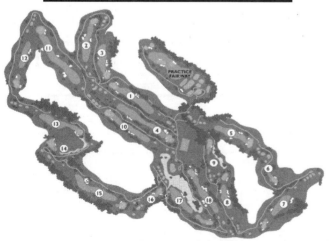

HOLE	1	2	3	4	5	6	7	8	9	Out	10	11	12	13	14	15	16	17	18	IN	TOT	HCP	NET
BLACK	373	203	430	377	215	419	412	510	310	3289	456	539	421	407	229	549	202	467	421	3711	7000		
GREEN	355	185	408	341	193	400	391	339	501	3113	418	536	400	388	201	520	170	438	399	3470	6583		
WHITE	331	166	390	320	190	370	359	319	473	2918	377	509	371	357	161	499	159	415	334	3182	6100		
GOLD	280	120	285	253	141	296	282	213	379	2251	297	416	323	269	92	411	122	288	292	2510	4761		
PAR	4	3	4	4	3	4	4	5	4	35	4	5	4	4	3	5	3	4	4	36	71		
M: HCP	18	16	6	2	14	4	10	12	8		3	13	11	15	9	17	1	5					
L: HCP	10	18	6	4	14	2	12	16	8		11	9	7	13	17	5	15	3	1				

| DATE: | | SCORER: | | ATTEST: | |

Willow Creek Golf Club
West Des Moines

515-285-4558

One of the few courses in the state to have 36 holes located in the same layout is Willow Creek Golf Club located on Army Post Road in Des Moines. This course was built to accommodate a great many golfers at once. Four new holes were built in 2000. The course has now expanded by the Hwy. 6 bi-pass. Three starting tees are close to the clubhouse. The course is laid out like three separate courses and the facilities can manage a crowd all day long. Willow Creek is a green fees course, with weekday green fees of $22. The clubhouse is a very nice area with a full line of equipment, including carts for rent plus a snack bar that serves drinks, grilled and microwave sandwiches. There is also a large area for catered meetings. The lower level area has a place to sit, relax, enjoy the view, and then get out for some more golfing. The characteristics for the entire 36 holes include nine ponds that come into play on fourteen holes, water is an important aspect of this course. They also have one sand bunker per hole and a tough rough along the fairways, around tees and greens. The above average number of trees are medium in size, 10-15 feet, and are generally scattered in the rough and around the tees. The landscaping of the course is one of the nicest in the area. Bushes and small trees adorn tees and pathways, flowers are present around the clubhouse, and the general condition of the entire course is good. The contour of Willow Creek is gently rolling. The fairways are narrow thanks to the lush rough. The greens also have a wide range of sizes and surfaces. The course was built in 1961. An expansion was made in 1991, which included an executive nine holes. This might be considered the busiest course in the city. Willow Creek is a very friendly course that has a courteous staff. This complex also has a driving range across the road that has an ample supply of driving mats. This is a good course to walk if you have the time. Willow Creek reinforces accuracy off the tee with the presence of the heavy rough and penalizes you for being places you hadn't planned on. The atmosphere is one of public golf, friendly but a little hurried. A well maintained and entertaining course that is very busy.

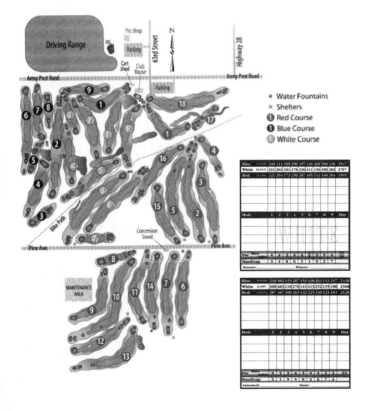

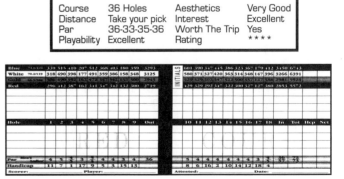

Course	36 Holes	Aesthetics	Very Good
Distance	Take your pick	Interest	Excellent
Par	36-33-35-36	Worth The Trip	Yes
Playability	Excellent	Rating	****

West Liberty Golf and Country Club

West Liberty

319-627-2085

The West Liberty Golf and Country Club is a public course located on the S.W. edge of West Liberty off Country Heights Road. The area in which the course is located would indicate a flat course but there is only one flat hole on the layout with the remainder fairly rolling. The course layout was an apple orchard in the forties. The only hazard on the course, besides the contour of the land, are the three sand bunkers and the trees. There are no water hazards and rough is cut mainly during the wet season. There is a considerable number of trees that come into play on every hole. The trees are not only plentiful but large in size. The fairways are tapering with trees closing in as you near the greens. The grass throughout the course is good despite the inclines found. Greens are medium in size and generally flat with a few sloping putting surfaces. The greens have a reputation of being hard to hold but easy to read once you get there. The line on West Liberty is that if you keep the ball straight you will have no trouble; now that sounds simple to me! The course was built in 1958 in a wooded, hilly area. The clubhouse offers a year round restaurant and is a very enjoyable place to eat. Golfers can order sandwiches and drinks from the bar area. Carts and golf supplies are available along with the opportunity to pay the reasonable green fees. This is an easy course to walk and score well on if you keep it between the trees.

Course	9 Holes
Distance	3032 Yards
Par	36
Playability	Good
Aesthetics	Good
Interest	Fair
Worth The Trip	Yes
Rating	★★+

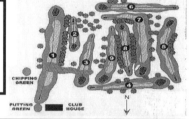

HOLE	1	2	3	4	5	6	7	8	9	OUT
WHITE TEES	478	140	221	335	387	307	501	300	363	3032
BLUE TEES	473	140	135	325	372	297	495	300	345	2882
HANDICAP	6	9	1	5	2	8	4	7	3	
PAR	5	3	3	4	4	4	5	4	4	36
RED TEES	378	135	130	315	367	290	485	300	335	2735
HANDICAP	6	9	1	4	8	7	5	3	2	
PAR	5	3	3	4	5	4	5	4	4	37

West Union Country Club

West Union

563-422-3482

The West Union Country Club is located two miles S.E. of West Union on a blacktop road. This is a nine hole course that is open to the public all mornings and most afternoons. One of the outstanding features of the course is the modern clubhouse. Inside the 160 members enjoy a full restaurant that is open the year round. This eating establishment caters many special functions for the course and for the community. There is a posh bar area that has lounge seating overlooking the course; plus snacks available to golfers during the day. Otter Creek runs the length of the course and shapes the layout. The stream really only affects two holes with water; but all the remaining holes come under the influence of the water because the land slopes to the ravine. Trees are scattered throughout the course and are medium in size with many new plantings added each year. Fairways are wide allowing you to spray the ball a little; but playing off the beaten path sometimes leads down the hill. Greens are medium in size and offer a variety of putting surfaces, generally sloping. West Union is a hard course to walk and a challenging course to play due to the hills and placement of trees. This is a placement course; position on the hill is very important for the next shot. West Union is a picturesque course that has a reputation of being difficult and subject to very windy conditions; nothing more enjoyable than a strong side wind to push your ball down the hill to the water; oh what fun.

Course	9 Holes
Distance	3144 Yards
Par	36
Playability	Good
Aesthetics	Fair
Interest	Good
Worth The Trip	Yes
Rating	★★+

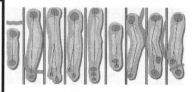

HOLE	1	2	3	4	5	6	7	8	9	Out
BLUE	138	407	485	356	455	182	378	360	383	3144
WHITE	135	402	475	350	434	175	370	350	363	3054
MEN'S PAR	3	4	5	4	5	3	4	4	4	36
HANDICAP	17	1	9	7	13	11	15	3	5	
+/- 0										
LADIES' PAR	3	5	5	4	5	3	5	4	4	38
RED	130	402	388	261	389	170	370	250	260	2620

Whittemore Golf Club

Whittemore

515-884-2775

The Whittemore Golf Club is a public nine hole course located one mile east of Whittemore and was built in 1969. There is one stream on the course running down the west side, coming into play three times. Very little sand exists but there is a two-inch rough bordering the wide fairways. Trees on the course are medium in size and line all the fairways, sparse in population though. The contour of the course is generally flat with a few swales present near the creek. Tees are elevated and large, greens are medium in size, presenting some rolling and sloping putting surfaces. The grass condition throughout the course is good, the entire course has a local reputation of being in good shape. This is a second shot course, good position for your approach shot makes the day go a lot easier. The clubhouse has an ample supply of balls, gloves, and some clothes. They also have carts for rent. Green fees are reasonable for a 9 hole course. The 200 members pay an initial stock of $100, then a yearly family fee of $355. This is an easy course to walk and a fairly easy course to score well on. Hazards are at a minimum, with only the trees on a few holes and the water on three others being of much threat. This is a small town course that has a lot of friendly members proud to be part of it.

Course	9 Holes
Distance	3034 Yards
Par	36
Playability	Fair
Aesthetics	Fair
Interest	Poor
Worth The Trip	Yes
Rating	★★

Hole	Men's Yards	Men's Par	Women's Yards	Women's Par
1	332	4	320	4
2	295	4	282	4
3	328	4	325	4
4	432	5	345	4
5	213	3	119	3
6	390	4	377	4
7	158	3	146	3
8	343	4	327	4
9	543	5	419	5
	3034	36	2650	35

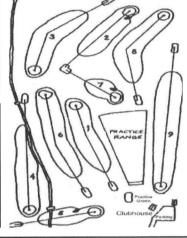

Sport Hill Country Club

Williamsburg

319-668-2225

The 180 members of Sport Hill Country Club in Williamsburg can enjoy a long challenging course that looks a lot easier than it really is. The course was expanded and totally redone in 2001. This gently rolling course has 3 ponds, 27 sand bunkers and no grass mounds. The small and medium size trees line the fairways and are more of a problem than they appear. They are small but cut off your entrance back onto the fairway if you happen to get off track. The fairway grass is good throughout the summer making the narrow fairways more enjoyable to hit your second shot from. Tees are small and flat as are the greens. These flat fast greens make your approach and putts more of an effort than a pleasure. Sport Hill is a long course over 3,417 yards - but fairly easy and enjoyable to walk. To many first time players this course can be a humbling experience; hidden breaks, small branches in the way, downhill lies, all can bring that score right up. The clubhouse has balls and gloves and a full bar with microwave sandwiches. The course is located in the S.W. corner of Williamsburg and is a nice place to play golf or enjoy an afternoon of swimming in their pool. Whichever you choose Williamsburg is a nice example of Iowa Golf. The changes to the course have made it very inviting and fun to play.

Course	9 Holes
Distance	3417 Yards
Par	36
Playability	Very Good
Aesthetics	Very Good
Interest	Very Good
Worth The Trip	Yes
Rating	★★★+

Hole	1	2	3	4	5	6	7	8	9	Out
Black	541	217	399	477	172	588	334	184	505	3417
White	536	205	391	469	167	580	327	168	498	3341
Red	518	184	354	429	141	523	297	153	475	3074
Blue	488	159	271	326	111	443	235	137	403	2573
Handicap	3	7	9	1	15	5	11	13	17	
Gold	418	120	266	319	95	437	227	107	397	2386
Par	5	3	4	4	3	5	4	3	5	36

Wahkonsa Country Club

Wilton and Durant

563-785-6328

Wahkonsa Country Club is a private club located three miles east of Wilton on old Highway 6. This is a family type course that was built out in the country on some flat farm land. It offers an alternative to the big city courses of Davenport. Dues for the 300 members are $530. The clubhouse has a dining room upstairs for special occasions and the bar and grill, for daily food, on the ground level. The public can eat in the downstairs eating facility any time. Wahkonsa course has one pond, six bunkers, and a two inch rough that is thinned out and does not hamper play. Evergreens run along a portion of the course; but most of the trees are new plantings along the wide fairways. This courses character has drastically changed in the past ten years with the new trees grown and now in play. Additional trees are added each year. Greens are medium in size and rolling and are known for being hard to hold and hard to putt. The course was built in 1967 and has an even contour. It is an easy course to walk, there are carts to rent; but a challenging course due to the length, the greens, and the presence of strong winds. A new irrigation system was added in the late 90's. The outstanding feature of this course would have to be the large amount of new trees that have been planted. In a few years this flat open field will become a wooded forest.

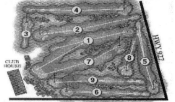

Course	9 Holes
Distance	3425 Yards
Par	36
Playability	Good
Aesthetics	Good
Interest	Fair
Worth The Trip	Yes
Rating	★★

HOLE	1	2	3	4	5	6	7	8	9	Out
Championship Tees	487	421	174	453	536	410	414	190	343	3428
Men's Tees	464	343	162	395	502	334	400	174	322	3096
Senior/Junior Tees	430	300	140	395	460	288	353	142	238	2746
Handicap	11	7	13	6	3	12	4	10	8	
Ladies' Tees	351	298	125	360	418	286	309	118	236	2501
Par	5	4	3	4	5	4	4	3	4	36

Twin Lakes Country Club

Winfield

319-257-6253

One of the more active couples and tournament clubs in Iowa is the Twin Lakes Country Club in Winfield. This nine hole public course is located on the N.W. side of Winfield and supports a 3325 yard course, a pool, and a year round restaurant. The restaurant is open 6 a.m.-10 p.m. during the golfing season and until 2:00 p.m. during the winter; a popular place since it is one of the only places in town to eat. The majority of space in the clubhouse is used by the dining facilities. The pro shop does have a few supplies and there are carts for rent. The 175 members pay a yearly fee of $475. Green fees are reasonably priced; when there are no tournaments. The characteristics of the course include two ponds, no sand, and a two-inch rough that is very fair. There are a few trees and the ones that do exist are small or new plantings. This is a fairly flat course for this area; with wide fairways and no steep hills. Tees are flat to the ground and small, the greens are small to medium in size, flat and are hard to hold. The course was built in 1966. This is a friendly course that is not very busy unless you happen upon it during a weekend tournament. It is a fairly long course that makes Twin Lakes a hard course to score well on unless you hit the ball long and straight. If you play in couples golf tournaments sooner or later you will play Twin Lakes, be ready for some friendly golf and some good food.

Course	9 Holes
Distance	3187 Yards
Par	36
Playability	Good
Aesthetics	Fair
Interest	Fair
Worth The Trip	Yes
Rating	★★★

MEN'S YARDAGE	149	495	445	370	293	531	444	160	300	3187
PAR	3	5	4	4	4	5	4	3	4	36
HANDICAP HOLES	9	4	1	5	6	3	2	8	7	OUT
LADIES YARDAGE	144	320	440	365	150	453	439	155	255	2721
LADIES PAR	3	4	5	4	3	5	5	3	4	36
HANDICAP HOLES	8	4	5	1	9	6	2	7	3	OUT
HOLE	1	2	3	4	5	6	7	8	9	

Lakeview Country Club

Winterset

515-462-9962

The Lakeview Country Club is a semi-private club located north of Winterset three miles near Cedar Lake; you can turn at Cedar Bridge County Park sign. Green fees are accepted from golfers living outside Madison county. The 270 members pay an initial stock of $200 then a yearly membership fee of $550 for a family. The clubhouse is a red block structure that has a nice bar area serving drinks and sandwiches. The dining room is open Wednesday thru Sunday for meals. There are no water hazards on the course but sand does come into play four times. Medium size trees line all the wide fairways with evergreens thrown in for a little variety. The contour of the course is rolling with only one fairway having a flat surface. Greens are small with rolling and tilted putting surfaces. Lakeview was built in 1946 and has supplied this community with quality golf for six decades. The course is fairly hard to walk, is maintained very well, and is a real challenge to play. The hills and trees causing the most troubles. Every hole is different, making you concentrate on your game at all times. The greens are tough to get on and tough to read and putt. Lakeview is one of the more challenging courses in the area. It is easy to get a tee time so try it out sometime. Cedar Lake and Cover Bridges are also worth a visit.

Course	9 Holes
Distance	2929 Yards
Par	35
Playability	V. Good
Aesthetics	Good
Interest	Very Good
Worth The Trip	Yes
Rating	★★★+

HOLE	1	2	3	4	5	6	7	8	9	Out
Men's Tees	417	530	334	306	203	403	251	304	132	2880
Par	4	5	4	4	3	4	4	4	3	35
Handicap	5	1	11	9	7	3	17	13	15	
Ladies' Tees	345	462	334	260	154	333	251	304	132	2575
Par	4	5	4	4	3	4	4	4	3	35

Buffalo Creek Country Club

Winthrop

319-935-3697

Buffalo Creek Country Club is a public nine hole course located three miles north of Winthrop on W 45. This is a family oriented course that is very relaxed and casual. The layout of the course is dominated by one stream that pierces the courses heart. It comes into play on five holes and has gained the psychological advantage over many of the members. There are also seven bunkers on the course, a short rough, and an average number of trees scattered throughout the course. The trees do line some of the fairways but in two cases perch right in the middle of the wide fairways blocking approach shots. The grass condition of the course has improved over the past few years and the putting surfaces are in good shape. Tees are small and close to the ground. Greens are medium to large in size and very flat in many cases. The clubhouse has carts to rent and a limited amount of supplies for sale. The bar area supplies sandwiches throughout the season and meals on special occasions. The 270 members pay an original stock of $200 and a yearly fee of $170. This is an easy course to walk and a fairly easy course to score well on if you pay attention. The layout is dominated by the creek, especially in the spring when it overruns it's banks. A nice small town course that offers what golf courses should, fun, exercise, and a friendly atmosphere.

Course	9 Holes
Distance	2713 Yards
Par	35
Playability	Fair
Aesthetics	Very Good
Interest	Good
Worth The Trip	Yes
Rating	★★★

HOLE	1	2	3	4	5	6	7	8	9	Total	Hcp	Net
BLUE	328	308	225	289	467	383	155	294	264	2713		
HANDICAP	5	11	15	13	17	3	9	7	1			
LADIES' HDCP	7	13	17	9	1	11	15	3	5			
RED	285	240	209	267	408	283	155	267	168	2283		
PAR	4	4	4	4	5	4	3	4	3	35		

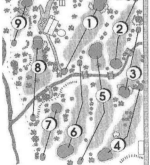

Shadow Valley Golf Course

Woodbine

712-647-3442

In 1998 a track of land in Woodbine was transformed into a 9 hole golf course called Shadow Valley. This was a difficult course to build, and at times impossible to build. But the dream was there, a housing development first and then a golf course that used the existing terrain and provided a fun place for golfers in the area. Shadow Valley is located one mile west of Woodbine on F20. The rolling and undulating greens average 7,000 square feet with a bent grass surface. Fairways are rolling, fully watered, and tight, providing the challenge needed in a new course. Hazards on the course consist of three sand bunkers, water on six holes and tiered rough. Forty-four trees were planted in 2003 and a plan is in place to line the fairways in the future with trees. People playing the course way shadow Valley is hilly, difficult to play, and fun to play. The clubhouse has a full café serving every day. Also in the clubhouse is a large convention center for meetings and parties. The driving range provides a place to warm up before your round. The 200 members pay an annual fee of $350. Green fees are $10 for 9 holes. This is beautiful young course that has a lot of water and side hill lies.

Course	9 Holes
Distance	3081 Yards
Par	36
Playability	Good
Aesthetics	Good
Interest	Good
Worth The Trip	Yes
Rating	★★+

HOLE	1	2	3	4	5	6	7	8	9	OUT
BLUE TEES	410	368	178	315	280	553	140	355	482	3081
WHITE TEES	374	348	150	286	257	527	132	327	445	2856
HANDICAP	2	6	10	11	16	9	18	4	14	
PAR	4	4	3	4	4	5	3	4	5	36
RED TEES	310	308	125	259	225	503	120	283	398	2531
HANDICAP	2	6	10	11	16	9	18	4	14	
PAR	4	4	3	4	4	5	3	4	5	36

Woodward Golf Club

Woodward

515-438-2198

The Woodward Golf and Recreation Course was built in 1968 and has matured into a fine young course. The contour of the course is flat with the fairways wide and open to almost any type of shot. Trees are scattered throughout the course and range from new planting size to medium poplars. There is one pond on the course and six bunkers. The rough is cut to three inches along the fairways but is fair and offers little resistance to the long iron shot. Greens are medium in size with a few tilted, a few rolling, and a few flat. This is a very enjoyable, easy walking course. It is also an easy course to score well on; mostly a short iron course. The clubhouse has balls, gloves, a few clubs, and carts for rent. The sitting area looks out over the course with sandwiches and drinks available. The 225 members keep this course fairly busy along with green fees players. Yearly family memberships are $577. Woodward-Granger golf teams also do their share of practicing, resulting in a state championship in 1987. The course is located on the S.W. side of Woodward and has a pool open to the public. This is a nice, easy course that is maintained well and offers a relaxed golfing atmosphere. This is a north-south course with a tough par 3 number one to get you on your way.

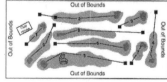

Course	9 Holes
Distance	3022 Yards
Par	35
Playability	Good
Aesthetics	Good
Interest	Fair
Worth The Trip	Yes
Rating	★★+

MENS PAR	3	5	3	4	5	4	3	4	4	35
YARDAGE RATING/SLOPE SE 67/104	207	480	173	280	540	366	160	456	360	3022
HANDICAP	5	3	7	9	2	6	8	1	4	
HANDICAP	6	5	8	7	1	2	9	4	3	
YARDAGE RATING/SLOPE 60.8/104	177	375	146	253	436	344	148	419	325	2623
LADIES PAR	3	5	3	4	5	4	3	5	4	36
HOLES	1	2	3	4	5	6	7	8	9	OUT

Little Bear Recreation Club

Wyoming

319-488-2559

Another wide open course that you can find in the eastern half of Iowa is the Little Bear Recreation Club on the north side of Wyoming. This is a gently sloping course that has very few trees but does have one pond and one stream that come into play on three holes. The wide fairways are in very good shape and outlined by 2 inches of rough on the sides. The tees are elevated and in good condition. You will find the greens flat and medium in size. The greens are also very true to read and present a lot of straight in putts. The course was built in 1966 and is developing into a golf course with a little bit of character. The clubhouse has carts for rent even though this is an easy course to walk, plus there are a few golf supplies available. The grill area serves great sandwiches and is open during the golfing season. The food is worth the trip. Weekday fees are very reasonable at $8. Members pay a family yearly membership of $350. The course is so popular because the cemetery is right across the road which means you can play until your last breath.

Course	9 Holes
Distance	2884 Yards
Par	36
Playability	Fair
Aesthetics	Fair
Interest	Poor
Worth The Trip	Yes
Rating	★★

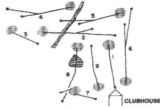

CLUBHOUSE

HANDICAP	9	8	3	1	5	7	4	2	6	PAR	Course Rating 33.6 Slope 104	
MEN'S YARDAGE	294	445	151	364	349	447	167	340	327	2884		
PAR	4	5	3	4	4	5	3	4	4	36		
0 - + WE												
HOLE NUMBER	1	2	3	4	5	6	7	8	9	TOTAL	HDCP	NET
PAR	4	4	3	4	4	5	3	4	4	35	Course Rating 33.7 Slope 103	
WOMEN'S YARDAGE	276	368	150	291	266	401	167	283	327	2529		
HANDICAP	7	1	9	6	5	3	8	4	2			

Twin Lakes Country Club Hole #1 -
My home course near Rockwell City

About the Author

My father introduced me to golf on the Twin Lakes course in 1962. Passing on the love of the game and the great golf tradition of golf at Twin Lakes, the fourth generation is now picking up the game on Twin Lakes Country Club. My father's Great Granddaughter Emma and Great Grandson Ethan have taken to their Mickey Mouse clubs like ducks to water. Even though their swings are a little wild, their feelings for the game are growing with each missed swing. Emma and Ethan are Iowa's golfing future. My dad, Homer Aegerter at 90, continues to pass on the passion and love for the game. I can only hope that I too, can pass along some of my love and respect for the game to the next generation. I taught golf at the high school level for many years and now, hopefully I can pass on some lessons to my Great Niece and Nephew. Whatever the case, it is great to see the very young get excited about the game.

PAGE	COURSE NAME	TOWN	COUNTY	TYPE
216	Lost Island Golf Club	Ruthven	Palo Alto	9
154	Malvern Golf Course	Malvern	Mills	9
155	Manchester Country Club	Manchester	Delaware	18
157	Manning - Manilla Golf and Country Club	Manning	Crawford	9
157	Manson Golf and Country Club	Manson	Calhoun	9
98	Maple Heights	Elma	Howard	9
244	Maple Hills Golf and Country Club	Tripoli	Bremer	9
158	Maquoketa Country Club	Maquoketa	Jackson	9
159	Marcus Golf Club	Marcus	Cherokee	9
160	Marengo Country Club	Marengo	Iowa	9
165	Mason City Country Club	Mason City	Cerro Gordo	18
146	Meadow Acres Country Club	Larchwood	Lyon	9
135	Meadow Hills Golf Course	Iowa Falls	Hardin	9
240	Meadowbrook Country Club	Sumner	Bremer	9
122	Meadowbrook Golf and Country Club	Hartley	O'Brien	9
258	Meadowbrook Golf Counrse	Wellsburg	Grundy	9
172	Meadows Country Club	Moville	Woodbury	9
53	Meadowview Country Club	Central City	Linn	9
94	Mescher's Rolling Knolls	Dyersville	Dubuque	9
95	Milne Memorial Park and Golf Club	Dysart	Tama	9
169	Monroe Gateway Recreation	Monroe	Jasper	9
170	Montezuma Country Club	Montezuma	Poweshiek	9
170	Monticello Golf Club	Monticello	Jones	9
171	Mount Ayr Golf and Country Club	Mount Ayr	Ringgold	9
171	Mount Pleasant Golf and Country Club	Mount Pleasant	Henry	9
174	Muscatine Municipal Golf Course	Muscatine	Muscatine	18
175	Nashua Town & Country	Nashua	Chickasaw	9
177	New Hampton Country Club	New Hampton	Chickasaw	9
178	Newell Golf Park	Newell	Buena Vista	9
180	Newton Country Club	Newton	Jasper	9
21	Nishna Hills Golf Club	Atlantic	Cass	18
119	Nishna Valley Recreation Area	Griswold	Cass	9
136	no card no info	Jackson Jct.	Winneshiek	9
180	Nora Springs	Nora Springs	Floyd	9
23	North Kossuth Golf Club	Bancroft	Kossuth	9
182	Northwood Country Club	Northwood	Worth	9
59	Oak Hills Par 30 Public Golf Course	Clear Lake	Cerro Gordo	9
208	Oak Leaf Country Club	Reinbeck	Grundy	9
118	Oakland Acres Golf Course	Grinnell	Poweshiek	18
182	Oakland Country Club	Oakland	Pottawattamie	9
111	Oakridge Recreation	Goldfield	Wright	9
12	Oaks Golf Club	Ames	Story	9
64	Oakwood Golf Course	Conrad	Grundy	9
235	Okoboji Vu Golf Club	Spirit Lake	Dickinson	18
148	Olathea Golf Course	Le Claire	Scott	9
189	Onawa Country Club	Onawa	Monona	9
79	Oneota Golf and Country Club	Decorah	Winneshiek	18
191	Osceola Country Club	Osceola	Clarke	9
16	Otter Creek Golf Course	Ankeny	Polk	18
110	Otter Valley Country Club	George and Boyden	Lyon	9
195	Ottumwa Cedar Creek	Ottumwa	Wapello	18
196	Ottumwa Country Club	Ottumwa	Wapello	18
27	Palmer Hills Municipal Golf Course	Bettendorf	Scott	18
198	Paullina Golf Club	Paullina	O'brien	9
200	Pella Golf and Country Club	Pella	Marion	9
200	Perry Golf and Country Club	Perry	Dallas	9
42	Pheasant Ridge Golf Course	Cedar Falls	Black Hawk	18
203	Pierson Golf Course	Pierson	Woodbury	Sand
166	Pine Creek	Mason City	Cerro Gordo	Par 3
142	Pine Knolls Country Club	Knoxville	Marion	9
96	Pine Lake Golf and Country Club	Eldora	Hardin	9
73	Pine Valley Golf Club	Creston	Union	9
156	Pioneer Town and Country Club	Manly	Worth	9
134	Pleasant Valley	Iowa City	Johnson	18
203	Pleasantville Golf and Country Club	Pleasantville	Marion	9
109	Plum Creek Golf Course	Fredericksburg	Chickasaw	9
205	Plum River	Preston	Jackson	9
205	Pocahontas Golf Club	Pocahontas	Pocahontas	9
260	Ponderosa Public Golf Course	West Des Moines	Polk	9
159	Prairie Creek	Maquoketa	Jackson	9
178	Prairie Knolls Golf Course	New Sharon	Mahaska	9
32	Prairie Rose	Brunsville	Plymouth	9
207	Primghar Country Club	Primghar	O'Brian	9
181	Quail Creek Golf Course	North Liberty	Johnson	9
176	Quail Run	Neola	Pottawattamie	9
207	Quimby Golf & CC	Quimby	Cherokee	9
208	Radcliffe Friendly Fairways	Radcliffe	Hardin	9
130	Raleigh Hills	Ionia	Chickasaw	9
250	Red Carpet Golf Course	Waterloo	Black Hawk	18
78	Red Hawk	Davenport	Scott	9
209	Red Oak Country Club	Red Oak	Montgomery	18
210	Remsen Golf Club	Remsen	Plymouth	9
144	Rice Lake Golf and Country Club	Lake Mills	Winnebago	18
210	Riceville Country Club	Riceville	Howard	9
218	Ridgestone	Sheffield	Franklin	18
239	River Bend Golf Course	Story City	Story	9
6	River Road Golf Club	Algona	Kossuth	9
3	River Valley	Adel	Dallas	18
140	River View Club	Keosauqua	Van Buren	9
100	Riverview Golf Course	Estherville	Emmet	9
212	Rock River Club	Rock Rapids	Lyon	9
212	Rock Valley Golf Club	Rock Valley	Sioux	9
213	Rockford Golf and Country Club	Rockford	Floyd	9
214	Rolfe Golf Club	Rolfe	Pocahontas	9
52	Rolling Acres Golf Course	Center Point	Linn	9
185	Rolling Hills	Norwalk	Warren	18
125	Rolling Hills Country Cllulb	Hull	Sioux	9
122	Rosman Glendale Farm Golf Course	Harlan	Shelby	9
115	Round Grove Golf and Country Club	Greene	Butler	9
97	Rustic Ridge Golf Course	Eldridge	Scott	9
216	Sac Country Club	Sac City	Sac	9
145	Sac County Golf and Country Club	Lake View	Sac	9
232	Saddleback Ridge	Solon	Johnson	9
217	Sanborn Golf and Country Club	Sanborn	O'Brien	9
222	Sandy Hollow Golf Course	Sioux Center	Sioux	9
217	Schleswig Golf Course	Schleswig	Crawford	9
268	Shadow Valley	Woodbine	Harrison	9
2	Shady Oaks Golf Course	Ackworth	Warren	18
108	Sheaffer Memorial Golf Park	Fort Madison	Lee	18
219	Sheldon Golf and Country club	Sheldon	O'Brien	9
40	Shoreline Golf Course	Carter Lake	Pottawattamie	18
219	Sibley Country Club	Sibley	Osceola	9
221	Sigourney Golf and Country Club	Sigourney	Keokuk	9
145	Silver Lake Golf and Country Club	Lake Park	Dickenson	9
194	Silver Springs	Ossian	Winneshiek	9
80	Silvercrest Golf and Country Club	Decorah	Winneshiek	9
226	Sioux City Country Club	Sioux City	Woodbury	18
8	Sioux Golf and Country Club	Alton	Sioux	9
142	Slippery Elm Golf Course	Klemme	Hancock	9
231	Sloan Golf Course	Sloan	Woodbury	9
244	South Hardin Recreation Area	Union	Hardin	9
251	South Hills Golf Course	Waterloo	Black Hawk	18
37	South Winn Golf and Country Club	Calmar	Winneeshiek	9
233	Spencer Golf and Country Club	Spencer	Clay	18
234	Spencer Municipal Golf Course	Spencer	Clay	18
35	Spirit Hollow	Burlington	Des Moines	18
265	Sport Hill Country Club	Williamsburg	Iowa	9
154	Spring Hills	Mallard	Palo Alto	9
109	Spring Lake Golf Course	Fort Madison	Lee	9
151	Spring Valley Golf Club	Livermore	Humbolt	18
88	Springbrook Country Club	DeWitt	Clinton	9
50	St. Andrews Golf Club	Cedar Rapids	Linn	18
236	Storm Lake Municipal Golf Course	Storm Lake	Buena Vista	9
98	Sun Valley Golf and Country Club	Ellston	Ringgold	9
230	Sun Valley Golf Club	Sioux City	Woodbury	Par 3
105	Sunkissed Meadows Golf Course	Fort Dodge	Webster	Par 3
189	Sunny Brae Golf and Country Club	Osage	Mitchell	9
252	Sunnyside Country Club	Waterloo	Black Hawk	18
28	Sunrise Golf Course	Bettendorf	Scott	9
240	Tama-Toledo Country Club	Tama	Tama	9
245	Tara Hills Country Club	Van Horne	Benton	9
7	Terrace Hills Golf Course	Altoona	Polk	18
113	The Hill	Grand Junction	Greene	9
187	The Inn	Okoboji	Dickinson	Par 3
93	The Meadows	Dubuque	Dubuque	18
241	Thornton Pleqasant Valley	Thornton	Cerro Gordo	9
128	Three Elms	Independence	Buchanan	9
148	Three Lake Municipal Golf Course	Lenox	Taylor	9
201	Thunder Hills Country Club	Peosta	Dubuque	18
202	Timberline Golf Course	Peosta	Dubuque	18
241	Tipton Golf and Country Club	Tipton	Cedar	9
215	Toad Valley Public Golf Course	Runnells	Warren	18
206	Tournament Club of Iowa	Polk City	Polk	18
119	Town and Country Golf Club	Grundy Center	Grundy	9
243	Traer Golf and Country Club	Traer	Tama	9
243	Treynor Recreation Area	Treynor	Pottawattamie	9
153	Tri- City Golf Club	Luana	Clayton	9
227	Twenty Seven Flags	Sioux City	Woodbury	27
266	Twin Lakes Country Club	Winfield	Henry	9
214	Twin Lakes Golf Club	Rockwell City	Calhoun	9
51	Twin Pines Municipal Golf Course	Cedar Rapids	Linn	18
228	Two Rivers Golf Course	Sioux City	Woodbury	18
245	Urbandale Country Club	Urbandale	Polk	9
61	Valley Oaks Country Club	Clinton	Clinton	18
11	Veenker Memorial Golf Course	Ames	Story	18
246	"Villisca Golf Club, Inc."	Villisca	Montgomery	9
246	Vinton Country Club	Vinton	Benton	9
266	Wahkonsa Country club	Wilton & Durant	Muscatine	9
85	Wakonda Club	Des Moines	Polk	18
43	Walter's Ridge Par 3	Cedar Falls	Black Hawk	Par 3
102	Walton Golf Club	Fairfield	Jefferson	9
36	Wapsi Oaks Country Club	Calamus	Clinton	9
13	Wapsipinicon Country Club	Anamosa	Jones	9
128	Wapsipinicon Country Club	Independence	Buchanan	9
253	Washington Golf and Country Club	Washington	Washington	9
43	Washington Park Municipal Golf Course	Cedar Falls	Black Hawk	9
254	Waukon Golf and Country club	Waukon	Allamakee	9
86	Waveland Golf Course	Des Moines	Polk	18
256	Waverly Municipal Golf Course	Waverly	Bremer	18
254	Webster City Country Club	Webster City	Hamilton	9
258	Wellman Golf Club	Wellman	Washington	Sand
259	West Bend Golf and Country Club	West Bend	Palo Alto	9
264	West Liberty Golf and Country Club	West Liberty	Muscatine	9
264	West Union Country Club	West Union	Fayette	9
179	Westwood Golf Course	Newton	Jasper	18
68	Westwood Golf Course Cub	Council Bluffs	Pottawattamie	Par 3
229	Whispering Creek	Sioux City	Woodbury	18
175	Whispering Pines	Muscatine	Muscatine	9
265	Whittemore Golf Club	Whittemore	Kossuth	9
55	Wildwood Municipal Golf Course	Charles City	Floyd	9
263	Willow Creek Golf Club	West Des Moines	Polk	36
80	Willow Run Country Club	Denver	Bremer	9
158	Willow Vale Golf Club	Mapleton	Monona	9
168	Woodlyn Hills Golf Course	Milford	Dickenson	18
96	Woodsedge Golf Course	Edgewood	Clayton	9
87	Woodside Golf Course	Des Moines	Polk	27
268	Woodward Golf and Recreation	Woodward	Dallas	9

PAGE	COUNTY	TOWN	COURSE NAME	TYPE
44	Linn	Cedar Rapids	Airport National	27
45	Linn	Cedar Rapids	Cedar Rapids Country Club	18
46	Linn	Cedar Rapids	Ellis Municipal Golf Course	18
47	Linn	Cedar Rapids	Elmcrest Country Club	18
48	Linn	Cedar Rapids	Hunters Ridge	18
49	Linn	Cedar Rapids	Jones Municipal Golf Course	18
50	Linn	Cedar Rapids	St. Andrews Golf Club	18
51	Linn	Cedar Rapids	Twin Pines Municipal Golf Course	18
52	Linn	Center Point	Rolling Acres Golf Course	9
53	Linn	Central City	Meadowview Country Club	9
161	Linn	Marion	Gardner	18
160	Linn	Marion	Indian Creek Country Club	9
172	Linn	Mount Vernon	Hillcrest Country Club	9
63	Louisa	Columbus Junction	Cedarcrest Country Club	9
247	Louisa	Wapello	Indian Hills Golf and Country Club	18
53	Lucas	Chariton	Lakeview Golf and Country Club	9
146	Lyon	Larchwood	Meadow Acres Country Club	9
110	Lyon	George and Boyden	Otter Valley Country Club	9
212	Lyon	Rock Rapids	Rock River Club	9
267	Madison	Winterset	Lake View Country Club	9
178	Mahaska	New Sharon	Prairie Knolls Country Club	9
192	Mahaska	Oskaloosa	Edmundson Golf Course	18
193	Mahaska	Oskaloosa	Elmhurst Country Club	18
191	Mahaska	Osklaoosa	Harvest Point	9
142	Marion	Knoxville	Pine Knolls Country Club	9
199	Marion	Pella	Bos Lander	18
200	Marion	Pella	Pella Golf and Country Club	9
203	Marion	Pleasantville	Pleasantville Golf and Country Club	9
162	Marshall	Marshalltown	Elmwood Country Club	18
163	Marshall	Marshalltown	Legion Memorial Golf Course	18
211	Marshall	Rhodes	Harvestor	18
237	Marshall	State Center	Lincoln Valley Golf Course	18
154	Mills	Malvern	Malvern Golf Course	9
111	Mills	Glenwood	Glenwood Golf Club	9
189	Mitchell	Osage	Sunny Brae Golf and Country Club	9
236	Mitchell	St. Ansgar	Acorn Park Golf Course	9
158	Monona	Mapleton	Willow Vale Golf Club	9
189	Monona	Onawa	Onawa Country Club	9
5	Monroe	Albia	Albia Golf and Country Club	9
246	Montgomery	Villisca	Villisca Golf Club, Inc.	9
209	Montgomery	Red Oak	Red Oak Country Club	18
173	Muscatine	Muscatine	Geneva Golf and Country Club	18
174	Muscatine	Muscatine	Muscatine Municipal Golf Course	18
175	Muscatine	Muscatine	Whispering Pines	9
264	Muscatine	West Liberty	West Liberty Golf and Country Club	9
266	Muscatine	Wilton & Durant	Wahkonsa Country club	9
207	O'Brian	Primghar	Primghar Country Club	9
198	O'brien	Paullina	Paullina Golf Club	9
122	O'Brien	Hartley	Meadowbrook Golf and Country Club	9
219	O'Brien	Sheldon	Sheldon Golf and Country club	9
217	O'Brien	Sanborn	Sanborn Golf and Country Club	9
219	Osceola	Sibley	Sibley Country Club	9
56	Page	Clarinda	Clarinda Country Club	18
99	Page	Essex	Essex Golf and Recreation	9
154	Palo Alto	Mallard	Spring Hills	9
112	Palo Alto	Graettinger	Hillcrest Golf Course	9
259	Palo Alto	West Bend	West Bend Golf and Country Club	9
99	Palo Alto	Emmestburg	Emmestburg Country Club	9
216	Palo Alto	Ruthven	Lost Island Golf Club	9
4	Plymouth	Akron	Akron Golf Club	9
32	Plymouth	Brunsville	Prairie Rose	9
141	Plymouth	Kingsley	Brookside Golf Course	9
149	Plymouth	Le Mars	Le Mars Golf Club	18
210	Plymouth	Remsen	Remsen Golf Course	9
123	Plymouth	Hinton	Deer Run	9
147	Pocahontas	Laurens	Laurens Golf and Country Club	9
205	Pocahontas	Pocahontas	Pocahontas Golf Club	9
102	Pocahontas	Fonda	Fonda Golf Course	9
214	Pocahontas	Rolfe	Rolfe Golf Club	9
7	Polk	Altoona	Terrace Hills Golf Course	18
13	Polk	Ankeny	Ankeny Golf and Country Club	9
15	Polk	Ankeny	Briarwood	18
16	Polk	Ankeny	Otter Creek Golf Course	18
204	Polk	Pleasant Hill	Copper Creek	18
206	Polk	Polk City	Tournament Club of Iowa	18
115	Polk	Granger	Executive Par 3 - Jester Park	Par 3
260	Polk	West Des Moines	Ponderosa Public Golf Course	9
138	Polk	Johnston	Hyperion Golf Course	18
114	Polk	Granger	Jester Park Golf Course	18
263	Polk	West Des Moines	Willow Creek Golf Club	36
262	Polk	West Des Moines	Glen Oaks	18
82	Polk	Des Moines	A.H. Blank Memorial Golf Course	18
245	Polk	Urbandale	Urbandale Country Club	9
261	Polk	West Des Moines	Des Moines Golf and Country Club	18
83	Polk	Des Moines	Echo Valley Country Club	18
84	Polk	Des Moines	Grandview Golf Course	18
85	Polk	Des Moines	Wakonda Club	18
86	Polk	Des Moines	Waveland Golf Course	18
87	Polk	Des Moines	Woodside Golf Course	27
23	Pottawattamie	Avoca	Avoca Golf and Country Club	9
40	Pottawattamie	Carter Lake	Shoreline Golf Course	18
67	Pottawattamie	Council Bluffs	Bent Tree	18
68	Pottawattamie	Council Bluffs	Cub Run Par 3	Par 3
69	Pottawattamie	Council Bluffs	Dodge Park Golf Course Riverside	18
70	Pottawattamie	Council Bluffs	Fox Run	18
71	Pottawattamie	Council Bluffs	Lakeshore Country Club	18
68	Pottawattamie	Council Bluffs	Westwood Golf Course Cub	Par 3
176	Pottawattamie	Neola	Quail Run	9
182	Pottawattamie	Oakland	Oakland Country Club	9
243	Pottawattamie	Treynor	Treynor Recreation Area	9
32	Poweshiek	Brooklyn	Brooklyn - Victor Country Club	9
170	Poweshiek	Montezuma	Montezuma Country Club	9
117	Poweshiek	Grinnell	Grinnell Country Club	9
118	Poweshiek	Grinnell	Oakland Acres Golf Course	18
171	Ringgold	Mount Ayr	Mount Ayr Golf and Country Club	9
98	Ringgold	Ellston	Sun Valley Golf and Country Club	9
145	Sac	Lake View	Sac County Golf and Country Club	9
216	Sac	Sac City	Sac Country Club	9
26	Scott	Bettendorf	Hidden Hills Golf Course	18
27	Scott	Bettendorf	Palmer Hills Municipal Golf Course	18
28	Scott	Bettendorf	Sunrise Golf Course	9
148	Scott	Le Claire	Olathea Golf Course	9
152	Scott	Long Grove	Glenns Creek	18
75	Scott	Davenport	Davenport Country Club	18
76	Scott	Davenport	Duck Creek Park Golf Course	18
73	Scott	Davenport	Credit Island Country Club	9
78	Scott	Davenport	Red Hawk	9
97	Scott	Eldridge	Rustic Ridge Golf Course	9
77	Scott	Davenport	Emeis Park Golf Course	18
74	Scott	Davenport	Crow Valley Golf Course	18
122	Shelby	Harlan	Rosman Glendale Farm Golf Course	9
121	Shelby	Harlan	Harlan Country club	9
8	Sioux	Alton	Sioux Golf and Country Club	9
190	Sioux	Orange City	Landswmeer Golf Club	18
125	Sioux	Hull	Rolling Hills Country Clulb	9
123	Sioux	Hawarden	Hawarden Golf Club	9
212	Sioux	Rock Valley	Rock Valley Golf Club	9
222	Sioux	Sioux Center	Sandy Hollow Golf Course	9
9	Story	Ames	Ames Golf and Country Club	18
10	Story	Ames	Coldwater Golf Links	18
8	Story	Ames	Homewood Golf Course	9
12	Story	Ames	Oaks Golf Club	9
11	Story	Ames	Veenker Memorial Golf Course	18
176	Story	Nevada	Indian Creek Country Club	9
127	Story	Huxley	Ballard Golf and Country Club	9
239	Story	Story City	River Bend Golf Course	9
95	Tama	Dysart	Milne Memorial Park and Golf Club	9
243	Tama	Traer	Traer Golf and Country Club	9
240	Tama	Tama	Tama-Toledo Country Club	9
24	Taylor	Bedford	Bedford Country Club	9
148	Taylor	Lenox	Three Lake Municipal Golf Course	9
4	Union	Afton	Lakeshore Golf and Country Club	9
72	Union	Creston	Crestmoor Golf Club	9
73	Union	Creston	Pine Valley Golf Club	9
140	Van Buren	Keosauqua	River View Club	9
195	Wapello	Ottumwa	Ottumwa Cedar Creek	18
196	Wapello	Ottumwa	Ottumwa Country Club	18
2	Warren	Ackworth	Shady Oaks Golf Course	18
183	Warren	Norwalk	Countryside	18
184	Warren	Norwalk	Legacy	18
185	Warren	Norwalk	Rolling Hills	18
129	Warren	Indianola	Deer Run	18
130	Warren	Indianola	Indianola Country Club	9
215	Warren	Runnells	Toad Valley Public Golf Course	18
253	Washington	Washington	Washington Golf and Country Club	9
258	Washington	Wellman	Wellman Golf Club	Sand
139	Washington	Kalona	Kalona Golf Course	9
66	Wayne	Corydon	Corydon Golf Club	9
126	Wayne	Humeston	Lake Side Golf Club	Sand
125	Webster	Humboldt	Deer Creek	9
105	Webster	Fort Dodge	Sunkissed Meadows Golf Course	Par 3
112	Webster	Gowrie	Gowrie Golf and Country Club	9
78	Webster	Dayton	Dayton Golf and Country Club	9
106	Webster	Fort Dodge	Fort Dodge Country Club	18
105	Webster	Fort Dodge	American Legion Golf Course	9
107	Webster	Fort Dodge	Lakeside Municipal Golf Course	18
36	Winnebago	Buffalo Center	Gruis Recreation Area	9
144	Winnebago	Lake Mills	Rice Lake Golf and Country Club	18
104	Winnebago	Forest City	Forest City Bear Creek Golf Club	18
37	Winneeshiek	Calmar	South Winn Golf and Country Club	9
194	Winneshiek	Ossian	Silver Springs	9
79	Winneshiek	Decorah	Oneota Golf and Country Club	18
80	Winneshiek	Decorah	Silvercrest Golf and Country Club	9
136	Winneshiek	Jackson Jct.	Jackson Heights	9
17	Woodbury	Anthon	Anthon Golf Club	9
66	Woodbury	Correctionville	Correctionville Golf Club	9
172	Woodbury	Moville	Meadows Country Club	9
203	Woodbury	Pierson	Pierson Golf Course	Sand
226	Woodbury	Sioux City	Sioux City Country Club	18
229	Woodbury	Sioux City	Whispering Creek	18
222	Woodbury	Sioux City	Hidden Acres Golf Club	9
223	Woodbury	Sioux City	Dakota Dunes	18
224	Woodbury	Sioux City	Floyd Municipal Golf Course	18
227	Woodbury	Sioux City	Twenty Seven Flags	27
228	Woodbury	Sioux City	Two Rivers Golf Course	18
231	Woodbury	Sloan	Sloan Golf Course	9
230	Woodbury	Sioux City	Sun Valley Golf Club	Par 3
225	Woodbury	Sioux City	Green Valley Municipal Golf Course	18
156	Worth	Manly	Pioneer Town and Country Club	9
182	Worth	Northwood	Northwood Country Club	9
25	Wright	Belmond	Belmond Country Club	9
57	Wright	Clarion	Clarmond Country Club	9
95	Wright	Eagle Grove	Eagle Grove Country Club	9
90	Wright	Dows	Dows Golf Course	9
111	Wright	Goldfield	Oakridge Recreation	9

Why Golf Courses Have 18 Holes

The following is not meant to offend hockey, tennis, basketball, football or soccer fans. It is rather, an attempt to put everything in its proper perspective.

Ever wonder why golf is growing in popularity and why people who don't even play golf go to tournaments or watch it on TV? These truisms may shed light:

• Golf is an honorable game, with the overwhelming majority of players being honorable people who don't need referees.
• Golfers don't have some of their players in jail every week.
• Golfers don't beat up on each other during the game.
• In golf you cannot fail 70% of the time and make $9 million a season, like the best baseball hitters (.300 batting average) do.
• Professional golfers are compensated in direct proportion to how well they play.
• Golfers don't hold out for more money, or demand new contracts, because of another player's deal.
• Professional golfers don't demand that the taxpayers pay for the courses on which they play.
• You can watch the best golfers in the world up close, at any tournament, including the majors, all day, every day for $25 or $30. the cost for a seat in the nosebleed section at the Super Bowl will cost around $300 or more.
• When golfers make a mistake, nobody is there to cover for them or back them up.
• Golfers do not gyrate all over the course after making a good shot, they expect that of themselves. A football player will dance for 5 minutes, jumping all over the field for making a simple tackle, did they not think they could do that.
• The PGA tour raises more money for charity in one year than the National Football League does in two.
• Golf doesn't change its rules to attract fans.
• Golfers have to adapt to an entirely new playing area each week.
• Golfers look at different pin placements each round, the goal line and the basketball hoop are always in the same place.
• Golf doesn't have free agency.
• You can hear birds chirping on the golf course during a tournament.
• Tiger Woods can hit a golf ball three times as far as Barry bonds can hit a baseball.

Finally, here's a slice of golf history you might enjoy.
Why do full-length golf courses have 18 holes, and not 20 or 10 or an even dozen?

During a discussion among the membership board at St. Andrews in 1858, one of the members pointed out that it takes exactly 18 shots to polish off a fifth of Scotch. By limiting himself to only one shot of Scotch per hole, the Scot figured a round of golf was finished when the Scotch ran out.

Now you know.

The above information was taken off the Internet; Author Unknown

The Game of Golf is 90% Mental and 10% Mental

- If you want to get better at golf, go back and take it up at a much earlier age.
- Since bad shots come in groups of three, a fourth bad shot is actually the beginning of the next group of three.
- When you look up and cause an awful shot, you will always look down again at exactly the moment when you ought to start watching the ball if you ever want to see it again.
- Any change works for a maximum of three holes and a minimum of not at all.
- No matter how bad you are playing, it is always possible to play worse.
- Never keep more than 300 separate thoughts in you mind during your swing.
- When your shot has to carry over a water hazard, you can either hit one more club or two more balls.
- If you're afraid a full shot might reach the green while the foursome ahead of you is still putting out, you have two options; you can immediately shank a lay-up, or you can wait until the green is clear and top a ball halfway there.
- The inevitable result of any golf lesson is the instant elimination of the one critical unconscious motions that allowed you to compensate for all your errors.
- If it ain't broke, try changing your grip.
- It's not a gimmee if you're still away.
- Everyone replaces his divot after a perfect approach shot.
- A golf match is a test of your skill against your opponent's luck.
- It's surprisingly easy to hole a 50-foot putt when you lie 10.
- Counting on your opponent to inform you when he breaks a rule is like expecting him to make fun of his own haircut.
- Non chalant putts count the same as chalant putts.
- The shortest distance between any two points on a golf course is a straight line that passes directly through the center of a very large tree.
- There are two kinds of bounces: unfair bounces, and bounces just the way you meant to play it.
- You can hit a 2-acre fairway 10% of the time and a 2-inch branch 90% of the time.
- Every time a golfer makes a birdie, he must subsequently make two triple bogeys to restore the fundamental equilibrium of the universe.
- If you want to hit a 7-iron as far as Tiger Woods does, simply try to lay up just short of a water hazard.
- To calculate the speed of a players downswing, multiply the speed of his backswing by his handicap. Example: backswing 20 mph, handicap 15, downswing 600 mph.
- There are two things you can learn by stopping your backswing at the top and checking the position of your hands: how many hands you have, and which one is wearing the glove.
- Hazards attract. Fairways repel.
- You can put "draw" on the ball, you can put "fade" on the ball, but no golfer can put "straight" on the ball.
- A ball you can see in the rough from 50 yards away is not yours.
- If there is a ball in the fringe and a ball in the bunker, your ball is the one in the bunker.
- If both balls are in the bunker, yours is in the footprint.
- Don't buy a putter until you have had a chance to throw it.

The above information was taken off the Internet; Author Unknown

For additional copies of

Golf Courses of Iowa - 3rd Edition

Please follow the directions below.

Please send a personal check, money order or cash in the amount of

$24.00 for one (1) copy
or
$42.00 for two (2) copies

(These Prices Include Postage, Handling and Tax)
Make checks out to Golf Courses of Iowa

Send to:

Gof Courses of Iowa
Box 65
Jefferson, IA 50129

If you enjoyed the book please pass this information along to other Iowa golfers. I am hopeful that Iowa golfers will find the information, pictures and descriptions interesting and useful. Every person that buys the book is my best customer. (I am one of those baby-boomers and I need the retirement money!) Thanks for your interest. There are 407 courses in the state, give me a call when you have played them all.

It's a Great Day for 36!